When the NHL
Invaded Japan

When the NHL Invaded Japan

*The Washington Capitals,
the Kansas City Scouts
and the Coca-Cola Bottlers' Cup,
1975–1976*

Steve Currier

McFarland & Company, Inc., Publishers
Jefferson, North Carolina

Library of Congress Cataloguing-in-Publication Data

Names: Currier, Steve, author.
Title: When the NHL invaded Japan : the Washington Capitals, the Kansas City Scouts and the Coca-Cola Bottlers' Cup, 1975-1976 / Steve Currier.
Description: Jefferson, North Carolina : McFarland & Company, Inc., Publishers, 2022. | Includes bibliographical references and index.
Identifiers: LCCN 2022022330 | ISBN 9781476687612 (paperback : acid free paper) ∞
ISBN 9781476645957 (ebook)
Subjects: LCSH: Coca-Cola Bottlers' Cup. | National Hockey League. | Washington Capitals (Hockey team)—History. | Kansas City Scouts (Hockey team)—History. | Hockey—Japan—History. | BISAC: SPORTS & RECREATION / Winter Sports / Hockey
Classification: LCC GV847.7 .C87 2022 | DDC 796.962/6409—dc23/eng/20220604
LC record available at https://lccn.loc.gov/2022022330

British Library cataloguing data are available

ISBN (print) 978-1-4766-8761-2
ISBN (ebook) 978-1-4766-4595-7

© 2022 Steve Currier. All rights reserved

No part of this book may be reproduced or transmitted in any form or by any means, electronic or mechanical, including photocopying or recording, or by any information storage and retrieval system, without permission in writing from the publisher.

Front cover photograph by Altrendo Images (Shutterstock)

Printed in the United States of America

*McFarland & Company, Inc., Publishers
Box 611, Jefferson, North Carolina 28640
www.mcfarlandpub.com*

Table of Contents

Acknowledgments vi
Preface 1

Period 1

1. Kicking and Screaming: An Introduction to Expansion in the NHL 5
2. In the Beginning 14
3. A Sandy Foundation: The 1974 Expansion Draft 24

Period 2

4. The Washington Capitals, 1974–75 49
5. The Kansas City Scouts, 1974–75 96

Period 3

6. The Washington Capitals, 1975–76 138
7. The Kansas City Scouts, 1975–76 173

Overtime

8. The Coca-Cola Bottlers' Cup 209
9. Aftermath 235

Appendix: Statistics 251
Chapter Notes 271
Bibliography 283
Index 285

Acknowledgments

Ironically, writing about two of the worst teams in professional hockey history was surprisingly enjoyable. It probably wasn't all that much fun competing for the Kansas City Scouts or Washington Capitals during that dreadful 1974–1976 period, but the players I interviewed for this book were quite happy to reminisce and regale me with their tales of woe. When I was writing my first book on the history of the California Golden Seals, former NHLer Howie Menard closed our interview by reminding me to always remember that hockey players are a good, respectful bunch of guys who are loyal to each other. I have continued to interview many former players since then and have even got to know a few on a more personal level, and I wholeheartedly agree with Howie's sentiment. Hockey players are almost always willing to sign an autograph through the mail, chat with you over Skype, or answer even your most mundane questions. They love reminiscing about their past glory and sometimes even their not-so-proud moments. These now-private citizens who have retired to the shadows of celebrity life thank you after interviews because you took the time to research their careers and ask about their past life.

First and foremost, I would like to thank the members of the Scouts and Capitals who granted me their time and allowed me to dredge up memories of all those 10–0 blowouts and 50-shot barrages that were surely no fun to experience. Many thanks to Ron Lalonde, Bernie Wolfe, Mike Lampman, Jack Lynch, Bill Mikkelson, Denis Herron, Robin Burns, and Henry Boucha for not only taking time out of their busy schedules to talk with me, but also provide me with articles, photos and other interesting (and in some cases rare) documents related to the NHL Japan series. Particular thanks to Burns for trusting me enough to send—on his own dime, I might add—a photo album loaded with rare personal and on-ice photos of the series. I honestly never thought I would ever see pictures like these, since I actually believed they had all been lost to the sands of time. I could not believe I was holding in my hands what are quite possibly the only remaining photos of the NHL Japan series. Ron Lalonde also took a huge risk sending me some rare Coca-Cola Cup artifacts, namely a game program, pennant, and several rare photos which you will now be able to see for yourselves. Thank you so very, very much!

I must also acknowledge Tim Beever for sending my way, free of charge I might add, not only a treasure trove of hard-to-find mid–1970s *Hockey News* articles, but also full media guides which were an absolute gold mine of information. I also owe a debt of gratitude to Lora Evans and Paul Patskou for organizing a Zoom event with former Capitals, notably Bill Mikkelson and Bernie Wolfe, who spun several yarns about the franchise's early years.

Mike Vogel of the Capitals was also an early supporter of this project and provided me with not only some great shots of the almost-mystical Coca-Cola Bottlers' Cup, but also a much-appreciated update as to the whereabouts of the trophy. He also suggested I contact the Capitals' director of hockey operations, Kris Wagner, whom I like to call the "keeper of the Coca-Cola Cup." He has taken good care of the quirky trophy, and he also arranged for the team's official photographer, Patrick McDermott, to take some great shots of the cup, in the middle of a pandemic no less! A large debt of gratitude goes out to all of you and to the very classy Washington Capitals organization for its support throughout this project.

Thanks also to the Society for International Hockey Research, particularly Kevin Shea, whose willingness to publish my original article about the long-forgotten NHL Japan series allowed me to get the ball rolling on this book in the first place. For those of you who have never heard of SIHR, it is *the* meeting place for anyone who is interested in reading, writing, or researching hockey history. Whatever difficult piece of information you're looking for, they've got it, and if they don't have it, someone will find it for you. If you want to connect with like-minded hockey connoisseurs and then get a warm, fuzzy feeling when someone you know has written a book, SIHR is for you.

Thank you to McFarland's Gary Mitchem, who took a chance by acquiring this book about two NHL flops and their peculiar, little-known trip to Japan. As I was writing this book, the thought that I was wasting my time crossed my mind many, many times. The subject of the Capitals' and Scouts' early years, and how the 1974 expansion draft indirectly led to the Coca-Cola Cup tournament, had always fascinated me, but would it fascinate others? After all, barely anyone even took notice of the event when it took place some 45 years ago. Apparently, there are lots of other weirdos out there!

Thank you also to the folks who created and have continued to update several great hockey websites that every researcher of the genre has consulted hundreds, if not thousands of times. I am eternally grateful to Dan Diamond and Associates, and Sports Reference LLC, who have helped make Hockey-reference.com one of the leaders in hockey statistics. I also depended a great deal on the Hockey Summary Project for information on individual games, not to mention NHL.com's fabulous database of game summaries, and Ralph Slate's Internet Hockey Database. These people have truly done a yeoman's work, and they have made life so much easier for hockey researchers everywhere.

Thanks to everyone who has supported my writing career over the last few years, and who has either bought a copy of my last book, borrowed it from the library, or borrowed it from a friend and passed on the good word afterwards.

Finally, I would like to thank my family for all their love and support over the years. Thanks to Mom and Dad for always encouraging me to write about what I love, and for always encouraging my sometimes obsessive quest to acquire just about any book or piece of memorabilia that is related to hockey. Thanks also to my brother Chris for his continued support of my writing career. I would like to end by acknowledging the love and support of my wife Hope, who has patiently put up with my constant need to type away on my laptop any time I can find free time. I am also grateful to my son Emmett for providing me with artwork for my basement pandemic office and to my daughter Laura for always making me smile. I am truly lucky to be able to do what I love near those I love most.

If you enjoyed this book, you may also enjoy *The California Golden Seals: a Tale of White Skates, Red Ink, and One of the NHL's Most Outlandish Teams* (University of Nebraska Press, 2017).

Visit my Seals tribute site (*www.goldensealshockey.com*) for other hockey-themed articles and fun, including the one and only Hockey Hall of Shame!

Preface

As the Washington Capitals and Kansas City Scouts lined up for the opening puck drop of the fourth and final game of the NHL Japan series, the players could only look back fondly on what had been an absolutely crazy adventure. Despite finishing the 1975–1976 season with, by a wide margin, the two worst records in the league, they had unexpectedly been gifted a golden opportunity to experience the beauty and diversity of Japanese culture, and to play hockey in front of enthusiastic crowds that simply could not get enough of their eccentricities, missing teeth, and flailing fists. Sure, games were played on top of an Olympic swimming pool complete with diving boards hovering over one end of the rink, and players risked life and limb checking each other into boards kept in place by nothing more than a few cement blocks, but competing in a foreign country while living it up in a luxury hotel was not supposed to happen to cellar-dwellers. Everyone who participated in the series was treated first-class by their hosts. There was talk that this series could become an annual event. There was also an all-expenses-paid stopover in Hawaii to enjoy on the way back home. For the first time in the clubs' two-year existence, life was pretty sweet.

Tommy McVie, the Capitals' insatiable head coach, had put his boys through the wringer the last three and a half months, but the torture worked wonders. McVie had eliminated the country-club atmosphere that had poisoned the dressing room since the team's inception. Now his boys were focused. They were ready to kick some Kansas City ass! McVie was absolutely convinced he had the better team. In his mind, this series was no vacation; it was an early training camp for the next season, and he couldn't wait for October to arrive so he could unleash his now-lean and mean team on the unsuspecting NHL.

On the opposite side of the rink, the Scouts could only wonder if this was the last time they would sport their outlandish blue, red and yellow uniforms featuring the proud Native American warrior on horseback. Prospects hadn't looked so hot in Kansas City as the Japan trip loomed. Attendance at Kemper Arena had been second-worst in the league, and the Scouts' many minority owners were jumping ship as the club desperately tried to sell enough season tickets to stay solvent. After the Scouts ended the season on an NHL-record 27-game winless streak, game four was an opportunity to salvage a little pride, not to mention send veteran defenseman Gary Bergman off into retirement a winner.

At the conclusion of the fourth game, the winning team would be awarded the

Coca-Cola Bottlers' Cup, a trophy that did not exactly measure up to the storied Stanley Cup. According to current Capitals director of hockey operations Kris Wagner, it looked like "a horse racing trophy" or what "a horse eats oats out of after a race." The oversized brass trophy had big, elegant horns on each side and resembled something Bjorn Borg would have captured in his heyday. The cup sat atop a wooden base whose brass name plate indicated the trophy's full name and the winner of the 1976 NHL Japan series. It was nothing of great note. Most everyone involved in the series still has no idea what happened to it all those years ago. The cup has become less than a footnote in the history of the NHL and the Washington Capitals.

So why bother writing a book on the story of one of the most inconsequential trophies in professional sports history? Despite its less-than-stellar reputation, the Coca-Cola Bottlers' Cup was a symbol of hope, a confirmation of big-league legitimacy, and a reward for hard work and determination. The original intention of the NHL Japan series may have been to spread goodwill and promote the game, but at the series' conclusion, it became obvious that the games had meant so much more to everyone involved. That's what this book explores, but to appreciate the story of the Coca-Cola Cup fully, and to recognize the uniqueness of the event, it is imperative to understand the unique series of events that led up to it.

One needs to look back to the root of this series, the 1974 expansion draft, whose conditions were so constricting, whose pool of available players was so poor, and whose very existence was so ill-timed and unnecessary that it spawned two franchises that were so utterly awful they were the only ones who could ever be invited to Japan. It was this needless expansion, one stemming from a combination of greed, spite, and lack of foresight, that eventually led to the Coca-Cola-sponsored series.

"There's an old saying, 'War is hell,' former Capitals coach Tom McVie once said. Expansion's worse."[1] With apologies to anyone who has ever lived through an actual war, McVie wasn't entirely wrong. After all, he had the misfortune of coaching the Caps during the latter half of the 1975–1976 season. As the schedule came to a close that year, the Capitals had played a grand total of 160 games in their short, two-year history ... and won *19*.

The Capitals' expansion cousins, the Kansas City Scouts, fared little better, winning 27. To put those numbers into perspective, the Caps and Scouts lost *74 percent* of their games those two years. In the first 320 games played by these two teams between 1974 and 1976, their overall record was an almost-impossible-to-believe 46–236–38, which becomes an even more depressing stat when one realizes that seven of those wins were against *each other*. Many teams win 46 games in a single season; it took the Scouts and Caps a *combined four seasons* to reach that mark! Yes, there were futility records a-plenty set in K.C. and D.C., many of which are likely untouchable thanks to the advances in coaching and goaltending, not to mention a salary cap, which have thankfully brought parity to the game.

Sports Illustrated's Alex Prewitt once described the Capitals' first season as having "reshaped careers and recolored legacies," but that phrase can easily apply to the Scouts as well.[2] To this day, several members of both clubs refuse to talk about their experiences. Many requests for interviews—from myself and other writers doing research—were either ignored or flatly turned down. Too many bad memories, which for some need to remain dead and buried.

The Capitals' and Scouts' first two seasons are quite fascinating in that never before or since have two teams been so closely linked in their ineptitude and hopelessness. Yet in April 1976, they were invited to Japan to compete in a one-of-a-kind four-game exhibition series. It was perceived as a minor affair, and it sadly remains a mere footnote in the history of hockey, but players from both teams left Japan with memories that would last a lifetime. The long-forgotten event was the seed that eventually sprouted into this book.

I had read about the series in a 1976 issue of the *Hockey News,* and I had always wanted to understand why in the world the NHL, Japan, Coca-Cola, or *anyone* for that matter, would want not only to invite what were undoubtedly the two worst teams in professional hockey, but *pay* them to promote the game in a land where the sport barely registered a pulse. It simply made no sense.

I interviewed several players who participated in the series to fill in some of the blanks so I could write an article for the Society for International Hockey Research's annual journal. The players I interviewed told so many incredibly funny stories about their experiences on and off the ice that limiting this research to a single article did not do justice to the Coca-Cola Cup tale.

In the mid- to late 1970s, professional hockey had plummeted to its nadir. "It was a mess," wrote Jeff Z. Klein and Karl-Erik Reif about the 1970s expansion boom in their 1998 book, *The Death of Hockey,* "First-division clubs routinely ran up double-digit scores against second-division sides," the latter of which included both Washington and Kansas City.[3] It hadn't always been this way. In 1967, when the NHL expanded from six to 12 teams, the new teams were somewhat competitive because there had been enough talent to supply six new franchises. Three years later, the league expanded to Buffalo and Vancouver, followed by the additions of Atlanta and Long Island two years after that. That same year, the World Hockey Association was formed, adding 12 more teams to the sporting landscape, bringing the overall number of hockey teams to 28, which put an enormous strain on the overall level of talent, thus hurting the flow and quality of the game.

Then came the expansion, or more precisely expansions of 1974: Washington and Kansas City in the NHL, *and* Indianapolis and Phoenix in the WHA, four new teams being birthed when there was simply no room for more offspring. How the NHL and WHA managed to find enough players to fill the rosters of 32 teams is mind-boggling.

To put things into perspective, in the NHL of 2022, there are now 32 teams, which isn't even an issue because the NHL has the luxury of drafting talented players from across Europe, including former Eastern Bloc countries such as Russia, the Czech Republic, and Slovakia. That was all but impossible in the 1970s, as those countries were closed off to North America. Other European nations such as Finland, Germany, and Switzerland had very few players of NHL caliber, and the United States only produced a few star players. That is no longer the case as the U.S. and Europe have since caught up to Canada in producing high-quality players.

In today's NHL, the ten-goal blowouts Klein and Reif alluded to are about as rare as unicorn sightings, and the NHL's salary cap makes it all but impossible for any team to plummet so far to the bottom of the standings that one would need a harness and a long length of rope to reach them. So one should not bet on ever seeing a reincarnation of the mid–1970s Washington Capitals and Kansas City Scouts ever again, and thus no reprise of the Coca-Cola Cup series, which makes the 1976 event even more unique.

In my conversations with members of the Scouts and Capitals, no one admitted that participating in the Coca-Cola Cup had ever been a career objective. The Coca-Cola Cup was the furthest thing from every professional player's ultimate goal, the Stanley Cup. After two years of abject failure and misery, however, the Coca-Cola Cup, while no priceless silver chalice, was a silver lining.

NOTE: Unless otherwise indicated, all quotes are from interviews conducted by the author for this book.

PERIOD 1

•• 1 ••

Kicking and Screaming

An Introduction to Expansion in the NHL

If the term "expansion team" were found in a dictionary, its definition would probably read something like "a collection of middling and fading athletes drafted for the purpose of competing fruitlessly for respect and an unattainable championship." Being part of an expansion team, no matter what the sport, is almost always an excruciating struggle. Think of Sisyphus pushing that giant boulder up a hill, only to watch it roll back down over and over again. Try as you might, you're never going to come out ahead. You're going to feel depressed. You might question your sanity. You might ask yourself why God has forsaken you and your teammates to a life of endless torture.

The world of professional sports is cold and cruel, and no one understands that fact better than a member of an expansion team. Ray Ferraro, for instance, was a member of the Atlanta Thrashers their first three years in the league. He had already proven himself a premier NHL goal scorer who had twice reached the 40-goal plateau and totaled 346 goals from 1984 to 1999, but after a so-so season with the Los Angeles Kings, Ferraro became a free agent. Despite his credentials, no one was interested in signing a once-prolific, 34-year-old centerman who was coming off a 31-point season.

Along came the Thrashers, who were gearing up for their inaugural NHL campaign in 1999–2000. The expansion draft had not been particularly kind to the newbies; the best offensive players they had picked up were Johan Garpenlov, who had hit the 50-point mark three times in his career, the last time in 1996, and Terry Yake, who had two 50-point seasons in 1993 and 1994. The Thrashers were almost completely devoid of skill, so they knocked on Ferraro's door, hoping he still had a few goals left in his stick. It didn't take long for Ferraro to realize that playing for an expansion squad could have a negative effect on one's psyche. A few weeks into the season, the Thrashers lost a close game in which they had played their hearts out, and Ferraro realized that the team had no hope of succeeding. "No matter how well you play, in most cases it just isn't good enough," he said. "It's a brutal feeling. You're happy to be in the league, but it's like going to work every day and having the door slammed in your face."[1]

Another trademark of an expansion team is the lack of consistency. From Day One, it feels as though no one is a part of the team's long-term plan, and there are no true building blocks other than the omnipresent first-round pick. He becomes the so-called "future" of the franchise who will take the rag-tag bunch of expansionists to the Promised Land, but who is probably being rushed into the lineup way too soon. In reality, an expansion team's roster is unstable and changes from game to game. "Guys that I'd never even heard of were showing up at morning skates," remembered Ferraro. "It was a complete mishmash from start to finish."[2]

Expansion can also be the sad, final stop on a long, professional sports journey. More than a few great players have toiled for an expansion team just to prolong their fading careers one more year. Doug Mohns, for instance, was a veteran of 1,315 games when he joined Washington in 1974, and he endured more ten-game losing streaks that season than he scored goals.[3] Years later, former Norris Trophy winner Doug Wilson was traded to the San Jose Sharks, who would win 28 games in their first two seasons combined. Then there was hard-working defenseman Brad Marsh, who had competed in over 1,000 games, but the last 59 of his career were spent with the woeful 10–70–4 Ottawa Senators of 1992–1993.

Examples like these are especially sad because each of these players had spent his whole career hoping to touch the Stanley Cup, only to see it slip away year after year. They were quality players, team leaders, and highly respected veterans who deserved to have their names etched on the mug at least once. They sadly realized that unless they were dealt to a contender, they would never get a sniff at the playoffs again.

Despite all the negativity that usually surrounds a first-year team, expansion has, on the other hand, opened the door of opportunity to players trapped in hockey purgatory. Since these teams are sorely lacking in talent, they have no choice but to give everyone a good long look. Brian Bradley's career, for instance, was going nowhere when he was drafted by the Tampa Bay Lightning in 1992, but once he bought himself a little suntan oil and a golf course membership, he notched a career-high 42 goals his first year in Florida. Ray Ferraro scored 76 points his second year in Atlanta. William Karlsson racked up 43 goals his first year in Vegas.

Expansion ain't all bad … but when it is, it's brutal.

Fools Build Houses… But Wise Men Won't Live in These

Since World War II, the NHL had existed as a six-team entity comprising the Montreal Canadiens, Toronto Maple Leafs, Detroit Red Wings, Boston Bruins, Chicago Black Hawks, and New York Rangers. That group is fondly remembered today as the "Original Six," even though plenty of expansion teams came and went in the NHL's first 25 years. The "Next Six," the California Seals, Philadelphia Flyers, Pittsburgh Penguins, Los Angeles Kings, St. Louis Blues, and Minnesota North Stars, entered the league in 1967. As with most ambitious business endeavors, this unprecedented expansion did not happen without controversy, namely the question of how the league could possibly maintain its reputation as the best and most competitive hockey circuit in the world when half of its teams had absolutely no chance of competing for the Stanley Cup.

1. Kicking and Screaming

The following "Three Little Pigs"–inspired parable,[4] written by Rick Pearson for the November 1972 *Hockey Illustrated*, perfectly describes the first half-decade of modern NHL expansion:

> Once upon a time there were six little men, each of them with a house built of bricks.
>
> Because their houses became so popular, they built and sold six more houses. But these six houses were made of sticks.
>
> "Don't worry," they said to the six new home owners, "the sticks are just as good as the bricks."
>
> But after a long winter, the houses made of sticks were never as strong as the houses of the original six little men.
>
> Despite the problems, there was even more demand for houses. So, the six little men (with the second six buyers sharing in the booty) built four more houses. These were houses built of straw.
>
> "Don't worry," they said to the four newest residents, "the straw is just as good as the sticks."[5]

Expansion's modern era got off to a decent enough start. Sure, the new teams were light on talent, and games were low-scoring, but with the exception of California and Pittsburgh, all the expansion teams drew decent crowds into the 1970s. As time went on, however, troubles multiplied.

As the NHL prepared to add Washington and Kansas City, Stan Fischler published *Slashing!* Having grown up watching the great players of the Original Six era, Fischler was no fan of what he believed had become a deteriorating sport. Fischler stated that hockey "went to hell" after expansion. He didn't go so far as to say expansion was a bad idea, but "the stupid management and the nearsightedness of hockey players … stripped the game of its inherent glamour."[6]

> The worst teams in major-league hockey are playing today—right now in the NHL and WHA … contemporary hockey is a shade of its former qualitative self.
>
> Expansion has done it. Expansion and a steadily decreasing talent flow that will only change in the next few years when more American-born players and more Europeans are lured to the North American continent.[7]

He was right. It would take years for the NHL to recover from its eight-year expansion frenzy.

A Brief History of NHL Expansion

From 1967 to 1974, it certainly seemed as though nothing got team owners more excited than approving new franchises and prepping for expansion drafts. After all, in just seven years the league *tripled* itself from six to 18 clubs, which is all the more shocking when one realizes that in the 25 years preceding the Great Expansion of 1967, the NHL showed almost no interest in adding new franchises. "Hockey was always conservative," explained Fischler. "Canadians are conservative-thinking people. They like the status quo. They liked the fact that they were selling out in every arena. It was a nice, comfortable situation. So why disturb it?"[8]

The league's fears were not unfounded. After all, in the 1920s and 1930s, the NHL had expanded several times, and while the Bruins, Black Hawks, Red Wings, and Rangers have all survived to the present day, several other expansion carcasses littered the hockey landscape. The Montreal Maroons, for instance, won two Stanley Cups during their 14-year history, but once the North American economy hit hard times during the Great Depression, it became obvious that Montreal could not support both the Maroons and Canadiens, and the former disappeared. The New York Americans were actually the first NHL franchise to set up shop in the Big Apple, but after 17 mostly mediocre seasons, the Amerks died as well. The NHL tried, through expansion or relocation, (and failed) to establish teams in Philadelphia, Pittsburgh, and St. Louis.

If you were a hockey fan in Montreal, Toronto, or Detroit, you were probably more than happy with the way the league was organized. The Canadiens, Leafs, and Wings won every Stanley Cup but one in the Original Six era's 25-year span. Chicago sleepwalked through season after season until the late 1950s, when Bobby Hull and Glenn Hall arrived and finally brought the Hawks a championship in 1961. As for Boston and New York, they wasted away in the NHL's basement so long, mold started growing in their equipment bags. Maybe, just maybe, it was time for the NHL's rich to start spreading their wealth.

Clarence Campbell had been the NHL's president since 1946, although he was really more of a mouthpiece for team owners, who held all the power behind the scenes. Campbell and the league's six owners oversaw the league's greatest period of stability. Attendance was strong in every market, and not one franchise folded or moved between 1942 and 1967. The NHL was a tight-knit organization, albeit one rife with corruption and collusion, as future events would reveal. Player salaries were kept low, and pensions were infinitesimally small. Owners had absolutely no reason to risk disturbing their perfect little club. In the early 1960s, Campbell had little interest in expanding the NHL: "Right now we're a pretty successful operation. When you come right down to it, nobody can match it. We'd only be buying a headache and what for?"[9]

In 1952, the NHL toyed with the idea of absorbing the American Hockey League's perennial Calder Cup contenders, the Cleveland Barons, but according to David Cruise and Allison Griffiths in *Net Worth: Exploding the Myths of NHL Hockey*, "the governors were only feigning interest to avoid charges of monopolistic practices."[10] Over the next decade, expansion talk quieted down to less than a whisper.

Clarence Campbell, for one, just couldn't comprehend how expansion could generate any income. He also feared expansion would invite the apocalypse. "Increasing the league doesn't increase your revenue 5 cents per club," he explained at one press conference.

> You'd simply have more hockey, and all diluted. If you expanded by only two clubs, each NHL team would have to provide six players. You just tell me what the result would be if you took six players off any team in the NHL. Any team! And what the hell do you think it's gonna do to the spectacle? ... It has to dilute it. These six players at the bottom echelon couldn't sell tickets, they couldn't sell a show, you couldn't put them on the ice by themselves. They are the fillers.[11]

Two other important issues that worried Campbell were travel and scheduling, which were indeed legitimate concerns. Although Major League Baseball had adapted to its expanded travel bubble after it placed teams on the West Coast in the 1950s, baseball's schedule had always been favorable to teams looking to keep travel costs low. East Coast ball clubs could travel to California to play a three or four-game set before moving on to another multi-game set somewhere else, but NHL teams played just one game against each opponent on a road trip, which meant a lot of packing, unpacking, and riding on trains every season. If the NHL had a team in, say, Los Angeles, it would be very expensive to travel all the way out to California for just one game, but if the league placed a few teams out there, that made good fiscal sense.

Unfortunately, Campbell was not the most forward-thinking person, and he was hung up on the potential travel issues of expansion. "You can't schedule Montreal or Toronto at home on Saturday and then on the Coast on Sunday," he explained. "Who the hell would run the risk? You could get snowed in ... and in order to go to the Coast, Toronto would have to give up three or four of its Canadian television dates and *that's revenue*."[12]

The Western Hockey League provided the NHL with the little nudge needed to push it down expansion lane. The WHL had entered into an agreement with the NHL to act as its minor-pro farm league, but when that deal expired, there were rumblings that the WHL, which already had franchises in major centers such as Los Angeles, San Francisco, Portland, Vancouver, and Seattle, was planning on competing directly with the NHL. "I haven't met with any NHL people lately, but there are other ways of presenting our case forcefully," said James Piggott, owner of the L.A. Blades. "And we do want in. And I can tell you it's not very far off, either."

Of course, there was also the little matter of television, a factor that simply could not be ignored; the upstart American Football League had signed a whopping $35-million deal with CBS. Even though the National Football League had been around longer and employed better players, the AFL was exciting and enticing, facts that quickly burst the NHL's bubble. "The NHL had long been operating on the comforting assumption that no rival league could get a national contract because it would be offering an inferior product," wrote David Cruise and Allison Griffiths in *Net Worth*.[13] If the less-talented AFL could eat away at the NFL's monopoly, why couldn't an upstart hockey league threaten the NHL likewise? The AFL eventually created so many headaches for the NFL that it forced a merger of the two circuits in 1970. The NHL had no interest in going down that road, so expansion was seen as a way to nip the WHL in the bud before it got too big for its britches.

Times were indeed a-changin', and hockey needed to modernize if it wanted to remain relevant. To make its mark and score that coveted national TV contract, the NHL needed more than four American markets, and some of those had to be outside the Eastern Time Zone. According to Cruise and Griffiths, New York Rangers president William Jennings, a big proponent of expansion, "spent many fruitless hours" lobbying NHL governors "to add at least two new teams to thwart the creation of a rival league, protect themselves from anti-trust action and lure network television. At least seven times between 1962 and 1964, Jennings tried to persuade the other governors to put expansion on the agenda at annual and semi-annual owners' meetings."[14] Just like that, after years of dawdling, hemming, and hawing, the NHL thought expansion sounded just grand! Charging each expansion franchise $2 million to enter the league likely greased those rusty wheels of progress just a bit.

Jennings believed it would be best not only to add two teams on the West Coast, but to add *four* more franchises and place them all in their own division where they would play the majority of their games against each other and, after a couple of play-off rounds, the last team standing would head to the Stanley Cup Final to face the best Original Six club.

Toronto Maple Leafs part-owners Stafford Smythe and Harold Ballard were not terribly enthused about expansion, but they were huge fans of the almighty dollar, so they were at least willing to listen. "Great idea," Smythe once said sarcastically. "You figure out a way to put the franchise fee in my pocket and I'll go along. But a bunch of guys in San Francisco who have never seen hockey aren't getting any of my players."

Ballard's views mostly echoed those of Smythe. "If the right kind of people come to us with $5 million and the right kind of plans, we'll listen," said Ballard. "We'd be crazy not to."[15] Then again, Ballard was also quoted as saying "Fuck 'em!" when asked what he thought about the notion of expanding the league, so he may not have been totally on board with the project.

Even though the players who would stock the new teams were never going to be All-Stars, nor were they even going to be in-their-prime third-liners, some general managers were incredibly concerned about losing their "fillers" and minor-leaguers. When the idea of allowing each Original Six team to protect just five or six players apiece was proposed, general managers balked. "We have our own interests and fans to consider," Montreal's Sam Pollock argued. "What is desirable, for the first few years, is that the new teams have an equality among themselves. Why should we give up a good kid to a new team when we haven't had a chance to look at him in the NHL ourselves."[16]

Detroit general manager Sid Abel also balked at being overly generous to the expansion clubs. "The new teams will be weaker and they ought to be," he said. "Why should the Red Wings spend millions to build up a franchise and then let these new guys move in on the same level?" One can only wonder if Abel remembered those words about a decade later, when he was at the helm of the Kansas City Scouts and kept asking why the league wasn't doing more to help his new team.

Clarence Campbell wanted the expansion teams to be competitive early on, so he suggested that each Original Six team protect nine players from the expansion draft. Some of the more deluded general managers responded with the ridiculous notion of protecting *14* players! In a stunning about-face, Stafford Smythe suddenly wanted to give a fighting chance to that "bunch of guys in San Francisco" who couldn't pick Gordie Howe out of a police lineup. "What we really need are rules to protect us from our own selfishness," Smythe believed. "I want the new teams to be competitive because they've got to be an attraction when they play in our buildings."[17] In the end, general managers and owners agreed that parity was in everyone's best interest, so they compromised: each established club would protect 11 skaters and one goaltender. The draft would follow the "claim and fill" system, meaning that when one player was selected from an established team, this club's general manager could add a new name to his protected list.

San Francisco–Oakland and Los Angeles were approved wholeheartedly because CBS insisted that the NHL establish franchises in California before signing a TV deal. Both markets had also played host to successful WHL teams, so local fans were reasonably knowledgeable. Placing a pair of teams on the West Coast was also practical for travel purposes, since teams could fly to California and play a pair of games before moving on. At the end of the day, the WHL's San Francisco Seals were sold to a group hoping to snag the Bay Area's NHL franchise, and after playing their final season as the California Seals, they essentially transferred to the NHL. The L.A. franchise went to Jack Kent Cooke, who named the team the Kings.

Another no-brainer expansion site was Bloomington, Minnesota, one of the hockey hotbeds of the United States. Even though the North Stars would be playing out of just the fifth-largest city in the state, it was also just a short drive from the Twin Cities of Minneapolis and St. Paul.

Pittsburgh was also a wise choice. The city had a long history of minor-league success and had once had an NHL team, the Pirates, from 1925 to 1930. Pittsburgh also had a major-league arena ready to go.

Philadelphia was a long-shot to get in, but after some convincing arguments from prospective owner Ed Snider and his associates, the league gave them the nod.

Vancouver was also considered a suitable location, but in the end, Canada's third-largest city was denied. Stafford Smythe and Harold Ballard were the alleged culprits in Vancouver's shocking rejection, because they were supposedly miffed that their proposal to build a 20,000-seat arena in Vancouver had gone belly-up. Smythe and Ballard planned to erect a hotel and build a race track on what they hoped would be free downtown property.[18] Perhaps Vancouver city officials felt unimpressed by the Toronto duo's proposal, or perhaps they were turned off by the Torontonians' brash attitude,[19] but the end result was a flat-out rejection, and the pair returned home with their angry tails between their angry legs.[20] Nevertheless, Vancouver remained on the NHL's radar, and the city was eventually granted a franchise that began play in 1970.

Then there was St. Louis, a curious case if there ever was one. Black Hawks owners Arthur Wirtz and James Norris owned the decaying St. Louis Arena, which they desperately wanted to unload onto some poor sap, and they figured the best way to accomplish this was by convincing league governors to grant a conditional franchise to St. Louis. Not that the city had any takers early on, but if someone stepped up to purchase the franchise by April 5, 1966, Wirtz and Norris's albatross would bid them goodbye. In the end, insurance tycoon Sid Salomon, Jr., his son Sid Salomon III, and Robert L. Wolfson paid the $2 million expansion fee.

Spinning Out of Control

Three years into the NHL's expansion era, Clarence Campbell could snap his britches and exclaim to the world that his league's ambitious endeavor had been such an overwhelming success that the league was going to expand once again.[21] The 1970 expansion, which added Buffalo and Vancouver to the NHL landscape, was a very good decision; both the Sabres and Canucks have been box office winners for decades even though neither team has yet to capture the Stanley Cup. When the NHL welcomed the Atlanta Flames and New York Islanders in 1972, however, warning signs hinted that the expansion bubble was about to burst.

This latest round of expansion was not undertaken under the noblest of terms. Nineteen seventy-two was the same year the World Hockey Association was founded, and as much as the NHL preached that the new league was small potatoes, the senior circuit was worried, and it reacted in much the same way Sheldon Cooper would if faced with a spider in the shower. In Klein and Reif's book, *The Death of Hockey*, the sportswriters explained that the WHA acquired "dozens of players of every level of ability from the NHL and scoured the minors for whatever the NHL hadn't already used to plug the holes," because the rapid expansion of pro hockey left them with no other choice. "The NHL, seriously concerned about the WHA's not inconsiderable star power and the rebel circuit's growth into a legitimate level, began cooking up expansion franchises like the carnival makes corn dogs, not because there was a demand for new teams, not because hockey was ready for more teams, but simply in a pre-emptive effort to put teams in cities before the WHA could."[22]

The WHA saw New York as the most desirable location to establish its flagship franchise, an absolute necessity for the league to be taken seriously. There was just one hitch: the fledgling New York Raiders couldn't secure a rink of their own because the NHL beat the WHA to the punch by planting its own team at Nassau Coliseum on Long Island, forcing the Raiders to become the New York Rangers' tenants at Madison Square Garden. The Rangers got all the best dates, so the Raiders were doomed from the start, eventually moving to New Jersey and then San Diego.

In the short term, the NHL's devious plan to shut the WHA out of New York worked. In the long term, however, the NHL paid dearly for its spiteful expansion. Adding two more teams before the league was ready to accommodate them simply widened the gap between the very best and very worst teams. Games became boring and lopsided, and before long fans became disenchanted, causing attendance to sag in many cities.

The WHA did what it had to do to survive, signing anyone who could lace up a pair of skates. One thing that was assured when jumping leagues was that a player would make a lot of dough playing in the "dubya." Everyone from superstars to fourth-line thugs lined up to sign inflated deals with the fledgling league. If a player didn't like the idea of jumping to a new league that might not last a year, they could always leverage the WHA's offer into a bigger NHL contract. Many NHL teams got fleeced into signing below-average players to ridiculous contracts, which just opened the door to other below-average players using the argument, "but look what *that* guy is making."

The New York Islanders, like most NHL teams, were not about to offer outrageous contracts to third- and fourth line schlubs, who unfortunately made up the majority of their first-year roster. As a result, the Isles suffered badly, losing a good portion of their expansion draft picks to the WHA, and consequently the 12–60–6

Isles resembled a minor-league outfit playing major-league opponents. Perhaps because the Atlanta Flames were a much more successful 25–38–15 their first year, the NHL convinced itself that the moribund Islanders were an aberration rather than a new norm for expansion teams. But that would not be the case, as the next batch of expansion teams would prove.

The next expansion phase could not have come at a worse time. Talent was stretched out thinner than it had ever been, and salaries were higher than ever, meaning the time was ripe for two new franchises that would crash harder and faster than any other. If the Original Six franchises were built with bricks, and the Next Six were built with sticks, and the second and third expansion phase franchises were built with straw, one could argue that when Washington and Kansas City joined in 1974, the 16 team governors essentially handed them a gingerbread house kit and gave them a hearty pat on the back.

"If you're the sort of person who likes to view NHL history in a glass-half-full way," wrote Sean McIndoe in *The Down Goes Brown History of the NHL*, "you could look at the 1972 expansion and say that hey, one out of two ain't bad. If you want to view the league's 1974 expansion through a similarly optimistic lens, you'd probably point out that at least nobody got run over by a Zamboni."[23]

2

In the Beginning

Long before the Scouts landed in Kansas City, the Midwestern city had played host to several professional hockey teams of varying success. The American Hockey Association's Pla-Mors were founded in 1927, and the team won league championships in 1930, 1933, and 1934. During the second championship season, the club was renamed the Greyhounds,[1] and in 1940, the Greyhounds became the Americans, but they never won another championship. The AHA closed up shop in 1942 and did not return until 1945 under its new name, the United States Hockey League. The Pla-Mors returned to the USHL that same season and won the league's first two championships. In 1945–1946, the club dominated the circuit with a 35–17–4 record, which also gave them the Directors' Cup as regular-season champs. The following year, the Pla-Mors slipped to second place with a 29–20–11 mark, but at the playoffs' conclusion, they marched off with the Paul W. Loudon championship trophy. Times were indeed good for a hockey fan in Kansas City, but they wouldn't last long. The Pla-Mors went through several name changes before finally folding in 1951 along with the rest of the USHL.

Kansas City did not host another professional hockey team until the St. Louis Blues established their Central Hockey League farm club at the American Royal Arena in 1967. The team's owner was Missouri Lieutenant Governor William S. Morris, and he was a good buddy of St. Louis owner Sid Salomon. Morris hoped that having a CHL team in Kansas City would eventually lead to the city getting an NHL team. Morris wanted his troops to play their home games at Municipal Auditorium, but no deal could be reached with the city to install ice-making equipment because of a pipefitters and plumbers strike, so the venerable American Royal Building would have to suffice. Unfortunately, the place literally looked and smelled like crap; since it was a livestock pavilion, there was manure everywhere. Like most barn-like structures, the place was not terribly warm, and the roof leaked. To join the NHL, Kansas City would have to do better than the American Royal, because the city could never convince NHL governors that letting Bobby Orr skate within walking distance of piles of cow poop was a good idea. So the search was thankfully on for an adequate site for a new arena.

Morris eventually gave up on owning a NHL franchise when he instead chose to run for the governorship of Missouri, which he ultimately lost to Edward Dowd. With Morris out of the running, that left three other groups competing for Kansas City's NHL entry. The first group was led by restaurateur Stan Glazer, the second by businessman Dr. Arthur Rhoades, and the third by real-estate developer Edwin G. Thompson.

Thompson had his heart set on building a new arena in nearby Overland Park, which was just a hop, skip, and a jump from the Interstate, but when citizens were asked to vote on a half-cent tax on food and beverages sold within five miles of the rink, the people of Kansas City gave the proposal one giant middle finger, and just like that, Overland Park was out. According to Ed Thompson, "somebody left out the word 'not' in the legislative package and the roof literally fell in."[2]

Thompson lobbied hard for a year and a half to get the Kansas City franchise, but he had stiff competition from Glazer and Rhoades. Thompson also had to deal with other franchise applicants from Cleveland, Cincinnati, and Washington. In late January 1972, when the 16 NHL governors sat down to determine who would be admitted into their exclusive club, it took them just 75 minutes to make their decision. Each new franchise required 12 affirmative votes, and according to reports in the next day's newspapers, the Thompson group's pitch was so effective, it was granted membership on the first of four ballots, earning 14 votes.[3] "When we started," Thompson said, "we were underdogs. And I mean underdogs. It's been one obstacle after another. When I was standing there [waiting for the announcement] my knees were shaking. When it was over, all I felt was grateful."[4] Looking back, Thompson was somewhat surprised the league put all their eggs in his basket, considering the lack of a concrete arena plan.[5] In hindsight, the NHL should have done its homework on Thompson and his group instead of paying the class nerd off with a fiver.

The league gave the Kansas City hopefuls until December 15, 1973, to decide where the new arena would be located, but when that deadline passed, the league extended the deadline to January 25, 1974. With just three days remaining until the hammer was scheduled to fall, the city council agreed to allocate $5.6 million for a new arena that would play host to the American Royal livestock show,[6] the sought-after NHL team, and the NBA's Kansas City Kings. R. Crosby Kemper, Jr., also donated $3 million towards building the new arena, part of which went to the American Royal so it could purchase land from the stockyards company. When the Scouts' and Kings' new home was finally completed in the fall of 1974, it had already taken on Kemper's name, two years after he died.

The only caveat was that the new arena would need to be ready in time for the start of the 1974–1975 season. Of course, there was also the matter of the franchise fee, which had skyrocketed from $2 million in 1967 to $6 million in 1972. Since Thompson's new franchise infringed on the territorial rights of the St. Louis Blues, the team would also be responsible for paying the Blues approximately $1 million.

The ownership group, known as Kansas City Hockey Associates, had 21 other stakeholders, none of whom owned more than 20 percent of the team. The largest share was owned by Murray Newman, whose father had co-founded the family-owned Hinky Dinky grocery-store chain. Lumber businessman Paul Hess, Jeff Jennings, son of New York Rangers president William Jennings, and Hank Stram, head coach of the NFL's Kansas City Chiefs, each owned 10 percent. Seven other men, including Thompson, owned five percent each, and ten others who each owned one percent, including legendary local baseball and football broadcaster Bill Grigsby. Thompson asked Grigsby to handle the business side of the Scouts and drum up sponsors, but he also some did some color commentary on Scouts game broadcasts. Grigsby used his charm to secure a $500,000 sponsorship from Seagram's, the famous whisky distillers, to help pay for a new scoreboard for the $22 million Crosby Kemper Memorial Arena. Unfortunately, his other contributions to the Scouts were rather limited as he lacked hockey expertise and was not a master promoter of anything unless it involved himself. Kansas Citians loved Grigs, however; he just wasn't a good fit with the Scouts. His lack of promotional skills cost the Scouts dearly as attendance began to plummet shortly after the first home game.[7]

At first, this convoluted ownership arrangement worked fine, but once the team began losing money due to low attendance, the partners, many of whom were small-time businessmen, were asked to pony up additional capital, and it became clear that having no primary owner was a problem.[8]

Despite being just a minority stakeholder, the young, good-looking Thompson was the team's main spokesman. Born in Kansas City March 18, 1935, Thompson grew up to be a tough and hard-working teenager. He sold vegetables as a 10-year-old, making "maybe $1 a day and all the bananas I could eat," he recalled. Later, he was a pump jockey at a 9th and Benton gas station. He was also saddled with a bad case of bulbar polio in the fall of 1954, but despite the threat of never walking again, having to spend 24 hours a day in an iron lung, and missing an entire month of school, he persevered and even became a star high school basketball player, scoring a Catholic League record 41 points in one game. He went to college, but when his mother became ill, he dropped out, never to return. The determined Thompson found steady work with a residential construction firm. At 19, he was helping lead a sales team of 27 employees.[9] He later founded Town and Country Home Improvement, which became a very successful business, and then he started the real estate development company Thompson Properties.

Thompson had many reasons for wanting to be a part of the NHL, and like most sports franchise owners, he spewed out many of the typical clichés that would later be printed in team media guides and game programs. He became an NHL owner because of the people of K.C., "the greatest sports fans in the world," who had already welcomed the Kansas City Blues with open arms and had enthusiastically purchased tickets to games hosted in a cold, foul-smelling minor-league rink.[10] How could the NHL possibly go wrong in a town where the fans were so clearly starved for hockey at the highest level? Thompson, his partners, and the NHL would find out soon enough.

The Front Office Takes Shape

The new team was hoping to call itself the Kansas City Mo-Hawks, which would have combined the postal abbreviation of Missouri (MO) with the popular Kansas nickname "Jayhawkers," but the Chicago Black Hawks protested due to the similarity to their own franchise name. Thompson explained that the Black Hawks "helped us [get] the franchise so we're happy to go along with their wishes and not use the word 'Hawks' in our nickname."[11]

The new franchise organized a Name the Team Contest, and about 15,000 ballots were cast, but only three names made it to the final round: Scouts, Tornadoes, and Crowns. On June 4, 1973, just five days short of the one-year anniversary of the league granting the franchise to Thompson, the team officially became known as the Scouts, a name that was suggested by contest winner James R. Maxwell. For suggesting the winning nickname, he was awarded a new car courtesy of Ford. The team's new nickname was inspired by a famous statue by Cyrus E. Dallin of a Sioux Native American called "The Scout," which still overlooks the city from Penn Valley Park. This statue would become a prominent part of the Scouts' logo.

Hall of Fame center Sid Abel, 55, was named the Scouts' first general manager. Nicknamed "Old Bootnose," Abel teamed up with fellow Hall of Famers Gordie Howe and Ted Lindsay to form the famed Production Line. In 612 career games, Abel scored 189 goals and 283 assists, won three Stanley Cups, was named to four All-Star teams, and won the 1949 Hart Trophy as league MVP.

Abel was traded to Chicago in 1952 and became the Black Hawks' player-coach, but he played in only 42 more games over two seasons. He later coached the Red Wings from 1957 to 1970 (with a one-year sabbatical in 1968–1969), and the team reached the Stanley Cup final four times. He became the Wings' general manager in 1962 and remained in the position until 1971. It was around this time that Red Wings owner Bruce Norris hired Jim Bishop to run the Detroit Olympia, and he gradually began taking up a bit too much space in the organization. Bishop was allowed to hire Ned Harkness, an old friend who had led a successful Cornell squad, and the my-way-or-the-highway bench boss took on Abel's old coaching duties. "I sure as hell complained right at the start of training camp," the affable Abel recalled. "I could see he wasn't running a professional camp. He was causing a lot of unrest in what had been a happy organization. He started bothering [Garry] Unger and [Pete] Stemkowski about their hair. The players weren't even allowed to smoke on the street." The writing was on the wall that Abel and Harkness could not coexist much longer, so Abel confronted Norris, who told the former Stanley Cup winner he was free to pack his bags if he so chose. Abel was proven correct as Harkness began dismantling the Wings from top to bottom, and the team would not fully recover from the "Darkness with Harkness" era until the late 1980s.

When Sid Solomon III, the son of the St. Louis Blues owner, approached him with a job offer, Abel agreed and became the club's general manager, but even though his overall experience there was positive, on April 13, 1973, Abel accepted a three-year contract to become the main decision-maker in Kansas City.[12]

Robin Burns, who played two years in Kansas City, felt Sid Abel was well-suited for the Scouts' general manager chair.

> You play the cards you're dealt with in the draft. I think Sid had done a great job in just trying to assemble a team to try and be competitive.
>
> I had Scotty Bowman as a coach in junior, and I knew Scotty very well, and I remember watching him, and someone said, "Scotty, what made you such an unbelievable, successful coach?" and he said, "Well, let me give you a few names that can also help you become

successful: Guy Lafleur, Mario Lemieux, and Steve Yzerman." He said, "It starts there." When you have those names, you have a pretty good foundation to be a successful coach. So, in Sid's case, he had Robin Burns, but there was only so much I could do.

Joseph Aldege Albert "Baz" Bastien became Abel's assistant GM in the summer of 1973. Bastien had been a three-time American League MVP and a fantastic young goaltender with a brilliant career ahead of him until an errant puck hit him in the right eye at the Toronto Maple Leafs' training camp in 1949. The damage was so severe that his eye was removed and replaced with a glass peeper. His on-ice career officially over, he turned his attention to the front office and became general manager and head coach of the minor-league Pittsburgh Hornets, with whom he had achieved his greatest success as a player. He later became Abel's assistant GM in Detroit before moving on to Kansas City with his good friend.

Up Expansion Creek Without an Orr

Abel hired 49-year-old former Boston Bruins coach Armand "Bep" Guidolin to lead his motley crew. Guidolin and Abel had grown up together in Timmins, Ontario, were teammates in Detroit from 1947 to 1949, and were then both employed by the Black Hawks. The story goes that Guidolin got his nickname because he was the youngest child in his family, and his Italian mother, who spoke very little English, often pronounced the word "baby" as "beppy," which was eventually shortened to "Bep."

Guidolin has the distinction of being the youngest-ever NHL player at 16 years and 11 months, appearing in his first game on November 12, 1942. The Boston Bruins, like most NHL teams during World War II, were short of players due to a large number signing up for military duty, so teenage Guidolin was handed a once-in-a-lifetime opportunity to suit up. In 519 career games with Boston, Detroit, and Chicago, Bep scored 107 goals and 171 assists.

After Guidolin's playing career ended, he returned to the Bruins and eventually signed a two-year contract to coach their farm team, the Boston Braves. "I could have made more money [in the WHA]," he admitted, "but—and I know this sounds corny—I believe I owe it to the Boston organization to stay with them." When the Bruins struggled down the stretch in 1972–1973, Guidolin replaced Tom Johnson behind the Bruins' bench. "A coach is hired to be fired," Guidolin said. "I've accepted this philosophy. A man can't coach the Bruins for the rest of his life. If I move up, I know the day will come when they'll want to replace me."[13]

Guidolin enjoyed considerable success with the Bruins, leading them to the 1974 Stanley Cup final. During his 104-game tenure in Boston, he compiled an impressive 72–23–9 record, so when it came time to renew his contract, Guidolin felt he deserved a five-year deal. It was against club policy to consummate such lengthy contracts, so the Bruins countered with a two-year deal. Guidolin believed he could do better elsewhere, so he resigned on May 27. Two weeks later, he signed a five-year escalating-contract with Kansas City starting at $40,000 and going to $45,000. He had fielded offers from several other teams, and there were even accusations that the Scouts had talked to Guidolin while he was still under contract with Boston, but those suspicions were never proven.[14]

"I hope I'm still around here when the day comes to drink champagne out of Mr. Stanley's cup," Guidolin said after signing with Kansas City. He also went so far as to rhetorically ask, "why can't we make this a Stanley Cup city in four or five years."[15] There was actually an answer to that question, and *Hockey News* correspondent Jay Greenberg probably put it best: "Guidolin [was] up expansion creek without an Orr."[16]

At the June 7 press conference announcing Guidolin's hiring, the former Bruins bench boss explained his philosophy about club rules. Drinking beer after a game was fine as long as it didn't interfere with team discipline. When he was asked about his stance on the longer hair professional athletes were sporting at the time, Guidolin scoffed at the notion that he would break out the clippers: "They don't skate with their hair. That's the style. What am I going to do, tell them to get a brush cut? It's 1974, not 1940.

"Performance is what I care about. If they don't perform like they're supposed to, then I'll get on them about that. But it's 1974, not 1940. People don't really care about things like that."[17]

Guidolin gave the impression that he was going to be a rather chill coach, but it was no secret that he had had his problems with the Bruins' more boisterous players, namely one Philip Esposito, defending scoring champion, whom Guidolin accused of phoning it in during the playoffs.[18] How Guidolin was going to react to the dregs of the league getting first-line minutes, overestimating their worth, and getting inflated heads was anybody's guess. He was often blunt, and sometimes a little too direct, especially after a loss, but he always told it like he saw it, no questions asked. "I'm all right after about 30 minutes or so.... Maybe I expect too much," Guidolin admitted.[19]

The Washington "Waterskates"?

While Kansas City was approved unequivocally as a new NHL member, few people expected the league to grant an expansion franchise to Washington D.C. But Abe Pollin defied the odds and persuaded the league to plant its flag in the Nation's Capital. Jimmy the Greek stated that Washington had a 600–1 chance of nailing down the NHL's second expansion team of 1974, but the highly-respected Pollin convinced 17 U.S. Senators and 42 House representatives to write to the NHL's board of governors, pleading to anyone who had any inside influence whatsoever that Washington would be a great addition. Pollin was so determined that he personally delivered his franchise application to the board of governors.

Abraham Pollin was born December 3, 1923, in Philadelphia, and he had been a citizen of Washington since he was eight years old. He graduated from George Washington University and in 1945, he joined his father's construction company. Twelve years later, he started up his own construction company, but sports were where his destiny lay. In 1964, Pollin and his partners, Arnold Heft and Earl Foreman, bought the Baltimore Bullets basketball team, and by 1968 Pollin had become the team's sole owner. Under his watch, the franchise was rechristened the Capital Bullets, and then the Washington Bullets on route to winning four conference titles between 1971 and 1979, and an NBA championship in 1978.

Pollin faced one major obstacle in gaining entry into the NHL: Washington did not have a suitable arena. That would all change thanks to Pollin, who envisioned building a large venue that could not only host NBA and NHL teams, but a plethora of concerts and other grand-scale events as well. In the 21st century, the decision concerning where to build a new arena is an easy one: it goes downtown, surrounded by lots of niche restaurants, bars, Whole Foods, and condos where rich people can dwell. In the 1970s, however, new stadiums were erected in the suburbs, as far from the din of downtown traffic as possible, convenience be damned. In Washington, the suburb of choice for Pollin was the farmlands of Landover, just off the Capital Beltway. "The location is certainly a great part of it," said Bullets executive vice president Jerry Sachs. "You don't have to drive downtown, and that is appealing. There is a tremendously large market right here and it's kind of opened up a whole new thing to fans of metropolitan Washington and northern Virginia."[20]

The 17,962-seat Capital Centre, which was shaped like a giant saddle, cost $18 million, took 15 months to build, and produced plenty of critics, but they quickly shut up when fans showed up in droves to watch the Bullets, who had been moved down the road from Baltimore. What made Capital Centre unique was Telscreen, a multi-million-dollar scoreboard consisting of four 12-by-16 foot screens which displayed full-color close-ups and instant replays. There were also 40 luxury sky suites, each with a reception area, a powder room, a wet bar, wall-to-wall carpeting, and closed-circuit and commercial television. Each suite provided a great view of the ice surface, and each could be accessed by private elevator. The arena also became a popular venue which hosted rock legends from AC/DC to ZZ Top.

"We have a NHL team … we have a place to play … but what we don't have is a NAME for the team," said Abe Pollin. "And since the team belongs to the fans, it only seems right to give the fans an opportunity to name it."[21]

And so until midnight January 17, 1974, everyone was encouraged to propose their ideas for a team name. Each entry had to be submitted by postcard, and only one name could be submitted per card. The winner, chosen by Pollin himself, would earn themselves a pair of season's tickets.

Of course, it is always a nice gesture when a sports team makes an honest effort to connect with its fans, but sometimes it is best to leave the fans out of the decision-making process. Some of the team names suggested were absurd, violent, or just plain baffling: Aardvarks, Apes, Atomics, Avengers, Belters, Blades, Buggers, Capital Abes, Caputs, Catfish, Chimney Sweeps, Colonials, Comets, Cutthroats, Cyclones, Delegates, Domes, Dum Dums, Eagles, Farmers, Gaylords, Girls, Gold Cuts, Growlers, Hookers, Ice Caps, Koo Koos, Metros, Pandas,[22] Pink Violins, Pollinites, Punishers, Sissies, Slapsticks, Snowflakes, Stompers, Streaks, Swingers, Troopers, Turtles, Warthogs, Watergate Bugs, Waterskates, Werewolves, Whips, and Wing Pings, whatever those are supposed to be. It can only be speculated that some of these submissions were either put-ons or the result of spending a weekend in a hot box. Luckily for Pollin and the Washington brass, the conservative NHL had the final say in all team names, and they likely wouldn't have approved of Gaylords, Dum Dums, Koo Koos, or the like. In the end, Comets, written out on 250 ballots, was the most popular choice, but was nixed.

Ruth Stolarick, born in Saskatchewan, but living in Alexandria, Virginia, earned herself two season tickets for suggesting the winning name ... sort of. "Washington Caps is what I had in mind. It's better than Capitals. It's easier to put on the jerseys." In the end, the name Pollin liked most was "Capitals," which, along with "Caps," was suggested by 88 different people. "We had thousands of names that were novel, clever, and extremely original," said Pollin. "It took me eight to ten hours, but I looked at every one. It wasn't until 11:30 last night that my wife and I came up with the final name."[23] The name itself wasn't terribly creative. In 1969–1970, there had been an American Basketball Association franchise called the Washington Caps. Before that, the Washington Capitols had been charter members of the NBA.

The NHL Capitals didn't have much of a creative crest either, simply consisting of the word "capitals" spelled out in lower-case letters and with the "t" shaped like a hockey stick chasing a teeny, tiny puck.[24]

Washington Commits to Schmidt

Milt Schmidt had already established himself as a bona fide NHL legend in the 1940s and 1950s, and he had plenty of experience as a general manager, so the decision to have him lead the Capitals in the same capacity made perfect sense. In April 1973, Schmidt signed with Washington under similar circumstances as Bep Guidolin's with Kansas City. Schmidt was hoping to sign a new three-year pact with Boston, but the Bruins refused to offer him more than a one-year deal. It was a difficult and sudden break for a man who had been a member of the Bruins since the Great Depression.

Schmidt had been one of the very best players in Bruins history. He entered the NHL in 1936 at the age of 18, and he won the 1940 league scoring title with 52 points in 48 games. "As a player, Schmidt combined finesse and clever stick handling with hard skating and body checking," said the Caps' GM's profile in the team's *Goal* game programs. "He gave 100% every minute and never gave up."[25]

He played center on the "Kraut Line" with childhood friends Bobby Bauer and Woody Dumart—the trio were all of German heritage—and together they played a big part in Boston's Stanley Cup victories in 1939 and 1941. Of course, these two Cups occurred while war was raging in Europe, and as the conflict dominated headlines in North American newspapers, the three teammates did their patriotic duty and enlisted in the Canadian military, sacrificing three full seasons in the process.

During the 1954–1955 season, Schmidt retired and took over the Bruins' coaching reigns, but he realized early on that success was much harder to achieve behind the bench. The mediocre Bruins of the 1950s usually hovered around the .500 mark and finished anywhere between second and sixth place. That sixth-place finish occurred in 1961, at which point Phil Watson went behind the bench, but after just

84 games, Schmidt took over again. Unfortunately, the coaching change did nothing to improve the team's fortunes, and the Bruins sputtered to a 73–157–46 record in Schmidt's second term. When expansion came calling in 1967, Schmidt was promoted to general manager, where he led the Bruins to Stanley Cups in 1970 and 1972.

Having a young lad named Bobby Orr leading the way certainly helped, but when Schmidt pulled the trigger on arguably the most lopsided trade in NHL history, the Bruins' forthcoming Stanley Cup success was sealed. Schmidt acquired future five-time scoring champ Phil Esposito, eventual 50-goal scorer Ken Hodge, and seven-time 20-goal scorer Fred Stanfield in exchange for Pit Martin and Gilles Marotte, both useful but not outstanding players, and backup goaltender Jack Norris. Unfortunately for Schmidt and the Capitals, there would be no such bounty available for trade this time around.

To draw the X's and O's on the Capitals' dressing room blackboard, Schmidt said he was looking for "a good fundamental man with a little Dutch uncle to him."[26] Schmidt believed Jimmy Anderson fit the bill best and signed him to a two-year contract on May 31, 1974. Anderson knew Schmidt well, having been a minor-league coach and scout with the Bruins, but this was also the 43-year-old's first NHL coaching job. Anderson was an American League legend who had plied his trade in Springfield for 14 seasons. He retired as the Indians/Kings' all-time leader in games played (943), goals (426), and points (821), and he was elected to the AHL Hall of Fame in 2009. He also had a brief stint with the L.A. Kings during their first season in 1967–1968, but at 37, his best days were behind him, and he was not in the team's future plans. After retiring, Anderson coached the Springfield Kings to the 1970 Calder Cup final, but the team was swept by Buffalo. In 1972–1973, he was behind the bench of the International League's Dayton Gems, who finished 44–25–4, but lost in the second playoff round.

One of the knocks against Anderson was that he was simply too nice to coach an expansion team as bad as this one would be. For example, during one trip to New York, Anderson ran into Derek Sanderson, an old friend from their days in Boston. Sanderson was frank with Anderson and told him straight up that he could not lead a team like Washington because he was too nice a person. Anderson scoffed at the notion, pointing out that he had pissed off Mike Bloom so much that the coach expected to be on the receiving end of a knuckle sandwich. "But he played one hell of a game afterward," Anderson said.[27]

Even in his early 80s, Anderson would spend time at the local park teaching children how to skate. "Those sessions at Amelia Park [in Westfield, Massachusetts] were so special to him," his son Bill recalled after Anderson passed away in 2013. "He did that right up until last October."[28]

Divisional Realignment

For the 1974–1975 season, the NHL divided its 18 teams into two conferences comprised of two divisions each. Geography was on Kansas City's side. The Scouts, located right in America's heartland, were placed in the Smythe Division along with the Chicago Black Hawks, St. Louis Blues, Minnesota North Stars, and Vancouver Canucks.[29] With the exception of Chicago, none of the Scouts' division rivals would pose much of a threat. "I think we got into the best division of all," said Scouts public relations director Bill Grigsby. "Vancouver has had problems and we don't know how strong they are going to be. St. Louis failed to make the playoffs, as did Minnesota. The Black Hawks are always tough…. We're not saying we're going to be one of the three teams from our division that makes the playoffs, but with Bep as coach and with the type of players we've been able to get, I definitely feel we will be competitive."[30]

The Scouts had a relatively decent chance of stealing a few games against their division foes, whom they would face 24 times, almost one-third of their 80-game schedule. That being said, Abel was not preparing a Stanley Cup parade in the near future. "In two or three years," he said conservatively, "we hope to make ourselves felt."[31]

The Capitals, on the other hand, drew a much shorter straw than their expansion cousins, falling into the Norris Division with the dominating Montreal Canadiens, the up-and-coming Los Angeles Kings, the up-and-down Pittsburgh Penguins, and the fading Detroit Red Wings. Already, it was shaping up to be a long season in D.C.

•• 3 ••

A Sandy Foundation
The 1974 Expansion Draft

"And everyone who hears these words of mine and does not do them will be like a foolish man who built his house on the sand. And the rain fell, and the floods came, and the winds blew and beat against that house, and it fell, and great was the fall of it."—Matthew 7:26–27

For those of you unfamiliar with expansion drafts, allow me to walk you through the process. When a new franchise joins a professional league, it starts with nothing but a front office staff, some stationery with the team's logo, and colorful new uniforms, but there is no real *team* yet. The franchise starts with a base of players who, theoretically, can make up an opening-day roster, but expectations are lower than a snake's reproductive parts, as the players provided in the expansion draft are riddled with question marks.

A few weeks before the draft, each established club decides which players it wants to protect and which players it is willing to part with. The expansion club selects its initial roster from all the players left unprotected. When a player is drafted from the roster of an established team, his former employer can protect one more player. This process continues until the new franchise has drafted two or three goaltenders and 17 to 20 forwards and defensemen, but the exact rules vary from one draft to another.

In theory, the expansion draft makes it easy for new clubs not only to build their initial rosters, but also to stock it with players of professional caliber. Unfortunately, most pro leagues' definition of "professional" and the expansion team's definition of said word are two very different things indeed. Sure, players are all professionals in the sense that they have been paid to play … by *minor* league clubs. In the expansion drafts of 1967, 1970, 1972, and 1974, the term "professional" was attributed to any player whose rights were owned by a NHL team; therefore many of the players chosen had never even seen a NHL game until gaining employment with an expansion team.

On the off chance that the player's name is remotely recognizable, there is probably something wrong with him, whether a history of serious injuries, a lack of foot speed, an inability to find the back of the net, an albatross contract, or just a good old-fashioned retirement waiting around the corner. For the most part, for the millions of dollars spent on gaining entry into a league, expansion teams are given the opportunity to construct their first roster with the rejects and problem children of every team.

An expansion draft is supposed to provide a new team with a few building blocks, but little more. The draft also offers the new team an opportunity to pick up a few bargaining chips, players who, if they prove themselves, may eventually be dealt at the trade deadline to a playoff contender for draft picks or a prospect.

The odds truly are against an expansion team. You may get lucky and hit the jackpot by sticking a coin in a slot machine, as some expansion teams have done through the draft, but chances are you will walk away empty-handed. NHL record books are littered with futility records set by expansion teams of the last 50 years.

No Fair Shake

The Washington Capitals and Kansas City Scouts were doomed to fail from the very beginning because they never got a fair shake. Washington and Kansas City were the victims of, among other things, bad timing and greed, and it took years for them to catch up to their NHL brethren. It didn't matter what they did June 12, 1974; there was not a lot of talent available in the draft, and everyone knew it.

Washington and Kansas City entered the NHL at a time when no one behind the Iron Curtain would entertain the thought of playing in North America, so forget about Czechoslovakia and the Soviet Union. Most general managers would only sign a Swedish or Finnish talent if someone twisted their arm. Forget about finding unmined talent in Germany, Slovenia, or Switzerland too, because they had almost none to speak of. There was also no Internet to help scouts unearth talented players lurking in the deepest, darkest corners of the planet. Washington and Kansas City would have no choice but to pick almost all their players from the North American ranks, and there simply weren't enough quality players left.

The WHA played a major role in draining the North American talent pool. The new league ruthlessly raided NHL rosters in 1972 and 1973, signing several star players to big contracts. Many players saw hockey as a means to an end, and many chose financial security over the Stanley Cup. Because so many star players had signed with the WHA, when the 1974 expansion draft arrived, NHL teams looked down their roster and protected the best players they had, leaving the Capitals and Scouts with nothing but the dregs.

The 1967, 1970, and 1972 Expansion Drafts

In 1967, each established team had been allowed to protect 11 skaters and a goaltender, and after a player was taken from an established club's roster, the club could protect one more player. The plan was perceived as unfair to the new teams, as the expansion teams got nothing more than depth players, injury-prone veterans, and slow-as-molasses defensemen, but compared to subsequent expansion drafts, the Original Six teams were as generous as Oprah asking her audience members to look under their seats.

The Original Six teams, even the bad ones, had deep rosters, and they had tons of players in their system who were good enough to play in the NHL, but with just 120 rosters spots available, American and Western Leaguers struggled to crack the rosters of Original Six clubs. Some tremendously talented players wasted away in the minors racking up goals, assists, awards, and championships, but because they often possessed some fundamental flaw, the minors were where they remained.

Ken Dryden has described expansion players as "players who were good enough for the NHL but had never been good enough before."[1] Those who were once deemed too slow or too injury-prone were now handed an opportunity to play major minutes at the NHL level because their new teams had no choice but to depend on them to score goals and bring them credibility. Other players had long NHL resumes, but because of injuries, inconsistency, or conflicts with their NHL teams, they found themselves buried deep in the minors with virtually no chance of ever getting back to the big league … until expansion pushed open the door.

Perhaps the NHL thought it unreasonable to ask the 1967 expansion clubs, who were still finding themselves, to expose half their rosters for the sake of stocking the Buffalo Sabres and Vancouver Canucks, so when the 1970 expansion draft rolled around the league allowed each existing team to protect 15 skaters and *two* goaltenders. With only about 250 players skating in the NHL there was still plenty of talent to properly stock two expansion teams. Even though the Canucks and Sabres were no world-beaters their first few years, they were at least competitive.

In 1972, the New York Islanders and Atlanta Flames were subject to the same draft conditions as the Sabres and Canucks. Once again, there was more than enough talent in the professional ranks, both major and minor, to stock two new teams, but outside forces intervened and mucked up the NHL's pretty little picture.

Before the Flames and Islanders even played a game, the WHA waltzed in with 12 teams of its own and immediately raided the rosters of every NHL team. The Islanders stumbled to a 12–60–6 mark their first season, not because they didn't draft well, but because defensemen Bart Crashley, Larry Hornung, and John Schella, and forwards Norm Ferguson, Garry Peters, Ted Hampson, and Ted Taylor jumped ship before playing even one game on Long Island.[2] The Flames, however, with a roster almost completely intact, enjoyed successful early returns thanks to the players selected in the draft.

The NHL's expansion plans had been relatively successful to that point despite a few hiccups, but when the WHA announced its arrival, the senior loop should have put a halt to its expansion plans. Of course, the NHL never believed the WHA was a serious threat, so there was no reason to panic, everyone thought, but the Clarence Campbell circuit would soon pay for its hubris.

3. A Sandy Foundation

The 1974 Expansion Draft

The Kansas City Scouts and Washington Capitals each paid $6 million to gain membership in the NHL, but neither received anything close to $6 million worth of talent. In the fall of 1974, there were about to be 32 NHL and WHA teams vying for players.[3]

To give you some perspective on the 1974 expansion draft, picture a delicious bucket of Kentucky Fried Chicken. Imagine that you and your friend haven't eaten all day, and all you want is a delicious, crispy, herbed-and-spiced chicken breast. Imagine that at the exact moment you insert your hands into the bucket of deliciousness you've been thinking about all day long, 30 very hungry and rather pushy friends start shoving their grubby mitts into the barrel. After the rummaging is over, all you and your friend manage to snag is a couple of scraps of chicken skin and maybe a greasy bone. That, in a nutshell, was the 1974 expansion draft, except it was actually *worse* than that chicken analogy because a bucket of fried chicken (a) doesn't cost $6 million, and (b) will not, in any way, lead to years and years of wandering aimlessly looking for respectability.

Signs had been popping up everywhere indicating that the Kansas City-Washington expansion was going to prove a disaster. The Islanders had been pillaged and plundered already, but the NHL simply ignored that and forged ahead with its expansion plans. While the WHA agreed in February 1974 to stop plucking players from the NHL unless their contracts had expired, these free agents (not to mention their agents) knew they still had more leverage than ever before; they could play one league off the other to get the best contract offer possible. The WHA may have been wonky, but it wasn't afraid to throw money around to fight off the mighty NHL, which angered the senior league to no end. Where the WHA got so much money is anybody's guess.[4] Being a hockey player in 1974 was akin to winning the lottery, because if a player didn't like his team's contract offer, there was always another league happy to pay him more. Players who had absolutely no business being paid like superstars were suddenly making thousands of dollars more than they were worth, simply because these two leagues were desperate for bodies and the talent pool was drying up like a wet sponge under a desert sun.

In the NHL's latest expansion draft, all existing clubs were allowed to protect 15 skaters and two goaltenders, just like in 1972. Each established team would part with three players, including a maximum of one goaltender. Furthermore, no player selected in the 1973 Amateur Draft was made available, so every established team could breathe a sigh of relief, knowing that their newest and youngest talents were exempt, and another spot on the protected list could be taken up by a veteran.

Another constraint was that all NHL teams that had lost goaltenders in the 1972 draft (Montreal, Chicago, Boston, and Los Angeles) could exempt themselves from losing another goaltender in 1974, if they chose. Montreal and L.A. chose to waive their right to protect their goaltenders. In the Canadiens' case, former All-Star goaltender, Ken Dryden, was returning from a one-year sabbatical, and they had a wealth of young netminders (Michel Plasse, Michel "Bunny" Larocque, and Wayne

Thomas) with NHL experience in their system, so the Habs were more than pleased to part with a goaltender rather than a skater.

Considering the upside of Montreal's young goaltenders, it seemed likely that the Scouts or Caps would pick one of them, but to make sure fate didn't have other plans, Montreal general manager Sam Pollock intervened. If the Scouts or Caps chose a Montreal goaltender, the Habs could happily protect prized defenseman John Van Boxmeer, so Pollock cut one of his famous backroom deals with Sid Abel: if Kansas City took Plasse with the first overall pick in the expansion draft, Montreal would send two of its prospects to the Scouts' training camp, and if the Scouts liked what they saw, they could sign them.[5] For the Scouts, there was little risk in taking Pollock's deal, since Plasse was already one of the better goaltenders available in the draft, but the players sent to Kansas City did little to impress.

In the end, 44 skaters and four goaltenders were chosen, which means Washington and Kansas City selected more players than any other expansion team had before, not that it mattered much since the surplus players drafted were hardly world-beaters. If the Capitals and Scouts had been allowed to select their team solely from the NHL's best rosters (Montreal, Philadelphia, and Boston, for example), they would have been in good shape, but that scenario would never play out. Since Washington and Kansas City were told to select three players from *each* team, that meant drafting a whole lot of bodies from (ahem) "powerhouses" such as the New York Islanders (19–41–18), Vancouver Canucks (24–43–11) and California Golden Seals (13–55–10). Having the pick of the litter really doesn't mean much when many of the puppies are sick and dying.

Scouting Around for Suitable Talent

The expansion draft was held June 12 at 2 o'clock at the Queen Elizabeth Hotel in Montreal. The Capitals won a coin toss to gain the right to select first in the Amateur Draft, so the Scouts picked first in the expansion draft. As in previous drafts, the players with the biggest upside were goaltenders, and the Scouts secured a couple of good ones.

The Scouts held up their end of the bargain with Montreal and took Michel Plasse with their first pick. Plasse had been selected first overall by Montreal in the 1968 Amateur Draft, but he didn't see much big-league action until 1972–1973. That didn't mean he didn't have his occasional moment in the sun. For instance, while playing for, fittingly enough, Kansas City of the Central League, Plasse became the first professional goaltender to score a goal. Down 2–1, the Oklahoma City Blazers pulled their goaltender, hoping the man advantage would help them draw even. Instead, as the Blazers peppered Plasse, the young goaltender grabbed the puck and shot it at the empty cage.[6] "I took it and threw it away," Plasse explained after the game. "Someone reached for it but missed. Then I saw it going straight up the middle. I could hardly believe it as it went into the open net."[7] Unfortunately, only 812 fans witnessed the historic goal as a blizzard battered Kansas City.[8]

In 1972–1973, as Ken Dryden's back-up, Plasse amassed a splendid 11–2–3 record and 2.58 goals-against average. The following year, Dryden temporarily hung up his skates, so Plasse was given a golden opportunity, but he struggled and finished the year 7–4–2 with a bloated 4.08 average despite playing behind a defense crew that included future Hall of Famers Serge Savard, Guy Lapointe, Jacques Laperriere, and a young Larry Robinson. Plasse frequently clashed with coach Scotty Bowman, so he was deemed expendable, especially after Dryden announced he was returning to the Canadiens for 1974–1975. "My ambition is to come back to Montreal, beat the Canadiens and hand Bowman the puck," Plasse admitted.[9]

The Rangers' Peter McDuffe was chosen to back up Plasse. The 26-year-old McDuffe was short on NHL experience, but long on credentials, having shared the CHL's MVP Award in 1970–1971 while playing for Omaha. That year he registered a 2.77 goals-against average and posted three shutouts. He moved on to Denver of the WHL, where he was named the circuit's top goaltender in 1971–1972. St. Louis gave him a 10-game tryout that same year, and he performed admirably, but he was traded to the Rangers the following year. In seven games with the Rangers over two years, he had a career save percentage of .911 and allowed just 19 goals.

The Scouts' goaltenders not only showed promise, they would prove to be a team strength, but how good would their forwards and defensemen be? Considering they were essentially getting the 16th-, 17th-, and 18th-best players of every other team, the Scouts would have been foolish to believe they would get any All-Stars in the draft. "Do you know what one 17th player on a team has in common with all the other 17th players?" asked Bill Grigsby, the Scouts' part-owner, broadcaster, and assistant to the president. "They are not very good."[10]

The following 22 rounds were reserved for forwards and defensemen, and aside from a few familiar names, there were not many reasons for optimism. The Scouts opened phase two of the draft by choosing former Philadelphia Flyer Simon Nolet. The *Hockey News*' Kansas City correspondent, Jay Greenberg, wrote that discovering Nolet in the expansion draft was "like finding the Mona Lisa at a garage sale," and he wasn't kidding.[11] Nolet was one of the few players available who had even a tad of offensive flair. At that point, he was third on the Flyers' all-time scoring list with 201 points in 356 games. He put up 22 goals and 44 points in just 56 games with Philadelphia in 1969–1970, 23 goals and 43 points in 1971–1972, and another 19 goals and 36 points in 52 games in 1973–1974. Nolet became the Scouts' first captain and represented Kansas City at the 1975 All-Star Game.

As the Flyers completed their transition from expansion pushovers to the fearsome Broad Street Bullies, the talented but not terribly aggressive Nolet did not fit into coach Fred Shero's plans. "They had it in their minds I was strictly offense," explained Nolet. "One year, they had me check Bobby Hull. How do you improve on that? You've got to play both ways to be good."[12]

Bep Guidolin, however, was impressed by what Nolet brought to the table: "smooth skaters like him last forever," he said. "It's so easy for him. No effort at all."[13] "He'll be our goal-scorer," said Sid Abel. "Simon will see a lot more ice time with us than he ever did in Philly, so we see him as a guy who could get 30 or 40 goals."[14]

In the 2nd round, the Scouts selected the player with the toughest hockey name ever, 24-year-old left wing Butch Deadmarsh, from the Atlanta Flames. Deadmarsh had been selected 15th overall in the 1970 Amateur Draft due in part to the impressive 37 goals, 70 points, and 361 penalty minutes he accumulated with Brandon of the Western Canada Hockey League. While those totals didn't quite translate to NHL superstardom (12 points in 117 career games), he was also coming off his best pro season, scoring six goals and earning 89 penalty minutes in 42 games.

He wasn't overly huge, only 5'11" and 186 pounds, but Deadmarsh was a tough customer. "Call him a tough guy, but don't call him a goon," wrote hockey historian Andrew Podnieks about Deadmarsh. "Say he can take care of himself, but don't say he goes looking for trouble. He's no policeman, he only plays the game hard. Call it what you will, Deadmarsh was a physical presence throughout the 1970s in both the WHA and the NHL."[15]

In round three, Kansas City picked up 31-year-old defenseman Brent Hughes from Detroit, and it was understandable why the Scouts coveted him. He was not a big scorer, but he averaged about 20 points per season, and he was a solid defensive player who gave the Scouts some credibility. He was also tough and resilient. On New Year's Eve 1972, he broke his leg in a game versus the Rangers, and while it took him two years to fully recover from his injury, he eventually returned and posted a career-high 22 points with the 1973–1974 Red Wings, his fourth team in two years.

The Scouts selected Paul Terbenche fourth from the Buffalo Sabres, but instead of toiling in Kansas City, he signed with Vancouver of the WHA.

In round five, the Scouts raided the roster of the NHL's bottom-feeders, the California Golden Seals, and selected Gary Coalter, who had played just four games for the Seals, but scored 38 goals and 69 points for Salt Lake City of the Western League. Unfortunately, Coalter would never duplicate that success in the NHL.

After misfires in rounds four and five, the Scouts wisely chose Gary Croteau from the Seals. Nicknamed "The Bull," Croteau was one of the hardest-working players in the NHL. The *Hockey News*' Ken Rudnick once described Croteau as looking "like he fell off the cover of a muscle magazine."[16] In the publication's next issue, Rudnick wrote that Croteau's style of play was "straightforward, dedicated wholeheartedly to the proposition that the shortest distance between two points is a straight line," and if "someone in a different-coloured uniform got in the way, there were 200 pounds on a 6-foot frame to deal with the obstacle."[17] He was also one of the most educated players in hockey, having spent four years at St. Lawrence University in Canton, New York. As a member of the Scouts, he worked towards a Master's degree in guidance and counseling at the University of Missouri.

Croteau had put up 15 goals and 43 points with California in 1970–1971, but he dipped to 12 goals and 24 points the following year, then played just 47 games in 1972–1973. His last year with the Seals, he rebounded nicely to 14 goals and 35 points, even though the team cratered. Despite a lack of natural goal-scoring talent, Croteau managed to stretch out a solid 684-game career in which he scored 144 goals and 175 assists. "Give me seven guys who hustle the way he does, and I wouldn't be far away from having a good club," Bep Guidolin said. "That's what a team needs, a bunch of guys who want to work."[18]

In round seven, the Scouts picked left wing Randy Rota from Los Angeles. A fan favorite during his short tenure in California, Rota was drafted for his offensive

Gary Croteau earned a reputation as one of the hardest-working players on every team he played for (Robin Burns collection).

potential. He had scored 11 goals and seven assists in 60 NHL games split between L.A. and Montreal, but as an American Leaguer, he had put up seasons of 31, 32 and 34 goals, and had been a point-a-game player in three playoffs with the Providence Reds and Nova Scotia Voyageurs.

He was only 5'8" and 170 pounds, so he was no heavyweight, but he could skate rings around the goons who were paid to intimidate him. The mild-mannered Rota, who hailed from Creston, British Columbia, had wheels, and he used them to score his fair share of goals, although he would never be considered a superstar. "Small but mighty," said his future coach, Eddie Bush. "He's a shooter and a skater. You don't have to be big to play this game." Being small did have its advantages though. "I crate [sic] more penalties than I take," he explained. "A guy will have his stick up to normal height and he'll high-stick me."[19]

In round eight, center Lynn Powis was plucked from Chicago's roster. Unlike many of the players selected in the draft, Powis had three things going for him: youth, upside, and a knack for finding himself on championship rosters. He was about to turn 25 when the draft rolled around, and he was coming off an 8-goal, 21-point campaign accomplished in just 57 games of limited ice time. He could play either at center or at left wing. Before coming to the Hawks, he had won a Calder Cup with Nova Scotia of the AHL in 1972, and an Adams Cup with Omaha of the CHL in 1973. An Avco Cup (WHA) championship with Winnipeg would find him in the late–1970s as well.

In the ninth round, the Scouts selected John Wright from St. Louis. He had scored 10 goals and 27 assists for the Vancouver Canucks in 1972–1973, but dropped to six goals and nine assists in 52 games the following year, which was split between Vancouver and St. Louis. He would play just four games for Kansas City before disappearing from the professional hockey scene.

The Scouts' 10th pick was Ted Snell, a right wing who had scored four goals and added 12 assists in 55 games for Pittsburgh in 1973–1974, but he had put up 64 points with Hershey of the AHL the year before, so he had some scoring potential. Unfortunately, it would never be realized in Kansas City or elsewhere.

In round 11, former K.C. Blues defenseman Chris Evans was snagged from Detroit's roster. Evans had somewhat of an offensive touch, scoring 24 points with Buffalo and St. Louis in 1971–1972, and another 21 points with the Blues the following year, before falling to four goals and nine assists in 1973–1974. He didn't last very long in K.C., participating in just two games, but the two assists he recorded technically put him at the top of the Scouts' all-time leader board for points per game.

In round 12, the Scouts snatched 26-year-old defenseman Bryan Lefley from the New York Islanders. Lefley had made his NHL debut in Long Island in 1972–1973 and scored three goals and seven assists in 63 games. The following year, like many of his new Kansas City teammates, he completely fell off his team's depth chart, seeing only seven games of action, but he did score 44 points in 58 games with Fort Worth of the CHL, so there was a chance he would rebound in K.C.

"A year ago," read his profile in the Scouts' 1974–1975 media guide, "[Lefley] was considered the best young defenseman on the Islander team" and "experience against NHL competition [was] all he [needed] to develop into a first line hockey player."[20] The sometime left winger, sometime defenseman from Grosse Isle, Manitoba, was a good hitter, although he was never much of a scorer. Some felt he did not compete hard enough night in, night out, but he had a sound hockey mind. After his on-ice career took him to Dusseldorf, Germany, he became a coach in Zurich in the early 1980s, and he coached in Europe for many years. Sadly, Lefley was killed in a 1997 car accident while coaching in Italy. In his book *Players*, Andrew Podnieks summed up Lefley's career rather poetically: "If you are a good hockey player, there are many options and possibilities outside the NHL. Hockey is a sport that crosses borders and one based on a common language that has sticks and pucks as its nouns and verbs."[21]

In round 13, Kansas City took Robin Burns from the Pittsburgh Penguins. Over three seasons, Burns had played 41 games with Pittsburgh and had registered all of five assists. "For three years with Pittsburgh I was on the toilet-seat run, up and down, up and down," Burns recalled.[22] He was not the most natural of goal scorers, but he got the job done in the minors. He scored 40 points in 46 games with Amarillo of the CHL, and in 1972–1973, he scored 47 points in 39 games with the AHL's Hershey Bears, followed by another 66 points in 74 games the next year. Burns also led the AHL playoffs with ten goals in 14 games, which may have helped persuade the Scouts to draft him.

Sid Abel understood that Burns could play a valuable role with the Scouts, but it was Burns himself who cleverly coerced his general manager into making him a better contract offer. "One of the interesting things was that when I told Sid Abel that I was my own agent, he said, 'That is so refreshing,' but what he didn't know was that in advance I had met with four or five different player agents.... I [negotiated my contract] myself, and Sid said, 'Just for not having to negotiate with a player agent, I'm gonna give you an extra five thousand a year,' and I signed a four-year deal." Burns added that Abel "was a gentleman. His wife Laurie was a beautiful lady, and Sid was always, always a positive person," a sentiment that was echoed by just about everyone who met him.

In the 14th round, the Scouts selected winger Tom Peluso, a fourth-round pick of the Chicago Black Hawks in 1972 who never played a single NHL game.

In the 15th round, Kansas City picked Kerry Ketter, a 6'1", 202-pound defenseman who played 41 games for the Atlanta Flames in 1972–1973 and recorded just two assists and 58 penalty minutes. He never played another NHL game, but later appeared in 48 games for Edmonton of the WHA.

The Scouts scored better in the next round when they selected 22-year-old left wing Norm Dube, a native of Sherbrooke, Quebec. Although he had yet to play a single NHL game, he had enjoyed two 30-goal seasons with the Springfield Kings of the AHL. "His form chart shows great skating and aggressive checking. He could become the Scout's [sic] scoring star of the future,"[23] said the team media guide about Dube, and in a way the description was accurate; he would become a scoring star of the future, and that future was December 1974. He played on a line with Richard Lemieux and Gary Coalter, and he briefly found his scoring touch, picking up seven points in ten games while Lemieux scored nine points during that same stretch. During one 28-game period, Dube scored a respectable 15 points, but his offense dried up in February as the Scouts' fortunes faded.

The Scouts drafted a rather large French-Canadian contingent that day. Temiscamingue, Quebec native Richard Lemieux, taken with the 17th pick, had put up 17 goals and 35 assists for Vancouver in 1972–1973, which was among the best career seasons of anyone in the draft, but Lemieux slipped to five goals and 17 assists the following year. It was obvious why the Scouts picked Lemieux; he possessed an impressive skill set that few of the exposed players could boast. He could skate fast, was productive on the power play, and won his fair share of face-offs. He also played with a chip on his shoulder. "At 5'8" and 160, Lemieux gives the impression he can be intimidated. Don't try it!" the Scouts' media guide warned.[24]

With their 18th pick, the Scouts hit a home run when they selected center Dave Hudson from the Islanders. Although Hudson was never a flashy scorer, he had put up 12 goals and 19 assists for the Isles in their first season, and he set team records for assists (4) and points (5) in a game, marks that stood for years. Like most of the players available in the draft, he had slipped badly in 1973–1974, scoring just two goals and ten assists. Luckily for K.C., Hudson would become one of its more consistent players, and he would remain with the franchise for four years.

With their 19th pick, the Scouts looked to Detroit and selected 26-year-old defenseman Ken Murray, whose 75 games of NHL experience went back to 1969–1970. He had scored just one goal and six assists during that span, so he was not going to see a lot of power-play time with the Scouts, but Murray was reputed to be a heavy hitter. "It's just the game I play," he said after being called up to Kansas City

Dave Hudson was a late expansion draft selection, but he was one of the most successful picks by either Washington or Kansas City, scoring 140 points in 277 games with the Scouts franchise (Robin Burns collection).

in January. "I go to the body. I knock 'em down if I can catch 'em." He was a bit "awkward during training camp," remembered Bep Guidolin, so he was sent down to the minors, but a week later he suffered a concussion, which ruined his chances of remaining in K.C.[25] When Claude Houde and Mike Baumgartner both went down with injuries, Murray was called up on New Year's Day, but he played just eight games, then headed back to the minors. He would play 23 games with the Scouts the following year, but he never scored a goal.

The Scouts fared better in the next round, choosing 24-year-old defenseman Dennis Patterson from the Minnesota North Stars. Patterson had been selected by Minnesota in the third round of the 1970 Amateur Draft, but he was sent down to the minors, and he remained there four years. He spent one year in Clinton of the Eastern League, where he put up a respectable 36 points. The Stars sent him to their AHL affiliate in Cleveland during the 1970–1971 season, and he played two more full seasons there before finding himself with the New Haven Nighthawks, the Stars' new AHL farm team. The 1973–1974 season was his best: eight goals and 25 assists in 70 games. There was a good chance Patterson would have seen some action in Minnesota in 1974–1975, but the Scouts grabbed him first.

While pickings became increasingly slim as the draft went on, the Scouts scrounged up a few keepers who would see lots of ice time in year one. One of them was 22-year-old center Ed Gilbert, taken from Montreal with the 21st pick. Gilbert had languished for two years in the AHL, where he put up 21 goals and 39 points as a rookie for Nova Scotia, and 30 goals and 74 points in 1973–1974. Like most prospects in the Canadiens system, Gilbert had little chance of graduating to the big club since the Habs were well stocked at every position. To become one of Montreal's top four centers, he would have had to supplant either Jacques Lemaire, Peter Mahovlich, Henri Richard, or Doug Risebrough, which was unlikely. "I had a pretty good minor league stint in Montreal, and Al McNeil told me to get in touch with an agent," Gilbert said. "My agent at the time told me to have a good second year and I had a good chance to get in with Washington or Kansas City."[26]

"I can't remember how many times I saw him," said Baz Bastien. "Maybe 10, maybe 12. But I thought he could be a helluva hockey player. Sid liked him, too. We made up our minds pretty much what we wanted, and he was the guy."[27] Gilbert would become one of the Scouts' power play specialists, but he also scored a couple of short-handed goals during the season. Gilbert was a very good skater who could set up teammates for goals.

With their final pick of the draft, Kansas City selected left wing Doug Horbul from the Rangers. "He can do it all," said an excited Sid Abel. The Rangers thought highly of Horbul, but agreed to let him go if K.C. chose Pete McDuffe, which they did. "He is an excellent skater, and the scouting report rates him an exceptional positional player," said the Scouts' 1974–1975 media guide. "Horbul should be around the National Hockey League for many years."[28] He lasted four games in Kansas City and scored one goal.

Crappy with a Capital "C"

Three weeks before the expansion draft, Milt Schmidt sounded pleasantly optimistic about the Capitals' chances of reaching the pinnacle of NHL success, a Stanley Cup championship, just like the Philadelphia Flyers were about to achieve against his old team, the Boston Bruins. He also seemed a bit naïve as to his prospects at the draft. "We're going to be taking a lot of players, and I've been told we're going to wind up with some that shouldn't be here," he said. "Well I'm determined that's not going to happen…. I'm not taking anyone just to be around."[29]

Like the Scouts, Washington chose wisely in the two rounds reserved for goaltenders. With their first pick, the Caps selected 24-year-old Ron Low from Toronto. "Lowtide" hailed from Birtle, Manitoba, and as a rookie, he briefly earned Toronto's number one goaltender job when Jacques Plante was dealt to Boston in March 1973 (for future considerations, which became goalie Eddie Johnston). Behind a mediocre Toronto squad that had already lost defensemen Rick Ley and Brad Selwood to the WHA, Low finished 12–24–4 with a bloated 3.90 goals-against average. The Leafs seemed to do everything possible to make sure Low never started another game, as they traded the rights to Bernie Parent to Philadelphia for Doug Favell, and then acquired Dunc Wilson from Vancouver. The Favell-Johnston-Wilson triumvirate held up, and the 1973–1974 Leafs finished 35–27–16, so it was no surprise Low was exposed in the expansion draft.

Low was arguably the most unfortunate goalie in the league, going from an Original Six team that boasted future Hall of Famers Darryl Sittler, Lanny McDonald, Dave Keon, Norm Ullman, and Borje Salming to a team of castoffs. When Low retired in 1985, his career record was a wretched 102–203–38, and he had just seven playoff games to his credit. The fact that his career spanned 12 years despite his sorry statistics speaks volumes about his talent and tenacity.

Thankfully, Low had experience playing behind a poor defense, but poor Michel Belhumeur, Washington's second pick, was in for the shock of a lifetime. In September 1974, before he even played one game with Washington, Belhumeur sued his former team for $1 million because he hadn't received his $19,000 Stanley Cup share as well as his $4,500 share for the Flyers' West Division championship. The problem, however, was that Belhumeur did not see even one second of action during the 1973–1974 season. A year earlier, he had been quite busy and had briefly earned his coach's trust.

Belhumeur was riding the pine November 26, 1972, when Boston tagged Doug Favell for six goals in 24 minutes. Fred Shero pulled Favell in favor of Belhumeur, and the 23-year-old shut out the Bruins the rest of the way. Shero gave the kid another shot the next game, and the result was 32 saves in a 2–2 tie versus Toronto. Belhumeur also won his next two games and six of his next nine to keep the Flyers in the playoff hunt, but by the end of January, Shero went back to Favell, and Belhumeur saw only spot duty the rest of the way. One thing he did *not* see the rest of the way, or at any other time in his future NHL career, was another win.

Unlike the Scouts, the Capitals chose to go with potential rather than name recognition, so many of the players Washington drafted had not seen a lot of NHL ice except from their couch watching *Hockey Night in Canada*. In the first round of forwards and defensemen, Washington selected left wing Dave Kryskow, an aggressive player with a great shot from the Chicago Black Hawks. "Kryskow's basic measurements are not much different from Bobby Hull's," wrote hockey historian Andrew Podnieks, "and it was as a potential Hull replacement that Kryskow made the Hawks in 1972–73.... Needless to say, Kryskow was no Hull."[30] Kryskow had shown some potential in the minor leagues, amassing 62 points in 52 games for the CHL's Dallas Black Hawks in 1972–1973. Even more impressively, he scored the first-ever *shorthanded* hat-trick in pro hockey history. When he was called up to Chicago for three playoff games, he scored two goals, but the following year, his first full NHL season, he managed a disappointing seven goals and 12 assists.

In the second round, the Caps smartly plucked the pugnacious Yvon Labre from Pittsburgh's roster. "Just call me Ivan," Labre would tell anyone who had trouble pronouncing his French name.[31] Considering he was almost exclusively surrounded by Anglophones, he probably heard his fair share of people call him "Yvonne."

Labre's Capitals career was the prototypical expansion success story. Expansion gave the hard-working, but light-scoring Labre an opportunity to play in the NHL full-time. From 1970 to 1974, the Sudbury, Ontario native got into only 37 games with Pittsburgh, but he would play seven years in Washington. "Hard work and relentlessness earned Labre every shift he ever played at every level," wrote Andrew Podnieks. "He had little talent ... but most of all he had miles of heart."[32]

"Yvon Labre wasn't the biggest guy in the world, but he fought everybody in the league," remembered Ron Lalonde, who played with Labre in Pittsburgh and Washington. "We didn't have any tough guys to go with him, and he wouldn't back down from anybody. And for the limited talent he had, he had a heart the size of the arena, and the fans got to really appreciate that."

Washington sportswriter Ron Weber wrote, "if you had to have fisticuffs with someone, then go on a week-long fishing trip with him, Ivan's your man. For one thing, he doesn't hold a grudge. For another, he's less than championship boxing material. 'I've got short arms,' he explains, while showing absolutely no reluctance to swing with the next adversary."[33]

Labre sometimes suffered brain cramps when facing opposing forwards, which put him into a position where he had no choice but to take the attacker down from behind, but Labre was a hard worker and a much-appreciated teammate. The problem with Labre was that the mind was willing, but the body was not always able to deliver. Injuries would eventually take their toll, and he played only two full seasons with the Caps, in each of which he led the club in penalty minutes. His perseverance and dogged determination helped him stretch out a career until 1980. Labre was so highly regarded in Washington that despite never leading the club to the playoffs, and scoring just 12 goals in 334 career games, he became the first player in franchise history to have his number retired.

In the third round, the Capitals hoped Pete Laframboise, snagged from the California Golden Seals, could repeat the 16-goal, 41-point performance of his 1972–1973 rookie campaign. The left winger was also the first player in Seals history to score four goals in one game. His second full season, however, saw his numbers plummet to seven goals and 14 points. It was the same old expansion story: another player once brimming with so much promise now looking for a fresh start.

Laframboise was just hoping to avoid the chaos that had almost consumed him in Oakland. He later described his two-year California tenure as "a complete farce" and a "paid holiday."

"You wouldn't believe the things that went on there," Laframboise said. "A common cold could keep a guy out 30 days. A guy would crack a bone, the docs couldn't find the crack, and he'd be out half a season." Laframboise was indeed thankful to leave the Seals, a team so badly neglected by owner Charlie Finley it was bought by the NHL just to get rid of him. Crowds were absurdly sparse even at the best of times. That said, the 19th-overall selection in the 1970 Amateur Draft had a seemingly bright and secure future. "I thought I was going to be protected," Laframboise recalled. "[Director of Hockey Operations Garry] Young told me to go buy a house, so I did, and I never even got to sleep in it once."[34] Poor Pete. By Christmas, the Oakland Coliseum would start looking like the fabled Montreal Forum.

The Caps' next picks were far less recognizable, and their lack of skill and experience strongly hinted at how the first season would unfold in Washington. In the fourth round, Washington selected forward Bob Gryp from Boston. While he had posted 38 goals for the AHL Boston Braves in 1972–1973, and another 30 goals the following year, those totals were never reached again, not even in the minors, which was unfortunate for the Caps, a team in desperate need of offense.

Next, it was L.A.'s turn to lose a player, in this case defenseman Gord Smith, who had not yet played a single NHL game. Like many of the others picked by Washington, Smith's minor-league credentials were enticing. His 1973–1974 season with

Springfield was impressive to say the least. Not only were his 67 points just five shy of the AHL record, and his 54 assists just two off the league record, he was voted the circuit's best defenseman. The Perth, Ontario native was the brother of Hall of Fame New York Islanders goaltender Billy Smith. While Gord would never be mistaken for Bobby Orr, he stretched out a 299-game career out of a limited skill set. The first 286 games of that career were played for the Capitals, making him one of the more successful selections from the expansion draft.

In the sixth round, the Capitals selected Steve Atkinson from the Buffalo Sabres. Unlike most of the other draftees, Atkinson had significant big-league experience, having once scored 20 goals for the Sabres when they (and he) were in their first year. Unfortunately, Atkinson never reached that magic mark again, falling to 14 goals in his second year, nine his third year, and six his fourth year.

In round seven, the Capitals looked to Philadelphia for their next pick, forward Bruce Cowick. "At one time," said Andrew Podnieks, "this fighter was in high demand. The era was the '70s. The stats were penalty heavy. The team was the Broad Street Bullies."[35] The Flyers were gearing up for one hell of an arms race, and they wanted every fist they could find. If it meant trading four assets (Jim Stanfield, Tom Trevelyan, Bob Currier, and Bob Hurlbut) to do so, so be it. Thanks to the 165 penalty minutes he accumulated in 1972–1973 with San Diego of the WHL, Cowick was expected to fit right in. He played eight playoff games for Philly the following year and looked good in his limited experience; he rammed the Bruins' Tasmanian devil, Terry O'Reilly, into the boards, in Boston, twice. Unfortunately, Cowick looked timid when draped in the star-spangled Capitals uniform, registering just 41 penalty minutes in 65 games.

In the eighth round, Washington picked one of the best players available, Toronto's Denis Dupere (pronounced "Doo-Pair-ay"). The mustachioed Jonquière, Quebec native was expected to carry Washington's offense after scoring 13 goals and 36 points in 61 games in 1972–1973. The following year, "Dupy" was on pace to match those totals, but he saw action in only 34 games and finished with eight goals and 17 points. He had potential for much more.

As the draft went on, the names got less and less familiar, to the point where it was almost impossible to evaluate the rosters of these new teams without a collection of media guides from across the continent. The Caps took Toronto defenseman Joe Lundrigan in the ninth round, but he would play only three games with Washington. In the 10th round, Washington chose 55-game veteran Randy Wyrozub from Buffalo, but he wouldn't see action at all with Washington.

In round 11, the Bruins' Mike Bloom became the Capitals' newest member. Bloom had been Boston's first-round pick in 1972 but failed to crack the Bruins' lineup, mainly because they were so stacked at every position. He had put up decent numbers in St. Catherines of the junior Ontario Hockey Association, and in minor-league San Diego he scored 25 goals and 69 points in 1973–1974, but as Andrew Podnieks put it, "the Beantowners left him high and dry in the Expansion Draft."[36]

In the 12th round, the Caps selected right wing Gord Brooks from the St. Louis Blues. While the 5'8", 168-pound right wing from Cobourg, Ontario was never going to send bodies flying into the crowd, he absolutely rocked one of the baddest fu-manchu mustaches of the era. He also had a bit of a scoring touch, exemplified by 16- and 21-goal campaigns with Kansas City of the CHL from 1970 to 1972, followed by 26 points in 23 games with Fort Worth. The latter season could have been much better had he not suffered a broken collarbone. He was called up to St. Louis in 1973–1974, and he scored six goals in 30 games.

In round 13, it was the Blues' Bob Collyard's turn to step up and claim his spot on Washington's initial roster, but that's about as far as he got, not playing a single game for the Caps.

In round 14, the Caps plucked defenseman Bill Mikkelson from the New York Islanders. If it is true that misery loves company, misery indeed loved spending time with the affable Mikkelson. He was part of the 12-60-6 New York Islanders of 1972–1973, at the time the worst expansion team in hockey's modern era, and now he was getting a first-class seat on the roller-coaster ride that was the Washington Capitals, soon to be the *all-time worst team* in hockey history.

The Neepawa, Manitoba-born defenseman had shown some promise as a junior player in the Western Canada Hockey League, putting up seasons of 41, 31 and 39 points even though he played no more than 59 games in a season. He had also scored 14 goals with the Brandon Wheat Kings in 1967–1968, but he was never able to repeat that success in the pros. As a member of the L.A. Kings system, he scored just two goals and nine assists with Springfield of the AHL before suiting up 15 times with L.A. in 1970–1971. With the Islanders, he saw a significant increase in ice time, but scored just one goal and 10 assists. That said, Mikkelson had more professional experience than most of his teammates, and his positive attitude was much appreciated, if not required, just to survive a season with an expansion team.

In the 15th round, Washington chose Boston Bruins right wing Ron Anderson. The Moncton, New Brunswick native had gone unnoticed for years due in part to his decision to play for Boston University when college hockey players were ignored in favor of junior hockey players. Eventually, the Boston Bruins took a flyer on the undrafted Anderson in 1972, but since he was fourth on the Bruins' depth chart behind stalwarts Ken Hodge, Terry O'Reilly, and Bobby Schmautz, he never got a sniff of the NHL until landing in D.C.

In round 16, the Caps picked up Mike Lampman from the Vancouver Canucks. Although he had but four career goals in 47 career NHL games, he found the back of the net regularly for Washington, albeit for a very brief period.

In the 17th round, Washington selected 26-year-old right wing Lew Morrison from Atlanta. Morrison had lots of experience, 332 games' worth, but he was not known for his offensive flair, never having reached the 20-point mark. He was, however, a good penalty killer, and he had won the Flames' Unsung Hero award for 1972–1973.

In the 18th round, star minor-league center Steve West was claimed from Minnesota, but he chose to sign with Michigan of the WHA instead.

In the 19th round, the Caps went with 22-year-old defenseman Larry Bolonchuk of Vancouver. He had all of 15 games of experience at the NHL level, but he was an aggressive player, amassing totals of 166, 139 and 174 penalty minutes in three IHL seasons.

In the 20th round, Washington chose another defenseman, 25-year-old Murray Anderson of Minnesota. He had yet to play a single minute of NHL hockey after puttering around the AHL for four years with varying degrees of success. He topped out at a decent 43 points with New Haven in 1973–1974, so once again, the Capitals were hoping those minor-league highs were a good omen.

In the 21st round, forward Larry Fullan was plucked from Montreal's roster, and as with so many selected before him, the Capitals were betting on his potential rather than his credentials. The 37 goals and 47 assists he recorded with AHL Nova Scotia looked promising, and with Richmond the following year, he scored another 65 points, so the NHL seemed like the next logical step for Fullan, but he would play just four games with Washington.

With their last pick, the Caps selected Jack Egers from the Rangers, which at first glance seemed like a smart, low-risk move. After all, Egers possessed a great shot which had earned him the nickname "Smokey," and he had a deft scoring touch, potting 23 goals in 1971–1972 with New York and St. Louis, and 24 the following year with the Blues. Despite his high skill level, Egers struggled mightily in 1973–1974 after knee surgery to repair a torn cartilage over the summer, but that didn't dissuade Schmidt. Unfortunately, Egers' career was all but over, and he played sparingly the next two years.

Expansion Draft Analysis

At the conclusion of the draft, sports writers unanimously agreed that the Scouts and Capitals were going to suffer greatly during their inaugural season, if not the next two or three as well. Some writers confidently claimed the two expansionists were the worst teams in the history of hockey, and they hadn't played a game yet. Media members across North America made snarky comments a-plenty regarding the embarrassing first season the Scouts and Capitals were about to endure.

After the draft, one Canadian columnist wrote that the Capitals were "only recognizable in their own mirrors."[37]

"If they think they've got a mess in Washington now[38] wait until they see the Capitals."[39]

Another Canadian columnist suggested that to avoid humiliation, the Capitals should "wear unlisted numbers."[40]

Windsor Star columnist Jim McKay imagined what might be written in a future newspaper after the first-ever game between the Capitals and Scouts: "Washington and Kansas City met last night in hockey for the first time. Hockey lost."[41]

NHL Players' Association head Alan Eagleson stated that the Scouts and Capitals owners should receive a complete refund of their $6 million expansion fee unless the league made better players available.[42] Russ White of the *Washington Post* wrote that it was "disgraceful" that Pollin "[couldn't] appeal to the Better Business Bureau."[43]

Pickings had been absurdly slim in the draft, but could the Scouts and Capitals have made wiser choices? Los Angeles' Bob Nevin, 36, remained exposed until the fifth round of forwards and defensemen. He would score 72 points in 1974–1975 and another 55 the following year, so his presence would have helped either Washington or Kansas City in the short term, and he could have been great trade bait come February when better teams load up for a playoff run.

Claude Larose was also available until the second-to-last round of the draft. Like Nevin, he only had a couple of years left, but he had a solid offensive touch, notching 137 points in 280 games after the draft.

Gary Bergman, a solid offensive defenseman, was available from Minnesota, and although he was nearing the end of his great career, he could have netted the Scouts or Capitals some interesting prospects or draft picks at the trade deadline.

Nevin, Larose, and Bergman would have helped the Scouts and Caps win a few more games their first few years, but they were cases of diminishing returns, much like investing in a ten-year-old used car. There was little chance Nevin, Larose, and company were ever going to repeat, let alone exceed their past glory. It made more sense to draft Dave Kryskow, Mike Lampman, Norm Dube, and Ed Gilbert, where there was a smidgen of hope they would become solid, long-term contributors.

From the results of the draft, it appeared as though Sid Abel privileged a what-have-you-done-lately mentality, since he plucked three players who had scored at least ten goals in 1973–1974. Thirty-two-year-old Simon Nolet was the oldest player drafted, and he was coming off a 19-goal season. He led all drafted players with 93 career goals, and he was the only player drafted to have scored more than 200 points in his career. Gary Croteau had potted 14 goals in 1973–1974 and had 129 points in 284 career games. Randy Rota had scored 10 goals in 58 games.

The Scouts' defense had some experience as well, but not much offensive skill. Brent Hughes, a 370-game veteran, was the elder statesman of the group at 30, and he could be counted on for about 15–20 points. Paul Terbenche had played 189 career games since 1967 but had scored just five career goals. The other defensemen chosen had but a few dozen games of experience combined.

All in all, this bunch was not going to set the hockey world on fire, but the hope was that with their experience level, they would at least put up a good fight and keep scores relatively close.

The Capitals, on the other hand, rolled the dice on young players who had very little NHL experience[44] but who had put up big numbers in the minors. Potential aside, stats-wise, no one on the Capitals screamed, or even whispered, "offensive superstar." Jack Egers, the wonky-kneed, 258-game veteran, led all Caps draftees with 58 career goals, 64 assists, and 122 points. Of all the Caps' draft picks who played in the NHL in 1973–1974, Denis Dupere led them all with a measly eight goals. Of all the defensemen they picked, Bill Mikkelson led the way with just 87 games under his belt.

All in all, the Scouts' draftees had far more experience, to the tune of 2,384 games (average of 108.4 per skater)[45] compared to the Capitals' 1,646 (78.4 per skater). In the goal-scoring department, the Scouts' selections scored 278 goals (12.6 per skater) compared to the Caps' 217 (10.3 per player). The Scouts' initial roster scored a total of 807 career points through 1973–1974, or an average of 36.7 per player. The

Capitals fared even worse with a sad 497 career points, or an average of just 23.7 points per player!

The Scouts' draftees had also been far more productive in the season prior to the draft, suiting up 753 times, for an average of 34.2 games apiece, while Washington fared much worse with 418 games played, just 19 per player. Kansas City's draftees lit the lamp 81 times and totaled 229 points (3.7 goals and 10.4 points per player), while the Capitals' initial roster counted just 40 goals and a measly 100 points (1.8 goals and 4.5 points per player).

Career Stats Before Draft, 1973–1974 Stats

Kansas City

Player	POS	From	GP	G	A	PTS	PIM	GP	G	A	PTS	PIM
Simon Nolet	RW	PHI	358	93	108	201	129	52	19	17	36	13
Butch Deadmarsh	LW	ATL	117	9	3	12	136	42	6	1	7	89
Brent Hughes	D	DET	370	14	99	113	397	71	1	21	22	92
Paul Terbenche	D	BUF	189	5	26	31	28	67	2	12	14	8
Gary Coalter	C	CAL	4	0	0	0	0	4	0	0	0	0
Gary Croteau	LW	CAL	284	52	77	129	53	76	14	21	35	16
Randy Rota	LW	LA	60	11	7	18	16	58	10	6	16	16
Lynn Powis	C	CHI	57	8	13	21	6	57	8	13	21	6
John Wright	LW/RW	STL	123	16	36	52	65	52	6	9	15	33
Ted Snell	RW	PIT	55	4	12	16	8	55	4	12	16	8
Chris Evans	LW/RW	DET	216	19	38	57	139	77	4	9	13	10
Bryan Lefley	D	NYI	70	3	7	10	56	7	0	0	0	0
Robin Burns	LW	PIT	41	0	5	5	32	0	0	0	0	0
Tom Peluso	LW/RW	CHI	0	0	0	0	0	0	0	0	0	0
Kerry Ketter	D	ATL	41	0	2	2	58	0	0	0	0	0
Norm Dube	LW/RW	LA	0	0	0	0	0	0	0	0	0	0
Richard Lemieux	C	VAN	192	29	61	90	68	72	5	17	22	23
Dave Hudson	C	NYI	132	14	29	43	24	63	2	10	12	7
Ken Murray	D	DET	75	1	6	7	97	0	0	0	0	0
Dennis Patterson	D	MIN	0	0	0	0	0	0	0	0	0	0
Ed Gilbert	C	MTL	0	0	0	0	0	0	0	0	0	0
Doug Horbul	LW/RW	NYR	0	0	0	0	0	0	0	0	0	0
Totals			2384	278	529	807	1312	753	81	148	229	321
Avg. Per Player			108.4	12.6	24	36.7	59.6	34.2	3.7	6.7	10.4	14.6
Avg. Per Game				0.12	0.22	0.34	0.55		0.11	0.2	0.3	0.43

Washington

Player	POS	From	GP	G	A	PTS	PIM	GP	G	A	PTS	PIM
Dave Kryskow	C/LW/RW	CHI	83	8	12	20	22	72	7	12	19	22
Yvon Labre	D	PIT	37	2	3	5	32	16	1	2	3	13
Pete Laframboise	LW	CAL	147	23	32	55	40	65	7	7	14	14
Bob Gryp	C/LW/RW	BOS	1	0	0	0	0	1	0	0	0	0
Gord Smith	D	LA	0	0	0	0	0	0	0	0	0	0
Steve Atkinson	RW	BUF	256	49	47	96	96	70	6	10	16	22

Player	POS	From	GP	G	A	PTS	PIM	GP	G	A	PTS	PIM
Bruce Cowick	C/LW/RW	PHI	0	0	0	0	0	0	0	0	0	0
Denis Dupere	LW	TOR	192	29	44	73	26	34	8	9	17	8
Joe Lundrigan	D	TOR	49	2	8	10	20	0	0	0	0	0
Randy Wyrozub	C	BUF	100	8	10	18	10	5	0	1	1	0
Mike Bloom	C	BOS	0	0	0	0	0	0	0	0	0	0
Gord Brooks	RW	STL	32	6	8	14	12	30	6	8	14	12
Bob Collyard	C	STL	10	1	3	4	4	10	1	3	4	4
Bill Mikkelson	D	NYI	87	1	11	12	51	0	0	0	0	0
Ron Anderson	RW	BOS	0	0	0	0	0	0	0	0	0	0
Mike Lampman	LW	VAN	47	4	3	7	2	29	2	0	2	0
Lew Morrison	RW	ATL	332	26	35	61	89	52	1	4	5	0
Steve West	C	MIN	0	0	0	0	0	0	0	0	0	0
Larry Bolonchuk	D	VAN	15	0	0	0	6	0	0	0	0	0
Murray Anderson	D	MIN	0	0	0	0	0	0	0	0	0	0
Larry Fullan	LW	MTL	0	0	0	0	0	0	0	0	0	0
Jack Egers	RW	NYR	258	58	64	122	138	34	1	4	5	12
Totals			**1646**	**217**	**280**	**497**	**548**	**418**	**40**	**60**	**100**	**107**
Avg. Per Player			**78.4**	**10.3**	**13.3**	**23.7**	**26.1**	**19**	**1.8**	**2.7**	**4.5**	**4.9**
Avg. Per Game				**0.13**	**0.17**	**0.3**	**0.33**		**0.1**	**0.14**	**0.24**	**0.26**

It became quite obvious to even the most amateur of hockey fans that these two teams had had no choice but to build the foundation of their $6 million mansions on a sandy beach. No matter how pretty that house looked on the outside, and no matter how much money the well-intentioned owners promised to dedicate to their houses' maintenance, these mansions were worthless because they were going to be swept into the ocean before long.

"It's not fair," lamented Milt Schmidt. "We paid $6 million to join the league, and look how little other teams have left for us."[46] Years later, Schmidt placed the blame for the Capitals' early struggles on Clarence Campbell. "He told us we were supposed to have the first choice of any player sent down to the minors. That wasn't so. We didn't get the players we were supposed to get."[47] Kansas City assistant GM Baz Bastien agreed. "With the other clubs protecting 15 players and the two new clubs being too close to the last expansion, there was just nothing left," he said two years later.[48]

In truth, the 1974 draft was no more unfair than the 1972 proceedings, but the circumstances surrounding the draft had changed drastically in two years, and they would have an even greater effect on Washington and Kansas City than could have been imagined. Dozens of former NHL players were plying their trade in the WHA, and in the two years since the WHA's inauguration, the NHL had not sufficiently replaced the talent poached by the renegade league. What all this meant was that the 17th- and 18th-best players on each NHL team in 1974 were not nearly as good as the 17th- and 18th-best players of each team in 1972. *Windsor Star* columnist Jim McKay described the players available in the draft as "little more than a bag of bones."[49]

Making matters worse, the rebel league was still snapping up free agents left, right, and center, which had a tremendously negative effect on the 1974 draft. Some NHL teams did not even bother protecting certain excellent players, knowing they were intending on jumping to the WHA. For example, before the draft took place, Frank Mahovlich had already made it clear that he was going to sign with the Toronto Toros, so Montreal protected another player instead, knowing the Scouts and Capitals wouldn't waste a pick on Mahovlich. The same went for Dave Dryden of Buffalo, who ended up signing with the Chicago Cougars. The result was that Washington and Kansas City lost out on a few quality players who could have made a difference.

The 1974 Amateur Draft

At the time, expansion teams were always given the opportunity to draft first, and luckily for K.C. and D.C., this was exactly the case once again. Unfortunately, the 1974 draft was widely considered the weakest in years, since there were no "can't miss" prospects who would dominate hockey for years to come. At the 1973 draft, only players born before January 1, 1954, were eligible to be drafted, but the WHA ignored the NHL's rules and signed 18-year-olds like Mark and Marty Howe, Dennis Sobchuk, Wayne Dillon, and Tom Edur. The following year, 19-year-old defenseman Pat Price was signed by the Vancouver Blazers.

The Capitals and Scouts desperately needed to hit a home run just to keep pace with the rest of the league, but they were walking to home plate brandishing a toothpick. The NHL reacted by lowering the cut-off date for first- and second-rounders of the 1974 draft to January 1, 1957, but the top juniors remaining were only now the cream of a weaker crop because the WHA had already scooped up the best talent. For the first time, the Canadian Amateur Hockey Association allowed the NHL and WHA to draft players under 20 years of age, but these players could only be selected in the first two rounds. Fourteen underage juniors were chosen in the first two rounds, and the teams drafting them ponied up $40,000 per player.

The 1974 Amateur Draft was unlike any other in NHL history. For one thing, the entire process lasted three days (instead of one), starting on the morning of Tuesday, May 28. Nothing was easy anymore thanks to the arrival of the pesky WHA, which had planned its own draft for May 31. Since the renegade league persistently tried to sign under-20 junior stars, the senior league wanted to get the jump on its competition. The NHL draft was held in secret, and picks were made via a wide-ranging phone network connecting each team to the league's head office in Montreal, but somehow, the player selections were leaked, and many names appeared soon after in newspapers across the continent.

Since the Scouts won the first pick in the expansion draft, the Capitals chose first in the Amateur Draft, and they bombed big time with defenseman Greg Joly, who would score just 97 points in 365 career games. "This is a great opportunity to play for a new team," Joly said. "It's better than being with one of the older, established clubs." He was wrong on all counts.

The poor kid barely stood a chance. In any other year, he likely would have been drafted much later, but with a weak draft class competing for first overall, not to mention Joly's Memorial Cup tournament MVP award (two goals, three assists in three games), the defenseman became an attractive prospect. He scored 21 goals and added 71 assists in his final year with Regina of the WHL, so he definitely had some skill. However, immediately after drafting Joly, the Caps committed the same error made by so many other teams who also drafted a first-round defenseman: they ludicrously compared him to the greatest rearguard of all time. "He's the kind of defenseman everyone has been looking for since Bobby Orr," said Milt Schmidt, dooming Joly before he played a single NHL game.[50] Not helping Joly in the least was the massive contract he signed: $800,000 over five years.

"Greg had a lot of potential, and it was easy to see that he had a lot of natural talent," said Doug Mohns. "He was the one player I felt sorry for. Had he been on a winning team, starting out, I have no doubt that he would have had a lengthy career in the National Hockey League barring injuries. He was only 20 years old and had very little support."[51]

Bill Mikkelson believed Joly's career was badly mishandled by the Capitals, and the teenager was unprepared for the pressures of being a top draft pick skating in the NHL. "Greg was a nice kid, really nice kid," remembered Mikkelson.

> I can't say anything bad about him, but…. I don't know whether he knew what a weight room was. He was obviously an excellent skater, but waist up, muscular? Not at all … not physically ready, but very deceptive, very good with the puck, tons of skill….
>
> And certainly, you know, even today, very good defensemen spend two or three years in the minors before they'll bring them up, and put them into limited playing situations … and then they sort of work their way up to more minutes and more responsibility playing against other teams' top lines. For us, being one of four defensemen [in the line-up every night] … it's just not fair. He should not have been put in that situation. Skill-wise, sure he was great, but it takes so much more than that…. I think other teams may have picked on him a little more than other guys, I don't know, being a well-known, high draft pick…. He was a happy-go-lucky kid … but I'm sure under the surface he must have been churning because so much was expected of him, way more than should have been laid on him, and like a bunch of us, he shouldn't have been there.

The Capitals had themselves one of the strangest Amateur Drafts in history. It seemed as though the Caps' goal was to completely drain the junior leagues. The Caps selected a whopping 25 players, including 13 of the last 45 players among the NHL-record 247 who were drafted. As the draft entered its latter stages, the Capitals just kept picking, and picking, and picking players like it was some sort of compulsion. One could understand their reasoning, however: the more players Washington drafted, the greater the chance one would succeed in the NHL. Unfortunately, since this was a weak draft, only six of Washington's 25 picks ever played a game in the NHL, and of those six, Joly's 365-game career would be the most successful.

Other than Joly, the only Washington draft pick to make any sort of impact was second-rounder Mike Marson, who had scored an impressive 35 goals and 59 assists in 69 games for the OHA's Sudbury Wolves. The Scarborough, Ontario native had the makings of a solid, if not excellent professional player, but one thing constantly held him back: he was black. "Mike wasn't as fortunate as me in regards to comments," said friend and teammate Bernie Wolfe, referring to the fact that he was Jewish. Wolfe admitted he had never been the target of anti-Semitic comments in the NHL, but Marson "had a much tougher time from other players and fans, and it was very sad."

"What a skater! He could skate like there was no tomorrow," remembered Wolfe. "He was a very talented hockey player." During a 2020 Zoomcast about the early years of the Washington Capitals, Wolfe told the story about when he and Marson bumped into Abe Pollin, his wife Irene, and another couple. "This is many, many years ago, of course, and Abe was a wonderful man," he recalled, "and he was bragging to his friends that he was the first owner to have both a Jewish player and an African-American player on the team, and I said, 'That's right, Abe, and you ruined us together!'"[52] Of course, Wolfe was only poking fun at his affable boss, but in all seriousness, Marson was doomed to fail in Washington.

As of September 1974, 12 times more people had walked on the moon than there had been black hockey players in the NHL. The only other black NHL player had been Willie O'Ree, who suited up 45 times for Boston but not since 1961. Schmidt had been O'Ree's coach in Boston, and the Bruins legend made an impression on Marson's father. During one interview for the Canadian Broadcasting Corporation, Schmidt explained that O'Ree was simply a Bruin like everyone else on the club, and not a *black* Bruin, so Marson's father was delighted that his son would suit up for the Hall of Famer's new club.[53]

At just 19, and with a lucrative five-year deal under his belt, the left winger was expected to put a few pucks in the net and lead the Caps to a few wins, but he was also asked to do so while deflecting racial slurs coming from all directions. Marson did himself no favors, however, by showing up to training camp 22 pounds overweight, and he did not score a point in his first 15 games. He shed the excess weight and became a solid contributor his rookie season, scoring 16 goals and 12 assists in the other 61 games he played, but everyone expected more.

"He was short, 5'9" or whatever, but he was about 5'9" wide too," remembered Bill Mikkelson. "Big arms, big legs, and a really strong guy for a kid his age. Usually you get into that size and strength in your mid-twenties or something like that. He was physically very mature and strong, and I don't remember him fighting that much, but I don't remember him ever backing down either or anybody intimidating him."

The Scouts fared much better with their first pick than the Caps did, going with 18-year-old Wilf Paiement, who would enjoy a respectable (and at times spectacular) NHL career. He was just coming off a 50-goal, 73-assist season with St. Catharines of the Ontario Hockey Association, so he was expected to inject a little pop into the offensively weak Kansas City lineup. Paiement was the prototypical "power forward," a guy who could score goals, but who would also drop the mitts and collect lots of penalty minutes. Ken Rudnick of the *Hockey News* once described Paiement as "a fine broth of a lad, a bull not to be trusted by even the most careless china shop proprietor."[54] Of everyone chosen in the 1974 draft, Paiement would score the third-most career goals (356) and points (814).

"Wilf, he was a big, strong kid," remembered teammate Robin Burns. "He was built like a brick shithouse.... I think his father was a lumber man, and he was a wrist wrestling champion of Ontario. He was just a mammoth man."

Paiement earned himself lots of space early on in his NHL career and began to build himself a bit of a reputation as someone who was not afraid to throw down. He was the youngest of 16 children, so he learned early on that to survive in the world, he would need to use his muscle and not let himself get intimidated. "You knew you'd better be ready if you were going to get into his face or do anything that irritated him," said broadcaster Jiggs McDonald. "There was a price to pay."[55] Years later, Paiement was coached by the flamboyant Don Cherry, who believed there was never anyone scarier under his tutelage. "The guy had those eyes like [one of his all-time favorites Bobby Schmautz]," he recalled to Al Strachan for the book *Hockey Stories Part 2*, "and I'll tell you, you didn't fool with this guy. He was the nicest guy off the ice, as a tough guy usually is, but nobody fooled with him."[56]

Hockey talent ran in Paiement's family; his brother Rosaire scored 34 goals for the 1970–1971 Vancouver Canucks, and as the younger Paiement was making plans to graduate to the pros, Rosie was a point-per-game player for Chicago of the WHA. "He used to give it to me all the time," Wilf admitted, "but with him gone, it was my older brother, Larry. Larry showed me a lot. He's the reason I play hockey.

"I used to go 20 miles all the time when I was 12 to play with the men. But I'd lost interest before. I didn't care about playing, so I sold the skates. My brother bought me another pair. I must have been a natural because I never really paid any attention until I was 14."[57]

The Scouts obviously had a lot of faith in Paiement, not only stitching hockey's sacred number 9 on his uniform, but signing him to a massive three-year contract worth an estimated $600,000. Like Greg Joly, Paiement became one of many "bonus babies," raw junior talents who scored some big rookie contracts resulting from the NHL–WHA war. "They came up with the money, and we weren't going to refuse," said Paiement. "They came up to what I wanted, so I'm satisfied." The Scouts were also in the unenviable position of having to throw extra dollars around just to keep their top prospect away from the Vancouver Blazers, but Paiement also explained that he preferred to play in the world's top league anyway and be a building block for the Scouts.[58] The Scouts also sweetened the deal by promising to fly in Wilf's parents four times a year to watch their son play.[59]

The rest of Kansas City's draft was pretty unspectacular. In fact, of the 13 players chosen, only five would play an NHL game, and of those five, only Paiement and Bob Bourne (582 points in 964 games) would enjoy successful careers.

While the draft was much weaker than usual, the expansion twins needed to shoulder part of the blame for their lousy draft lot. In fact, future NHL stars such as Pierre Larouche, Bryan Trottier, Charlie Simmer, Danny Gare, Ron Greschner, Guy Chouinard, Mario Tremblay, and Clark Gillies, among others, were selected in the first three rounds and would have helped the Scouts and Capitals immensely, but somehow slipped through their fingers.

With the Amateur Draft concluded and the Capitals' and Scouts' rosters stocked, all that was left was to get the historic 1974–1975 season under way. For the first time, 18 teams would compete in an 80-game schedule that would stretch from October 9 to the Stanley Cup–clinching game on May 27. Needless to say, neither Kansas City nor Washington would be a part of the celebration. Because of the NHL's sorry excuse of an expansion draft, not to mention arguably the worst Amateur Draft in history, the Capitals and Scouts were well on their way to fighting over Japan's Coca-Cola Cup, though that was still nearly two years away.

PERIOD 2

•• 4 ••

The Washington Capitals, 1974–75

> It's one thing to be an underdog, but it's quite another to find oneself in a situation where a team has so little talent and so little cohesion that no amount of hard work can overcome *anything*. The smothering gloom of that self-knowledge undermines all motivation; at such abysmal levels, competition seems not even a difficult struggle but a pointless demonstration.—Jeff Z. Klein and Karl-Erik Reif in *The Klein and Reif Hockey Compendium*[1]

For most expansion teams, expecting to succeed is simply an exercise in futility. The losses pile up quickly. There isn't enough talent to pull a team out of a prolonged funk. The forwards seem armed with pea shooters. The defense seems to be skating in mud. The goaltenders face a virtual firing squad every night. As Capitals coach Jimmy Anderson later put it, "You can't take hockey players named Flotsam and Jetsam and win games. You can't make an apple pie out of a barrel of lemons."[2]

Before the first puck had even been dropped, the Capitals' brass was already complaining about how they had been shafted in the conscription of their initial players. "When will someone on an established club admit that the expansion draft as it's run now is a disgrace?" asked Abe Pollin.[3]

Milt Schmidt was no happier than his boss. "We paid $6 million and look how little the other teams left us," he exclaimed. "You'd think they'd want to help us get off to a good start in the NHL, which would help the league and help fight the WHA."[4] Schmidt's tone had certainly changed since the expansion draft, when he declared, "I am very pleased with everything.... Many other clubs had to go through the same thing we are going through. They had to start from scratch and so do we. But if they want to protect 15 players, maybe they shouldn't be allowed to fill." Before skedaddling into the pity zone, he changed course, explaining, "But then the draft laws shouldn't be changed for the benefits of two teams when the other clubs had to go through the same thing."[5] He was certainly speaking more graciously than he should have. After all, Washington had drawn from a talent pool shallower than in previous expansions. There were signs that the Capitals would not be just another expansion team; this outfit would be one for the ages for all the wrong reasons.

Speaking of *outfits*, authors Jeff Klein and Karl-Erik Reif wondered if it was "some sort of inside joke in Washington when the team entered the league in 1974 with 'capitals' spelled out across the players' chests in *lower-case letters* ... with the 't' forming a little hockey stick, of course."[6] In the first edition of their book, *The Klein and Reif Hockey Compendium*, the authors described the Caps' threads thusly: "Like the New York Americans of the twenties and thirties ... the Caps take to the ice clad in sweaters that look like the debris after the explosion of an American flag."[7]

One important detail Klein and Reif forgot to mention, or perhaps chose to erase from their memory banks, was the Capitals' pants. As a general rule, the only time white looks good on a hockey uniform is when it is the primary color on a jersey. White should *never* be the primary color on any other visible part of a player's uniform. The California Golden Seals tried painting their skates white in 1971–1972, and the result was players looking like they were skating on stumps when they appeared on television. By the following season, the Seals wisely added some green to their white skates before finally returning to all-black blades. The Capitals, however, ignored the Seals' fashion faux pas and dressed their players in white pants, which would be worn on the road with red jerseys.

Not only did the white pants look goofy in the first place, but when they got wet, they became as transparent as Saran Wrap, and fans could easily see the brown padding underneath. Sometimes, if a player wasn't wearing long underwear, fans could see a whole lot more, if you know what I mean.[8]

Tommy Williams was acquired from Boston a few weeks after the expansion to provide the youthful Capitals with much-needed veteran leadership. Here, he models the Caps' infamous white pants, which were discarded after just four road games early in 1974–1975 (Doug McLatchy collection).

If that wasn't bad enough, after a couple of periods of game action, the unfortunate-looking pants made it look like the players had soiled themselves. You see, when players sweat, slide on the ice, and have all sorts of blood, boogers, phlegm, and puck marks leaving stains everywhere, white pants become a real bad idea real fast. Yes, you could figuratively *and* literally say the Capitals looked like shit. The pants were mercifully retired after the Caps lost to Chicago on October 23, 1974, and even though the NHL had a rule prohibiting uniform changes in the middle of a season, the league relented. The Capitals could have gone the traditional route and chosen blue pants to go with their red away jerseys, but no, they defied all logic and went with red instead. This new uniform looked equally ridiculous, so four road games later, the Caps chose the only other option left in their color palate, which went over much better with fans, and remained a part of their uniform for over two decades.

Filling in the Gaps

As confounding as the Capitals' uniform situation was, it paled in comparison to the major question marks Milt Schmidt and Jimmy Anderson had concerning their roster. It was so incredibly weak that soon-to-be 41-year-old defenseman Doug Mohns was invited to training camp on what Schmidt called a "look-see basis" even though Mohns was still under contract with Atlanta. "He was Grandfather Time," said defenseman Murray Anderson. Coming off a back injury and operation, Mohns reported to camp early and performed well enough that the Caps purchased the last year of his contract from Atlanta.[9] The Capitals indeed had a reason for feeling concerned about the state of their defense. Mohns had 1,315 games of NHL experience under his belt; number two on the defensemen experience list was Bill Mikkelson, with 87 big-league games to his credit. Yvon Labre's 16 games played in 1973–1974 were second to Mohns' 28. No other Caps defenseman had played a single minute that season in the NHL.

In the Capitals' early days, Mohns was the most recognizable name on the lineup card. He had been in the NHL seemingly forever, starting out as a 13-goal, 14-assist Boston Bruins rookie in 1953–1954. He was very versatile, often suiting up at left wing rather than his more natural defense position. He possessed a booming slap shot, tremendous speed, and an ability to dish the puck precisely to teammates. With Boston, he often teamed up with Fern Flaman on the blue line and Don McKenney on a forward unit. In 1956–1957, he finished fifth in voting for the Norris Trophy, given to the league's top defenseman. After scoring 118 goals and 229 assists in 711 games with Boston, he was traded to Chicago in the summer of 1964, where he would go on to even greater success. Between 1965 and 1969, Mohns broke the 20-goal mark every year, playing on the "Scooter Line" with center Stan Mikita and right wing Ken Wharram.

After Wharram complained of chest pains, was diagnosed with myocarditis, and had to retire, Mohns found it difficult finding the back of the net. He went from 22 goals in 1968–1969 to six in 1969–1970 and just four the following season, so Chicago traded him to Minnesota late in 1970–1971. He never regained his scoring touch although he remained a respected leader on and off the ice. He became the Capitals' first captain, but he wouldn't receive the "C" until 37 games had been played. For his dedication, perseverance, and sportsmanship on and off the ice, he became the Caps' nominee for the Bill Masterton Trophy at season's end.

Nelson Pyatt joined the Capitals late in the season, and Mohns treated the young forward much like a father would. Mohns noticed that Pyatt was sartorially inept, so to speak. In fact, he owned just one suit, a lovely corduroy number, which led to much finger-pointing and laughter. Mohns, who believed the youngster needed to dress like a professional hockey player, brought Pyatt to a tailor he knew in Montreal, and Pyatt added three beautiful new designed suits to his wardrobe.[10]

Even though Mohns was universally respected by his teammates, he was not spared the indignity of being the butt of a few jokes. Mohns was, shall we say, folically challenged, so he wore a toupee ... even under his helmet. To make sure it didn't come off and expose his nearly naked scalp as he removed his lid for the national anthem, he would simply salute the flag. One time, however, as the Caps were skating off the ice for the intermission, Mohns removed his helmet, but the toupee somehow got stuck inside. Garnet "Ace" Bailey, a practical joker and shit disturber *par excellence,* joined the Capitals later in the season, and he just could not help himself. "Jesus Christ," he shouted to Mohns, "don't let them blow the top of your head off, it's just a frigging game."[11] On road trips, Mohns used to carry his precious hair piece in a little red box, and when it went AWOL one time, Mohns nearly blew a gasket.[12]

If the Caps' blue line looked thin, the offense was in an even bleaker state. Schmidt had little choice but to shop around for anyone who could put the biscuit in the basket, so he picked up 34-year-old Tommy Williams from Boston in another cash transaction which turned out to be his best pre-season move.

Williams had been a good offensive player in the Original Six days, often finishing in double-digits in goals, and as a 19-year-old was part of the gold-medal-winning 1960 U.S. Olympic team, scoring 10 points in seven games. In 1963, now in the NHL full-time, he scored 23 times and added 20 assists for Boston. Most years, he was good for about a point every two games. When expansion arrived, his totals went up. First, it was 50 points in 68 games for Boston in 1968; two years later, he exploded for 67 points as a member of the Minnesota North Stars.

When Williams' wife suddenly passed away, however, he struggled both personally and professionally. He had trouble handling alcohol, and his relationship with coach Jackie Gordon soured. He was dealt to California in February 1971, and in the 18 games he played there to close out the season, he scored 17 points, but the rejuvenation didn't last long. After a slow start the next year, the Seals sold him to Boston, and then he signed with New England of the WHA. He rebounded nicely with 21 goals and 58 points in his second season there, but there were doubts that he had much left in the tank.

Doug Mohns had played with Williams in Boston and remembered him as "good at handling the puck" and a "better than the average player when it came to his skating ability," a skill Mohns believed "kept him in the league."[13]

"For a guy that was at his stage in his career," recalled teammate Ron Lalonde, "he was a really good skater ... [but] he had what we called flight patterns, you know, a play. We'd do it on the chalkboard, drawing the lines up, and this was Tommy Williams' flight pattern, and you got to hit him with the puck up here, but he could skate and he could score.... He was an interesting character for sure."

Williams was also a bit unpredictable off the ice. His nickname was "The Bomber" because once, as a member of the Seals, he unwisely told a customs agent he was carrying a bomb, and he was promptly arrested. On another occasion, while

Williams and roommates Denis Dupere and Ron Low were renting a nice house, they often hosted team parties. The house had a beautiful fireplace, but the three bachelors lacked firewood. Undaunted, the resourceful Washington players tore the cedar shingles off the basement walls, grabbed a few old chairs, and chucked them all into the fireplace to help get a roaring fire started. "I felt sorry for the owner," admitted Lalonde, "but it was pretty funny at the time."

The Capitals also purchased the contract of left wing Bill Lesuk from Los Angeles. Early in his career, Lesuk seemed to have the makings of a pretty good goal-scorer. In Philadelphia, he played on the "LBJ Line" with Serge Bernier and Jim Johnson, and for a short period they lit it up regularly. In 1970–1971, Bernier, Johnson, and Lesuk finished second, third, and seventh in team scoring. Lesuk finished his first full NHL season with 17 goals and 36 points, but the following year he dipped to seven goals and 13 points in 45 games before being shipped off to L.A., where his numbers continued to disappoint. The Capitals were hoping Lesuk could resurrect his career and return to his double-digit goal-scoring, but he didn't record his first goal until December 20.

The Capitals also acquired center Neil Murphy, a 13-goal scorer with the AHL's Boston Braves, but he never made it onto the Washington roster.

What Do a Chef, a Lightbulb, and Johnny Bower Have in Common?

Players from all over the place converged on the Capitals' training camp in London, Ontario, hoping to earn a roster spot. It was like the freakin' Island of Misfit Toys got a good deal on some hockey equipment. There was Jiri Bar, a former Czechoslovakian junior who was "an overweight chef in Philadelphia," Tim Conway, known as "Commie," who was invited to camp as a favor to a Caps minor owner, and Terry "Lightbulb" Wasson, who, based on his nickname, was wasting his time competing for a goaltender job.[14]

The Montreal Canadiens granted prospects Peter Sullivan, Guy Delparte, and Kevin Ahearn the opportunity to practice with the Capitals, and if Jimmy Anderson and Milt Schmidt were impressed, they had the Canadiens' blessing to keep them. After all, it wasn't like Sullivan, Delparte, or Ahearn had a prayer in Montreal considering the Habs' depth. Delparte and Ahearn never amounted to much at the big-league level, but Sullivan had some serious skills. Schmidt was hoping to take on a larger centerman, however, so Sullivan was sent back to Montreal. They sent him down to their AHL affiliate in Nova Scotia, where he promptly scored 104 points before joining the WHA's Winnipeg franchise the next year and scoring 295 points in 313 games.

Doug Mohns was the first veteran to report to camp, which opened on September 9. Officially, it was a rookie camp, so he was joined by young newcomers such as Greg Joly, Mike Marson, John Paddock, Paul Nicholson, Jack Patterson, Brian Kinsella, and Johnny Bower, son of the great Toronto goaltender of the same name.

For some players who had already been around the NHL block a few times, training camp meant an opportunity to shine. "We began with a lot of enthusiasm at training camp," recalled Denis Dupere later in the season. "So many guys were getting a chance to play."[15] Anderson had held two practices a day for three weeks to whip his players into shape. "The game," said one Caps player, "was our easiest day. We had the rest of the day off."[16]

It did not take long for players to realize that being part of the first edition of the Washington Capitals would be the hockey equivalent of going over the top and charging through No Man's Land, only to be met by German gunfire. Mike Lampman, for one, did not feel Anderson was the right person to be coaching this rag-tag bunch: "I just thought Jimmy didn't come with enough coaching experience to handle an expansion team like this. He was a nice guy and I know he coached in the minor leagues, but that clearly wasn't enough. All I remember was, in training camp and the early games, he seemed to be overmatched as a coach."

The Capitals' pre-season started off quite ominously as the team geared up to play its first game, against Buffalo, in St. Catharines, Ontario. Right wing Steve Atkinson choked on a piece of chicken or steak (depending on the person you ask), which required a barium solution at the hospital to get it dislodged.[17] "I was too damn excited to get going," he said.[18] With all due respect to legendary comic actor and writer Larry David, Atkinson definitely should have curbed his enthusiasm just a bit; the near-death experience was a harbinger of very dark days ahead. The cover of one Capitals exhibition game program mistakenly called the NHL's newest franchise the "Washington Generals," the lovable losers who almost never beat the barnstorming basketball legends, the Harlem Globetrotters.

John Paddock, described in the *Hockey News* as "a big youngster with a nose as red as Rudolph the Reindeer's," opened the scoring on a 20-foot slapper at 4:36 of the first period. "I didn't expect it to come on my first shift," Paddock said. "I was so excited that I almost went into the net after it."[19] Jack Egers scored on a power play to give Washington a 2–0 lead. While the Sabres ultimately skated away with a 4–2 victory, the Capitals looked all right, but the Sabres were just gearing up for what would become a 113-point season, and they were not going to become Washington's first prey. Despite a good initial showing, when the Caps faced those same Sabres on September 25, they could not have looked more like an expansion team. Not only did they lose, 3–1, but Bob Gryp failed to score on a penalty shot, and the Caps got nabbed twice for having too many men on the ice.

If anyone judged the Capitals' future success on their performance in their first pre-season game in D.C. September 28, they surely would have expected them to be Stanley Cup champions in no time. Tommy Williams grabbed the puck on an errant Montreal pass and beat Ken Dryden just 11 seconds into the contest, capitalizing on the typical early-season errors that plague so many teams. "I believe it hit off one of our defenseman's skates," Dryden explained. "I never got a decent look at it." Just 30 seconds later, Andre Peloffy put Washington up, 2–0, and the Habs headed into the first intermission wondering what had gone wrong. "Those guys are obviously shooting for a place on the roster," Montreal coach Scotty Bowman said about the Washington players. "That's the pattern with almost all the new teams. It is amazing how deep some guys can dig."[20]

Unfortunately, the Capitals didn't dig quite deep enough as Montreal roared back and eventually took a 4–3 lead with two minutes left. Denis Dupere feathered a pass to Steve Atkinson—in his first game with Washington, and now fully recovered from his unfortunate bout with that piece of chicken—who shot a 14-foot backhand past goaltender Wayne Thomas to knot the game at 4–4 with just 1:23 remaining, which sent 8,119 D.C. fans home very happy. Needless to say, that game was an anomaly, as there would be very little success against the Montreal Canadiens, or anyone else for that matter, for the next few years. Years later, Yvon Labre remembered that the players were "high as kites" and brimming with confidence, but that feeling would fade away fast as games began to count in the standings.[21]

Greg Joly had a particularly difficult start to his NHL career, and the media was ruthless. "Greg Joly makes $3,769 a week. In his first two weeks as a Washington Capital, the prized rookie has done just about nothing to earn it," said the *Baltimore Evening Sun*'s Phil Hersh. "Joly cruised through the one-week rookie season, partly because he came to training camp out of shape and partly because as top draft pick, is assured of making the team."

Joly also missed half the team's practices, and the first four exhibition games, due to a strained Achilles tendon. After injuring his foot, he was given a day and a half to rest before he participated in an 80-minute scrimmage which caused further damage to his foot. There were accusations that management, upset with Joly's lackadaisical approach to fitness, pressured the 20-year-old defenseman into practicing a bit too hard when he should have been resting, but Anderson denied any wrongdoing, stating that any player earning six figures could only remain on the sidelines so long. "He skated that much on his own, then found out it was sore," said Anderson. Doctors were consulted, and Joly was told to sit for a short spell. Joly admitted he was to blame for aggravating his injury. "I think I just went back too soon. It's nothing serious, just a pulled muscle. I've just got to let it rest."[22]

Milt Schmidt was depending on Joly to recover from his injury, since the rest of the Caps' defense did not have much offensive skill. "We're a much better team with Joly in," he said. "He's the guy we're relying on to get the puck up the ice by the tough forecheckers in this league."[23]

The Caps' other prized rookie, Mike Marson, also arrived in camp out of shape, and like Joly, he was earning big bucks: a five-year, $500,000 contract. Marson was determined to make the Capitals and prove to everyone that he was worth every penny. "I'll be on the ice for the National Anthem on Opening Night in New York," he said early at training camp. Marson worked his tail off and got rid of the excess pounds, usually two or three a day, partly a result of hard work, but also due to skipping the odd meal. "He began to get involved physically," Schmidt said. "He realized that there was more to this game than just putting the uniform on." His efforts paid off as he became the first Capitals player to score a hat-trick in a 6–4 win over Detroit on October 3. "Mike needed that game," Anderson said. "It was the confidence builder for him. He is just a kid and he'd been nervous. Sometimes it takes a veteran player four or five exhibitions to get untracked." Ironically, the right winger's first and only career hat-trick may have led to the premature end of his NHL career. Schmidt was on the verge of sending Marson to the minors, which would have given the kid a chance to develop his skills. Instead, because of his big night, he was told he would stick with the big club.

"I'm 19, have some money, and it's up to me now to play it all right," Marson said after earning his spot. "If I do, I can go through life without having to work at anything but hockey. It's what I've always dreamed of doing."[24] Marson felt confident he was on the right track, and while he indeed possessed the skills to succeed in the NHL, his work environment would hinder his development.

The Numbness Begins

All in all, the Caps had looked pretty good in the pre-season, going 3–4–1, including a three-game winning streak to conclude the exhibition schedule, but the good fortune would be short-lived. The Capitals wouldn't win three in a row again until 19 months later, and even then, those three wins would not officially count in the standings.

The Capitals opened their 1974–1975 season October 9, 1974, against the New York Rangers, who had finished the previous season with 94 points, so few people expected a happy ending for Washington. In fact, as the team was boarding the plane to the Big Apple, Bruce Cowick noticed an airline agent helping an elderly passenger. Thinking he was funny, he commented that teammate Joe Lundrigan also needed some help. The agent, thinking he was funnier, responded, "Your whole team needs help."[25] Who knew that airline agents were expert hockey analysts!

Bill Mikkelson remembered how a future Hall of Fame defenseman took him down with a clever quip in the early stages of the Caps' franchise opener. "I took a penalty against Brad Park…. He skated by me as I was going to the penalty box, and I said, 'Nice dive' to him, and he said, 'Yeah, first one this year!'… a quick-witted thing on his part … so off I went to the [penalty box], not too happy."

Jim Hrycuik (pronounced "Huh-RYE-chuck") scored the first regular-season goal in Capitals history at 5:06 of the first period. The rookie stole the puck from Rod Seiling and took off towards the Rangers' goal with Dave Kryskow on his flank. New York had just one defenseman back, and he chose to cover Kryskow, so Hrycuik had a perfect shot at the cage. He closed in on Ed Giacomin, deked him out of his jock strap, and put in a backhand shot. "I got so excited I didn't know what to do with myself," Hrycuik said about what was also his first NHL goal, on his first shift, and on his first shot.[26]

Hrycuik's historic marker gave Washington the lead for exactly 37 seconds until Rod Gilbert fed a pass to Greg Polis, who beat Ron Low for the tying goal. Both teams scored a goal in the second period, but in the third period, almost everything went the Rangers' way. The Capitals' tight defense soon fell apart, and the Rangers outshot the Caps, 19–1, in the final frame. Rick Middleton put New York up, 3–2, just 1:11 into the period, but Kryskow tied it up 0:32 later. Just two minutes later, Rod Gilbert skated into Capitals territory and lured several Washington players towards him as he dished the puck over to Polis, who tucked the puck into the left corner of Low's net. Middleton scored his second goal at 16:13 to make it 5–3, and Gilbert wrapped up the night's scoring with a goal 0:29 later to seal the Rangers' 6–3 victory.

"It could've been worse—but not much," said a tired Ron Low, who faced 43 shots compared to the Capitals' 12 on Giacomin. Low's quote was actually one of the most uplifting related to the 1974–1975 Capitals.

"The defense just fell down, that's all," Low continued, trying to rationalize the loss. "But you've got to expect that. We're brand new. Half the time we didn't know what we were doing. We had lines skating together for the first time." Low believed, however, that this was the making of "a pretty good team," but they just "played a better one."[27]

Low probably had no idea, but this night was just a microcosm of the Caps' entire first season, and the fatigue he felt would stick with him like a permanent tattoo "I'm numb. I've been numb for 30 minutes or so. I can't say I'm proud. We lost, didn't we? But what the hell, we ran out of shots."

Jimmy Anderson was thoroughly impressed by his team's effort, even though the Rangers dominated the game pretty much from start to finish. "They always talk about how expansion dilutes the quality of play," he chirped after the game. "But these kids really looked like they belonged out there. I think we're going to give some teams a lot of trouble."[28]

"The worst moments," Hrycuik said, "were when we got trapped in our own zone and couldn't move the puck out. They swarmed all over us. They hit us, they muscled us. I never realized how strong some of the guys are who are in the league."[29]

A 75-point scorer with Hershey of the AHL, Rostern, Saskatchewan native Hrycuik was acquired in the intra-league draft in June 1974. Milt Schmidt had scoured North America looking for anyone who could score a few goals, and while he was in Hershey, he took notice of Hrycuik. "I knew a lot of scouts were coming to our games," Hrycuik admitted. "I didn't know they were looking at me. We had a lot of guys who could come up to the NHL."[30] Despite his early flourish, Hrycuik was not long for the Washington Capitals' world. In November, he was shunted off to AHL Richmond, where he scored seven points in seven games. He was called back up to Washington and scored four points in seven games before running into a goalpost and injuring his knee. He never played another NHL game.

Low tried to look on the bright side despite a tough finish. "It's not going to be like it was tonight all year," Low said as he swallowed salt tablets.[31] He was 100 percent right in saying game one would not be repeated all season long; it would actually get much worse, and this loss would be nothing more than a drop in a very full bucket.

Dupy Bumps a Rump and Smokey Goes in the Dump

After a humiliating 6–0 shutout at the hands of the Minnesota North Stars three days after the season opener, the Capitals returned home on October 15 and tied Los Angeles, 1–1. The home opener was attended by a disappointing crowd of just 8,093, in part because the team's sales department expected a lot of last-minute ticket purchases, so no one believed it would be necessary to paper the house with free tickets to make the event seem like an overwhelming success. Only 6,000 season tickets had been sold by the end of October. "It's an interesting phenomenon," said Capitals and Capital Centre vice-president Jerry Sachs about the low season-ticket sales. "I guarantee you we didn't lie about the 30,000 requests. They were very real."[32]

The Capitals' brass was not worried about the disheartening early-season turnout. "Washington will beat the Flyers' first year gate," boasted assistant GM Edgar "Lefty" McFadden. "When the Redskins finish, the Capitals will be the thing in this town. The Bullets will have their night on Saturday. The Capitals will have Sunday. There's no doubt in my mind that the hockey team will average over 10,000 a game."[33] In the end, McFadden was right ... barely; the Caps averaged 10,004 customers per game, and those aforementioned Flyers provided the Capitals with their only two sell-out crowds of the season.

The Capitals took to their home ice October 17 to take on the Chicago Black Hawks before 9,471 fans, and they were treated to an entertaining contest. Germain Gagnon gave Chicago a 2–1 lead 0:54 into the second period, but the Capitals fought back. Denis Dupere had earned a reputation as a hard worker, but his slap shot couldn't break a pane of glass, and most of his goals were scored in close. In fact, Dupere's first goal as a Capital, at 12:04 of the opening frame, was scored by banking a shot from behind the net and off the skates of goaltender Mike Veisor. Dupy's second goal, which tied the game at deuces, bounced off the ass of Hawks defenseman Doug Jarrett who, when Dupere joked, "A fine shot, eh?" was quick to retort, "No big deal, I have the biggest rump in the league."[34]

Less than two minutes later, Ron Anderson put the Caps up by a goal. Gagnon and the Caps' Mike Bloom were both sent to the penalty box for spearing with under seven minutes remaining in the period, and 0:14 later, Bill Mikkelson was chased for tripping, giving Chicago a 4-on-3 power play. Dennis Hull capitalized on the opportunity and tied the game at 3–3.

Not wanting to lose a single point to the NHL's newest club, the Hawks peppered Ron Low with 18 third-period shots, but they couldn't find a hole. Jack Egers brought the crowd to its feet with the game-winning goal at 8:46 of the third, and the Caps could now boast a "1" in the victory column. "Not far from our nation's capital," wrote the *Chicago Tribune*'s Bob Verdi, "where earth-shaking events are daily propositions, a landmark of sorts was established when the Capitals recorded their first National Hockey League victory." Lefty McFadden could not get over the atmosphere in the Capitals' dressing room after the big win. "They were measuring one another for ring sizes. It was like they took the Stanley Cup."[35]

Unfortunately, with the season just a month old, Egers began to feel pain in his leg caused by a ruptured disc in his back, and eight weeks after surgery to repair the disc, he ruptured it again in practice, forcing him to miss the remainder of the season. "You were treated like a piece of meat," Egers would say about his time in Washington. "I wonder if I had been given that year off, if I would have had three or four more years."[36]

Like a Bunch of Sunday School Kids Wearing Their Communion Outfits

The Capitals went for broke in the first few weeks of the season, employing an aggressive, wide-open style of play that earned them a few points. Of course, the early-season success against Montreal, Los Angeles, and Chicago may have also been due to the "sneak factor" often associated with teams not expected to do well. Every year, in almost every sport, there are one or two teams that prognosticators expect to land near the bottom of the standings, yet in the first few weeks of the season, there they are, floating to the top of their division if not the entire league, and everyone starts doing double-takes in response to the shocking turn of events. Before long, however, the sneak factor disappears and reality sets in.

Washington's 1–2–1 record actually put them ahead of Montreal, who at 0–2–2 were languishing at the bottom of the Norris Division standings. That abnormality did not last long, but no one could have predicted just how bad things would get in D.C. Jimmy Anderson believed the win against Chicago was "a reward for hard work," and he also thought the Caps' historic achievement would catapult them to greater success. "Now they know they can do it, so if the guys don't win more, I'll be able to kick their butts."[37] By mid-season, Anderson's feet were likely ready to fall off because those things must have done *a lot* of kicking!

At least the Capitals had themselves a couple of decent goaltenders who did their darnedest to keep the team in most games. In the 1–1 tie against L.A. on October 15, the Capitals were outshot, 34–20, and Kings coach Bob Pulford praised Ron Low for his heroics: "That guy was fantastic," he said. When the Caps beat the Chicago Black Hawks, coach Billy Reay said, "No question—Low beat us." On October 23, it was Michel Belhumeur's chance to shine. The Capitals were in Chicago and as usual were badly outshot by a 42–12 margin. Not only did Belhumeur keep the score close, only losing 3–2, but he established a new NHL record by stopping *two* penalty shots in one game. Those shots weren't taken by shmucks either, but rather all-star Jim Pappin and future Hall of Famer Stan Mikita. "The guy had some sort of night," said the Hawks' Dale Tallon. Some Chicago players even said they had thought of taking Belhumeur out for a couple of drinks on Rush Street!

"Maybe I'm a sadist," said Low, "but I enjoy playing goal. It's satisfying to beat a good team, to win any game. If you play a good game and you lose, you can look at yourself and say 'I did the best I could.'"[38] Of course, early in the season, when everyone has a realistic chance at the playoffs, attitudes remain positive and everyone feels hopeful, but as the losses pile up, the players' resolve is tested.

The Capitals' losing streak was up to six games when they took on the 0–8–1 Scouts on November 3, and the Scouts overcame 3–0 and 4–2 deficits to win their first NHL game, 5–4. Joe Gross of the *Annapolis Capital* did not mince words:

> The Capitals played like a bunch of Sunday School kids wearing their communion outfits ... they're so scared to hit anyone it's ridiculous.... You have to shoot when you get an open shot, but the Caps play pitty-pat and try to show off their non-existent passing skills.
>
> The power play is hockey's biggest scoring threat, with one team being one man short.

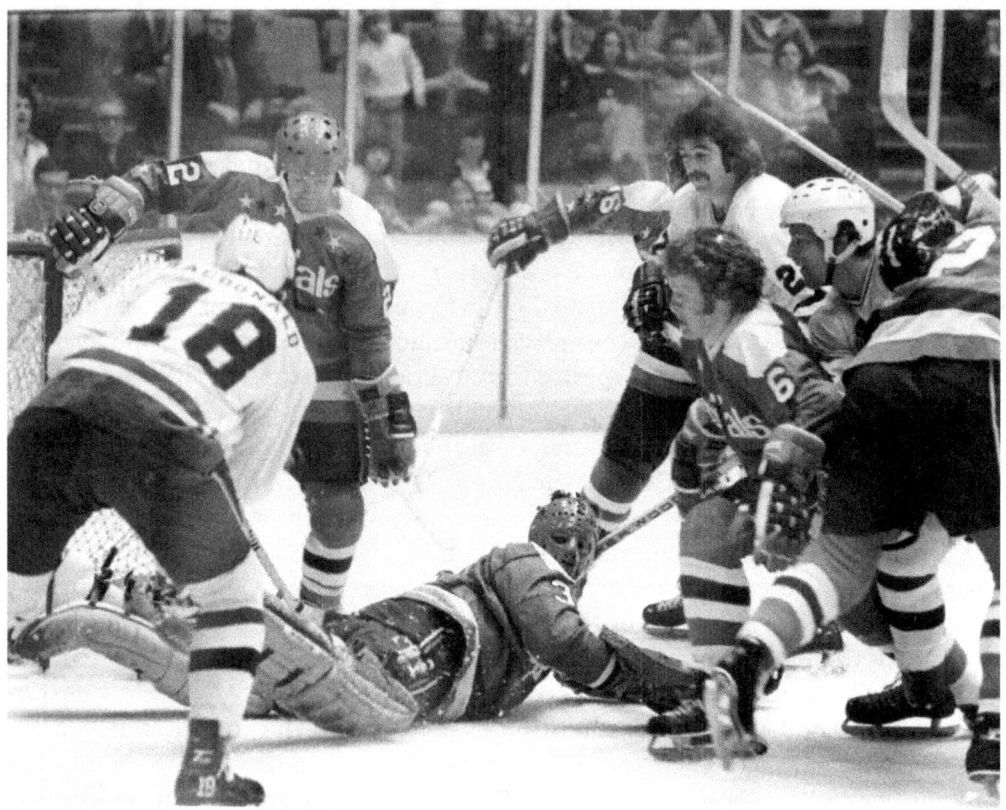

Goalie Michel Belhumeur desperately tries to keep Pittsburgh's Lowell MacDonald from slipping the puck into the Washington net as Doug Mohns (#2) and Gord Smith (#6) try to keep two other Penguins at bay during the 1974–1975 season (Ron Lalonde collection).

> When the Capitals are on a power play, the opposition usually outshoots them and there ain't no way that's right.[39]

Despite posting a "1" in the win column early in the season, by November 18, that number hadn't changed. But the loss column? Oh, its number changed all right, and frequently. In fact, at the 18-game mark, the Caps' record stood at a miserable 1–15–2. Opponents were lighting the red lamp so often that Low and Belhumeur could have been poster boys for Coppertone. Opponents averaged *eight* goals a game the first four contests in November, and the average for November was over six. That stretch included a 10–4 defeat to the Boston Bruins and an 11–1 setback to Montreal, plus five shutout losses. Denis Dupere probably summed up his teammates' feelings best when he explained that everyone on the team knew "it wouldn't be easy with a new team. But I don't think any of us knew just how rough it would get either."[40]

Legend has it that NHL president Clarence Campbell wrote to Park Anderson, the Capitals' official scorer, to ask why the expansionists' opponents were being credited for a disproportionately small number of assists. The reason: the Caps coughed up the puck so frequently that opponents scored unassisted goals a-plenty.[41]

In the 10–4 loss to Boston, Bobby Orr lit the Caps for three goals and three assists. The score was 2–1 when Orr went ballistic. "The team was just in awe of them," Anderson said. "Playing the Bruins, playing in Boston Garden, a kid like Mike Marson watches those guys pass the puck around and he's just in awe."[42]

It was no secret to anyone that the Capitals were struggling tremendously, so much so that other teams were starting to take pity. Early in the third period, and with the score 9–3 in favor of Boston, Orr took it upon himself to sabotage his own goaltender's goals-against average just to make the Caps look competitive. "I passed to Denis Dupere," revealed Jack Egers many years later, "and Orr just kept backing in on Gerry Cheevers and saying, 'Shoot, Dupy, shoot.' He backed in so close Cheevers was screened and Denis put it in.[43] That's how sympathetic other teams looked at us."[44]

Against Montreal, it was the same story; the Caps looked utterly astonished as their superstar opponents racked up points by the bushelful. Henri Richard skated away with five points, and Guy Lafleur scored two goals in what was, at that point, the worst beating any team had suffered this young season. The Habs led 3–0 after 20 minutes, then 9–0 after 40. Montreal outshot Washington, 42–17. Mike Bloom told Alex Prewitt of *Sports Illustrated* that on the plane ride back to D.C., Quebec native Denis Dupere told him how his mother and sister had come to watch him play, but the massacre left them crying.[45] Yes, the Capitals were so horrendous that year that even meaningless regular-season games could lead to tears of despair!

The Best AHL Team in the NHL

Even though it was only November, there was a feeling brewing that maybe the NHL's latest expansion was a mistake. Jimmy Anderson knew all too well what kind of hell could only be reserved for a member of an expansion team. He believed the NHL had expanded too fast, and it was going to take "three to four years for these kids to do anything."[46]

"All we have is an American Hockey League team," he lamented weeks later. He also accused the NHL's established teams of hoarding talent, preventing the Caps from becoming competitive. "They're hiding players they're not using. They have players who could help us and they're just letting them sit there. We think they should almost be giving them to us to help the league. They want an arm and a leg." He was right. The league had developed a serious disparity problem. Never before had there been such a wide gap between the league's biggest powers and cellar dwellers.[47]

Lefty McFadden could only wonder why 17,007 fans would bother showing up at the Philadelphia Spectrum November 9 to watch the Flyers barely break a sweat in their 6–2 win over Washington. "How can they come and watch this kind of hockey?" he questioned. "Rather, the question should be, how much longer will they stand to come and watch this kind of hockey?"

The Capitals were barely a month old, and already they were begging the NHL for better players. McFadden believed the Caps had some "nice kids" but that this meant little since "the world [was] full of nice kids." What the Caps needed was legitimate hockey players, he opined, but few had been made available in the expansion draft. Despite the Caps' and Scouts' combined two wins at this point, the NHL already had visions of expanding to Denver and Seattle, and McFadden feared a repeat of the morass Washington and Kansas City found themselves in unless the NHL loosened its restrictions on how many players each established team could protect.[48]

Ron Lalonde joined the Capitals in mid-season, and in 2019, he recalled what Tommy Williams thought about the Capitals. "[He] was a real character, and one of our better players. He used to joke, 'You know, we've got a good team,'" he said, "and then he'd pause for effect… 'The problem is we're in the wrong league; we should be in the AHL.'"

About the only bargaining chip Milt Schmidt had at his disposal was the Caps' first-round draft pick, which was already shaping up to be a first-overall selection. Anderson agreed that the Caps and Scouts had been betrayed by the NHL, but he cautioned against trading draft picks in a desperate attempt to bolster their rosters with what would be considered middling talent languishing on other teams. "Sure, it would be nice to find one or two players who can complement this team, but what are we going to have to give up to get them?

"But if we have to give up draft choices for a 25-year-old established player, then we will do it. I know I would like to have a player like [the Flyers'] Bill Clement on our team."

Philadelphia coach Fred Shero agreed with Anderson. The Flyers had once been an expansion team, and they struggled in their early years too, but they steadfastly refused to deal away draft picks for immediate help, and they stayed the course until finally finding their way to the Stanley Cup. "Jimmy is doing as well as he can with what he's got," Shero said. "Sure, he should try to make a deal now, but who's going to give him anything?" He also suggested that Anderson tell his players "they should be proud to be in the big leagues, that 99 percent of them wouldn't be here if it wasn't for expansion, and they should work twice as hard to stay here."[49] While that was some good advice, Shero was not speaking from experience. In fact, no one in NHL history had ever been in the same position Anderson found himself in, and it would take more than a pep talk or two to get the Capitals thinking like champions.

Hitting the Seiling

Before the calendar even turned to 1975, Milt Schmidt begged and pleaded with anyone who would listen to be merciful and give the Capitals someone, *anyone*, who could make them better. Unfortunately for Schmidt, everyone knew the Capitals were desperate and that their best trade asset was shaping up to be the number one overall draft pick. Schmidt knew he would likely need to part with his first-round pick, but he had no interest in dealing it for the "garbage" other teams were offering up.[50]

Schmidt was in negotiations to acquire Minnesota centerman Fred Stanfield, who had scored over 20 goals every year but one since 1967. Since he was mired in a horrible slump and watching games from the press box, he could have been had for a

4. The Washington Capitals, 1974–75

song. Then he scored a hat-trick one night against Detroit, and the deal fell through. "I was happy for Stanfield, but his timing was awful," Schmidt said.[51] In the end, had Schmidt been more patient, he might have gotten Stanfield after all; in January, the Stars traded him to Buffalo for Norm Gratton and a third-round pick.

Some players around the league feared being traded to Washington more than being stricken with stage four lung cancer. At one point during the Capitals' formative years, there was a rumor that Ron Low was heading to Boston for the "Tasmanian Devil," Terry O'Reilly. According to D.C. radio host Phil Wood, "It reached a point where O'Reilly pleaded with the Bruins not to send him to Washington, and Low's wife asked the Caps if she should prepare to move."[52]

Even when the Capitals managed to make a move, there was still a distressing cloud hanging over the American capital. For instance, the Rangers' Rod Seiling was placed on waivers after he made some derogatory comments about Big Apple fans who had clamored for more aggression from the mild-mannered defenseman. For a measly $30,000, Schmidt upgraded his blue line corps significantly. "We'll build our defense around him," he said. Adding a player of Seiling's skill and experience could only benefit this expansion outfit. The stalwart had been a full-time Ranger since 1964, and he had scored 248 points in 644 games, which were both more than anyone on the Capitals roster except greybeards Tommy Williams and Doug Mohns.

The former Ranger suited up for Washington October 31, the day after he was acquired, and he worked his tail off, supposedly losing ten pounds in the process.[53] Seiling said all the right things to the media, how great his new teammates were, and how he was going to do his best to make the Capitals better ... and then he was traded to Toronto for Tim Ecclestone and Willie Brossart.

Apparently, the Seiling deal was just a ruse to get the more coveted Brossart, but both Schmidt and Rangers GM Emile Francis denied that the Toronto deal had already been prearranged. Nevertheless, McFadden was very impressed by what Schmidt's behind-the-scenes shenanigans had produced. "We got a tough defenseman, some cash and a future consideration. We gave up nothing."[54] Well, not exactly. In his 12th game with Washington, Brossart scored his first and only NHL goal, then broke his ankle. He would be out the rest of the season. As for Ecclestone, he was sold to Atlanta the day he was acquired by Washington, so in the end, the Capitals had absolutely nothing to show for their trade. *Hockey News* columnist Russ White wrote that Washington "had three NHL players in their possession in a revolving door episode and came out of it with the least valuable player of the threesome.

"Seiling, to be sure, was the best of the lot. He could have helped the Capitals. He can move the puck, he can play defense.... He was certainly better than what Washington had."[55]

Later that season, the Capitals were still badly in need of some quality defensemen, so Schmidt acquired Jack Lynch from Detroit, and it took him even less time than Brossart to land in the infirmary. During his first weekend with the team, an errant shot from the Rangers' Gilles Marotte struck Lynch below his left eye and damaged some facial bones, which put him on the shelf two weeks. When Lynch returned, he wore a special lacrosse-style helmet the rest of the season, and it took months for his face to feel normal again.

The Capitals had little choice but to stick with the talent they had and hope for the best. The first line of Williams, Dupere, and Kryskow, sometimes referred to as the Gazelle Line because of their speed, was the only unit providing any consistent offense. At the 28-game mark, Dupere was leading the Capitals with 13 goals and 22 points, while Williams also had 22 points, including a team-leading 14 assists. Kryskow was third on the team in goals (5), assists (11), and points (16). Other than this trio, no one else was contributing much on the scoresheet. Light-scoring Yvon Labre, who had two goals and nine assists, led all defensemen, providing points from the back-end was supposed to be Greg Joly's job.

Steve Atkinson had once been a 20-goal scorer with Buffalo, but with Washington he forgot how to find the net, and he was demoted to Richmond after a *literally* slow start. Following the Caps' 6–0 loss to Minnesota on October 12, Schmidt remarked that Atkinson was as slow as a snail, which was not far off from the truth. He was sent down to the minors in mid–October and called back up to Washington a month later, but after 12 games he had scored just one goal and two assists. On February 1 against Vancouver, "The Snail" would earn the distinction of scoring the first penalty shot goal in Capitals history, but he didn't exactly set the world on fire with his foot speed. "They'll have to speed that up to play in slow motion," Atkinson cracked.[56]

On Thin Ice

A big part of the Capitals' future was 19-year-old left wing Mike Marson. He had been given an incredible chance to be a key figure on this young and undertalented expansion team, but cashing in on this opportunity would be extremely challenging for even the most talented prospect. It wasn't enough that he was one of the players the Capitals most counted on to score goals, but he also had to overcome the racist taunts that were still very prevalent in the 1970s. Marson would always be bothered by how fans, opponents, and teammates perceived him. "It's all so bizarre," he said in a November 1974 interview, "when people talk about the first to do this or the second to do that; or worry about somebody's race.

"It's not just in sports, but all through society."

Barely a day went by when an article went out of its way to mention he was black, which had absolutely no bearing on his skills or competitiveness. Marson struggled early on as he adjusted to life in the big leagues. Some critics believed Washington drafted Marson as a publicity stunt that would generate some buzz for the first-year club.[57] Marson was paid handsomely, to the tune of $100,000 a year, which made him a magnet for criticism, especially after his first 16 games, which he described as "brutal." The Caps should have read the writing on the wall and sent him to minor-league Dayton to gain some experience and prepare him for the next NHL season, but they refused.[58]

Marson didn't see much ice time, roughly five minutes a game, the first few games of the season, so his confidence dipped. "For a while, I began having second thoughts about my ability," Marson admitted. "I thought maybe I should have played another year in the juniors."[59]

Cecil Harris wrote the 2003 book *Breaking the Ice*, an enlightening look at the experiences of some notable black hockey players. Marson explained how some teams put a bounty on his head, which anyone who injured him could collect. One time, Detroit's Dennis Hextall, a rabid wolverine of a hockey player, speared Marson so hard the blade of his stick broke. Marson received one threat that looked more like a ransom note: letters cut out of a magazine and pasted to create a threatening message: "You're on thin ice black boy.... The n***r is going to die."[60] From time to time, between 1974 and 1976, Marson would play with Bill Riley, another black hockey player. Riley remembered the two of them "getting high-sticked and slashed. Those things cut Michael's heart out."[61]

Unfortunately, the 19-year-old rookie received little support from some teammates. In Philadelphia, someone called the Spectrum and said he was going to kill Marson. His teammates responded by joking about not wanting to sit too close to him on the bench. Another time, Marson was filming a TV commercial, and Dave Kryskow joshed that if he "[got] his face painted," he could have been the one appearing on screen.[62]

Marson's teammates probably believed they were just being funny. After all, hockey players are notorious for ribbing and taunting each other mercilessly, whether by shaving a strapped-down rookie's entire body in the dressing room, or by embarrassing a buddy through some sort of prank involving public nudity. The fact is that the jokes sent Marson's way were incredibly hurtful and cut him deeply. He lost faith in those who were expected to have his back; teammates are supposed to look out for each other and stand up to any injustice that may come their way.

Years later, when Milt Schmidt was informed that Marson felt isolated by his teammates, the general manager was surprised. "I don't know if he felt uncomfortable, and if he did he never mentioned anything like that to me,"

Mike Marson, the NHL's second-ever black player, was the unfortunate victim of both racist taunts from fans as well as unrealistic expectations to become a superstar on a team devoid of talent (Doug McLatchy collection).

he said. "He was very well-liked by his teammates and there was no reason in the world he should have felt uncomfortable among his own players."

Marson was upset to hear Schmidt's comments. "That's his opinion," Marson said. "Sometimes you don't know something because you don't want to know something."[63]

When Marson was interviewed by *colorofhockey.com* in 2016, around the time the Capitals honored him before a game, he explained that he had managed to put aside some of those hard feelings. "For me, it's interesting to have put away all the negative things that transpired so many years ago—we're talking over 40 years ago—when the world was a totally different place."[64]

Sabre-Rattled

The Capitals' losing streak ended at ten when they tied Atlanta, 2–2, on November 12, but their winless streak continued on to a whopping 14 games, which, believe it or not, was their third-longest streak that season. On November 19, Marson finally broke out of his season-long slump, scoring two goals as the Caps beat the Seals, 6–4, for win number two. "Marson is playing better hockey each week," said Anderson. "As long as he checks his man, he'll get ice time."[65]

Washington followed up the victory with an 11-game winless streak which included a trio of setbacks to the Buffalo Sabres. In the first of those games, November 20, the Sabres unleashed a 50-shot attack at Ron Low, while the Caps tested Gary Bromley just 14 times. As would become the norm over the next two weeks, the Sabres' French Connection Line of Gilbert Perreault, Rene Robert, and Richard Martin dominated the Capitals, scoring eight points between them.

When the two teams met again December 3, Low was out with a broken toe, and Michel Belhumeur had the flu and a 105-degree temperature, so third-stringer John Adams got the call. How did Adams react when he received the news that he needed to leave Richmond for Washington? "Oh no," he said. "I know who they're playing tonight."[66] Adams' fears were certainly justified as the Sabres' outshot Washington, 46–29, en route to a 5–3 win, and the French Connection Line counted nine points, including four goals by Martin.

The Sabres almost let the game get away, however, as they let Washington mount a comeback from a 4–1 deficit. Pete Laframboise scored his fourth goal of the season at 15:06 of the second period, and Dave Kryskow potted his fifth at 1:21 of the third to put fear into the Sabres' eyes, but Martin ensured the Sabres' victory with his fourth goal of the game at 15:52.

"After Martin got his third goal, I had his number—for about 40 minutes," said Adams. "But unfortunately, it's a 60-minute game." Adams also said he was "looking forward" to the Caps' next encounter with Buffalo. That would come just two days later, and afterward he probably thought he was crazy for having looked forward to the onslaught he suffered.[67]

The Sabres won handily, 9–2, bringing Washington's overall record to a dismal 2–21–3. This time, the Capitals were outshot, 45–17, and the Sabres' famed trio scored ten points. "I'm glad I won't see the 'French Connection' for a while," said Adams.[68]

Things would not get any better two nights later versus St. Louis as the Blues unleashed a 60-shot barrage on Belhumeur. Surprisingly, it was Washington that *figuratively* drew first blood, as Bill Mikkelson drove the puck towards the net, and the rebound was picked up by Denis Dupere, who scored his 12th goal on a power play at 12:39.

Then, St. Louis *literally* drew first blood. Mike Marson skated hard to beat out Barclay Plager for the puck behind the St. Louis net, but Garnet "Ace" Bailey came in hard from the other side, and as he checked Marson, his elbow connected with the rookie's face, breaking his nose. Bailey would be off to the penalty box for the next five minutes, but it didn't really matter much since Doug Palazzari scored a short-handed goal just 0:33 after Dupere's goal. Chuck Lefley made it 2–1 for St. Louis at 17:52. During Bailey's five-minute penalty, the Blues had seven shots on goal to the Capitals' three. Then the game got ugly as the Blues whipped three more shots past Belhumeur. After the fifth St. Louis goal, Bruce Cowick scored for Washington, but at 5–2, there wasn't much chance of a comeback.

Belhumeur took a delay-of-game penalty early in the third period because he fell on the puck behind the goal line. Garry Unger scored on the ensuing power play to become the Blues' all-time leading goal-scorer. St. Louis scored two more quick ones in the first three minutes of the third period to make it 8–2.

Roadkill

As the Capitals slowly circled the drain, preparing to be whisked away into insignificance, a few newspaper and magazine articles announced the fact that Washington had yet to win a game on the road. The Caps' road struggles were approaching comedic levels. Case in point: November 27 versus the 7–10–4 Minnesota North Stars.

With the score tied, 4–4, Steve Atkinson shot the puck through Cesare Maniago's five-hole. It hit the back of the net, dead center, and bounced back out. The Capitals' bench erupted, but the celebration was premature since neither the goal judge nor the referee saw the puck go in the net, so the score remained tied. "I've never been surer of anything in my whole life," Doug Mohns exclaimed after the game, which the Stars won, 6–4. Maniago's response to Mohns' accusation of thievery? "I don't speak English," Minnesota's British Columbia–born goaltender said to a Washington reporter after the game.[69]

As frustrating as losing to Minnesota had been, the Capitals, to a man, would have gladly replayed that game a hundred times if they had known what embarrassment awaited them against Boston on December 14. All was well for the first 7:02, but the moment Bobby Orr ripped a 50-foot slapper that deflected off Mohns's stick and past Low, the game was essentially over. Before the first period was over, the score was 5–0, Boston. Jimmy Anderson took pity on Low and inserted Belhumeur into the Washington goal to start the second stanza, and the Caps responded with such a better effort that they got outscored only 2–1. Dupere ruined Ross Brooks' shutout with a power-play goal 0:15 seconds into the frame, thanks to a great pass from Kryskow streaking down the right wing. All Dupere had to do was snap it home just eight feet in front of the net.

Belhumeur probably thought Low had absorbed the worst of the debacle, but in reality, as the *Boston Globe*'s Francis Rosa put it, Belhumeur got "that clay pigeon feeling."[70] Dave Hynes and Andre Savard both scored to put Boston up, 7–1, but the beating was not over yet. Don Marcotte scored twice, and Ken Hodge added another, and there were still more than nine dreadful minutes remaining on the clock. Carol Vadnais made it 11–1 at 13:10, and finally John Bucyk potted another at 14:21 to wrap up the scoring and seal the Bruins' 12–1 victory. Seven different Bruins scored at least three points in the game.

The same day as the humiliating 12–1 shelling against Boston, Schmidt sent right wing Lew Morrison (four assists in 18 games) to Pittsburgh for Ron "Newsy" Lalonde (three assists in 24 games). "Newsy" had a decent offensive touch, having scored 10 goals and 17 assists in 1973–1974, but he fell out of favor with the Penguins when young Pierre Larouche cracked the line-up and started eating up valuable minutes. Lalonde fit right in with the Capitals, scoring 12 goals and 14 assists in 50 games, which put him among the team's scoring leaders at the end of the season. The Capitals' 1977–1978 media guide had this to say about Lalonde: "As far as the Capitals are concerned, dependability and durability are both spelled L-a-l-o-n-d-e." From his arrival December 14, Lalonde would suit up for 144 straight games before an eye injury cost him four games. "The secret behind Ron's longevity is simple," the guide continued. "He uses persistent forechecking at both ends of the ice to drive the opposition's forwards to distraction. In addition, Ron sees frequent service as a penalty killer. He is also the team's leading faceoff artist."[71]

One would think that after the 2-24-4 Capitals stumbled home from their humiliation in Boston, the fans would hesitate to come back in large numbers, but a season-high 11,526 fans greeted the Caps and Maple Leafs on December 15. Ron Ellis, coming off a hat-trick in his last game, scored his 13th goal near the end of the first period to give the Leafs a 1–0 lead, but that was all the Leafs would get on their former teammate, Ron Low. Mike Bloom scored his second goal of the season at 17:21 of the second period to knot the game at 1–1, and Paul Nicholson put Washington up, 2–1, with his third of the campaign. The Leafs' George Ferguson didn't help matters much by picking up an interference penalty three minutes after Nicholson's goal, and Jim Hrycuik scored his fifth goal on the ensuing power play to give Washington a 3–1 victory.

Despite halting their 11-game winless streak, the Caps were unable to turn the corner on their miserable season. Rather, they responded with three straight losses, 4–2 to the surging Canucks on December 17, 4–1 to the surprising Kings on December 19, and 5–2 to the perennially miserable California Golden Seals on December 20. If there was a positive takeaway in that last one, it was that Bill Lesuk and Ron Lalonde scored the first two shorthanded goals in Capitals' history, just 0:32 apart in the second period.

You know your season is going badly when you can lose, 4–0, and take something positive out of it. The achievement in question: keeping Buffalo's vaunted French Connection off the scoresheet. "You feel you've accomplished something any time you hold Buffalo to four goals and shut out the 'French Connection,'" said Anderson.

"I was very pleased with the job that Bruce Cowick and Bill Lesuk did on those three, holding them scoreless. They kept them bottled up all evening and thoroughly distracted."[72] Don Luce and Craig Ramsay, however, scored three shorthanded goals.

The next time the two teams met, on February 21, the Sabres won 9–4 and the French Connection scored three goals and three assists, giving them a grand total of 33 points in five games versus Washington, an average of 6.6 points per game.

Another problem the Capitals had early on was drawing fans ... their *own* fans, that is. The Caps didn't draw their first sellout crowd until Philadelphia came to town on December 26, along with about 6,000 of their fans making the trip to D.C. The Philadelphia fans were just as loud and rowdy at Capital Centre as they normally were at the Spectrum.

The sell-out crowd got to witness history that night as Bill Riley, a black right winger from Amherst, Nova Scotia, was called up from Dayton just for this game. He went back to Ohio afterwards, and he wouldn't become an everyday NHLer until two years later, but on this night, he and Mike Marson became the first black teammates in league history.

The night got off to a horrible start for Washington as Reggie Leach deflected a Jim Watson shot past Ron Low for the opening goal just 0:12 into the contest. Low was forced to make several big saves in the first period just to keep the Caps in the game, but eventually the Flyers broke through. The Flyers went on the power play late in the second period, and they bombarded Low with seven quick shots before Bobby Clarke scored at 18:28. "That was a bleep bleep call by [referee] Brian Lewis against Bill Lesuk," Anderson fumed. "That was not a trip. Everyone is pulling dives—they're taking acting lessons—they're going to Stan Makita's [sic] acting school." Just 1:07 later, Bill Clement made it 3–0 Philadelphia, and the game was basically over at that point. The two teams exchanged goals in the third period, making the final score 4–1 in Philadelphia's favor.

"From a coaching standpoint, it was our best game of the year," said a proud Anderson, but then he remembered the power play goal and lost his marbles. "We can't afford those bleep bleep penalties. No expansion team can afford penalties like that, and they keep calling them on us."[73]

Good Riddance, 1974

The Capitals hoped that as the calendar turned to 1975, they could also turn the page on what had been arguably the worst start by a pro sports team ever. As the Capitals floundered, Doug Mohns was named team captain. "Mohns will be Anderson's right-hand man," said Schmidt. Mohns had never been captain during his career, but he was more than ready to accept the challenge. "So far, I have not had the authority to intervene in anything," he said. "Now, as captain perhaps I can help."[74]

It had also been difficult building a cohesive team because the players didn't live close together; some lived near Capital Centre, while others lived in Virginia near the team's practice facility.

If there was one person in hockey that no one in their right mind was envious of, it was poor Jimmy Anderson, but the coach did his absolute best to look at the bright side and take solace in the fact that almost everyone pitied him for falling into such a horrible situation. "There is a lot of mail," he said. "People write to say that they are pulling for us, saying prayers for the team."[75]

Anderson was in way over his head trying, and failing, to keep this outfit running smoothly. Anderson was too nice a guy to be responsible for whipping a bunch of misfits into a cohesive unit. The constant losing made everyone feel agitated, and players complained about the numerous line combinations. Schmidt grew frustrated that the team couldn't commit to "one style of play." Anderson encouraged a bit too much roaming and free-flowing offense (not that the Caps were scoring many goals) while Schmidt preferred a tighter checking system. Schmidt didn't see the purpose of trying to outgun other teams, since all the Caps possessed were slingshots with broken rubber bands.

The Capitals had dropped to 3-31-4, miles behind the surprisingly respectable Kansas City Scouts, but Mohns believed there was still time to right the ship and achieve some level of respectability: "We realize the problems. We realize what we are up against. What we might do, what we cannot do. It is important that we do not lose confidence in ourselves as players. We have been disorganized and now must organize. In time we can pull ourselves together on and off the ice."

"Maybe we have some new year's resolutions like everyone else," Mohns mused, but despite the airing of grievances, and the hope of turning a corner in 1975, like most New Year's resolutions, nothing changed. In fact, things may have actually gotten worse.[76]

Washington closed out 1974 with a demoralizing 7-0 loss to the surprising New York Islanders at Capital Centre before travelling to Long Island for the second game of their home-and-home series. The result was a little better, but a 5-2 loss was nothing to brag about.

A date with the Montreal Canadiens at the fabled Forum was hardly what the doctor ordered to fix the ailing Caps, especially considering that the Caps had yet to win or even tie a single game on the road. That trend would not end on this night. Not even close. The Habs outshot Washington, 47-17, but that wasn't even half the story.

"Larry Robinson was there and he looked at me," Dave Kryskow recalled years later. "I smiled and asked, 'What's the over/under on tonight's game?' He said, 'Ten.' I said, 'Sounds about right.'"[77]

Montreal got their party started with a Guy Lafleur power-play goal just 1:59 after the opening faceoff, and they never looked back. Murray Wilson added another power-play marker at 7:08, Yvon Lambert capitalized at even strength at 7:55, and Guy Lafleur added his 27th of the season at 15:23.

The second period was worse than the first. Peter Mahovlich put Montreal up 5-0 with another power-play marker at 1:05, and Mario Tremblay made it 6-0 nine minutes later. Doug Risebrough scored the Habs' fourth power-play goal at 11:03, and Lafleur completed his hat-trick, again on the power play, at 14:52. As though the Capitals hadn't been punished enough, Guy Lapointe scored his 16th of the season at 18:55, and Jacques Lemaire scored at 3:47 of the third period to make the final score 10–0. Lafleur finished the night with three goals and three assists, while Lapointe had a goal and four assists, and Mahovlich scored a goal and three assists.

The following night, the Flames served up a 3–0 shutout which brought the Capitals' latest losing streak to nine games. And then, like a babbling brook in the middle of an endless desert, came one brief shining moment of hope. The Bruins had 1–0, 2–1, and 3–2 leads in the game, but the Capitals rallied each time. Mike Marson scored his seventh goal in the opening period to knot the game 1–1, and he scored his eighth at 11:55 of the second. The Bruins' Don Marcotte put Boston up by one just 0:31 into the final frame, but Pete Laframboise tied the game, 3–3, three minutes later, giving him a goal and two assists on the night. Marson also finished the game with three points.

While the Caps' gutsy effort halted their losing streak, they followed it up with seven straight losses to bring their latest *winless* run to 17 games! It was undoubtedly difficult for the players to endure night after night of losing, usually by extremely lopsided scores. Some coaches around the NHL made it quite clear in newspaper interviews that they viewed the Capitals as the most pathetic outfit stinking up the professional ranks. Tommy Williams, however, shrugged off the comments, and even though many of his teammates could not help thinking about losing game after game, Williams had a perfectly good reason not to worry. In a *Weekend Magazine* expose about the Capitals' horrendous first season, Dan Proudfoot wrote that Williams was not at all worried about what he would tell his grandchildren if they asked him whether he played on the worst team of all time. He could always claim it was the other Tommy Williams, the one who was playing for the L.A. Kings![78]

After Kansas City shocked Boston with a 3–2 win in late January, Scouts coach Bep Guidolin hammered home the fact that the Capitals lagged so far behind the rest of the pack when he claimed that the victory was no more special than "beating Washington or anyone else."[79] Other coaches believed it wasn't worth the effort to play hard against Washington. Philadelphia coach Fred Shero thought his team should have played a little more loosey-goosey when it shut out the Caps, 4–0, on January 16. "I don't know why they[80] think they have to kill everybody," Shero complained.

"When you get easy opposition, that's the time to skate easy, make some good plays, have some fun. You save the fighting for the tough teams."[81] Shero even took the NHL's resident goon, Dave "The Hammer" Schultz, who was leading the league with 278 penalty minutes, out of the lineup.

Despite spotting the Flyers a 1–0 lead early in the second period, the Capitals' defense withstood Philadelphia's relentless attack for two periods. Then the third period arrived, and the wheels fell off the track. Washington managed just one shot on goalie Bernie Parent, and Reggie Leach scored the first Philly goal in the period, followed by Rick MacLeish, and a third by Bill Clement, and the Capitals had another shutout loss under their belts.

The only hope the Capitals had was an encounter with another team that was almost as bad as them, but those moments were few and far between. There was always a decent chance the Caps could beat their fellow expansionists from Kansas City. The sad sack California Golden Seals, who had been rebuilding ever since the WHA raids in 1972, were always ripe for the taking. The Minnesota North Stars were on a steep slide into putridness. Then there were the legendary Detroit Red Wings, who were smack dab in the middle of the "Dead Things" era of their history.

The 1974–1975 season was shaping up as one of the Wings' worst. After a quick 5–1 start, which was more of an illusion than an accurate measure of their talent (two of those wins came against Washington, one against California), the Wings came crashing back down to Earth, going 6–24–8 before hosting Washington at the venerable Olympia Stadium for the first of a home-and-home series.

The first game was not much of a surprise. The game was not played in Washington, which of course meant another Capitals loss, this time 5–2, extending their overall winless streak to 17 games. The following night, as the Caps prepared for the back end of the home-and-home series, captain Doug Mohns was quite adamant that he did not want to be associated with what was shaping up as the longest winless streak in NHL history. The 1944 New York Rangers and 1950 Chicago Black Hawks had both gone 21 games without a win. "I've been in the league 22 years, and I don't want a crumby record like that tagged to my name," he said.[82]

The thing that is perhaps most bizarre about a losing streak is that even though one game has absolutely no effect on the next one, there exists an omnipresent feeling that no matter how much momentum is built in any one game, everything will inevitably fall apart, and the streak will continue to grow. Players grip their sticks a little tighter. One-timers are thwarted by an ill-timed broken stick blade a little more often than usual. Everyone worries about how much it will hurt if the streak grows by just one more game.

Bill Lesuk scored 0:24 into the game to put Washington up, 1–0, and Dupere gave the Caps a two-goal lead with a power-play marker ten minutes later. The Wings' Hank Nowak whittled the gap to one goal at 8:55 of the second period, but Kryskow and Lalonde put Washington up, 4–1. Detroit's Bill Hogaboam made it 4–2 on a power play, but Tommy Williams scored a short-handed goal to restore Washington's three-goal lead. Realizing they were risking losing to the worst team in NHL history, the Wings came out firing early in the third period, and Hogaboam scored his second goal of the night in the first two minutes. The Caps refused to fold, however, and Bruce Cowick put Washington up, 6–3. Despite being outshot, 38–23, Washington earned win number four and put an end to their winless streak.

Teams on losing streaks are incredibly fragile and can come apart at the seams in a heartbeat. Bill Lesuk recalled after the game that the Wings had almost scored very early in the game, but "it took a whale of a save" by Ron Low to keep the score 0–0. "I hate to think what would have happened if Detroit had beaten us to that first goal. No…. I just won't think about it."

Anderson rewarded his players with a day off before the team left for California to play the Kings. "I only wish I could repay all of them for what they have done," he said, "rather than mope about what they haven't."[83]

Revolving Door

Despite the merciful end to one of the worst stretches in NHL history, the Capitals were hopelessly out of a playoff spot, so Schmidt started wheeling and dealing, hoping one trade or another would create a spark. "We've been busting our bottoms to make it more entertaining," Schmidt said during the trading spree. "Our phone bills the past four days are going to put Mr. Pollin back a few more dollars. We're down in the dumps but we're still kicking."[84] While none of the trades made major waves in Washington or elsewhere, Schmidt received, for the most part, a lot more assets than he gave up.

Schmidt had already acquired the versatile Ron Lalonde before Christmas, and on January 21, Pete Laframboise (five goals, 10 assists) was sent to Pittsburgh for Ron Jones (one goal, one assist), who would play just 21 games for Washington, scoring two points. Despite the incredible struggles of the Capitals, Laframboise was disappointed to be traded. "I'm sorry to be leaving Washington," he said. "It's going to be a winning team and I'd like to be around when it happens."[85] The trade was somewhat of a surprise since Laframboise had just started to gel on a line with Mike Marson and Mike Bloom. Fans started calling the trio the Blood Line due to their rough style of play. "We've been together since day one," Laframboise said about his road roommate, Marson. "It was only a matter of time before we clicked."[86]

Marson and Bloom both picked up their game in January and February. Marson got into a scrap with the Islanders' Ernie Hicke, which impressed Anderson. "That's the type of player Marson was in the juniors," the coach gushed. "We want him to be physical, to be aggressive. It makes his whole game better."

"I'm no headhunter," Marson said. "But if I get a stick in the face or a cheap hit, I come back with something in return. I enjoy getting hit, hitting back. It's pow, pow, pow and I'm in the game. It's what hockey is all about. I feel I can be more valuable to the team when I'm involved." Marson scored two goals and an assist in the Capitals' shocking 3–3 tie against Boston earning himself the game's first star.

Both Marson and Laframboise explained, however, that it was Bloom who really made the unit go. He liked mucking it up in the corners and making life miserable for opponents. He also got himself into a world-class slobberknocker with Montreal's 6'2" 205-lb. Pierre Bouchard during the Habs' 10–0 rout of Washington. Bloom's recent surge may have been why Schmidt dealt him. After all, sometimes it is best to strike while the iron is hot, and Bloom's value was at its highest. Bloom took his seven goals and 19 assists to Detroit for 22-year-old Blair Stewart, whose true value would not be known until the following year, since he was sidelined for the rest of this season with a broken ankle.

On February 8, disgruntled Dave Kryskow (nine goals, 15 assists) was also moved to Detroit for defenseman Jack Lynch (two goals, 15 assists). Kryskow had been unhappy about the amount of ice time he had received, but he had been fairly productive the first few months of the season. His production slipped in the second half, and he was also growing frustrated by never-ending losing. Jimmy Anderson once asked Kryskow's opinion on the team's overall talent level, and Kryskow was very frank in his opinion. "We were in California, and he asked my opinion, and I said he should send these young bastards down to the minors and get some guys who knew how to play the game."[87] Whether or not this conversation led to Kryskow's trade to Detroit is unclear, but a few days later, he was gone.

Jack Lynch, on the other hand, had a decent offensive touch and a great attitude. "When the trade was announced in New York a neutral observer stated he wasn't sure the Capitals had gotten a great player for Dave Kryskow, but he was positive they had gotten a fine human being," wrote Ron Weber in the *Hockey News*.[88] It's a good thing Lynch had such a positive attitude, because playing for a loser could easily cause a professional athlete to crack.

Lynch did, however, bring a little humor to the team. When he scored one of his rare goals, Lynch would break out his patented "Stork Shuffle" to celebrate. "I scored a goal, the winning goal, against Atlanta, and I remember it distinctly because … my daughter took the picture that was in the front page of the *Post* and had a mouse pad made of that picture and [Bob Fachet said] it looked like the mating dance of a Malibu stork.… I just got really excited when I scored because I'd never been a goal-scorer."

Continuing the carrousel of departing and arriving players, on February 28, Schmidt acquired center Nelson Pyatt for a 1975 3rd-round draft pick going to Detroit. The pick Schmidt gave up turned out to be Al Cameron, whose best NHL season topped out at just 16 points, so no harm, no foul. Pyatt had never scored a point in 14 career NHL games, mostly due to a lack of ice time. The Red Wings were in shambles at this point, and they proved it by allowing Pyatt to stew in AHL Virginia. Pyatt went back home to Thunder Bay, Ontario, and he remained there until eventually agreeing to return to Virginia if his trade request was accepted. "I didn't sleep for the first two nights after the trade," he said. "Then Jack Lynch came to me and pointed out this was an expansion team and if you make mistakes, you'll get another chance.… The toughest thing in the NHL is getting confidence."[89]

When Pyatt got his chance in Washington, he found the back of the net six times in 16 games. "I wish I had 10 more forwards like him," said chief scout Red Sullivan. Pyatt has the distinction of scoring the first penalty-shot goal in Capital Centre history in a 4–2 loss to Toronto on March 9. The Capitals, who took just 13 shots on goal that night, had looked flat the entire game, but with just 3:17 left to play, Leafs goalie Gord McRae threw his stick to make a save, and Pyatt was awarded the free shot. Pyatt immediately went to Ron Low, the former Leaf, to learn the book on McRae. "He can take them and stop just about anything because of his reach," Low told Pyatt. "Forget the deke. Skate in and shoot."[90] He was right.

Minus 82

Next out the door was defenseman Bill Mikkelson (three goals, seven assists). While he was not traded away in the final weeks of the season like many of his teammates, after 59 games he was sent to the AHL, where he would spend most of the next two seasons before playing one final year in Mannheim, Germany.

It had been a very tough season for Mikkelson, both on and off the ice. His brother was tragically killed in a car accident in October. He received the devastating news during the warm-up to a game. "As soon as I heard, I hid from the players," Mikkelson recalled. "I went in behind the furnace room. Somebody came in … and I just said, 'Let me know when the players are gone,' so [afterwards] I went out and changed and left, and that's it," contrary to reports that he broke down in the dressing room and began throwing his equipment around. Mikkelson handled his emotions in a very private manner, not letting his teammates see him in his emotional state. "As far as crying goes, yeah, I did a lot of that, but I didn't do it in front of any players."

In a book about the 1974–1975 Washington Capitals, Mikkelson's unfortunate place in NHL history cannot be overlooked. When he was demoted to Richmond, he already owned the league's all-time worst plus/minus mark of -82, meaning he was on the ice for 82 more even strength goals against than the Capitals scored themselves at five-on-five. His mark is a negative standard that will undoubtedly stand the test of time since fewer goals are scored in the NHL these days, and players with embarrassingly low plus/minus marks are usually demoted in short order.

Despite holding one of the most dubious records in NHL history, Mikkelson holds a positive view of his record and his spot in hockey immortality. "If somebody said I had a choice not to play in the NHL or hold the NHL record for the worst plus-minus, I'd take the worst plus-minus," he said. "At the very least, I can say I was there, and it was special."[91]

Years after retiring, Mikkelson was interviewed by *Sports Illustrated*'s Michael Farber, and even though Mikkelson had been previously asked dozens of times to speak about "minus 82," the former Caps defender still had a great perspective on it. It's a stat that hasn't really bothered him over the years. He freely admits that the number was "earned," even though few individual players should truly be blamed for a goal against in what is supposed to be a *team* sport. Mikkelson once described the plus-minus system as being similar to crossing the street and getting run over by a driver who has ignored a red light. "You're still hit, but it's not your fault," he reasoned. He added, "In the grand scheme of life, it's so far down there you can't even see it. It's in the Marianas Trench."[92] When his children were teased at school about their father's record, he always had a great response: "I would always tell them to ask the kid who was bothering them what *their* father's NHL plus-minus had been."[93] Does Mikkelson have any regrets about his place in NHL history? Absolutely not. "I played against Phil Esposito and Bobby Orr in Boston … in retrospect I was quite grateful to have had that opportunity to be minus 82," he told Farber.

"I got to play. And the price I paid, I would pay it 100 times over."[94]

St. Louis Deals an "Ace"

For the most part, Schmidt's trades helped the Capitals improve somewhat, but none had the impact of the trade he pulled off on February 10 when All-Star Denis Dupere (20 goals, 15 assists) was sent to St. Louis for Garnet "Ace" Bailey and Stan Gilbertson. Dupere was very disappointed to be leaving Washington during a career-year. He felt under-appreciated, but Schmidt explained that the Capitals "did appreciate what Denis did for [them] and he should be flattered that the team made as good a deal for him as [they] were able to."[95]

Getting Bailey and Gilbertson was a real coup as both played great hockey with Washington and finished 1974–1975 on a tear. Bailey had scored a career-high 41 points in 49 games with St. Louis, and he would score another 17 points in 22 games with Washington. He had a reputation as a good checker, a hard-working player who wasn't afraid to dig in the corners, and he could play either wing. He was also skilled at dishing the puck to teammates. According to the Capitals' 1977–1978 media guide, "Bailey and Billy Kilmer both have one thing in common—they can both thread a needle with a pass."[96]

Denis Dupere was enjoying a career season with Washington when he was traded to St. Louis in February 1975 for Stan Gilbertson and Garnet "Ace" Bailey. In this photograph, he is wearing the short-lived, all-red Capitals road uniform (Doug McLatchy collection).

Bailey was also known to clown around a lot of the ice. Whenever he had the chance, he would pull some sort of prank, host an illegal party, or throw out a smart-aleck quip to break up the dressing room. He was always a very popular teammate, wherever he went. Bill Mikkelson played with Bailey for just a brief period, but the Capitals' after-hours ringmaster left a lasting impression on him. "I think every team should have an Ace Bailey," Mikkelson explained. "You talk about being a down season and everything, it just seemed like Ace was always up; he was always … the happy-go-lucky, cheerful, party guy. He was kind of a magnet personality, and a good guy to have on the team as long as people can, I guess, maintain their own discipline around him."

Gilbertson had also once been part of the Bruins organization, but he was acquired by California in 1971, where he scored 88 points in 235 games. As the Seals put their worst-ever season behind them and promoted several young kids to the NHL, Gilbertson struggled mightily, scoring just five points in 15 games before being shipped off to St. Louis, where he scored five points in 22 games. In Washington, however, the rejuvenated left winger notched 11 goals and 18 points in 25 games. "Maybe," Schmidt mused hopefully, "it'll be like the Esposito trade the Bruins made."[97] Gilbertson hailed from Duluth, Minnesota, the same town where Tommy Williams, four years his senior, was born. In fact, the future teammates grew up on opposite sides of the same playground. "My house was behind home plate, his out beyond center field," Gilbertson remembered.[98]

Like a Transmissible Disease

While the Caps had put their wretched 17-game winless streak behind them, one streak that was still alive and kicking was their road losing streak, which by February 10 had reached an NHL-record 28 straight games. Jimmy Anderson tried to put a positive spin on what was already shaping up as the worst season in NHL history, if not the entire history of professional sports. Players around the league couldn't help but feel pity for their brethren languishing at the bottom of the standings. "It's awful tough, awful tough for them," said the Rangers' Derek Sanderson. "They work hard but until they develop a system, they'll continue to have troubles." Unfortunately, the Capitals had almost no identity and no cohesiveness, which is normal for an expansion team. "The hard part," Sanderson explained, "is developing that nucleus. Right now the Capitals have players drafted from all over the lot, players who have played in different systems.

This devilish smile says everything you need to know about Garnet "Ace" Bailey, the life of every Capitals party and the perpetrator of just about every off-ice prank (Doug McLatchy collection).

"What they need is a good nucleus of their own players first, then they can develop a power play and penalty killers." At one point, the Capitals went 60 straight power plays without scoring a goal.[99]

How did the Capitals stack up against the worst

teams in other professional sports? The Capitals' 4–45–5 record on February 11, 1975, put them 179th among 179 teams in operation that season, which included Major League Baseball, the NFL, WFL, NBA, ABA, WHA, NASL, and World Team Tennis. The Caps were even worse than the expansion New Orleans Jazz of the NBA, who had won just seven of 51 games. According to UPI sports editor Milton Richman, one Washington sports writer "suggested that since both the Jazz and the Caps end their seasons the same day in the nation's capital, they stay over one day and play each other in some neutral game like tennis or baseball to decide which is the worst."[100] By season's end, the Jazz would count 23 wins, so no neutral-site game was necessary to prove the Caps were the poorest club of all.

The Capitals were so bad that their ineptitude was even beginning to rub off on opponents. It was claimed that coaches talked about the Capitals as if their very presence rubbed off negatively on their opponents, like a flu bug. On February 8, the New York Islanders beat the Caps, 5–1, but the next night in Boston, the Isles looked flat and were defeated soundly by the Bruins. Isles coach Al Arbour explained his team's subpar performance: "We caught [the Capitals'] bad habits."[101]

The Red Sullivan Era Begins...

Long ago, the Capitals had given up hope that the season could be saved. In the 1975 article "And the Last Shall Be First" for Canada's now defunct *Weekend Magazine*, Dan Proudfoot wrote that the Capitals seemed to decide that individually, they would continue "to show up for their games, give it a good effort, and hope for nothing more than spring, a southern vacation and a switch from Bloody Marys to icy cool banana daiquiris."[102]

A common topic of conversation in the Capitals' dressing room and in media scrums was losing, and what it felt like to be the worst team in the NHL. "The game isn't fun any more," said Ron Low as the losses piled up. "It's just work."[103]

The Capitals' play was also affecting Anderson. In Proudfoot's article, Anderson admitted to secluding himself and screaming his lungs out until the pain went away.[104] Luckily for the Caps' beleaguered coach, his torturous tenure behind the bench was coming to an end. After leading the Capitals to just four wins in 54 games, Anderson was replaced by 45-year-old chief scout George "Red" Sullivan, who had played nine seasons in the NHL in the 1950s and 1960s. The former Rangers and Penguins coach had been the first employee hired by Milt Schmidt.

"This didn't exactly jump up and hit me cold," admitted Anderson. As the Capitals lost yet another game, this time against Los Angeles at the Great Western Forum, Anderson stared up at the stars and pondered his future, which could not have looked bleaker. He knew changes were imminent and that he would not survive the season. "There I was, standing alone and hearing things," he remembered. "We had lost. I was running out of time. It was a game we should have won."[105] The day he was dismissed, Anderson had planned to meet a friend at the race track before getting down to brass tacks and preparing for the visiting Rangers, but Schmidt called Anderson to his office at Capital Centre first.[106] Gentleman that he was, Anderson accepted the bad news gracefully. Anderson would remain with the club as a scout, and Schmidt even offered his former coach a two-week holiday, but Anderson took just a few days off to regroup before getting back to work.

"I appreciate his work and regret this move," Schmidt said during a press conference announcing the coaching change.[107]

"It hurts," Anderson said after flying back home to his family. Red Sullivan praised Anderson for the work he had done. "Jimmy is an astute hockey man. He has had a tough job. I have never seen a club with such injuries. We're lucky he did the job he did. I'm tickled he is still with us."[108]

Bill Mikkelson believed Anderson "was a very nice guy" who did not want to torture his players with tongue lashings that could have been likened to beating the proverbial dead horse. Anderson's demeanor "was his approach to dealing with a bunch of guys who were being beaten and deflated on an almost nightly basis ... maybe he felt we did not need him piling on us like the fans and the media were. Maybe he thought we needed a positive voice and not somebody else kicking us."[109]

Anderson would never get another chance at coaching an NHL team, probably due to his awful 4–45–5 record, which no one in their right mind would see as a reason to hire him, but it wasn't fair to judge his coaching skills by his statistics. Most expansion team coaches get at least a full season, if not two, to prove themselves, but Anderson got just 54 games. One shouldn't also forget that he had been saddled with one of the thinnest rosters in NHL history and had arguably been set up to fail from the minute he was hired.

The Capitals were also rumored to have been an undisciplined crew due to Anderson's too-soft touch. "It may be just what the club needs," the deposed coach said of Sullivan's appointment behind the bench. Sullivan would never be accused of being too nice to his troops. "He scares the hell out of me," said one Capitals player.[110] Captain Doug Mohns, however, was more positive regarding the coaching change. "We welcome Red," he said after Sullivan's second game behind the Capitals bench. "He may spur us to smoldering coals, it not a flame."[111]

Sullivan had stood behind the Pittsburgh Penguins' bench for two years, and the *Hockey News*' Pittsburgh correspondent, Lou Prato, said the coach "wasn't gruff. He was up front with everything. He didn't try to evade. He probably did criticize players, but I don't think he criticized them openly." He also described Sullivan as "very likeable," but he expected his troops to put out a maximum effort.[112] Penguins GM Jack Riley once said that Sullivan would "blister the plaster off the walls if [the players weren't] moving." One-time Penguin Dick Mattiussi described Sullivan as "a fiery guy" who "kicked the wastebasket a few times."[113] When Earl Ingarfield was traded from Pittsburgh to Oakland in 1969, he described the move as "like getting out of jail" and said that "Sully couldn't fire up a furnace."[114]

The players had every reason to be concerned about their new bench boss, because based on the following story, some players were hardly in game shape despite already having played more than half a season. While Anderson often stopped practices to teach players fundamental skills, Sullivan preferred to use practice as a means of getting his players into tip-top shape. One of his drills consisted of getting his players to skate two full lengths of the rink without collapsing, but results were mixed at best. "Three guys got sick to their stomach in one practice," remembered Doug Mohns. "And one guy got cramps and another guy got so tired he fell to the ice and couldn't get up."[115]

As the team's chief scout, Sullivan was mostly responsible for the player selections that had been made since the beginning, so he had extra motivation to get the Capitals on track. Sullivan's primary goal was to make sure the Capitals did not finish the season as the worst team in NHL history; the 1972–1973 Islanders held that distinction, picking up a sad 30 points their first year. At the rate the Capitals were crawling, they were on pace for an astonishingly low 19 points. To avoid the shameful title of "Worst Team Ever," the Caps would need to post 16 points in their final 25 games, indeed a formidable task for this bunch.

The coaching change took everyone by surprise, including Sullivan, who was reading the morning paper at home in Peterborough, Ontario, when he received a call from Schmidt asking if he could make it to D.C. for puck drop that night! Sullivan claimed he had to drive through two blizzards to reach the Toronto airport, but he made it to the rink on time.

Most, if not all players, had no idea Anderson had been replaced until about 6 o'clock, when they arrived for their February 11 game against the Rangers, the second of a home-and-home series. The coaching change frustrated Ron Low, who, as the Caps' number one goaltender, had been facing 40-plus-shot barrages since Day One. He grumbled to reporters that he had no idea whether he would get the nod in goal. Then, without missing a beat, Low's attention turned to his rumbling stomach. No kidding. "All I know is I'm hungry," he admitted. "I don't eat the day of a game and I'm starved."[116]

Anderson had been a little lax when it came to curfews and getting to the team bus on time, which did little to help improve the players' overall discipline. When Mike Marson and Yvon Labre arrived late for the bus that was to take the team to JFK Airport, Anderson laughed it off and stated that he charged $25 for a wake-up call, in reference to the fine for early-morning tardiness. He went back into the hotel to look for his missing players, who claimed to be late because the hotel failed on its promise to wake them up on time.[117]

No one knew how Sullivan would react to tardiness. After his debut against the Rangers, the new coach told his players he wanted them back at the hotel at curfew. One player asked Sullivan if there would be a practice the next morning. Flexing his new muscle as bench boss, Sullivan responded yes, and he would let them know later on exactly when it would take place. With a twinkle in his eye, he let everyone know he would be knocking on doors before bedtime. No one missed the bus the next morning.[118]

Sullivan did have a soft spot for his players, though. After dropping a tough 3–1 decision to Pittsburgh, yet another road loss, Sullivan came into the dressing room, but he didn't tear a strip off anyone's hide. Instead, he told his players to meet him in his hotel room later that night. When the players arrived, Sullivan was nowhere to be found. Suddenly, a bellboy knocked on the door with a big, covered cart. Sullivan walked in a short time later and whipped off the cover to reveal a couple of cases of beer. "Congratulations, boys," he said. "You tried hard. Unfortunately we didn't make it."[119]

Over time, Sullivan had apparently mellowed quite a bit. "He was a player's coach," Jack Lynch remembered.

> Just a great, great guy.... Really a good communicator. He realized that the team was lacking in talent. He appreciated good hard work. He did the very best he could with what he had... [He] just tried to keep everybody together because they were going through arguably the toughest part of any one of their careers. You look at the guys who had success like Doug Mohns and guys such as that in other organizations, and between those players that had had success and Red, they tried to keep a really good environment, and Red worked really, really hard, but I think it almost killed him.

Even though Sullivan remarked that he wasn't "going to turn this team around overnight," he actually did. The problem was that the turnaround lasted all of one game.[120] Sullivan actually won his debut behind the Capitals' bench, giving him a perfect 1–0 record as Washington's coach, but the game almost didn't happen because the maintenance crew, made up of high school students, had trouble removing the white paint left behind after an Ice Capades show. The ice-cleaning machine had to have its scraper blades removed every so often because the paint kept dulling them. The blue and red lines had to be repainted, which forced the Capitals and Rangers to wait until 10 o'clock to begin play. Rangers GM and coach Emile Francis believed that under the circumstances, the game should have been cancelled, but considering the Caps were on pace to lose about $1 million this season, cancelling the game would have meant shelling out more precious dough to pay for the Rangers' hotel, air fare, and meals. Abe Pollin had no desire to be the good guy on this night, and the game went ahead as scheduled.[121]

Whether the delay helped the Capitals is anyone's guess, but the Rangers had every chance to bury the Capitals and failed. The Rangers stormed out to a 4–1 lead in the second period, making a Washington comeback improbable. After all, they very rarely scored more than two goals in a game, let alone three in a period and a half, but lo and behold, the Caps *did* battle back. Steve Atkinson scored his ninth goal of the season just 1:42 after Derek Sanderson put the Rangers up 4–1, and Tommy Williams scored his 15th on a power play in the final minute of the period to make it 4–3. Gord Brooks broke out of a season-long goal-scoring slump by potting his first goal at 2:35 of the third to tie the game, 4–4, chasing Eddie Giacomin from the net. Mike Marson scored on Rangers back-up Gilles Villemure at 7:18 to put Washington up by a goal. Then Mike Bloom made it 6–4, and Atkinson added his second of the night at 18:56 to make the final score 7–4.

For the Capitals, it was sweet revenge for the 7–3 loss the Rangers had handed them at Madison Square Garden just two days earlier. It would also represent the high-water mark of the Red Sullivan era of Capitals hockey. Two days later in Kansas City, the Caps went looking for two in a row and their first win on the road, but the still-winless Michel Belhumeur got no help from his teammates, who looked flat in dropping a 5–1 decision. The *Kansas City Star*'s Ken Rudnick pointed out the next day that Jimmy Anderson "went out dangling a carrot and Red Sullivan came in wielding a stick, but it may take more than a coaching change to bring anything approaching laughter to the dressing room of the Washington Capitals."[122]

Three days later when the two teams met up again in D.C., the only team that did any laughing was the Washington Capitals, who recorded their first-ever shutout, a 3–0 victory. This was small potatoes considering the Scouts were a woeful 13–37–7, but a shutout is a shutout. Ron Low gave much of the credit to defenseman Yvon Labre, who despite a limited skill set was enjoying a tremendous season thanks to his never-give-up attitude and physical presence. "Yvon was always around to help, clearing the puck and getting it down ice. The wings were backchecking [but] the defensemen never let them get a second chance."[123]

One would think such an achievement would cause one to celebrate, but Low took it all in stride, Capitals style! "It wasn't that I felt so good—I just felt like I do when I don't feel lousy."[124] Kansas City wouldn't register its first shutout until its *fourth* season, so the Caps at least had *something* they could hold over the heads of their expansion cousins.

The good times did not last long, and the results of most subsequent games were predictably embarrassing. On February 22, Chicago outshot Washington, 43–15, in a 10–3 pasting. Three days later when the Black Hawks came to D.C., the Capitals at least put up more of a fight. Literally. The teams combined for 44 penalty minutes in a fight-filled third period. Marson high-sticked Chicago's Phil Russell, and the ornery Hawk wanted revenge the way he knew best: by dropping the gloves. The 19-year-old Marson happily obliged and stood toe-to-toe with the toughest Black Hawk. "It would have been pick 'em," said Yvon Labre. "Marson is a human bowling ball. If he and Russell could have had a longer go, you'd have seen some crisp uppercuts. Russell would have taken a few solid belly punches."[125]

Mike Bloom, who had not yet been traded to Detroit, and who had scored 12 points in his last 12 games, took on Darcy Rota. Red Sullivan was disappointed that a few Hawks stepped in to break up the fight. "If Mike got loose with a stick in his hand, he'd have chopped down a half dozen heads," he said.[126]

The Inevitability of Defeat

The two losses to Chicago in late February were just part of a six-game stretch in which the Capitals allowed a whopping 38 goals! Not included in that sequence of games was the 7–3 loss to Vancouver, the 8–0 whitewashing against Boston, and the 8–4 drubbing in Montreal at the beginning of March. However, according to hockey writers and statisticians Jeff Z. Klein and Karl-Eric Reif, there is one game that perfectly sums up the Capitals' entire first season. On March 1, 1975, the 6-54-5 Capitals were in Toronto to take on the 24-29-11 Maple Leafs.

The Leafs dominated the flow of the game, launching 34 shots on Low, but somehow, the game was 3–3 in the third period. Stan Gilbertson put Washington up, 4–3, at 4:45, with assists going to Tommy Williams and Ron Anderson, but victory was anything but a sure thing. As Klein and Reif put it,

Immediately following Gilbertson's goal, play became ragged for a few minutes. Then the tide turned in favour of the Leafs, and at some indefinable point, in an invisible but somehow palpable way, it became undeniably evident that the Capitals possessed no idea of how actually to win the game, even though they were leading ... without completely falling apart in any sudden way, it had nonetheless become obvious that the Caps had lost every clue about how to play hockey *as a team*.... Toronto's edge in territorial play did not improve dramatically, nor did their number of shots increase drastically. But each successive scoring chance was better, and the Caps became more tentative and confused. They still led by 4–3 when they took a penalty with five minutes to play, but they killed it off, and with three minutes to go, they still led. But it didn't matter. Dave Keon scored to tie it with a minute and a half to go: 4–4. Time dwindled, but no problem for the Leafs. With seven seconds to play George Ferguson scored, and the inevitable had come to pass. The inevitability of defeat—worse than the routs, worse than the records, worse than the frustration—is the most bitter, paralyzing symptom of the disease of losing.[127]

According to Bob Fachet, in a 1989 article for *Inside Hockey*, "Ron Weber, who [had] seen every game the Capitals [had] played, was silent for 62 seconds after Ferguson's goal."[128] The Capitals' 33rd straight loss away from home was, as *Hockey News* columnist Russ White put it, "a professional sports record ... that probably goes all the way back to when the lions dominated the Christians."[129]

And then there was March 15 in Pittsburgh, when the Caps played what may have been the worst game in franchise history. After a six-day layoff, they couldn't have looked more out of sorts. Not only did the Capitals get outshot, 65–24, which was bad enough, but the final score was even uglier. "We were moving the puck all night," said Penguins coach Marc Boileau. "It was like a pinball machine out there."

Syl Apps scored the Penguins' first goal on the first shift of the game. Just 1:36 later, Pierre Larouche made it 2–0 on a play "during which everyone seemed in suspended animation," wrote the *Pittsburgh Press*'s Dan Donovan. Defenseman Barry Wilkins took an innocent-looking, waist-high shot at Michel Belhumeur, but the Caps' cage cop barely even acknowledged its existence, and Larouche nonchalantly tipped it in. Rick Kehoe's goal at 6:37 foreshadowed just how bad this night was going to become. According to Donovan, "Ron Schock kept the puck in the zone and passed it to Vic Hadfield. The left wing passed in front to Kehoe, whose high shot went just under the crossbar. Instead of standing up for the shot, Belhumeur ducked."[130]

With the score 5–0 and less than 15 minutes expired, Sullivan removed Belhumeur and threw Ron Low to the wolves. Low managed to keep the Penguins off the scoreboard the rest of the period, but the game's result was never in doubt. Labre made it 5–1 early in the second period on an awkward shot that eluded a Pittsburgh defenseman and found its way through the legs of goaltender Gary Inness.

The rest of the second period was all Pittsburgh. Exactly 24 seconds after Labre's goal, Vic Hadfield broke away all alone on Low and sucked the goaltender out of his crease, leaving the cage completely empty. Hadfield couldn't have missed the net even if he had tried. Bob Kelly made it 7–1 a little over two minutes later, and light-scoring Bob McManama put Pittsburgh up by seven.

The humiliation continued in the third period as Hadfield, Larouche, and Kehoe all scored their second goals, and former Cap Lew Morrison closed the scoring at 11:14, making the final score, 12–1. As if suffering one of the worst 60-minute ass-kickings in the history of professional sports wasn't enough, Kansas City coach Bep Guidolin, whose Scouts were just coming off a horrible 6–1 loss to St. Louis and were in the midst of a 16-game winless streak of their own, couldn't help rubbing a little salt in the Capitals' fresh wounds. "I would never go for what I saw here last night," he said. "They didn't put out at all."[131]

Three nights later, the Flyers visited D.C., and events didn't go much better than in Pittsburgh. The Flyers were up 4–2 after 40 minutes, but Red Sullivan was not about to let his troops give up. "I was prancing up and down the dressing room," he recalled in the May 1989 issue of *Inside Hockey*. "I'm saying, 'They're only human. They put their skates on the same way we do. We got another 20 minutes. Anything can happen, just keep working, they're not that good.'" Then Ace Bailey, who was always at the ready to murder any kind of serious, momentum-encouraging speech just for shits and giggles, was quick to respond, "That's right, Red, but they're not that bad." Sullivan had to leave the room so the players couldn't see him laughing hysterically.[132] The Flyers won the game, 7–2.

... And Ends

On March 20, the Capitals lost their 61st game, 5–1 to Minnesota, breaking the single-season NHL record. The officiating that night was supposedly so atrocious that Sullivan blew up to reporters afterwards. "When you're down, they figure you can't win," he said. During a two-minute span in the third period, the Capitals were called for three penalties resulting in two power-play markers. The result was two power-play goals. Making matters worse was the fact that Minnesota scored another power-play goal later in the period, not that it mattered anyway since the game was already out of reach, and there were only eight seconds left on the clock. "That was the worst officiated game I've ever seen," Sullivan continued. "We had a good hockey game going, the people were up and all of a sudden zip-zip-zip and the ballgame was over."[133]

When Sullivan was promoted to coach, he said he hoped "to be able to stay behind the bench for 10 years."[134] He lasted exactly 19 games, posting a 2–17 mark. The last 15 games of the Red Sullivan era were very easy to summarize: 15 losses. The last of those defeats was an 8–2 thrashing at the hands of the Boston Bruins on March 22. Bobby Orr led the way with three goals and an assist as the Bruins outshot the Capitals, 41–19.

Sullivan had asked Milt Schmidt to relieve him of his duties four days earlier, and Schmidt announced Sullivan's departure shortly after the Boston game. At the time of Sullivan's resignation, the Capitals sat last with an almost impossible to believe 6–62–5 record. "I can't hack it anymore," Sullivan explained. "The old stomach is all buggered up. I'm not eating properly; I'm not sleeping properly. I can't do it anymore at my age."[135] Yup, he was a veritable senior citizen at a ripe old 45 years.

There were other warning signs he was not going to last long behind the bench. One night, broadcaster Ron Weber called up Sullivan, who was dozing away. Weber innocently wanted to know who that night's starting goaltender would be, but

Sullivan reacted by pitching the phone across the room. Another time, when Montreal's Dorval Airport was closed due to a snowstorm, the team was forced to take a bus to Burlington, Vermont, but Sullivan had forgotten not only his green card, but his coat too, so he had no choice but to walk through the snow to a nearby immigration post. He eventually got back to the team, and a reporter said to him, "I see they let you go."

"Yes, darn it," answered Sullivan.[136]

Sullivan realized he had made a huge mistake in accepting the challenge of leading the worst expansion team of all time, admitting he "got involved in too much, too soon" and wasn't "mentally or physically conditioned to go behind the bench" after spending close to six years away from coaching. Sullivan went right back to scouting, where he could avoid the pressure of answering the media's questions about why the Caps were so bad. Before leaving the spotlight, however, he wanted to clear the air about one thing: "I want you to know I wasn't fired this time," he joked, referring to his previous coaching gigs in Pittsburgh and New York.

"It would be senseless to put Red to any more misery," said Schmidt. "He's a nervous wreck. This has put an awful strain on him. He simply held too much inside. He's got to get away from it."[137]

Uncle Miltie Takes Over

With only a handful of games left in the season, Schmidt decided to take on the extra responsibility of coaching the rag-tag bunch he had assembled. Schmidt had lots of coaching experience, and he very nearly started the season as the Caps' bench boss, but decided to go with poor Jimmy Anderson instead. Now that the Caps had not only burned right through Anderson but Sullivan as well, Schmidt was going to find out for himself why this outfit he put together had failed so miserably.

When Schmidt took over behind the bench, the Caps' 15 consecutive losses had already tied the NHL record set by the 1930–1931 Philadelphia Quakers. It wouldn't be long before the Caps smashed that mark too, posting losses in Schmidt's first two games as coach. "I have been sitting upstairs and cursing all year," he said. "I had to go down to the bench and try to do something myself." He admitted, however, that it was "going to take more than coaching" to turn this team around.[138]

Coming into their March 28 game with the Seals, the Caps were riding a 37-game losing streak away from home, which tied the league record for futility set one year earlier by these aforementioned Seals. *Hockey News* columnist Russ White compared the Capitals' plight to the famous Wilbur Mills–Fanne Foxe sex scandal that had erupted in October. After Foxe became famous, she had more gigs than she knew what to do with, which led to a great line from White: "Her road record was a lot better than that of the new Capitals ice hockey team, which gets undressed almost as often as Ms. Foxe.

"Trouble is the Capitals don't have as much up front as the Tidal Basin Bombshell."[139]

Even though the 19–45–12 Seals had been eliminated from the playoff picture long ago, they were usually competitive at the Oakland Coliseum, so it seemed unlikely that the Capitals would end their ignominious losing streak. Perhaps knowing another awful historic moment was staring the Capitals square in the face, the boys in red, white, and blue got out in front, 3–1, and the Seals barely seemed to notice.

In the second period, the Seals woke up and reduced the Caps' lead to 3–2 on a goal by Charlie Simmer, and Dave Gardner made it 3–3 five minutes into the third period. Washington stormed back less than two minutes later on a goal by Nelson Pyatt, but the Seals could not get the tie and salvage their pride. Pyatt scored an empty netter at 19:28 to seal the deal, and Washington skated away with a shocking 5–3 win. Ron Low tore the mask off his face and revealed a smile that stretched from ear to ear. Schmidt proclaimed the victory "sweeter than the Stanley Cup."[140]

Needless to say, Seals coach and director of hockey operations Bill McCreary was none too impressed by the end result. "With the good weather, [the players'] minds seem to be on golf and tennis," he said after the game. For former Seal Stan Gilbertson, who went from playing for arguably the worst team in the expansion era just one year earlier to playing for the absolute worst team in league history, he finally had a reason to hold his head up high. "When we got those two quick first period goals, we thought we had a chance to win," he said. "We've been beaten so often, it's really good to win. I spent enough time with the Seals, and we always seemed to be setting negative records."[141]

It was a bittersweet night for the Seals' Butch Williams, who had played a great game. "I got to play against the Capitals, my brother's team.... I ended up with a few points [one goal and two assists]," he recalled. "I was the first star and Tommy [two assists] was the second star.... Our dad was listening to the game over his short wave and that made it special.... Tommy marched a garbage can around their dressing room like it was the Stanley Cup."[142]

The story of the garbage can "Stanley Cup" has been told countless times, but Ron Lalonde shed some new light on the famous post-game celebration.

> We came in the dressing room, and we were quite happy, and one thing led to another. We all signed—it was a plastic green garbage can[143]—and then somebody suggested taking it out, and they actually took it out back into the arena and skated around the ice with it. There was nobody left in the rink, but we made a big deal of this garbage can. I think [the Seals] were in the league for the next year, and that garbage can was still there with all our names on it.

Jack Lynch remembers that night fondly as well. "We got back to the hotel," he wrote in an e-mail correspondence, "and partied like hell until the wee hours!!"

Even old Milt Schmidt got in on the fun. He drank Coors beer like it was his first celebratory drink after his release from prison. Players kept cheering "Break up the Caps" as they hoisted the garbage can over their heads. Even the new guys could appreciate the significance of the victory. "It may be the end of the year," said Nelson Pyatt, "but finally it is a start."[144]

Predictably, the Caps lost their subsequent home-and-home series against Detroit. In the first game, in D.C., the Capitals still had some leftover adrenaline from their big win in Oakland, and they stormed out to a 5–2 lead thanks in part to

Ron Lalonde's hat trick, the first in Capitals history. "Scoring the Caps' first hat-trick was a highlight for me that first year," Lalonde admitted in a 2019 interview.

> It happened towards the end of the year, and that's a record that Ovechkin can't break. Looking back, and I didn't think of it at the time, being the first hat-trick, but it was an accomplishment for me. I had one in a pre-season game, but I'd never had an NHL hat-trick. It was an achievement for me that I still talk about today. My grandsons like to tell people, "My grandpa, he scored the Washington Capitals' first hat-trick." So, it's the answer to a few trivia questions in around Washington every once in a while.

It looked as though the Capitals were assured of their first-ever two-game winning streak, but reality set in as the Wings clawed their way back, and then some, with *six* unanswered goals to take the game, 8–5. The Caps' defense wasn't big league the following game either as the Wings took it easily, 8–3, in Detroit, setting up the team's final road trip of the season.

With Regards to Richard Lewis ... the Road Trip from Hell

If it wasn't already obvious by this point, the Capitals were not exactly the most talented bunch, but they had also endured more bad luck than just about any other franchise in existence. They were given nothing but scraps in the expansion draft. They were left with a shallow talent pool in the Amateur Draft. Key players like Greg Joly and Ron Anderson found themselves on the shelf for long stretches. Even worse, on the road the Caps were victimized quite often.

> "I remember in Oakland, we arrived at the airport late," recalled Ron Lalonde. Typically, when you get off the plane you go out, the bus is waiting for you there, the team looks after the equipment, you might have an overnight bag or whatever, you get on the bus, and off to your hotel. We get there and it's eleven o'clock at night, and it's like crickets; there's nothing happening, there's no bus.... We had to make our way to Oakland where we were staying, and it was a fair trip from the airport. I think the airport was in San Jose if I remember correctly. We were ... trying to find cabs at that hour. There were a number of things like that that happened, that shouldn't normally happen to any team in the National Hockey League, but if those things were happening it was usually on the road, and you weren't able to play your best.

All that was nothing compared to the mother of all God-awful road trips, the curtain closer of the Caps' road schedule.

After the humiliating 8–3 defeat in Detroit on April 2, one of the worst spring snowstorms ever ravaged the area, closing the airport, so the Caps boarded a train in nearby Windsor, Ontario, and travelled to Montreal for an April 5 game, assuredly another humiliation in the making. Before the lambs were killed, however, they had to trudge their way through a vast, snowy wasteland that stretched from Windsor to the slaughterhouse called the Montreal Forum. No one on the Caps was quite ready for this kind of weather. The mercury had reached a balmy 70 degrees when they left Washington for Detroit, and everyone was dressed in their summer attire. Broadcaster Ron Weber, whom Jack Lynch described as "not much of a dresser," unwisely chose to wear matching white pants, belt, and shoes. When Weber emerged from the train station located under the Queen Elizabeth Hotel in Montreal, the city was buried in snow, and he looked like he was only dressed from the waist up!

Montreal was at a standstill. Hotels were completely booked, so some unfortunate souls slept in lobbies, but the Capitals were lucky enough to have rooms already reserved. They must have slept comfortably because when the hotel finally remembered to wake up Ace Bailey and Ron Lalonde, it was 9:30 a.m., just a half-hour before a team workout was set to begin.[145] In order to avoid a $25 fine, Bailey and Lalonde rushed to the front of the hotel, only to discover there were no cabs, so they convinced a police officer to drive them through snow- and ice-covered streets to the Forum, where they arrived for the team workout with about a minute to spare.

Despite almost arriving late for practice, a real no-no in hockey, Bailey, the team's resident clown, couldn't resist goofing off one more time. Michel Belhumeur, who was injured, bet Stan Gilbertson a whole quarter that he couldn't score on Ron Low during a team scrimmage. Well, wouldn't you know it, there went Gilbertson barreling down the ice on Low, and he planted himself in front of the goaltender, hoping for a pass or maybe a slap shot that would deflect off his stick, his shin, his butt, anything. The problem was that old Ace had overheard Belhumeur and Gilbertson's conversation, so there was no way Gilbertson was getting that puck. According to sports columnist William Barry Furlong, a smiling Bailey dished a pass to Gilbertson "that would demand an advanced degree in acrobatics to handle." The always sharp Bailey spun right around, skated towards Belhumeur, and told him that he wanted "half the action."

While Bailey and Lalonde narrowly escaped paying a $25 fine, Bob Gryp had no reason to worry about sleeping in because he was recovering from a nasty bout of diarrhea that kept him plenty awake. According to reports, Gryp was found wandering the third floor of the hotel at midnight wearing nothing but a gold bedspread, like "the ghost of King Midas lost," wrote Furlong. Gryp figured he had been to the bathroom about 25 times since arriving in Montreal, but he may have been exaggerating. "It was an expression of the surrealism—and the adversity—that surrounded this team," wrote Furlong. After all, the Capitals had set such an obscene number of negative records that "the disasters of this road trip gave it a sense of possession and expression that might be denied the successful." As Gryp was, well, *gripping* his kingly robe, several Caps were running in and out of their rooms ... naked. Surprisingly, no one complained.[146]

If Washington couldn't keep the pathetic "Dead Things" from racking up 16 goals in two games, their chances of beating the mighty Canadiens in Montreal were just about nil. If winning a second away game in hockey's capital wasn't a daunting enough task, the Habs needed two more wins to clinch first place overall, so they were surely tickled pink to be hosting Washington; in five games against Montreal thus far, the Caps had been outscored, 39–7. "As I told the players this morning," Schmidt said, "they have an obligation to themselves, their families, and the team owners to go all out against Montreal, to do the best they possibly can. Just because we've got a bad record is no reason not to give everything they've got."[147]

For the first 14 minutes, the Caps went shot for shot with the superior Canadiens, but once the Habs broke through the Washington defense, it was game over.

The Capitals looked so outclassed that one TV announcer accidentally referred to Montreal's opponents as "the Washington Craps." Who was the lucky goaltender to suffer this latest embarrassment? Michel Belhumeur was injured, and John Adams was given the start against Detroit just to give him some ice time, so that meant it was Ron Low's lucky night to stand in front of the firing squad. When Schmidt informed Low that he, not Adams, would be starting against Montreal, Low responded, "Thanks a lot." Newspaper reports do not always account for tone when quoting people, but it can safely be assumed Low was being sarcastic. Low's stomach was often in knots the day of a game, and on this Saturday, he ate nothing more than a poached egg for breakfast. Luckily for Low, after he allowed eight goals on 31 shots over two periods, Schmidt yanked him and threw in Adams after all. Not surprisingly, Washington was outshot, 45–18, and got bombed, 10–2, bringing the six-game season series goal differential to an unfathomable 49–9!

If only the Montreal beatdown had been the worst part of the road trip, but oh no, the trip actually got worse! The only remedy that would do the Caps any good was a nice, home-cooked meal and a familiar, warm bed, but on the final road trip of the season, how could the Capitals break from the ignominious tradition of hardship that had been firmly established the first night they stepped on enemy ice? The Capitals may have provided John Hughes with the inspiration for the film *Planes, Trains and Automobiles*, because this trip from Montreal to D.C. could not have been more convoluted and painful.

The team had planned to take a charter flight to Baltimore after the game and land around 2:30 a.m., but it was deemed too expensive to charter a 180-seat plane for just 24 people, so the team considered flying commercial, which under normal circumstances would be perfectly acceptable. Unfortunately, the commercial flight was scheduled to leave Montreal at 7:30 a.m., which also wasn't a huge problem under normal circumstances. Montreal, however, was still buried under a mountain of snow, so there was no guarantee that runways would be cleared, which meant the Capitals would risk missing their season-ender on Sunday against Pittsburgh.

The Capitals must have felt like they had been demoted back to the minors when Schmidt told them he was thinking of hiring a bus driver to take the team to Boston, from where they would fly to Baltimore. "That was as popular with the team as bone surgery," said William Furlong. An alternative solution was to take a bus to the airport in Burlington, Vermont, and take a plane to Baltimore, but to get to Vermont's largest city before takeoff, the team would have to leave Montreal around 4 a.m.

When Schmidt woke up to make the morning wake-up calls, he was informed that the runway in Montreal would be cleared after all, meaning the players could sleep in until 5 o'clock, which would give them enough time to board the 5:45 a.m. bus that would take them to the airport. Of course, this was not the end of the story. Far from it. Schmidt woke up late, and as he embarrassingly boarded the bus, he said, "My watch says 17 minutes to the hour." Bill Lesuk was the last person to board the bus, 15 minutes late, because he had to run back to his room to collect his false teeth!

When the Capitals arrived at the airport and the players perused a U.S. Customs immigration form, one player paraphrased one of its questions: "Do you or your family have cash or checks or negotiable instruments in excess of $500,000?" He then pointed at beleaguered, but highly paid Greg Joly, who was still sitting on one goal for the season.

The team finally landed in Baltimore at 10:30 a.m., but the team bus could not leave to take everyone home because Belhumeur still had to clear his status. Under normal circumstances, this is not taxing, but Washington's still-winless back-up goalie had lost his bag, his visa, and all his identification papers.[148]

There were, of course, a few positives to be drawn from the Capitals' tedious road trips. Mike Marson remembers the long treks out West as being a wonderful opportunity to bond with teammates and a chance to put aside the pressure of performing for home town fans: "I have fond memories of getting to know some of the guys on a more personal note. At that time, the West Coast swings were 14 days long. You really get a chance to know or find out who these guys are as teammates."[149] Despite the incessant losing and never-ending hardships, many of the players remain close to this day, much like soldiers who went through the hell of Vietnam together. Only a member of the 1974–1975 Capitals could truly understand the suffering the guy sitting next to him on the bench or in the locker had endured. For many, it was an opportunity to finally play in front of NHL fans, and that was something no one could ever take away from them.

Crazy Eights

There was just one game left, against Pittsburgh, who had thrashed the Caps, 12–1, the last time the two teams met, but not only did Washington get a measure of revenge on the playoff-bound Pens this time around, they set a few team records along the way.

Vic Hadfield opened the scoring for Pittsburgh at 10:10 of the first period, but Tommy Williams responded on a power play 2:31 later. It wouldn't be the last time he appeared on the scoresheet that night. The Pens' high-octane offense began to pummel Ron Low like they had a few weeks earlier, and again the goals came quickly. First, Ron Stackhouse made it 2–1 at 14:08, and Lew Morrison scored 1:47 later, while teammate Chuck Arnason was in the penalty box for slashing, to put Pittsburgh up by two goals. Ron Lalonde answered back 0:28 later with a power-play marker to pull the Caps within a goal.

In the second period, Stan Gilbertson and Tommy Williams took over the contest. Just 2:36 into the frame, Gilbertson scored his tenth goal, with assists coming from Ace Bailey and Williams. Less than two minutes later, Bob Gryp scored his fifth goal of the year to put Washington up, 4–3. While Stackhouse scored another goal at 17:18 to tie the game at 4–4, the Penguins had little left in the tank at that point. Williams retaliated 0:36 later, and the Capitals never looked back.

The game remained 5–4 until 13:50 of the third period, when Gilbertson found offensive talent he never knew he had. He scored his second goal of the game on the power-play with assists by Williams and Yvon Labre. Gilbertson scored again at 16:58 on assists from Williams and Bailey, and he added a fourth goal 0:18 later, with yet another assist by Williams. "I wanted Tommy to get it," Gilbertson admitted. "He had two goals. He never had a hat trick before. I looked to feed him the last one.... It would have been great for Tommy to get it."[150,151] At the end of the day, Washington won their eighth game of the season, 8–4. Bailey had four assists, while Williams finished with a franchise record six points. The late-season outburst bumped Williams' team-leading point total to 58. Gilbertson's last three goals were scored in a team-record span of 3:26.

Ron Lalonde had scored a hat-trick just days earlier and had been the Capitals' record-holder for most goals in one game. "The record lasted one week. I guess it was because I broke the ground that they realized they could do it, so Gilbertson had to go and score four," he joked.

If anything, the season's final game gave the Capitals reason for optimism for the following season. "It's nice to go out a winner," said Gilbertson, who, like 11 other Washington players, was about to become a free agent. "Let's hope this is a preview of things to come next year."[152]

Gilbertson may have been pleased by the sudden turn of events that concluded the Capitals' first season, but he also never forgot the route he had to take to get to his four-goal game. The Seals had dispatched him to St. Louis, who sat him on the bench for most of the 22 games he played there. The Blues sent Gilbertson to Denver of the CHL, where the pissed-off winger promptly scored 11 goals and 15 points in 10 games. He had every intention of signing with a WHA club for 1975–1976, but the trade to Washington, and his late-season flurry, convinced him that his NHL days were not over yet. Gilbertson suddenly had value, and there was no guarantee he was going to re-up with the Capitals, even though they essentially saved his career. "I'm unemployed as I take this uniform off the last time," he explained. "Loyalty can go so far. Loyalty hasn't paid any bills. I'll listen to the WHA, and I'll listen to what Washington might have in mind."[153] Gilbertson was sick and tired of losing, having spent the majority of his NHL career with the last-place Seals, but something must have tickled his fancy because when October rolled around, there he was, front and center in a Capitals uniform, a freshly signed two-year contract under his belt.

Underwhelming Results

As the Capitals were gearing up for their season finale against Pittsburgh, Ron Low was asked what had been the highlight of the season. He could have mentioned the memorable road win in Oakland or the shutout he posted against Kansas City, but he overlooked both of those moments and said, "It'll come tomorrow night when this damn thing ends."[154]

"Usually you don't like to see the season end," Schmidt said. "But, under those circumstances, in a situation like that, it was a blessing."[155] Washington scored just 181 goals, the lowest mark in the league, and they allowed a league-record 446 goals, nearly *two-and-a-half times more* than they scored. Ron Low was an unfortunate victim of playing for the worst defense in the history of professional hockey, but he also found some benefits. "I'm a better goaltender than I was when this all began," talking as though "this" was the worst form of torture a human being could be subjected to. "I've learned and gotten something out of every game. Sure, I still foul up but not as much anymore."

"I've seen a lot of rubber," Low said. "I don't think I'll ever see as much again. At least I hope not."[156] Low finished the season with a shockingly bad 8–36–2 record, a bloated 5.45 goals against average, and a historically low .855 save percentage. He also faced 1,622 shots, a ridiculous average of 37.6 per game.

"He'd play his heart out in goal every night and in practice," said Ron Lalonde, "and you wanted to play for him … The effort that Ron Low put out at practice and dared you to score on him translated in the games."

Jack Lynch echoed his long-time friend and teammate's view of Low.

> We had a great goaltender, and I say it to this day, a *great* goaltender in Ron Low. That old line, "He saw more rubber than the Michelin Man," was certainly true. His goals-against average was brutal. I always looked at the goals against as a team stat, not so much a goalie stat, but he gave it everything he had every single night...Considering the barrage that he faced every night, he truly was inspirational to me as a guy that just gave it everything he had every night, and you wanted to do the best you could for him because he was truly on the line every single night on the worst team in NHL history.... Everybody along the way always respected him.

The Capitals' fan club voted Low the club's MVP. Now, he was expecting to be paid accordingly. "I am an NHL goaltender and expect to be paid like one," he explained matter-of-factly. "Three years ago when I signed a three year contract with the Toronto Maple Leafs, I acted hastily. I should have taken more time, signed for only two years.... I'm getting American Hockey League pay. I want NHL pay. I believe I deserve it."[157] The WHA offered Low an opportunity to star in the rebel league, but Low put his faith in Schmidt and signed a long-term deal with Washington.

As the old saying goes, the heroic Ron Low saw more rubber than a dead skunk on the Trans-Canada highway. In 1974–1975, he faced an average of 37.6 shots per game, which predictably resulted in a gaudy 5.45 goals-against average and .855 save percentage (Doug McLatchy collection).

While Ron Low may have been dealt an unlucky hand, Michel Belhumeur was arguably the unluckiest goalie to ever *live*. In what can be described as the ultimate irony, the French name "Belhumeur" roughly translates to "good mood," something he was probably not in very often during his time in D.C. Belhumeur finished the season a soul-crushing 0–24–3, with a 5.37 goals against average, .861 save percentage, and 1,165 shots against for an astounding average of 38.6 per game! The only real victory he could claim was a minor one, and it occurred off the ice, so it was never registered in the record books. He won a dollar from Tommy Williams playing pool one time, and he savored that victory like it was a world championship. He taped the winning dollar bill over his spot in the dressing room and added a note that read, "Thanks, Bomber" alongside a drawing of the normally hard-luck goaltender reeling in a fish labeled "Bomber."[158]

Of course, the Capitals' eight wins and 21 points were modern-day lows and their claim to infamy. Their 67 losses were an all-time high that stood until the 1992–1993 Ottawa Senators and San Jose Sharks both incredibly cracked the 70-loss mark.[159] Not once did the Capitals win or even tie two in a row. They also had a 17-game losing streak, which set another NHL record, and 11-, 14- and 17-game winless streaks. There was also their 1–39 record on the road, another dubious record that stood alone until the dreadful 1992–1993 Senators picked up a single duke away from home.[160] The Capitals also lost more home games (28) than any other NHL team in history. The 94 power-play goals the Capitals surrendered broke the previous record by an incredible 13. The 18 shorthanded goals given up were four more than the previous record. The power play sucked, and at one point it went 60 straight opportunities without rippling the twine. How bad was the power play? Consider the following quote from Jimmy Anderson, where he lowered the bar in his definition of the word "asset" by explaining that Steve Atkinson's value as a power-play specialist was that "At least he [didn't] give up the puck."[161]

The Capitals were also the unfortunate victims of the injury bug. Jack Egers missed most of the season with a back injury, Jim Hrycuik and Greg Joly missed time with bum knees, Willy Brossart and Blair Stewart both nursed broken ankles, and Ron Jones injured his shoulder.

The Caps' plight was best portrayed by veteran winger Ace Bailey in a film the team distributed showing some of the highlights and lowlights of the season. "In this particular segment depicting one of the games near the end of last season," wrote Milton Richman of the San Rafael, California *Daily Independent Journal*, a rival player faked out Bailey so completely that the Washington winger fell to his knees as his opponent skated around him and scored. Bailey then raised his stick over his head and smashed it into a half-dozen pieces against the ice "in a picture of absolute frustration.... Bailey look[ed] at it sadly and sh[ook] his head. Looking at the Capitals ... that's about all anyone [could] do."[162]

The only thing the Capitals had going for them was attendance. The team drew over 400,000 fans for their home games, a number which could have been much higher had Abe Pollin not demanded full payment for season tickets when fans started asking about them early in the season. "If people will pay to see the Washington Capitals, they'll pay for anything," said Skip Feldman, the general manager of the WHA's Baltimore Blades, who moved from Michigan to Maryland in January and promptly closed up shop at the end of the season. The Capitals actually sold more tickets than the Washington Bullets, who had won five straight division titles and would advance to the NBA final in 1975. The *Washington Post* had an explanation for the anomaly: "Losers, yes, but losers with crash and dash…. The Capitals are fun because they give the impression that they are really trying."[163]

Yvon Labre remarked that even though the Capitals were a last-place team, "all we hear[d] [were] cheers," and he also wondered "if this [was] all real."[164]

Despite their fans' enthusiasm, the Capitals still lost enormous sums of money. Only three times did over 14,000 fans show up at Capital Centre, and only one of those games was a sell-out. The Caps bragged about having had 30,000 season-ticket inquiries, but in the end, only 6,800 people took the plunge. It also didn't help that Abe Pollin required season-ticket purchasers to fork over the entire amount at once, and during tax season no less.[165] Average attendance was just a tad over 10,000 per game, putting the Caps near the bottom of the league, which was bad news since the average player's salary kept escalating thanks to the ongoing NHL-WHA war. In 1974–1975, the average NHL salary was $81,000, which was an understandable expense for contenders needing to spend money to keep their best players in the fold. For the Caps to retain the services of their highly touted prospects, the team grossly overspent. Although the Caps had little talent to speak of, the team's average salary was almost $65,000. The oft-injured Greg Joly was just one year into his five-year, $800,000 contract, and Mike Marson, who showed promise with 16 goals his rookie season, was just a year into his five-year, $500,000 pact.

The Capitals did their best to cut corners here and there, which was unpleasant for the players who were already suffering plenty. One time, the team told their travel agent to purchase the least expensive tickets possible, but they probably didn't realize that the reason why these tickets were so cheap was because there was no in-flight meal. Broadcaster Ron Weber remembered that when flight attendants were handing out the other less economical passengers their meals, the high-paid but hungry Capitals comically moaned and groaned like they hadn't eaten in days. Weber also recalled that when one flight attendant walked past him, Ace Bailey asked her, "Can you go by a little slower, so we can at least smell it?" Another time, the former Stanley Cup winner and beloved former Boston Bruin, wondering how much stingier the Capitals could get, suggested that he and his teammates "start wearing tennis shoes. The next flight we might have to stand up."[166]

Early in the season when the Capitals realized they were short on dough, they had no choice but to send Peter Sullivan, acquired from Montreal in exchange for not selecting certain players in the expansion draft, back to *La Belle Province*. That move saved the team $100,000 even though, according to Robert Fachet of the *Washington Post*, "Sullivan was the best center in camp." The team saved another $150,000 when they got rid of Rod Seiling after just one game. According to Fachet, the Capitals had had no idea Seiling had been earning so much.[167]

Although he had little chance of drafting a competitive club though the expansion draft, Milt Schmidt fully accepted the blame for the debacle that had unfolded before his very eyes. Schmidt thought he had come up with a smart draft strategy, but it backfired badly. "We went for big guys and Kansas City went for skaters in the expansion draft," he explained. "I figured the big thing was not to get pushed around. The trouble was, the big guys I drafted—they don't like to fight."[168]

Ron Lalonde believed he knew why the Capitals struggled so much their first season:

> Washington got the 18th or 19th player off all the rosters, and it wasn't a good pool of talent to choose from, so it was a challenge from that standpoint, and you're taking 18 different organizations, bringing players, trying to meld them together to play as a team, and I think that was the biggest challenge that we had that first year. We weren't on the same page. We had guys from all these different organizations, they all had different stages of their career, different mindsets, different motivations, and to try to get them to play together as an expansion team, with winning in mind, was a challenge.

While this generally explains why most expansion teams struggle their first season or two, Kansas City had also drafted its players from the same talent pool, and they iced a far more competitive squad. The fact of the matter is that Schmidt drafted players with minor-league credentials hoping this would translate to success at the NHL level, but Kansas City's strategy of drafting a combination of savvy veterans and promising youngsters proved to be the winning plan, relatively speaking.

Defenseman Murray Anderson added a different twist on the Caps' first-year woes. "I was just a small cog in a very small wheel, because it was just too many small cogs to make a big wheel. Does that analogy make sense?"[169] That, in a nutshell, tells you all you need to know about the 1974–1975 Washington Capitals.

5

The Kansas City Scouts, 1974–75

As training camp loomed closer and closer, the Kansas City Scouts still had no rink to call home. The Scouts had a good plan in place to ensure their future success, but even the best-laid plans can go awry. The Scouts planned on building a new arena in the Stockyards section of town where the American Royal building, home of the Kansas City Blues hockey team, was located. "The setup for the Scouts will be much, much better in every way," said Bill Grigsby, the Scouts' public relations director. "The parking area and the access roads will be vastly improved. There'll also be lots of restaurants nearby."[1]

Unfortunately, in April and May, several local unions picketed the Kemper Arena project, stalling its completion. Only the Bricklayers Union came to an agreement with the Kansas City Builders Association, thanks in part to K.C. Mayor Charles Wheeler, Jr., who asked the workers to remove their pickets. "We are very grateful to the bricklayers," said Scouts president Edwin Thompson. "They're showing that they do have some civic responsibility. I'm also grateful that the mayor stepped in. It would have been nice if it had been done six weeks ago."[2]

The NHL was starting to lose patience with the whole construction strike because it put the league's entire schedule in jeopardy. "The [home opener] must be played [November 2]," explained league president Clarence Campbell. "There's no way, once the schedule is agreed upon, that you can just drop a game and say we'll pick it up and play it later."[3] That being said, one Montreal writer didn't think it would be much of a catastrophe if the Scouts were prevented from taking the ice at all. "It will be a break for Kansas City if they can't find a building to put this team in," he wrote, taking a jab at the Scouts' pitiful expansion roster.[4] When the NHL schedule was finally published, the Scouts found themselves starting the season on an onerous eight-game road trip.

"Imagine, all this was going on and we still had to start putting together a hockey team," recalled Edwin Thompson. "There was the job of educating a lot of Kansas City people on the game itself. Tickets to be sold. Advertising. Suites. Our Arena Club to build. It's all on schedule now, but as I look back—ouch!"[5]

Despite these initial hiccups, Sid Abel was optimistic that the Scouts would be successful in what he believed would be "a great hockey city." He believed the response in ticket sales had been "terrific" and that "Any time we can have over 5,000 sales without having a player or a place to play ... that's something."⁶

Damn Those Vancouver Blazers!

There were signs early on that this was not going to be an easy first season. For one thing, not everyone selected in the expansion draft was enamored with the idea of playing for a team sure to land in the basement. Already, the Scouts' blue line was not looking too spectacular, but when Paul Terbenche, a decent enough defenseman with 189 games' experience, signed a five-year contract reportedly worth $500,000 with the WHA's Vancouver Blazers, he left the Scouts with a big void on the back end. Abel accused Terbenche of being in kahoots with Blazers coach and general manager Joe Crozier in an attempt to secure his release from Kansas City. "I won't do it," Abel snarled. "He's a signed hockey player and he's committed here for this year." Abel threatened to trade Terbenche's rights to another NHL team if push came to shove, but in the end, Abel relented, likely because trading away a player on a long-term contract in *another* league wasn't going to bring much back in return.⁷

Terbenche would have received tons of ice time in Kansas City, but playing for an established team, even in a less reputable league, was much more enticing. According to an article in the *Vancouver Sun*, Terbenche didn't expect the Scouts to win more than 15 games. Crozier had also been Terbenche's coach in Buffalo, and Crozier thought highly of him. "Last year Turbo was the best skater on my club. He's got a good attitude and can play forward as well as defence," the coach said. He also described Terbenche as "a good team man."⁸

Left wing Butch Deadmarsh was another training camp holdout. Of the 50 players invited to Port Huron, Michigan, he was the only one to not show up. There were rumors that he too was considering signing with the WHA because he wasn't able to renegotiate the contract he had already signed with Atlanta, the team that held his rights before the expansion draft. "His attorney was talking like he was a Frank Mahovlich," Abel said. "He was telling me what he was going to get from the W.H.A. and he was trying to bluff me." Abel assured everyone that Deadmarsh would be ready to play for the Scouts, and said the defenseman wasn't at camp because Abel just didn't know where Deadmarsh was! Deadmarsh, on the other hand, made it quite clear, from his Penticton, British Columbia home, that he definitely was not reporting to training camp and had already signed a four-year deal with the Blazers that would start in 1975–1976. Deadmarsh stated that he was originally "very happy and excited" to be a part of the expansion Scouts, but was left feeling disappointed and unwanted when they "didn't show any interest" in him. "They didn't even phone me to tell me and welcome me," Deadmarsh accused. Abel disagreed with Deadmarsh's claim and said that he, like all other players picked in the expansion draft, had received a welcome letter. "And it was sent registered mail, too," Abel said. "To all three of his addresses. He signed for it. We know he got it." Deadmarsh, however, had every intention of sitting out the season if he had to. "I've got to look out for myself," he said.⁹ Cooler heads eventually prevailed, and Deadmarsh, who still had one year left on the contract he had signed a few years earlier with Atlanta, ended his holdout after the first exhibition game. Before long, however, like Terbenche before him, Deadmarsh would also be on his way to Joe Crozier's Blazers.

Defenseman Brent Hughes was planning a more long-term exit strategy by signing with the WHA for the 1975–1976 season. You read that right; Hughes signed a deal with another team *before* his current contract expired. If there was a smidgen of consolation, at least Hughes hadn't signed with the damned Blazers, but with the San Diego Mariners, meaning that three of the Scouts' top four expansion draft picks had already made concrete plans to leave Kansas City behind in the next 12 months!

Hughes said he had wanted to sign a long-term deal with Kansas City, but the Scouts were not prepared to give many, if any, of their expansion draftees more than a two-year contract. A lucrative multi-year contract from San Diego was too tough to pass up. Hughes was 31, nearing the end of the road, and only had so many more productive years left. That said, Hughes had made a commitment to the NHL when he signed his not-yet-expired contract, so he prepared himself to join the Scouts even if it was for just one year.[10]

The Scouts' contract issues highlighted what had become an all too common problem in professional hockey. "Hockey was a great game before Alan Eagleson and the flock of attorneys, agents, and other salary scavengers came along," lamented hockey writer Stan Fischler in his 1974 book *Slashing!* "Players thought of their teams first and themselves last. Money was a secondary concern. Finishing first and winning the Stanley Cup was primary ... a big-league hockey player knew that he had to claw and continue clawing if he wanted to stay in the NHL. He made a decent salary if he was a journeyman. If he was a superstar, he might make $20,000 to $25,000 a year and consider himself the luckiest guy in the world."[11] In the 1970s, financial security and dreaming of something called the Avco World Trophy apparently fueled the competitive fires just fine. How times had changed. Confronting the coach or general manager was once believed to be career suicide, but by 1974, players showed no fear since there was always another major league willing to pay big bucks to anyone who could handle a puck.

The roster openings gave the Scouts' Amateur Draft picks a golden opportunity to shine. Eighteen-year-old Wilf Paiement, who was signed for about $200,000 a year thanks to a bidding war with ... you guessed it, the Vancouver Blazers, was a lock to make the team, but his signing was anything but easy or quick. *Kansas City Times* reporter Jay Greenberg criticized Ed Thompson for diddling on the Paiement contract. "He [Thompson] wants to sign Paiement, sure, but isn't convinced of its urgency. He gives lip service to building a winner, but hasn't come to grips with what it is going to take. He leaves the impression he feels he can throw six Canadians and a puck on the ice, and that the majority of his patrons won't know the difference. He's right in the short run but tragically mistaken in the long."

If Thompson wasn't serious about signing Paiement, there were other NHL teams, namely the Buffalo Sabres, who were more than interested in having him on their roster. Even though it was prohibited from trading number one draft choices for two years, the Sabres went so far as to acquire Wilf's brother Rosaire to try to entice the rookie to sign with Buffalo. Wilf had indicated he was thrilled about the idea of playing with his sibling, but in the end, the Sabres stood down and did not challenge the NHL's two-year trade embargo.

Although Jay Greenberg believed Paiement and his agent Bill Watters (who worked for Alan Eagleson's law firm) were asking the Scouts for an exorbitant sum of money, Greenberg believed that the Scouts could not afford to tighten the purse strings and contest the troubling trend of rising salaries. Paiement was not Paul Terbenche or Butch Deadmarsh; he was a seriously skilled player and a potential franchise cornerstone who needed to be signed at any cost: "$500,000 or $600,000 ... is too much to pay an 18 year old," wrote Greenberg. "But within context of the times, Eagleson is not asking anything out of line. The Scouts say it is a matter of business sense, that signing Wilf wouldn't bankrupt them.

"Let's hope it's only a matter of principle, and let's also hope Thompson and the Scouts change their minds. Because if they can't afford Wilf Paiement, Kansas City Hockey Associates can't afford to be in the hockey business anyway."[12] As the months went by, these words would unfortunately prove to be an omen rather than a sports writer's simple musings.

Initially, it seemed as though Paiement had very little interest in signing with Kansas City, but he did. According to Greenberg, on September 6, the Scouts' greatest offensive hope, his parents, Bill Watters, and Alan Eagleson "walked into a Kansas City motel lobby. Wilf looked anything but excited. His doubts were well-rehearsed and easily recognizable and, although he said little, his eyes told a lot, darting back and forth as if trying to explore the place to which he had been delivered.

"'I don't want to talk about the money," Paiement said. "'I just hope I'm happy here.'"[13]

The following day, Paiement signed a three-year deal with Kansas City, and the youngster became the highest-paid freshman in NHL history. Ed Thompson would learn very quickly just how expensive being a part of the NHL was.

The Scouts Take Shape

The Scouts arrived in Port Huron for training camp, not quite knowing what to expect. There should have been a huge banner that read: "Abandon all hope ye who enter here" hanging overhead; it was a foregone conclusion that silver Stanley would not be hobnobbing with the Scouts anytime soon.

On Day One of camp at McMorran Arena, Bep Guidolin imposed an 11:30 curfew, but he also preached positive thinking and togetherness. He made it clear that if the players worked hard enough, the playoffs were an attainable goal in the weak Smythe Division. "Three of the five teams in our division didn't make the playoffs last year," Guidolin said. "We can do it."[14] Guidolin could speak from experience, having lost the Stanley Cup just months earlier to an inferior, but hard-working and highly motivated club. The Philadelphia Flyers had not been expected to win it all, but they beat the Boston Bruins at their own game by outhitting and outhustling them. They showed no fear and gave no quarter. The Flyers were also fortunate to have under contract one of the greatest NHL captains of all-time in Bobby Clarke, Vezina Trophy-winning goalie Bernie Parent, and future Hall-of-Famer Bill Barber, but the rest of their line-up was above average, and their defense a collection of no-names.

If the Scouts had any hope of reaching the playoffs, they would have to concentrate on moving the puck out of their own end, hitting the opposition hard every chance they got, and winning games by committee. There were no superstars on this team. "We're going to have to have our defensemen hit," Guidolin said. "We're going to have to do it early, get off to a good start and build up a reputation so people will say when you go to play K.C. and try to cross the blueline, they're going to cork you. We've got to get that reputation."[15]

During that first training camp meeting, Guidolin also expressed his hatred of the World Hockey Association. According to Jay Greenberg of the *Hockey News*, "the WHA jumper, in Bep's scale of values, was only slightly ahead of the child molester." One would think Brent Hughes, future WHA contract in his back pocket, might have felt targeted by his coach's vitriol, but Hughes took it all in stride. "I would have been worried if it was an established club," the defenseman said. "It being a new one, and not knowing what to expect, it really didn't bother me coming to camp." Guidolin's little speech caught Hughes off guard, but he refused to take it personally, believing "it was meant for the younger guys."[16] Everyone put on their uniforms and got ready for pictures and physicals. Irv Blehm of the NHL's security office talked to the players about avoiding well-known athlete vices such as gambling and drugs.

Guidolin planned to put his players through two workouts a day and to whip these guys into shape even if it killed them. A shudder would run all the way down the spines of Bruins players, remembering practices where everyone was either keeled over or running for the bathrooms. "Breakfast and the first day of a Bep Guidolin practice were never meant to go together," wrote Jay Greenberg in the September 16, 1974, edition of the *Kansas City Times*. That was Boston, a veteran team loaded with superstars. What did Bep have in mind for what his new collection of castoffs? "Everybody goes," Guidolin said. "Everything moves. No stopping. They're going to be tired."[17] He wasn't kidding; sometimes, the players would practice four hours a day; they probably couldn't wait to face NHL competition just to get a bit of a break.

During camp, the Scouts had a scrimmage against the AHL's Baltimore Clippers, and Guidolin was not at all impressed by the effort put forth by his defensemen, claiming they "didn't hit anybody…. Just when you think you've got everything pretty well set, they go back to playing the same way they did when we got them." Guidolin set the bar high for the upcoming season by forcing not just his defense crew but his entire team to undergo a grueling series of skating sprints. "We just have to let them know we don't stand for that kind of thing. It was the defensemen mostly, and it's too bad the other individuals have to suffer for the other guys."[18]

On September 21, the Pittsburgh Penguins travelled to Port Huron to take on the Scouts in their first pre-season game. The Scouts players had only had four days to get to know each other, but Guidolin was not worried. "It's not too soon," he said.

"I wish we could play tomorrow night, Saturday night and Sunday night. We've got to be able to see what they can do under game conditions. There are players who just don't practice well, not even in scrimmages, and you can't tell how good theyre [sic] going to be until we get them into game competition."

Paiement was unquestionably the most natural goal scorer on Kansas City's roster. He would make his NHL debut just shy of his 19th birthday, but he relished the opportunity to impress the veterans around the league. "That's what you have to remember about Paiement, how young he is," said Bep Guidolin. "He's going to be an experienced NHL player at a time when most kids are just coming out of junior."

"He's a tough kid, too," Guidolin continued. "He's the kind of guy you can build a team around—big and strong, too. But give him a chance. He's just a growing boy."[19] Sid Abel was incredibly impressed by the overall package Paiement brought to the rink. "Wilf would be playing back in the old days when there were only six teams in the league," he said. "He's not a stick-handler, but he moves the puck out of trouble and he can shoot. He doesn't have finesse, he just runs over people."[20]

Paiement would score his first NHL goal in the Scouts' fourth game of the season, a 4–2 loss to Atlanta, and he scored a goal in six consecutive games from October 23 to November 5. In his first 21 games, he scored 11 times.

Others, such as Robin Burns, who had played four years with Pittsburgh, had something to prove. "Of course," he admitted. "It's always going to be that way, with the team that lets you go. You want to show them they made a mistake. It would be great. Stand the old team on their rears and say, hallelujah, brother."[21]

The Scouts' first exhibition game did not go well at all. The disappointment was not that they lost 4–1 to Pittsburgh, but rather the way in which they lost. Pittsburgh led, 2–1—Norm Dube scored the first goal in Scouts history—in the third period when the Scouts made it quite clear that this was the very first game in club history. Not only did they give up two shorthanded goals in the final four minutes, costing them the game, but they put the second of those goals in their own net. In the last minute of the game, the Scouts pulled their goalie to give themselves a 6-on-4 advantage, but when Randy Rota passed the puck toward the blue line, no one was there to receive it, and the puck slid all the way into the empty Kansas City cage.[22]

First-game jitters aside, the Scouts fared well in the pre-season, including a convincing 6–2 win September 25 against Pittsburgh in which Lynn Powis scored three goals. "I was starting to get tired," said Michel Plasse, who recorded the win. "When we got the fifth goal I was very happy."

After the Pittsburgh game, the Scouts embarked upon a six-hour bus trip followed by a 90-minute flight to Austin, Minnesota, for a contest against the North Stars. McDuffe and Plasse were each expected to play half the game, but McDuffe was cut in the face for four stitches, so Plasse handled the goaltending duties himself. He was up to the task, stopping 31 shots in a come-from-behind, 3–3 draw.

The Stars had jumped out to a 3–1 lead on an unusual goal by Bill Goldsworthy. According to the *Vancouver Province*, "Goldsworthy's goal came on an experimental free shot, under which a team is awarded a free shot from one of the faceoff circles if a player deliberately holds the puck against the boards or a goalie holds the puck too long."[23] The *Minneapolis Tribune* described the goal thusly: "Goldy drilled a swift shot between the closest pipe and the goalie when Michel Plasse moved out just a step as the big right winger swung for the shot."[24] The bizarre rule was extremely unpopular with players and coaches, so it was never formally adopted by the league and remains a footnote in NHL history.

Three nights later, the Stars travelled to Port Huron for the back half of a home-and-home series, but the Scouts were more than ready, scoring an impressive 5–1 victory to bring their exhibition record to 2–1–1. "In June I just thought there was no way we're going to have a good team this year," admitted Michel Plasse. "But now I think we're going to surprise people." Guidolin, however, was not surprised by his team's early success: "I told you we're not that bad a team…. Once we get our lines set, we can play with anybody in this league. We're going to be inexperienced around the net, but things will come together."[25]

The Scouts concluded the pre-season with a 2–3–1 record, but with the team facing an eight-game road trip to start the season, wins would be much tougher to come by.

The Scouts did their best to build a decent defense through the expansion draft, but it was clear that the players drafted would not do, so on June 27, the Scouts signed free agent and St. Paul, Minnesota, native Jim McElmury. One of many college-educated players on the Scouts' roster, the 24-year-old had just seven games of NHL experience under his belt, all with the North Stars, but he had scored eight goals and 23 assists in 76 games with Portland of the Western Hockey League. The Scouts were obviously excited about McElmury's potential. In the team's 1974–1975 media guide, it was pointed out that he "learned to skate at an early age in the biting cold of Minnesota winters and he learned his lessons well, as one of his brightest assets is his puck carrying ability. He has a strong shot from the blue line."[26]

Two months later, the Scouts acquired 25-year-old Roseau, Minnesota, native Mike Baumgartner in a cash deal with Montreal. "Mike is aggressive, knows where the open man is and has potential to become a regular in his first year," stated the Scouts' 1974–1975 media guide.[27] Like McElmury, he had enjoyed some minor-league success, scoring 47 points with Dallas of the Central League and 43 points with Omaha the following year.

Finally, in late September Abel sent the club's third-round Amateur Draft pick, Bob Bourne, to the New York Islanders in a bit of an odd deal. The Islanders told the Scouts they would send back a defenseman, but they hadn't decided which one! "I only hope they send me a guy I want," said Guidolin. According to Jay Greenberg, "Speculation [ranged] from Bart Crashley, the former Kansas City Blue, to Jean Potvin or Gerry Hart, but other than the fact that the Scouts [were] looking for the rugged type … there [were] no clues from the brass who the player [would] be."[28]

In the end, the Islanders chose Crashley, who had spent the last two years plying his trade in the WHA. The 18 goals and 45 points Crashley put up with the 1972–1973 L.A. Sharks were enticing, as were the 30 points he scored the following year. "I had re-signed with the New York Islanders, who had drafted me two years previously," explained Crashley. "Los Angeles was moving to Michigan to become the Stags. I signed a nice deal with Bill Torrey and was in training camp when I was traded for Bob Bourne."[29]

What was even more baffling about this deal was that Abel would want Crashley in the first place; they didn't see eye to eye when they were employed by the Red Wings. "I was teamed with Gary Bergman," Crashley recalled in 1972 before Kansas City even had an NHL franchise. "I would work a full shift one night and nothing the next. Sid Abel and Baz Bastien were in charge. They told me that if I carried the puck across the blue line they'd bench me. That wasn't my style of play." He also admitted that one of the reasons he signed with the WHA was because he "didn't want to get into another Sid Abel situation."[30]

While the Scouts' blue line was about as anonymous as it got, they were a competent bunch who would make it difficult for opposing teams to run up the score. Unlike Washington, which tried to put emphasis on offense and failed miserably, Kansas City stressed the basics and keeping the opposition honest. The only question was if this "honesty" would lead to enough wins to qualify for the playoffs, but in the weak Smythe Division, anything was possible.

Season One Gets Underway

The Scouts were originally scheduled to open the season October 5 against Minnesota, but the construction strike nixed those plans. Instead, game one took place at Maple Leaf Gardens in Toronto on October 9, and Sid Abel couldn't have been more wound up. "I'll be glad when they drop the puck and get it over with," he said before the game.[31] Normally, the loosey-goosey Robin Burns was anything but uptight, but this game meant a lot to him and his teammates. "Pitter, patter, we'll get at'er," he said at practice the morning of the game.[32]

The Scouts' first-ever line-up included Michel Plasse in goal and Peter McDuffe as his back-up. Brent Hughes, Bart Crashley, Mike Baumgartner, Bryan Lefley, and Jim McElmury made up the defense, and John Wright, Richard Lemieux, Wilf Paiement, Ted Snell, Dave Hudson, Robin Burns, Lynn Powis, Simon Nolet, Butch Deadmarsh, Norm Dube, Ed Gilbert, and Randy Rota were the forwards. If you're thinking that this line-up wouldn't strike fear in anyone, you would be correct. In fact, at one point during the game, a TV announcer even said, "I came out to watch the Scouts practice today and I didn't recognize anyone."[33]

The Leafs, on the other hand, had stars Darryl Sittler, Lanny McDonald, Dave Keon, Norm Ullman, Ron Ellis, and Borje Salming, among others, in their lineup, so a negative Kansas City result was predictable, but the Scouts put up a valiant effort. "The Scouts suffered their initial rites into the National Hockey League stoically last night and with a minimum loss to their adolescent dignity," wrote Jay Greenberg.[34]

After two periods, the Scouts were holding their own against the far more experienced Toronto sextet. Plasse held down the fort, stopping 27 of 29 shots in the first two stanzas. Just 0:56 into the second period, McElmury fed a pass to Hudson, who skated toward the Leafs' goal. He dished the puck over to Nolet streaking down the right wing, and the captain ripped a 25-foot shot between the legs of goaltender Doug Favell to make it 2–1, Leafs. Later in the period, Favell had to come up big to thwart a scoring chance by Dube, sitting to the right of the goal crease.

The Scouts began to crumble early in the third frame when defenseman Jim McKenny launched a tricky 35-foot shot that eluded Plasse. "I lost it," the Scouts' goalie admitted after the game. "It looked to me like it was going into his glove and curved," Nolet added.[35]

Kansas City took a few penalties in the period, two of which cost them dearly. While Crashley was in the penalty box for hooking, the Leafs' power play went to work. Lefley blocked a point shot from Lyle Moffat, but Keon rushed in to grab the loose puck behind the net. He fed a sweet backhand pass to Sittler, who was parked in front of the net, and the future Hall of Famer slapped the puck behind Plasse for his first goal of the season to put Toronto up, 4–1. Less than three minutes later, Ian Turnbull deflected a point shot from Inge Hammarstrom past Plasse to make it 5–1. With a win now out of reach, Rota took the puck and eluded the aggressive checking of Willie Brossart while racing down the left-side boards. Rota thought about blasting the puck at Favell, but instead chose to feather a beautiful pass to the streaking Powis, who tipped the puck past the helpless Leafs goaltender. Keon countered, however, with the Leafs' sixth goal in the dying minutes, bringing the final score to 6–2.

"Kansas City played well…. They really went after us," said Leafs coach Red Kelly. "It was a tough game until we broke it open in the third period. They took the play away from us in the second period…. I think Kansas City surprised a lot of people here…. They're going to give a lot of teams trouble."[36]

The Leafs outshot Kansas City, 46–28, and despite Plasse's fine performance, he was disappointed in the final result. "I'm a little angry," he said. "I don't like to lose, but you can't expect to win all the time anyway."[37]

The Scouts may not have won their debut, but they made a good impression nonetheless. Red Burnett of the *Toronto Star* wrote that the Scouts displayed "guts and dogged determination" against the vastly superior Leafs, and that the expansionists had impressed with "pestiferous checking liberally sprinkled with clutch-and-grab tactics." Burnett also relieved Leafs fans with the news that the pesky Scouts would return to the Gardens just one more time, heady praise indeed for a first-year outfit. Lawrence Martin of the *Toronto Globe and Mail* was just as effusive in his game report. "In gaudy gold, red and blue uniforms, the new Kansas City Scouts looked ugly but for two periods of last night's opener they didn't play that way. They had the worried Leafs saying, 'Heh, who are these guys.'"[38]

Poor Robin Burns had himself a difficult debut. In a 2019 interview, he looked back on that historic first game and how, for the first and only time in his career, he led the NHL in a major statistical category:

> I led the NHL in penalties after the first game. I remember my parents were there. It was just an incredible, incredible feeling, and in those days they brought out the drum corps, the bagpipes, you know, the back watch, and they march onto the ice, and they had a ceremony. I played in Maple Leaf Gardens against the Marlies in junior, but to play in Maple Leaf Gardens under a packed, packed house, the opening game of the year with all the ceremonies, and…. I guess my adrenaline was pumped up pretty good. I ended up getting three penalties…. I was pissed and I fired the puck down the ice and [referee Bob Myers] gave me ten minutes, so I think I had 16 minutes that first game.

"There's been a lot of people who have tried to tell me I was three-quarters crazy," Burns said. "Well, I think you've got to be half nuts to play this game, anyway."[39] If you find a newspaper or magazine article on the history of the Kansas City Scouts, you can bet your bottom dollar Robin Burns was interviewed. Of all the players who wore the Scouts uniform, Burns is easily the most eager and enthusiastic to chat about his brief moment in the sun and the teammates he skated alongside.

"To say that Robin Burns plays the left wing with delicate balance would fall somewhere in the same genre as telling the Pope he isn't [a] good Catholic," read his bio in the Scouts' 1975–1976 media guide. "Robin's game is hard work, forcing his man out of the play and putting the puck in the net."[40] According to hockey historian Andrew Podnieks, the Montreal, Quebec native "was always the funny guy, the guy who'd goof around in hotel lobbies and airport areas, keeping the team loosey-goosey. He wore number 13 just for the hell of it ... he was known for his sandpaper touch around the net. One writer of the day observed that Burns couldn't score into the Grand Canyon."[41]

Burns enjoyed every moment he spent in the NHL. "There are a lot of people who would be upset about the No. 13," he said in a December 1974 issue of the *Hockey News*. "But no one I every [sic] played for accused me of not being serious when I put on the skates and go out and play the game." No matter where he went, however, his primary objective always seemed to be cracking up his teammates. When Burns was toiling with Hershey of the AHL, he had a teammate named Steve Andrascik who could speak Czechoslovakian. One time, Burns and Andrascik were being interviewed by a naïve, young radio host, and they convinced the kid that Burns was really a Russian player named "Boris Strongkof." Burns even garbled a few phrases of fake Russian to convince his interviewer that he indeed hailed from behind the Iron Curtain. Andrascik "translated" the entire time. When the kid asked "Boris" how he had become such a great player, Burns blah-blahed a few more phony words, and Andrascik translated: "When he was very young he used to skate down the river!"[42]

The first 16 games of the season, playing mostly on a line with Simon Nolet and Dave Hudson, Burns certainly did more than provide a few laughs in the dressing room, scoring 13 points, including four multi-point games, but he then went 12 games without a point.

In game two, the Scouts fell to the Islanders by the same 6–2 score as in the season opener. Game number three was a special one, however, as Simon Nolet made his return to Philadelphia after being exposed in the expansion draft. "It sure is going to seem funny," the captain said before his first appearance against his long-time team. "I'm trying not to think about it." When the game began, Nolet, then the Flyers' third all-time leading scorer, received a standing ovation from the normally hostile Philadelphia Spectrum crowd of 17,007. "The fans here never booed me," Nolet said. "They always liked me, and I always tried my best for them. But I never thought I'd get that."

The game was tied 1–1, and the Scouts were killing a penalty, but that didn't stop Nolet from showing off his offensive skills. He took a pass from Deadmarsh and skated effortlessly past a stunned Bobby Clarke, but his shot was blocked by goaltender Wayne Stephenson. Nolet grabbed hold of the rebound and jammed it home to put K.C. up, 2–1. "He went through me like I wasn't there," Clarke said. "I should know he was too good a player to beat him like that."[43] Despite Nolet's impressive performance, the Flyers showed why they were the defending Stanley Cup champions and came from behind to win the game, 3–2.

At 32, Nolet, from St-Odilon, Quebec, was the Scouts' elder statesman and most reliable offensive producer. "He is no bulldozer, it is more his style to dip a shoulder, pirouette, fly by and arrive delighted," wrote Jay Greenberg in the October 25, 1974, issue of the *Hockey News*. Nolet was typical of any expansion team's best player: there was always a young building-block player just getting his feet wet—in this case Wilf Paiement—but before the hotshot rookie could claim the mantle of the team's best player, Nolet would act as a "life preserver" who would "keep the Scouts from drowning while they build."[44]

"He's got more responsibility now," said Clarke after Nolet's first game against the Flyers. "He's with a team now where he probably won't make the playoffs for the rest of his career, but at [least] he'll get his share of goals and recognition." Coach Guidolin was obviously impressed by what Nolet brought to the table when he named him captain of the Scouts, a role that suited the former Flyer well.[45]

Road Weary

The Scouts began their first season, as expected, scoring few goals. The first four games all resulted in losses, and the Scouts were outscored, 19–8. The schedule would only get tougher as the winless Scouts travelled to Los Angeles to face the Kings, who at 2–0–3 were off to their best-ever start. Bob Berry opened the scoring just 2:24 into the game, and the Kings kept the Scouts at bay the rest of the way. Dan Maloney and Juha Widing scored power-play goals to ice the game, 3–0, and back-up goaltender Gary Edwards picked up the shutout for L.A.

It didn't take long for the Scouts to dream about one day returning to Kansas City and slipping under the blankets of their very own warm beds, but their eight-game road trip was only half over. While getting ready for a workout at the L.A. Forum before the fifth game of the season, the players just had to chuckle at their lot in life. In the tiny visitors' dressing room, players were practically climbing over each other just to get out the door. Robin Burns noticed a bunch of ants on the floor. "I think some are coming along for the ride in my pants," he joked. "All aboard."

"Cheer up," responded trainer Gordie Marchant. "A week from today, we'll be on the plane and going home." Bart Crashley walked by Marchant at that moment and shot back, "Where's home?"

When the players were on the bus waiting to leave their Los Angeles motel, someone noticed an armored car nearby, so one of the players called out to the team's highly paid superstar rookie, "Hey, Wilf, they've come to pay you."

Even captain Nolet was ribbed during that initial road trip. One time, the Scouts were on the bus and Nolet was counting heads as he always did, but players were changing seats left, right, and center so Nolet couldn't do his job. "He can't count, for bleepsakes," one of the players yelled, while others jokingly clamored for a new captain.[46]

Indeed, it had been one hell of a tough start for the fledgling club. The Scouts had stayed just three days in Kansas City since the start of training camp, and it was mostly to find places to live. Others took the time to drive their cars in from where they had played the previous year. "I think the toughest thing was our families," explained Burns.

> It was so difficult because we went to training camp and then everybody was scrambling, families and wives in Kansas City.... We really didn't know when the arena would be ready, so that made it pretty difficult to start, and ... it seems like everywhere we went for that next week or so, we ended up at the team's home opener. It was the first time a lot of these teams were opening in front of their fans and everything like that, and in come the mighty Scouts. Well, needless to say, people don't like losing their home openers, and having the Kansas City Scouts as the opponent didn't help us in any way, shape or form.

A Point Well Taken

The Scouts broke their five-game winless streak by tying the California Golden Seals on October 23. The *San Mateo Times'* Hugh McDonald wrote that the Seals "fell behind 4–1 as they played the role of hosts to a fault—many faults."[47] Dave Hudson opened the scoring at 5:15, but Stan Weir responded for California at 11:34. Then, according to McDonald, the Seals "parlayed some stupidity and loose defensive play" into three straight trips to the penalty box, which at one point resulted in a two-man advantage for the expansionists in the dying minutes of the first frame.[48] With Bob Stewart and Dave Hrechkosy in the penalty box, Wilf Paiement scored his second goal of the season at 19:36 to send the Scouts back to the dressing room with a 2–1 lead.

The Seals again looked sloppy in the second period as Ed Gilbert scored just 0:29 into the frame after Ron Huston lost a faceoff and two of his defensemen whiffed when attempting to clear the puck. Nolet delivered what looked to be a knockout punch to the struggling Seals with another goal just 0:24 later, but instead, the goal seemed to rouse the Seals from their slumber, and they pressed Michel Plasse.

Stan Weir finally broke through the Scouts' defense and scored his second goal of the night at 15:45, and then Larry Patey followed up with his third of the season at 17:18. "The defensemen went down," he said. "and I held my shot until the goalie was going the other way."[49] Just 1:33 into the final period, Huston pulled the Seals even at 4–4. The Scouts had one last chance to win it, but goalie Gilles Meloche stoned Paiement with a sprawling save with just 1:36 left in the game.

Seals director of hockey operations[50] Bill McCreary was unimpressed by his team's effort. "It was our worst game this year," he said. "The comeback means nothing. We had to have a save on a breakaway to avoid losing to a team which hasn't won a game all year."[51]

"Maybe it'll convince them in the future that playing teams like Kansas City, Washington and Vancouver you have to prepare for like any other team," said Seals coach Marshall Johnston about his players and the sorry effort they put forth. Bep Guidolin saw this comment as an insult, as though the Seals did not take the Scouts seriously. Guidolin believed that anyone who could make such a comment surely had "rocks in his head," but he had a lot more to add in his tirade, accusing Johnston and Seals management of not being capable of "get[ting] that team up for seven years" and "putting people to sleep all over the National Hockey League." The insulted Scouts coach even went so far as to say that they would not need seven years to overtake the Seals, but that in two years his team would "smoke right by them."

That being said, the Scouts had finally rid themselves of the pesky zero in the points column. "The pressure is off," Guidolin continued. Blowing a three-goal lead to the Seals and losing would have been a true rock-bottom moment: "it's a good thing we held on and got the tie, because if we would have lost, we would have been so down that…," and then his voice trailed off.[52]

Of course, these games were played on the road, putting the Scouts behind the eight ball right from the get-go, but their scrappy attitude kept them in most contests. "They'll surprise a few teams if they keep playing like that," said Atlanta's Pat Quinn after his Flames narrowly beat the Scouts on October 18.[53] Larry Popein, Vancouver's assistant coach, was at the Kansas City–California game on October 23. "That Kansas City team hasn't much talent, but it sure works hard," he admitted after the game.[54]

Popein was definitely right about the Scouts' hustle. Two nights after the Scouts finally broke the goose egg in the points column, they travelled to Vancouver to take on the surprising Canucks, who for the first time were gunning for a division title. The Canucks easily outshot the Scouts, 44–24, but every time Vancouver took the lead, someone in a K.C. uniform tied it up. Dennis Ververgaert opened the scoring with his sixth goal 2:06 into the game, but a Jim McElmury shot from the point bounced off Butch Deadmarsh's skate past goalie Ken Lockett. Wilf Paiement put K.C. up by a goal with his third of the season at 13:46. The rookie was standing behind the Canucks' net and tried to pass the puck to a teammate, but it deflected off defenseman Dennis Kearns' stick and just over the goal line.

Even though John Gould and Garry Monahan gave Vancouver a 3–2 lead in the second period, Simon Nolet scored on a power play to tie the game at 3–3. The captain skated the puck up the right wing, undressed Lockett with a beautiful move, and backhanded a shot into the vacant cage. The Canucks regained the lead at 1:26 of the third period on a goal by Paulin Bordeleau, but the Scouts pushed back. Not long after Bordeleau's goal, the Scouts went on the power play again, but Lockett stoned Nolet cold. The puck bounced out to Richard Lemieux, who rang a shot off the post. Later in the period, Lockett stymied Ed Gilbert on a partial breakaway, and Nolet banged the rebound right into the fallen goaltender. The Scouts gave it everything they had but couldn't even the count, and Chris Oddleifson finally popped in an empty-net goal at 19:41 to seal the Canucks' 5–3 win.

Sitting 0–6–1 entering their October 27 contest at Boston, the Scouts could only hope for a better result. Bep Guidolin returned to the Hub City for the first time since signing with Kansas City, and the Bruins were coming off a couple of tie games against lightweights Pittsburgh and St. Louis, so the Scouts were hoping to catch the Stanley Cup finalists flat-footed. Bobby Orr and his comrades had other plans as they jumped out to a commanding 4–0 lead in the second period. Bart Crashley remembered one fan commenting on the Native American scout on the K.C. crest as he directed a jeer at Guidolin: "Hey, Bep! What's that Indian looking for? The first win?"[55] Considering the final score was 8–2 Boston, the fan's theory was not all that far-fetched.

The still-winless Scouts didn't have much to offer on the trade market, so Sid Abel started making low-key deals to try to shake the roster up a bit. On October 29, Abel traded Chris Evans to St. Louis for Larry Giroux, who sported a wicked Ogie Oglethorpe coiffe a good three years before the Syracuse Bulldog popularized the look. Guidolin, however, was surprisingly cool with Giroux's hairdo.

"Do you think you should trim it up a little bit?" Guidolin asked Giroux.

"How's it look?" responded Giroux.

"Not bad," said Guidolin. "Heck, times are changing," the coach added. "You go along with it."

The Giroux trade was hardly earth-shattering, but it was the best the Scouts could do considering their lack of top-end trade bait. When Giroux arrived for his first practice in Kansas City, Burns greeted him. "How does it feel to be our saviour?" he asked jokingly.[56] Not surprisingly, Giroux was not the Scouts' saviour, as he played just 21 games (no goals, six assists) in Kansas City before being shipped off to Detroit.

Around this time, Guidolin pared the team's roster down from 23 to 20. Doug Horbul, John Wright, and Norm Dube were the unlucky ones heading to the farm in Providence.

Breaking in Kemper

The Scouts played their long-awaited first game at the $22 million Kemper Arena on November 2, but the night didn't go off without a few hitches. For one thing, the arena's interior was not yet completed, and there were only 2,000 parking spots available. As a result, some people arrived three hours early, but not just in cars; they came in buses, bicycles, and on foot as well! About an hour before puck drop, over a hundred residents of the West Side blocked traffic on the 23rd Trafficway and chanted, "We want 23rd!" while brandishing signs and handing out leaflets explaining why they were getting in fans' way.[57] Nevertheless, the Scouts could finally say they had an official home to break in. "It was culmination night for the Ed Thompson follies, the end of years of merry-go-rounds and roller coasters concerning franchise applications, referendums, lawsuits and construction strikes," said *Hockey News* correspondent Jay Greenberg.

"It has to be the biggest thrill of my lifetime.... I'm just excited to be a part of it. Only and [sic] idiot wouldn't be," said Thompson.[58]

Those problems aside, the Scouts outshot the Chicago Black Hawks, 35–29, in a spirited affair before 14,758 fans, which must have pleased the Kansas City brass immensely. Chicago's Ivan Boldirev scored the first goal at Kemper just 3:06 after the opening face-off, and Jim Pappin scored his ninth of the season five minutes later. Wilf Paiement scored his fifth goal at 14:58 on an assist from Jim McElmury to cut the lead to 2–1. In the second period, Rich Lemieux tied the score at 2–2, but the Scouts' happiness was short-lived as Cliff Koroll scored less than two minutes later to put the Hawks up by one. Koroll made it 4–2 mid-way through the final period. Ted Snell scored his first goal of the season at 12:22 to put the Scouts just one behind. Kansas City outshot Chicago, 14–8, in the third period, but Tony Esposito was up to the task and held the Scouts off the scoresheet the rest of the way.

The Scouts' home opener did not end in a win, but the night was still an overwhelming success. "I think they got their money's worth," said Robin Burns.

"They were great," said Guidolin. "Just tremendous for a first-night crowd."[59]

"Super," said Ed Gilbert. "Just super. It was all brand new. It was heart warming to see the people turn out for us." That said, Gilbert was starting to grow frustrated with the constant losing. "It's starting to get me mad," he said. "We should have won three or four already. It's disheartening to play so damn good and not be rewarded by winning."[60]

Luckily for Gilbert and his teammates, game number ten was against their expansion cousins from Washington, who were a woeful 1–8–1 and had already been shut out four times. Early on, it looked as though the Capitals would rout their cousins as Greg Joly scored his first NHL goal, on a power play, 4:47 into the game. Jim Hrycuik scored at 14:49 to make it 2–0, Washington, but Gary Croteau responded with his first goal as a Scout at 16:53. In the second period, Simon Nolet, who had been firing on all cylinders since opening night, scored his sixth goal of the season, on a power play, at 3:28. Washington stormed back later in the period and took a 4–2 lead thanks to goals by Denis Dupere and Dave Kryskow, but Bart Crashley reduced the lead to 4–3 with his first marker of the season just 0:35 after Kryskow's goal.

The Scouts looked inspired in the third period, racking up 12 shots to the Capitals' seven, and before long Kansas City had tied the score on a goal by Paiement at 7:16. Deadmarsh then got his name in the Scouts' record book by scoring the first game-winning goal in franchise history at 12:19. Gilbert and Burns both had solid games as well, finishing with two assists apiece in the Scouts' historic first win. "We were working hard, even when we were losing, and it finally paid off," said Gilbert.[61]

The Scouts must have felt a twinge of pride after win number one, because they looked positively inspired two nights later against Pittsburgh. The expansionists peppered Penguins goaltenders Bob Johnson and Gary Inness with a team-record 48 shots, but the netminding tandem was up to the task.

Inness started the game for Pittsburgh and stopped all 13 shots he faced, but the good times came crashing down when teammate Syl Apps hooked Robin Burns, who lost control and accidentally drilled the goaltender in the face with his leg. Burns hit Inness so hard the Pittsburgh netminder was briefly knocked unconscious. In came Johnson, who kept the overwhelmed Penguins in the game. "B.J. saved us," said Pens coach Marc Boileau. "Especially when he made some big plays right off the bat on the power play."

The Penguins jumped out to a 2–0 lead on goals by Apps and Jean Pronovost, and the score remained that way into the second period. When Vic Hadfield took a roughing penalty with less than five minutes to play in the frame, the Scouts found themselves in position to whittle the gap to a single goal. Burns scored his first goal of the season on the man advantage to give the Scouts some hope, and Barry Wilkins fully opened the door of opportunity by taking a slashing penalty with less than a minute remaining. Paiement capitalized on the opportunity and scored his seventh goal of the season to knot the game, 2–2.

In the third period, Hadfield deflected a shot from Ron Schock that found its way past Plasse, and the Pens went up by a goal, but the lead did not last long. Three-and-a-half minutes later, Nolet scored his second of the night, and the game was tied at 3–3. The teams remained deadlocked until 14:25, when Schock shocked Plasse with a well-timed shot from the nearby faceoff circle that sailed over the goalie's shoulder. In the final minute, Hadfield made a nice pass to Rick Kehoe, who put the puck into an empty net to seal the Pens' 5–3 victory.

"We had a lot more chances than Pittsburgh did," said Burns, "but Inness made some good saves and B.J. was terrific. He stopped at least five sure goals. He was so unbelievable. He looked like the B.J. of last year when we were teammates on the Hershey team that won the Calder Cup."[62]

After win number one in Washington, the Scouts returned to their losing ways and dropped three in a row to Pittsburgh, Vancouver, and Buffalo, bringing their home record to 0–4. Coach Guidolin expected his team to struggle in its first season, but he was growing frustrated with his players' supposed lack of effort. "We've got to get more second effort," he said after the Scouts' 6–1 loss to Buffalo November 9. "We've got to get rid of that attitude."

"How do you do that?" someone asked him.

"You've got to keep reminding them."

"And if that doesn't work?"

"Then you make some changes."

Guidolin really did take losses personally. After the Scouts won, jubilant Bep would puff cigars and happily chat it up with reporters, but when his team lost, he was brooding and cranky, like someone had just drunk the last beer in the fridge. "I don't like to lose and I'm eating my heart out when we do," the Scouts' coach admitted, but he looked forward to a brighter future when Kansas City would have enough talent to win games consistently. "One of these days when there's a half-decent team here, I want to be able to say that I was a part of building it."[63]

We're Going Streaking!

Luckily for Guidolin, the home losing streak would not last much longer. In fact, not only did the Scouts finally win a home game, they did something they definitely would not become known for: they put together a winning streak.

First, the Scouts shocked the St. Louis Blues with a 5–3 win at Kemper on November 13. After spotting the Blues a 1–0 lead, Gilbert and Burns scored power play goals to put the Scouts up, 2–1, at the intermission. Floyd Thomson tied the game at 7:33 of the second, but Jim McElmury and Rich Lemieux scored within a minute of each other to give the Scouts a 4–2 lead, and Gilbert scored his second goal of the night at 6:00 of the final frame to snuff any potential Blues rally.

To say the least, the Scouts were a happy bunch back in the dressing room. "I knew we were gonna win tonight," said Burns, as he put on what *Maryville Daily Forum* sports columnist Steve Cameron described as a "psychedelic black and white overcoat."

"Do you think I'd dress like this if we were gonna lose?" Burns continued.

Bep Guidolin was not about to steal his players' well-earned thunder. "Don't talk to me," he said to reporters after the game. "Talk to the players. It's their night."

The game seemed to signal a turning of the tide as the Scouts started getting breaks here and there. "We played well enough to win against Chicago and Pittsburgh, but we couldn't get the break," said Nolet. "The puck would hit the post." On this night, however, pucks found the back of the net. Gilbert felt things were going so well for him that he "could have had five goals."[64] Defenseman Dennis Patterson, called up from AHL Baltimore, also played a strong game, breaking up a 3-on-1 St. Louis charge and sliding across the ice to foil another scoring attempt.

The fourth goal, scored by third-liner Rich Lemieux, was particularly noteworthy in that it showed that the Scouts had begun to evolve from sad-sack expansion team to full-fledged NHL club. When Lemieux won the face-off just in front of goalie Eddie Johnston, instead of passing the puck back to the point, Lemieux hammered it at the St. Louis net and backhanded the rebound into the net. Pittsburgh's Ron Schock had pulled off the same trick a week earlier, and now the Scouts were adapting their game to better compete with other teams. Normally, the Scouts would have just passed the puck to the point, but now they were showing signs of aggression.[65]

For a while, the Scouts certainly were an improved hockey team. Two nights later, the win streak was complete, and this time the New York Islanders were the victims. The Isles were an up-and-coming team that had matured considerably in this, their third NHL season, but on this night, the Scouts were the dominant club. New York had a 2–1 lead in the third period, but Paiement and Nolet put the Scouts up, 3–2. As the game wound down, Nolet added an empty-netter to give Kansas City a much-deserved 4–2 win.

Of course, since the Scouts were an expansion team, this win streak was not supposed to last very long, and it didn't. The next night, the 3-11-1 Scouts travelled to Minnesota and lost, 3–1, followed by three more losses, but only one of those defeats left a lasting impression. On November 22, the Montreal Canadiens arrived at Kemper for what they likely thought would be an easy two points, but the Scouts had other plans.

Dave Hudson put Kansas City up 1–0 just 0:20 into the contest, and the Habs must have thought, "OK, let's not let the Scouts get too big for their britches." Forty-three seconds later, Doug Risebrough tied the score, 1–1, and the floodgates opened. Yvan Cournoyer, Pete Mahovlich, and Mario Tremblay all scored before the period concluded, and the game seemed completely out of reach. The Canadiens outshot the Scouts, 19–7, and with a 4–1 lead, the Habs seemed in complete control and on the verge of sending 9,177 Kansas City fans home disappointed.

"Seemed" is really the key word here as the second period told a completely different story from the first. Ed Gilbert scored two power-play goals, at 8:51 and 10:03, to close the gap to 4–3, and 0:43 later, Robin Burns completed the scoring blitz with his fourth goal to tie the game at 4–4.

Unfazed by the suddenly explosive Scouts, Jim Roberts put Montreal back up by one 0:46 into the third period, but Wilf Paiement responded with his tenth goal 25 seconds later to make it 5–5. The pesky Scouts just would not tap out, and the seesaw battle continued. Jacques Lemaire scored at 5:49 to put the Habs up, 6–5, but Simon Nolet returned the favor with another power-play goal at 14:49. The Scouts hung on for dear life, hoping to take the tie score to the end of regulation, but the desperate Habs pulled out a 7–6 victory thanks to a second Risebrough goal with just over two minutes remaining. "We scored six goals against the Montreal Canadiens," said coach Guidolin. "It's a moral victory. It was the best game we played this season. We deserved a better fate."[66]

Goodbye, Good Vibes

After the shocking performance versus Montreal, the Scouts came crashing back down to earth and began playing like an expansion team all over again. The following night in Chicago, the Scouts most definitely got what they deserved if the scoreboard was any indication. The Hawks ran roughshod over the expansionists in the first period, outshooting them, 23–5, which included a 16–1 run during one ten-minute span. When the final buzzer sounded, the Hawks claimed a one-sided 6–0 victory thanks to a 51–16 advantage in shots.

The Scouts' luck and effort were both much better three days later when they took on another division rival, the 13–5–4 Vancouver Canucks. Gerry O'Flaherty opened the scoring at 4:52 of the first period, but Lynn Powis tied it up on a power play at 17:57. The Canucks retook the lead on a goal by Bobby Lalonde just before the midway point of the game. Less than five minutes later, Ted Snell scored a shorthanded goal, and the game was tied at deuces. In the third period, the Scouts jumped ahead thanks to a Randy Rota goal at 3:49, but just 1:11 later, Greg Boddy made it 3–3.

At one point, Bart Crashley was skating towards the Vancouver zone when he unleashed a slap shot from just outside the blue line. Goalie Ken Lockett misplayed the shot, and suddenly the Scouts were up, 4–3, with about ten minutes to play. The Canucks pulled Lockett soon after and replaced him with Gary Smith, but what Vancouver really needed was another goal, so with less than a minute remaining, Smith skated to the bench and the Canucks sent out another attacker.I It was all in vain; the Scouts earned win number four.

And then just like that, the good vibes disappeared. On November 27, the Scouts somehow recorded *zero* shots on goal in the second period, which wouldn't have been so bad if the Atlanta Flames hadn't launched 20 shots at poor Pete McDuffe. The Scouts surprisingly made a contest of it, losing only 4–2, but in the process dropped their overall record to 4–16–1. Those sorry performances against Chicago and Atlanta were just the tip of the iceberg.

On December 1, one day after falling 1–0 to the horrible Detroit Red Wings, the Scouts suffered what was arguably the worst defeat in franchise history, a 10–0 whitewashing by the Flyers in the City of Brotherly Love. The *Philadelphia Inquirer*'s Chuck Newman described the contest as "a game that should erase all thoughts of further expansion."[67]

The Scouts fell behind, 5–0, before the end of the first period and 9–0 at the end of two. The *Philadelphia Daily News*' Bill Fleischman accused the Scouts of employing a "stare and shrug defense."[68] The game was so out of reach that Flyers coach Fred Shero found it difficult to do his job. "Believe it or note [sic], it was a hard game to coach," he admitted. "You've got to stop the players from going goofy."[69]

As for Bep Guidolin, he was in no mood to stick around and chit-chat with the Philadelphia media after the game. Moments after the final buzzer, the Scouts' bench boss grabbed his coat, muttered a quick "Gotta go," and disappeared into the night.[70] According to the *Kansas City Times*' Jay Greenberg, he and Chuck Newman took off after Guidolin, looking for a quote, but Guidolin would have rather French-kissed an enraged porcupine than talk about the game. "You saw it, you write it," he hollered.[71]

Poor Peter McDuffe played the entire 60 minutes, and his stat line unfortunately absorbed all ten Flyers goals. A few days after the rout, Guidolin was asked why he had left his helpless young goaltender to fend for himself, and the coach responded rather cryptically that McDuffe didn't "deserve to be pulled. Sunday night, he's getting bombed like the second world war [sic]. I'm going to put him right back in. Plasse will get his chance to be bombarded, too."[72]

Sure enough, three nights later as the Scouts faced off against the Black Hawks in Chicago, McDuffe was right back in goal to face another difficult test, and Guidolin wouldn't be any happier with the end result. Stan Mikita broke the scoreless deadlock 2:25 into the game, and the Hawks never looked back. Darcy Rota scored his ninth goal two minutes later, followed by goals from John Marks, Jim Pappin, Bill White, and another from Pappin in the last minute of play. With Chicago up, 6–0, after 20 minutes, Guidolin tore into his troops during the intermission: "I let them know in no uncertain terms after the first period that I was still in charge and ... that when we have a game plan, I expect them to follow it."

The Scouts scored three goals of their own, two by Randy Rota and one by Simon Nolet, to make the score 6–3 around the midway point of the game, but when Darcy Rota scored his second of the game at 13:04, that was all she wrote for the Scouts. The 7–3 loss dropped Kansas City to 4-19-1. "We came back to life in the second period, but in the first period they looked like they didn't know what was going on," admitted Guidolin.[73]

The Scouts definitely looked like they knew what was going on December 6 against the same Philadelphia Flyers who had run roughshod over them just days earlier. Reggie Leach and Bob Kelly put the Flyers up 2–0 less than four minutes after the opening faceoff, but the Scouts cut the deficit to one goal when Lynn Powis scored his third of the season. In the second period, Rota shocked the Flyers with his fifth and sixth goals, scored in the span of ten seconds. The Flyers, desperate to avoid a humiliating loss, dominated the play in the final frame and eventually, Leach scored the equalizer at 12:12. For the Scouts, losing the extra point surely stung a bit, but keeping the Patrick Division leaders from gaining a "W" still felt good.

After the 3–3 tie against Philadelphia, the Scouts took on the Islanders and Bruins, but ended up on the wrong end of both decisions. Losing to New York and Boston was not at all surprising, but neither was the Scouts' 5–3 victory over the visiting California Golden Seals on December 12. The Seals were sitting in last place in the Adams Division with a sorry 6–18–5 record and possessed a roster akin to that of an expansion team. Since the start of the 1973–1974 season, the Seals had won just three road games, so the odds were actually *against* the Seals on this night despite taking on an opponent with just four wins.

It was not a good night to be a Seals fan. "I've often said that I haven't been disappointed in the team this year," said Seals coach Marshall Johnston. "We had far better chances, but it would have been an injustice if we had won." The Scouts outshot the Seals, 40–29.

"We lost on a poor effort," Johnston added. "In the second period we had nothing at all."[74] Rich Lemieux scored his fourth goal at 5:42 of the middle stanza, and the hot-shooting Randy Rota scored his seventh. The Scouts outshot California, 15–8, in the period, and in the third, the expansionists continued to control the flow of the game. Simon Nolet scored his 13th goal just 0:31 into the frame, and Jim McElmury increased the lead to 4–0 about a minute later, but the Seals came on strong when the game seemed completely out of reach. Warren "Butch" Williams made it 4–1 at 2:44, and Len Frig brought the Seals to within two goals at 3:57, followed by a Dave Hrechkosy goal at 10:55 that made the score 4–3, but that was as close as the Seals got as Lemieux scored again just over a minute later.

Abel Clips a Wing

Despite the impressive showing against California, it was no secret that the 5–21–2 Scouts were struggling badly in the cream-puff Smythe Division. The Scouts had already been shut out five times and had scored two goals or less 14 times. After 26 games, Simon Nolet and Wilf Paiement led the club with 11 goals, while Nolet led with 20 points. Ed Gilbert had scored seven goals and eight assists, which was in line with expectations for him.

Randy Rota had seven goals to his credit, but more had been expected of him. He had so much speed to burn his nickname was "Rocket," but he didn't pot goals like another famous "Rocket" had done for Montreal decades earlier. The Scouts employed Rota at right wing, which turned out to be a mistake since he was a left-handed shooter. *Hockey News* correspondent Jay Greenberg described Rota's troubles thusly: "Time after time, Rota has turned on the burners, gotten a half-step on a clutching defenseman, then been faced with the tedious task of having to bring the puck back across his body to get his good shot away. By the time he does that, he's too deep to do anything about it, and any goaltender can smother the shot before it starts."[75]

Making matters worse, assistant captain Butch Deadmarsh, the second forward chosen by the Scouts in the expansion draft, quit the team after 20 games and decided to wait until his contract expired so he could join the WHA's Vancouver

Blazers. The Trail, B.C. native started the year with five points in nine games, but he went into a deep slump afterward. When he didn't provide the muscle he was known for, he was demoted to the fourth line and penalty-killing duties. The Scouts finally gave up on Deadmarsh and placed him on waivers, and the Blazers scooped him up a year early. They even paid Kansas City the NHL's $30,000 waiver price, so instead of losing Deadmarsh for nothing at season's end, the Scouts at least got something in return. It was a historic deal in that it was the first official transaction between NHL and WHA clubs.

"We were all disappointed," Sid Abel said. "He didn't give us the kind of hockey he was supposedly capable of. He's building a home in Vancouver and playing here it just seemed like he was putting the year in."

"I've never seen a hockey player so pleased to leave a team before," Bep Guidolin added. "He played but not up to what I had seen him do in the minors."[76] Little-used Glen Burdon was called up from the minors to replace Deadmarsh, but after just three days and very little ice time, Burdon left the team when it touched down in Chicago on the way home from Philadelphia. Abel fined the rookie and sent him to Providence of the AHL, and that was it for Burdon's NHL career.

Something needed to be done to shore up the offense, and Abel came through for his boys. The best trade the Scouts ever made occurred on December 14, 1974, when they sent Bart Crashley, Larry Giroux, and Ted Snell to Detroit for Guy Charron and Claude Houde. The Scouts were desperate for offense, and with Dave Hudson recently going down with a hairline ankle fracture, the club had only two natural centers left: Ed Gilbert and Richard Lemieux. Abel and his Washington counterpart, Milt Schmidt, had talked about making a massive trade with each other just to shake things up, since no other team in the league was offering up players who would help them, but when the reeling Red Wings came calling, Abel could smell a steal.[77] Despite being described years later by a member of the Colorado Rockies staff as "efficient, but … about as exciting as a dial tone," Guy Charron was by far the best player the Scouts ever employed.[78] From the moment he put on a Scouts uniform, Charron became the offensive sparkplug the team had sorely lacked since the beginning, and his career trajectory immediately changed for the better.

The Montreal Canadiens had dealt Charron, Mickey Redmond, and Bill Collins to Detroit for the legendary Frank Mahovlich in 1971. Charron got more ice time, and his point totals increased every year, from 12 to 25 to 36, and finally to 55. As the Red Wings stumbled through a horrendous 1974–1975 season, Charron scored just one goal in his first 26 games. He also reportedly had some defensive shortcomings, but he was quick to defend his skill set. "Sometimes I wonder why they say something like that when I really had one of the best records on the club as far as minus goes," he argued.

This roster mismanagement happened smack dab in the middle of the infamous "Detroit Dead Things" era, so the one-sidedness of this transaction was in keeping with then–Red Wings tradition. "It's a big question mark in my mind," Charron said. "But he [coach Alex Delvecchio] is the one who called the shots. I was pleased when I found out about the trade. Very pleased. I just wanted a chance to play regularly."[79]

Tragedy and Loss

Guy Charron's arrival in Kansas City would have a profound, positive effect on the Scouts, but as the team returned from a road trip in early December, some terrible news would shake the team to its core. Trainer Gordie Marchant had shown signs of depression for quite a while, according to some of his colleagues, but no one had been able to help him, if he had in fact confided in anyone. To the shock of everyone on the team, Marchant died of a self-inflicted gunshot wound at the farmhouse he shared with his assistant, James Kraus. A .38 caliber pistol was found next to Marchant's body, but he left no suicide note.

Years later, assistant trainer and long-time friend Dale Graham remembered a moment when Marchant may have been indirectly trying to reach out for help, but there was no way of knowing the extent of Marchant's troubles. "We'd gone to dinner just days before in Chicago. He talked about our relationship. Looking back, I think he was saying goodbye. It makes me emotional to talk about it all these years later. Gordie was my mentor.... He motivated me to get a college degree, which was rare for athletic trainers in those days. His death was really hard on me."

Just before the Scouts were scheduled for a team practice on December 9, Sid Abel told the players and staff what had happened. The players were devastated to hear of Marchant's sudden passing. "There was dead silence in the locker room, and it continued as the players were slowly getting ready to practice," recalled Graham. "I think it was Simon Nolet that suggested to Bep to cut the practice short," and the coach obliged.[80]

Letting Points Get Away

Despite Charron joining the team and immediately becoming a key contributor, wins did not come easily. In fact, after the impressive 5–3 win over California, the Scouts went on an eight-game winless streak further cementing their spot in the Smythe cellar. One of the low points occurred on December 18 versus the surging L.A. Kings, who were challenging Montreal for first place in the Norris Division. For the first 20 minutes, both teams failed to locate the back of the net, but once the Kings solved Michel Plasse, goals came fast and furious.

Juha Widing broke the scoreless deadlock at 8:29, and a minute and a half later, it was Bob Berry's turn to light the lamp. Before the ink dried on the scoresheet, Mike Murphy scored his 11th goal, and at 11:59, Bob Nevin scored his 12th. The Kings were not exactly known for their offensive prowess, but on this night, they scored four times in 3:30 and outshot the Scouts, 15–2, in the second period. With the game far out of reach, Gene Carr and Murphy added goals to make the final score 6–0.

The next night against Pittsburgh, the Scouts were much better, but the final score was just as difficult to digest. Nolet and Burns each scored two goals, and just like that, a mere 2:31 into the second period, it was 4–1 Kansas City. One thing the 1974–75 Penguins were known for, however, was an extremely potent offense, and it was on display the last 21 minutes of the game. Light-scoring Nelson Debenedet drew the Penguins to within two at 19:51 of the second, and as any hockey fan knows, those last-minute goals can be momentum changers.

Sure enough, the Penguins took control in the third frame, and defenseman Mario Faubert scored his first NHL goal at 7:29. With time winding down, rookie Pierre Larouche beat McDuffe for his tenth goal, and the game ended in a 4–4 draw.

The Scouts' habit of letting games slip away in the third period was becoming quite bothersome. Case in point, the night of December 21 in St. Louis. K.C. entered the final frame up 4–3 thanks to a Robin Burns power play goal at 19:56 of the second period, but 49 seconds into the third period, Chuck Lefley picked up his sixth goal, and it was all downhill from there. Ken Richardson put St. Louis up, 5–4, with 6:58 left in the game, and Garry Unger risked a potential icing call by shooting the puck the entire length of the ice to seal the 6–4 victory with an empty-net goal at 19:21.

After three disastrous outings in a row, things would not get better as the Scouts' next four opponents were playoff contenders. First up, against the Islanders, the Scouts took a 1–0 lead on a power-play goal by Norm Dube at 17:10, and 47 seconds later Brent Hughes scored his first of the campaign. Very suddenly the Isles were down by two goals, but as had been the norm the last few weeks, the Scouts could not preserve the lead. Billy Macmillan tickled the twine 0:34 into the second period, and then the flood gates opened. Bob Nystrom tied the game at 2–2 at 13:02, and in the final frame, Billy Harris, Andre St. Laurent, and Garry Howatt each picked up singles to give New York a 5–2 win.

Following the collapse on Long Island, the Scouts visited Montreal on December 28 and limped away with a 7–2 thrashing under their belts. The Scouts travelled back south to take on the Rangers the next night, and while the score was much closer, the Scouts still blew a 1–0 first-period lead on their way to a 2–1 defeat.

Leggy and the Milkshake Kid

After another heartbreaking 2–1 loss, this time at home versus St. Louis, wins started coming a bit more regularly. In fact, compared to Washington, the Scouts started looking like a powerhouse! Between January 4 and February 13, the Scouts put together an 8-15-5 stretch, which for an expansion team is about as good as it gets. For the most part, the scores were close. On January 4, the Scouts picked up win number six, 2–1 over Detroit, and then number seven against Minnesota before a Kemper Arena crowd of 9,047, one of the largest of the season.

Even though the Scouts lost their next game, 6–1, to the New York Rangers, ending their winning streak at two games, the expansionists rebounded nicely January 11 versus Washington. It was the second meeting between the NHL's newest teams, and like the first time, Kansas City emerged victorious over the still-winless-on-the-road Caps. Mike Marson gave Washington a 1–0 lead early on, but Ed Gilbert scored his tenth goal at 11:28, and the teams retreated to their dressing rooms tied. In the second period, Ron Lalonde slipped the puck between Pete McDuffe's legs, but Simon Nolet and Robin Burns scored within 19 seconds of each other to put K.C. up, 3–2. Dave Kryskow evened the score at 15:40, but Dave Hudson regained the Scouts' lead with a power play goal at 18:15. Rich Lemieux scored another power play goal early in the third period to give the Scouts a 5–3 win.

As the Scouts gained some real momentum and made a charge at fourth place in the Smythe Division, Sid Abel acquired 22-year-old goaltender Denis Herron and defenseman Jean-Guy Lagace from Pittsburgh for Michel Plasse. Plasse had performed admirably for Kansas City, despite his 4–16–3 mark and 4.06 goals-against average in 24 games, but he and Abel were unable to come to terms on a long-term contract. Plasse was looking for a six-figure deal, but rumors suggested that the Scouts were losing money and thus would never give him that kind of scratch, so he was shipped to Pittsburgh, although Abel sang a different tune to the media. "I'm pretty well positive we could have signed him," the general manager said. "I've talked to his attorney. This has nothing to do with his contract at all.... Had he played well all the way through, it might have been different."[81] Abel was referring to questionable goals Plasse had allowed in three of his last four starts.

Herron, on the other hand, had only 26 games of NHL experience under his belt and an unspectacular 8–11–2 record, but he was highly motivated, and he had potential to be an excellent professional goaltender even though he had a few areas that needed refining. "I go out too far," he admitted. "I have to control my rebounds. When guys are so close, I have to try to keep the puck." Other than all that, the guy was a solid goaltender even though he didn't look the part at all. In fact, he looked *nothing* like a hockey player should, or even a professional athlete for that matter. Herron was not what you would call a beefcake. "I was walking down the street the other day," Herron would say in November 1975, "and a fellow says, 'Hi. Who are you?'

"I say, 'I'm the goalie for the Kansas City Scouts,' and he looks at me and says, 'You're kidding.'"[82]

To say Herron was nothing more than skin and bones was not an exaggeration. He was 5'10" and an almost lighter-than-air 160 pounds, which plummeted to an anemic 143 by the end of the season. The *Hockey News*' Ken Rudnick described Herron as the not-very-imposing kid "getting sand kicked in his face by the bully at the beach, the 'Before' in an add [sic] for a body-building course."[83]

The Scouts' medical staff had a foolproof plan to beef up their young goaltender, which the Scouts' media guide described as "a high protein calorie diet that included up to eight milk shakes a day," but that Gary Croteau claimed was actually up to *ten* shakes a day![84] Herron and Croteau spent much time working out in Croteau's basement over the summer, and by the time the next season started, Herron had gained back ten pounds. Herron was also a dependable, hard-working player who had earned his coach's respect. Guidolin once described his young goaltender as physically "hard" and "a bear for work."[85]

Being a goaltender on an expansion team is almost never a walk in the park, so Herron was either mildly delusional or a glutton for punishment, because he actually relished the opportunity to be overworked. "I want lots of shots," he said shortly after his arrival. "Lots of work. I want lots of experience." In his first two games with the Scouts, the young goaltender faced 75 shots, gave up 12 goals, and, as Jay Greenberg put it, at the end of each game looked "like he had overslept in a sauna, exhausted, beaten, but still asking for more." Guidolin quickly became a fan of his new goaltender. "We had some great goaltending on our side," he said after one of those losses, 5–0 to Buffalo on January 19. "I told him he's going to see a lot of rubber and by the end of the season we'll have a goaltender. That's the best workout he's had. He's an eager, aggressive kid, and he could turn out to be a heck of a goaltender for us."[86] All Herron wanted was to give his team a chance to win, even though the chances usually fell somewhere between slim and none. Herron wanted his teammates to rely on him, and as he would find out, that's exactly what they did, allowing over 40 shots to reach his body on an almost nightly basis. Herron fit in well with his teammates, and they knew early on they could depend on him. On more than one occasion, he single-handedly kept the Scouts in games they had no business being in.

Robin Burns got to know Herron well during their time together with Pittsburgh's AHL farm team in Hershey. Burns grew up in Montreal and spoke French fluently, so he was able to help the young *Québécois* goaltender feel comfortable with his new AHL team.

> When Denis was with the Pittsburgh organization, he hardly spoke any English. Using the F word in French is no big deal because actually the translation for a "seal" in French is *phoque*. So he comes over to dinner and he's sitting down, and my wife makes spaghetti for him, and he turned around afterwards, and her name was France, and he says, "France, that's the best fuckin' spaghetti I ever had." My kids were sitting there, and their eyes were bulging. So in the dressing room the next day, I had to kind of say to him, "You know, Denis, you gotta be really careful when you're using the F word."

As promising as Herron was, Abel felt the real prize in the deal was Jean-Guy Lagace. "He's a hard-nosed defenseman, a hitter," said Abel.[87] He and Baz Bastien had coveted the 29-year-old defenseman at the expansion draft, but because of bad timing, they weren't able to secure his rights. After choosing Simon Nolet and Butch Deadmarsh with their first two picks, the Scouts hoped to snag their first defenseman, but Washington used its second pick on Pittsburgh's Yvon Labre, so the Penguins reacted by adding Lagace to their protected list.

Lagace had some experience, and he would score 11 points in 19 games for Kansas City that season. "He starts things and he's contagious," said Gary Croteau. "He is really the type who motivates, not only verbally, but by the way he plays, too."[88] In the team media guide published at the end of the season, "Leggy" was described as the team's "holler guy," who added "color to the dressing room and leadership on the ice…. He immediately became a 'hit' with his aggressive play and a hip-check that had charging forwards spilling all over Kemper Arena ice."[89]

The story of how Herron and Lagace found out about the trade to Kansas City is an interesting one. "Most of the people found out before I found out," Herron explained. Herron was playing for the Hershey Bears when he was called up to the NHL as an injury replacement. As the club was warming up to play Atlanta one night, Herron was initially told he was starting in goal, but when the Penguins retreated back to their dressing room while the Zamboni cleaned the ice, the coach suddenly informed Herron and Lagace that neither would play that night. "I really, really got upset," said Herron, "because it was a chance for me to prove myself … and I told Jean-Guy Lagace also that he was not playing, and Jean-Guy really, really

5. The Kansas City Scouts, 1974–75

got upset also. Anyway, I sat on the bench, Jean-Guy got undressed, and sat in the stands…. My wife at the time was in Montreal [and she] found out in the news…. Even the referee knew about the trade. After the game, they came to see me and they said, 'You've been traded to Kansas City.'"

Herron must have been wondering what kind of miserable situation he had been cast off into when he got his first start January 16 in Detroit. The Red Wings were still sputtering along directionless, and it looked as though the Scouts would hand the venerable franchise one of its worst defeats of the season as they jumped out to a 4–1 lead after 20 minutes. Guy Charron not only stuck a knife in his former team when he scored his first goal, but he twisted it around a bit as well with his second marker. Wilf Paiement and Ed Gilbert notched the Scouts' other goals. The Scouts seemed well on their way to win number nine, but Detroit closed the gap to 4–3 in the second period and tickled the twine four times in the final frame to ice a 7–4 comeback win. Herron faced 16 shots in the third period, while his reeling teammates could only manage seven. If there was a silver lining in Herron's first game as a Scout, it was that he at least was not under contract to the Washington Capitals, where he would only have been so lucky as to have a 4–1 lead to blow in the first place.

Bep's Finest Hour

On January 18 and 23, the Scouts played some inspired hockey and defeated Chicago, 4–1, and Boston, 3–2, in Beantown to bring their record to 10–31–4. In the latter contest, Bobby Orr looked to begin an onslaught early by scoring just over a minute after the opening face-off. The Bruins continued to press, peppering Denis Herron with 19 shots in the first 20 minutes, while the Scouts managed just five, but one of those five, coming off the stick of Randy Rota, tied the score, 1–1, before the teams headed to intermission. Ed Gilbert and Gary Croteau scored in the second period to put the Scouts up, 3–1, and the unthinkable suddenly seemed possible: the Kansas City Scouts could beat the Boston Bruins.

The Bruins were determined not to let this expansion outfit embarrass them. Early in the final frame, Ken Hodge darted into the Scouts' zone, hoping to grab possession of a loose puck, but Herron charged out of his net to cut him off. Unfortunately, the Scouts' young goalie slipped near the puck, allowing Hodge to take it. He shot the puck toward the empty Kansas City cage but rang it off the post.

Johnny Bucyk scored at 5:47 of the third period to put a real scare into the Scouts, but Herron was outstanding the rest of the way and gave his team the opportunity to pull off the upset. "It was very, very long," Herron admitted. "I looked up at the clock every minute." In the final minute, the desperate Bruins sent out Bobby Orr, hoping he could weave his magic one more time, but it was not meant to be on this night. "I saw him coming in by himself," the goalie recalled. "But he came in too fast. All I had to do was go down. He was in too close."[90] Herron stopped 34 of 36 shots to preserve the most shocking win in Kansas City's short NHL history. "We deserved to win," said Guidolin. "We worked so damned hard for it."[91]

Guidolin, the former Bruins coach, may have been the happiest member of the

K.C. Scouts the night of the upset, but he didn't provide much in the way of memorable quotes; he waited two more days for that. "Ever hear of Winston Churchill?" he asked, "Well, this was my finest hour." Guidolin had waited to pour salt on the Bruins' wounds because he knew they would be coming to Kansas City on the 27th. "I didn't want to give them any ammunition," he said.[92]

Ed Gilbert remembered this game fondly, and he believed "you couldn't have had a better coach for that team at that time than Bep. Boston needed to win but they were thinking it was an automatic win. That was a real physical goal, and I think I ended up in the back of the net with the puck somehow. They came at us both guns blazing and it was such a huge win. My dad called me up the next day and told me that I was in the *Globe and Mail*.... That was pretty cool."[93]

Herron recalled the game like it was yesterday.

> Boston at that time had an incredible team. Esposito, Orr, Cashman ... the Chief, everybody were there. We're playing in Boston ... a minute in the game, Bobby Orr was coming down straight in the middle and he shot the puck from the red line and I missed the puck and it went right in the net, almost from the red line, and I said, "Oh my gosh, that's gonna be a long game." It was almost like a wake-up call. We beat Boston in Boston, 3–2.... After that, I never looked backward, because that boosted my confidence so high.... I think that game changed my career and changed my confidence and everything.

Herron was a standout in the shocking victory. "When the puck was in the Scouts' end as much as it was all night at the Garden," wrote Jay Greenberg, "three goals

Denis Herron was one of the most underrated goalies of the mid to late 1970s because he played on so many middling teams, but coaches around the league were often quick to praise his talents (Robin Burns collection).

weren't meant to be enough." He added that Herron "kept his cool and wouldn't let his teammates' magnificent efforts crumble."[94]

For hard-working penalty-killer Gary Croteau, his second-period goal provided immense relief. According to the Scouts' 1975–1976 media guide, Croteau "rattled more goal posts than football fans after the Super Bowl," and he hadn't scored since November 3 against Washington, a span of 34 games.[95] "It had to be the worst start of my career," he said. "When you start going 10, 15, 20, 25 games without a goal … you start to worry. When I was pressing, I was coming close, hitting a lot of posts. That made it more frustrating."[96] Croteau's confidence returned, and he scored his third goal of the season a few nights later in a 4–4 tie with Atlanta.

Even though Croteau was struggling offensively, there was no way Guidolin was sending him to the press box; he was too valuable in so many other ways. Croteau played the majority of games alongside Ed Gilbert, and together, they provided the Scouts with a surprisingly effective penalty-killing unit which allowed just 53 goals. "He's a bear for work," the coach said. "That's what a hockey club needs—a bunch of guys who're willing to work."[97] In fact, of all the players Kansas City selected in the expansion draft, Croteau would become the longest-tenured Scout, suiting up for 390 games over six years.

Unbeknownst to back-up goaltender Peter McDuffe, while he was on the road his wife and 16-month-old son returned to their apartment only to discover the place had been completely cleaned out by burglars. Pretty much everything was taken except for an electric tea kettle, some Canadian money, and the lid to their sewing machine. McDuffe's wife Mary, seven months pregnant, had tried to contact her husband in Boston, but it took two days for the message to reach him. Police believed the robbers had planned their visit when McDuffe was on the road, which left the apartment ripe for rummaging, especially since the couple did not own a dog. Luckily for Mary, the other players' wives were incredibly supportive, particularly Brent Hughes' wife Sandra, who took her and her son in.[98]

Fluking a Tie and Blowing Leads

The win over Boston put Kansas City just four points out of fourth place, held at that time by Minnesota. The trade for Guy Charron had clearly made a big difference. In the 15 games he had played in Kansas City, he had scored 19 points. After 44 games, Simon Nolet was still lighting it up with team-leading marks of 18 goals, 19 assists, and 37 points. The Scouts also got solid contributions from Ed Gilbert (12 goals, 11 assists), Robin Burns (10 goals, 13 assists), Richard Lemieux (10 goals, 13 assists), and Wilf Paiement (15 goals, 6 assists). Dave Hudson would have been among the team scoring leaders had he not missed so many games due to injury. He began his Scouts career scoring 14 points in his first 15 games, and he looked well on his way to doubling his career highs in most offensive categories, but a mini-slump followed by a hairline fracture that occurred during a December 6 game versus Philadelphia derailed Hudson somewhat. He nevertheless managed 20 points in 34 games.

Four nights after the big win over Boston, the Bruins travelled to Kansas City with revenge on their minds, but once again, they found themselves struggling to keep up with the pesky Scouts. Norm Dube and Guy Charron lit the lamp in the first period to put the Scouts up 2–0 before the Bruins woke up and mounted an attack of their own. Rod Graham scored his second and final NHL goal less than a minute after Charron's marker to pull Boston to within one.

Phil Esposito evened the score at 7:49 of the second period with his 46th goal, and the Bruins outshot K.C., 12–8, in the frame. In the third period, the Scouts continued to play the Bruins tough, giving up only nine shots, and Robin Burns scored at 14:36 to put the Scouts just minutes away from their second straight victory over Boston. Unfortunately, the Bruins had much pride on the line and refused to concede. As players piled into Denis Herron's crease, Wayne Cashman took an innocent-looking shot from the right boards, and the puck found itself in the player scrum. Carol Vadnais and Esposito both hacked away at the puck, which hit Don Marcotte and bounced into the net at 19:14.

"The puck hit Don Marcotte's skate," Herron explained. "Am I sure it hit his skate? Yeah, I'm sure. That's illegal. I'd like to see a replay.

"I tried to protest to the official but he said the puck wasn't kicked … it ricocheted, and that's legal." Herron looked on the bright side, however, admitting, "Those guys are very experienced. It makes me feel good to play them so well."[99]

Even though the Scouts had blown the lead in the dying seconds of the contest, a 3–3 tie against one of the NHL's best teams was a reason to hold their heads high. "All I know," said Guidolin, "is that we played two good games against the Bruins…. We didn't fluke a tie. They fluked a tie—not us."[100]

Two nights later, the Flames paid a visit to Kemper, and even though the Scouts failed to beat the visitors, they still took the lead four times in the game. That said, the Scouts should have won the contest. With less than two minutes left, Dennis Patterson took a shot from the point. Flames goalie Phil Myre fumbled the puck, and as it fell behind him, he reached back to grab it, but it was too late. Referee Dave Shewchyk immediately called it a goal, a first in the NHL for Patterson, and despite protests from the Atlanta players on the ice, the Scouts found themselves up, 4–3. "It never went in," Myre said. "No way…. I was in good position, too."

Under normal circumstances, a go-ahead goal with less than two minutes on the clock would have sealed the victory, but the Scouts had a terrible tendency to blow leads late in games. "Maybe that's why you call it an expansion team," explained Denis Herron.

> Experienced teams know that in the third period they need to push a little harder…. You need to play in the offensive zone to score, and that, I think, is what happened … all of a sudden the other team just started to push a little bit harder, and we were backing up on our heels and we were getting so many shots [against] in the third period that all of a sudden they score…. The games that we won, we didn't win by that many goals … or we had a very good start and by the time the team realized that, trying to catch up, we managed to hold on to a win.

On this night, there would be no Kansas City win. The Flames' Noel Price took a shot that completely missed the net, but Jean-Guy Lagace "tried to pick it out of the air," according to Peter McDuffe, and the puck was redirected towards the goal crease.[101] McDuffe, fully expecting the puck to head into the corner of the rink, now had his back towards the loose puck, and Tom Lysiak simply needed to tap it into the empty cage for the game-tying goal with 1:35 left.

Poor Pete McDuffe. He had played his heart out in the first two periods as the Scouts got outshot, 33–14, yet the score was 2–2 thanks to a couple of power-play goals by Simon Nolet and Lynn Powis. McDuffe's teammates didn't find their game until the third period, when they outshot Atlanta, 17–8, and took the lead on two occasions, but such disappointments are just another part of life for an expansion team.

The "Golden Age of Scouts' Hockey"

It must be said that unlike the poor souls residing at the Capital Centre in D.C., the Scouts had done little to embarrass themselves since the start of the season. Most nights they were competitive, even against the NHL's elite. They had already beaten the Islanders, Bruins, and Canucks, all playoff-bound clubs. They had also tied Vancouver, Pittsburgh, and most impressively, the Stanley Cup champs from Philadelphia. "I think you've got to give Bep and Baz an awful lot of credit," said Sid Abel. The Scouts came into the season well-prepared despite the long odds against them. "There wasn't anyone in the draft we didn't have a book on."[102]

Between January 1 and February 4, the Scouts' 5–8–3 record, while not spectacular, was the second-best mark in the Smythe Division, and their 49 goals scored were tops during that period. It was, as Jay Greenberg wrote in the *Hockey News*, the "Golden Age of Scouts' Hockey," a high point in the franchise's short history, but there were still a few stumbles on the road to respectability.[103] The Scouts played division front-runners like Vancouver, Boston, and Chicago like their lives depended on gaining a point in the standings, but the Buffalo Sabres were a different story. "We seem to be all right against the clubs that try to work the puck in, but Buffalo attacks aggressively and we make mistakes in our zone," said Abel.[104]

Just a few days later, on February 2, Abel's words proved prophetic as the Sabres showed the Scouts just how aggressively they could attack by launching a team-record 58 shots on Denis Herron, who did his best to keep the Scouts in the contest, including stopping the first-ever penalty shot against Kansas City, but ended up on the losing end of an 8–1 score. In the next game, against Chicago, the Scouts again proved Abel right by tying the Hawks, 3–3. The Scouts also put out solid efforts against Toronto, California, and Washington soon after for wins number 11, 12, and 13.

In early February, Abel was still looking for some extra toughness, so he picked up minor-league enforcer Doug Buhr off waivers from the L.A. Kings. Buhr would not only cost the Scouts the $40,000 waiver fee, but also the services of defenseman Roger Lemelin, although just until the end of the season. The 6'3", 215-pound 25-year-old Buhr was not exactly the second coming of Bobby Orr, putting up a paltry 18 goals in two-and-a-half seasons, but he had accumulated triple-digit penalty minutes every year. "He may turn out to be what we want," said Guidolin. "We've got nothing to lose." The Scouts could only hope Buhr would provide some much-needed

Guy Charron was the best player the Scouts ever had. With 113 points in 129 career games in Kansas City, he is the Scouts' all-time leading scorer (Robin Burns collection).

muscle, because he didn't bring much else to the table. "Not too mobile," said Guidolin. "But he can shoot a puck. Who knows, a guy like that, it may turn his whole life around. We have everything to gain. At least we're getting some size."[105]

Lemelin, however, was shocked to learn he was changing addresses. The young defenseman was not getting much ice time with the Scouts, so it was believed that sending him to the minors to get some experience would be beneficial, even though they had promised him he would play out the season in the NHL. Making matters worse, Lemelin had already moved all of his things to Kansas City, and his father was also visiting him at the time of the trade.[106] Kansas City would not give up on Lemelin, however, as he would return to Kansas City the following year.

On February 6, the Maple Leafs met the Scouts in Kansas City, looking to solidify their hold on third place in the Adams Division. In the previous weeks, the Scouts had blown late leads three times, and on this night they came damn close to making it four. Nolet scored his 22nd goal, on a power play, which gave him a team-high and career-best 44 points. Dave Hudson accepted a beautiful pass from Lagace, who was standing out near the blue line, and "Hud" blasted a 20-foot shot that struck goaltender Doug Favell's glove before bouncing into the cage. Then Doug Buhr grabbed the disk at the Scouts blue line and drove hard past the Leafs' Jim McKenny. Buhr crossed into the Leafs' zone and dished the puck over to Hudson, who shuffled it over to Gary Coalter, skating in on the right side. Coalter fired the puck past an overwhelmed Favell for his first NHL goal, and the Scouts' third in a span of 6:27.

The Scouts held a 3–1 lead and a 27–13 edge in shots on goal, but in the third period the Leafs pressured Herron. Tiger Williams scored just 1:07 into the period to give the Leafs some life, and 12 minutes into the period, Inge Hammarstrom rang a shot off the post, so the score remained 3–2 into the final minute. In the dying seconds, Ron Ellis stood to the right of Herron, but the goaltender made a great save. The puck hit the crossbar, and as Charron put it, "rolled across it. I thought it would never come down." The puck landed on top of the net, leading to a face-off in the Scouts' zone. Charron won the draw from Darryl Sittler and shoveled the puck to Dennis Patterson, who cleared the puck out of the zone to preserve the win. "You always think about things like that," Patterson said. "It's about time we did it." Herron was the hero once again, making 14 saves in the final period before 7,128 fans.

For the Scouts, it was quite a relief to put their string of late-game letdowns behind them. "Four in a row like that," admitted Rich Lemieux, "would have been very, very hard to take."[107]

On February 9, the Scouts put out another inspired effort against the Golden Seals. Despite their putrid 2–21–2 record away from home, it was the Scouts who embarrassed the Seals, who were in free fall following an impressive December. Robin Burns was providing a little shade for goalie Gary Simmons, and in the process the Scout tipped the puck into left side of the net for his 12th goal of the campaign. Wilf Paiement put K.C. up by two goals at 9:13 of the middle frame. Brian Lavender helped bring the Seals to within a goal by dishing a nice pass over to rookie Charlie Simmer, whose 20-foot shot beat Pete McDuffe, but that was all the Seals would get as McDuffe made 33 saves in the 2–1 win, one of his finest outings of the season.

"It was one of our better games," said a pleased Bep Guidolin. "We have been playing really well for the last seven weeks. Our young players just aren't making the same mistakes that they did early in the season."[108]

After losing to Vancouver, 4–0, to close out their three-game road trip, the Scouts returned home, where the Washington Capitals, who were coming off an impressive 7–4 win in coach Red Sullivan's debut, were hoping to win two in a row for the first time. Randy Rota opened the scoring on a power play at 18:03 of the first period, but Yvon Labre tied it up for Washington at 7:51 of the second. That was all the offense the Capitals could muster on the night. The Scouts took a 2–1 lead into the third period, when Wilf Paiement scored his second goal of the night on a power play 0:24 after the opening face-off. About ten minutes later, Burns potted his 13th, and Ed Gilbert capped off a great night for Kansas City with his 14th while Rich Lemieux was in the penalty box for slashing. The 5–1 victory brought the Scouts' record to 13–36–7.

Like an Egg Rolling Out of the Playoff Race

After the Scouts won their 13th game, reality set in and the Scouts started looking like an expansion team again. In what would become a franchise tradition that lasted well into the 1980s, the Scouts ended the season in a big-time funk, in this case winning just two of their final 24 games. The good news was that crowds started getting bigger in the final quarter of the season. In the 1974 portion of the schedule, the Scouts' average attendance was an underwhelming 7,907, but in the final 24 games of the season, attendance jumped to 8,939 per contest.

As the season wound down, a troublesome new habit started raising its ugly head: getting shut out. Between February 7 and March 2, the Scouts were blanked six times in 12 outings. The Seals shut out the Scouts on February 15, which was tough to stomach since the boys in Pacific blue and gold were not nearly as competitive as Montreal or Philadelphia, but what happened next was far more embarrassing. The Scouts flew to Washington for a one-game road trip, hoping they could get back on the winning track, but the game turned into a nightmare.

The Midwest sextet dressed just four defensemen for the game, because Brent Hughes was nursing an injured hand and Jim McElmury had twisted his ankle. The situation became dire when Jean-Guy Lagace fractured his ankle in the first period and was lost for the remainder of the season. For the rest of the game, the Scouts were down to just three defensemen, and Dennis Patterson was playing with strained ligaments in his left shoulder. Nevertheless, newspaper reports stated that Patterson played over 50 minutes that night! Making matters worse, Bryan Lefley, who had just been called up from Providence of the AHL, had to leave the game with a knee injury. Guidolin was so desperate that he put center Guy Charron on defense just to give some of his injured bodies a rest. The only healthy body on the blue line, Claude Houde, must have felt it was just a matter of time before he went down too, but he made it through to the final buzzer with all his body parts intact and in working order.

Considering the wonky state of the Scouts' defense, not to mention that leading scorer Simon Nolet was also out with a bruised calf, the Scouts put out a tremendous effort to keep the Capitals from winning their sixth game of the season. K.C. fired 32 shots at Ron Low, but the goaltender blocked them all en route to the Caps' first-ever shutout, 3–0. It also marked the 11th time the Scouts had been skunked.

Two nights later, the Scouts put together what Guidolin called "a hell of a team effort" against New York. Rangers All-Star Rod Gilbert drew first blood at 8:14 of the first period by tipping a Gilles Marotte shot past McDuffe. Charron scored his 11th goal to knot the game 1–1 at 14:07 of the second period, and just 1:09 later, Randy Rota also scored his 11th. The score remained 2–1 until disaster struck with just over ten minutes remaining. Lynn Powis was battling for the puck near the right boards and lost possession to Greg Polis, who took a 25-foot shot that eluded McDuffe.

Guidolin was quite upset with Powis, whose gaffe cost the Scouts a win against one of the NHL's best teams. "Our player had the puck inside the blue line," Guidolin said. "All he had to do was dump it out. I'm not going to name him. If you were watching the game you know who he was. He didn't play much after that, anyway."

Powis tried his best to control his emotions after hearing that Guidolin was less-than-impressed with him. "They scored," Powis said after the game. "That's the way the egg rolls."[109] Powis' quip proved to be prophetic. Opponents scored a lot more than the Scouts did the rest of the way, and the Scouts continued to roll all the way down to the NHL's basement.

After a 6–3 dismantling courtesy of the Canadiens on February 20, the Scouts hosted the 17-35-6 North Stars. Charron got the ball rolling with a goal at 1:27 on assists from Rota and Burns, and Burns followed that up with a power play goal of his own at 13:22 to put the Scouts up, 2–0. Norm Gratton whittled the Scouts' two-goal lead with a goal at 15:39, but the Scouts took control of the game in the second period and never looked back. Claude Houde scored his first NHL goal 0:27 into the second frame, and Burns made it 4–1 early in the third period to ice the Stars. McDuffe stopped 24 of 26 shots in a 4–2 Scouts victory.

Unfortunately, there was little reason to celebrate the rest of the season. One win against another mediocre team wasn't going to reverse the Scouts' negative trend. After the win against Minnesota, the Scouts embarked upon a 16-game winless streak which began with a 4–2 defeat in Toronto February 26, followed by a trip to the Philadelphia Zoo, a.k.a. The Spectrum, home of the Broad Street Bullies.

The Scouts were so badly outclassed by the defending Stanley Cup champions, the *Philadelphia Inquirer*'s Chuck Newman wrote that Flyers goaltender Wayne Stephenson "played Saturday night against the Kansas City Scouts. No, make that *dressed* against the Kansas City Scouts, because a goalie actually playing seemed rather superfluous in the Flyers' 3–0 victory." The Flyers outshot the Scouts, 45–16, and the Scouts mustered only eight shots through 40 minutes, so Stephenson had a hard time staying focused. At times, as he played the puck behind the net, he chatted with his defensemen just to make things interesting, but his counterpart Pete McDuffe, was anything but bored. McDuffe kept the Flyers off the scoresheet for 39:28 until Rick MacLeish finally broke through and scored his 24th goal. McDuffe did his best to keep his team in the game, but Andre Dupont scored two minutes into the third period, and Terry Crisp put the game out of reach eight minutes later.[110]

A Blue Line Band-Aid

With many WHA teams teetering on the brink of extinction, NHL teams welcomed many players who were either out of work or preparing to find a new employer. Thirty-one-year-old defenseman Larry Johnston was one such player. Johnston's arrival couldn't have come sooner, as the Scouts' blue line was suffering badly due to its almost unprecedented rash of injuries. There was also the little matter of replacing Brent Hughes, who was preparing to move to the WHA after the season.

"It was a nightmare," Johnston said about his WHA experience. "I'm anxious to get back to the NHL. There's no comparison, really." According to *Hockey News* correspondent Jay Greenberg, when Guidolin heard Johnston's words, the coach "turned into a lighthouse. The ships at sea could find their way from the beam emanating from his face."

"That's all I wanted to hear," Guidolin said, but his excitement over having Johnston in the lineup would be short-lived.[111] Before long, the coach and defenseman would be at loggerheads and sniping back and forth at each other in person and through the media.

After a salary dispute with the Detroit Red Wings, Johnston signed a four-year, $240,000 deal with the Michigan Stags in July 1974, but after just 49 games with the cash-starved Stags, who had already uprooted and moved to Baltimore, Johnston signed a contract with Kansas City on March 1. Johnston accused the Stags of not always paying him on time, so he was more than happy to cut ties with the WHA's weakest link.

Skip Feldman, executive director of the soon-to-be-defunct Baltimore Blades, was highly critical of Johnston, claiming he had underperformed and was "just going through the motions." Feldman opined that the Stags could not deal Johnston for anyone of value because his salary was too hefty for most teams to absorb. Needless to say, both parties agreed it was time to tear up Johnston's contract, making him a free agent.[112]

Johnston already had 207 games of NHL experience between 1967–1974. One thing he was known for was his aggressiveness. "Oh, he was one of the bad ones, all right," wrote hockey historian Andrew Podnieks, "one of the baddest of them all."[113] With Detroit from 1971–1974, he had seasons of 111, 169, and 139 penalty minutes despite missing significant time in two of those seasons. He was also +21 in 1971–1972 and +6 the following year, so he could handle things on the defensive end as well.

Johnston was an even more ornery character in the minors. Ornery to the tune of 356 penalty minutes with EHL Johnstown in 1963–1964, 262 minutes with Tulsa of the CPHL the following year, and several more triple-digit penalty minute totals in the AHL throughout the 1960s and early 1970s. Aside from 100-penalty-minute-man Wilf Paiement, the Scouts were not a particularly aggressive bunch, but expecting the team's 19-year-old star-in-the-making to play the enforcer's role was not conducive to winning, so Johnston's toughness was more than welcome.

The Scouts' next game, March 2 in Atlanta, was a letdown although the Scouts put up a better effort than they had recently. Johnston was in the Scouts' lineup for the first time, but despite the reinforcement on the blue line, the game got off to a rotten start as Curt Bennett tipped an Ed Kea shot that beat Herron at the 40-second mark. The goal, Bennett's 23rd, tied the mark for most goals by an American-born player, set by Tommy Williams in 1963. Bennett eclipsed the record at 6:04 of the third period to give the Flames a 3–0 lead, and Jacques Richard closed out the scoring 2:35 later. Once again, the Scouts were on the wrong end of a shutout, this time 4–0.

Falling Flat

The losing continued throughout March. The Scouts could have put an end to their winless skid on March 11 against the suddenly reeling Vancouver Canucks, but they blew it ... again. Peter McDuffe was outstanding through two periods as the Canucks buzzed relentlessly and launched 26 shots on goal. Lynn Powis scored his ninth goal at 4:22 of the second period to give K.C. a 1–0 lead. Gary Croteau then shocked goalie Gary Smith with a quick 30-foot shot that smacked the middle of his trapper but fell out and landed in the net, just nine seconds into the third period.

Croteau's goal could have easily deflated the wilting Canucks, but Don Lever responded a minute later to make the score 2–1. Powis scored again at 10:51, and it seemed as though the determined Scouts would defend their two-goal lead and end their winless skid, but the Canucks had been watching their Smythe Division lead shrink dramatically the last few weeks and were just that much hungrier. Luckier too.

At 12:24, Leon Rochefort scored on a weak 60-foot shot that sneaked past McDuffe while he was screened. "He [McDuffe] never moved until it was in the net.... I think he was looking for a high shot, but because I didn't hit it like I wanted to it went along the ice," Rochefort said about his flubbed shot.

Now it was the Scouts who seemed deflated. Lever scored 2:44 later to make it 3–3 and steal a point from their division rivals and extend their winless streak to eight games, but Guidolin looked on the bright side. "That was our best game in about three weeks," he said. "We'd like to finish as strong as we can, especially against teams in our own division, to give our guys some confidence for next season."[114]

Not only were the Scouts falling apart late in games, they were in a complete free-fall in the standings too. Jean-Guy Lagace's ankle fracture affected the team more than anyone would have expected. The Scouts gave up far more goals after he went down. Furthermore, they missed his offensive skill from the blue line, and they missed his persistent checking. "From his very first appearance in a Scouts' uniform," wrote Jay Greenberg in the *Hockey News*, "Lagace became a traffic cop, giving the power play a point man who could both shoot and pass the puck. The power play has been abysmal since he was lost."[115]

With Simon Nolet out of the lineup for eight games, not to mention that it took him a few more games to rediscover his scoring touch, the Scouts had little in the way of firepower in late February and all of March. Without Nolet, his linemate Charron stopped finding the net too. "I didn't think," said Guidolin, "especially on a team like this, that any player could ever mean that much to us."[116]

The other problem plaguing the Scouts was that other teams had learned how to beat them, and it had become more and more difficult for the Scouts to catch a team taking a nap. Making matters worse, the Scouts were served a steady diet of games against Montreal, Los Angeles, Toronto, Pittsburgh, and other playoff contenders. The league's new playoff structure, which guaranteed a playoff spot to the top three teams in each division, meant that just about everyone in the league, with the exception of California, Kansas City, Washington, Minnesota, and Detroit were putting everything on the line. "Every club we played needed the points," said Baz Bastien. "Like the other night against the Islanders I thought we played a good game. But they're a contender. They needed the points."[117]

The Scouts' winless streak reached double digits as they completed a four-game road trip in Pittsburgh on March 16. The Penguins were in the midst of their best season ever thanks to a very potent offense, and on this night the Pens stormed out to a 5–0 lead on goals by Ron Schock, Vic Hadfield, Rick Kehoe, and two from Lowell MacDonald.

With the game almost completely out of reach, the Scouts woke from their slumber. Simon Nolet scored his 23rd goal (and his first in 18 games) at 13:23, and Randy Rota followed up with his 12th 26 seconds later, but the game's outcome was never in doubt despite the Scouts' 19–11 edge in shots in the second frame. Goalie Gary Inness kept the Scouts' scorers at bay and preserved the Penguins' 5–2 lead.

Kehoe scored for Pittsburgh at 6:32 of the third period, making Gary Croteau's goal six minutes later totally obsolete. "We missed a lot of chances, but it's encouraging to see a team play like this," said Bep Guidolin. "They were skating better, digging in the corners, really playing well. There have been some nights when it's been discouraging. But you look at it all-in-all, you've got to be pretty proud of them, really. Most of the time, 95 percent of it, they've given me all they had…. Really, I can't complain."[118]

Despite Bep Guidolin's optimism, five more losses and a tie followed, bringing the Scouts' winless streak to 15 games. One of those losses proved rather historic. On March 29, the Scouts travelled to Montreal, which of course meant they would leave with zero points, but this time, the Habs' win was their 1,000th at home. Guy Lafleur also scored his 50th goal, something he would achieve five more times in his career. The Scouts may not have been doing a lot of celebrating, but at least their opponents were making memories.

Game number 77 against the New York Rangers was one Peter McDuffe likely wanted to forget. It was no secret that the Rangers were a once-great team on the decline. The Rangers had won two in a row just once since late January, and they were in danger of missing the playoffs if they didn't get their act together quick.

"When you give up so many goals, something's got to be done," said Rangers goalie Gilles Villemure.

"It was time for a little soul searching," added Brad Park.

"We talked things over, discussed what was wrong," said Steve Vickers.

The Smythe Division cellar-dwellers were exactly what the Rangers needed to pull them out of their funk. McDuffe faced 24 shots in the first period, 18 more in the second, and another 17 in the third. Surprisingly, the Scouts held a 2–1 advantage thanks to a short-handed marker by Gary Croteau and another goal by Wilf Paiement, his 25th of the season. "When that happened," Vickers said, "I was a little upset."[119] That's when he started teeing off on McDuffe, scoring once in the second period and twice more within 28 seconds in the third. He added his fourth goal, and 41st overall, with just 2:38 remaining. Rod Gilbert finished the night with five assists. New York outshot Kansas City, 59–18, and ran the Scouts out of Madison Square Garden with an 8–2 loss under their belts.

The Scouts' last win of the season, and their first since February 23, came on April Fools' Day. The surprising L.A. Kings, fighting neck-and-neck with Montreal all season long for first place in the Norris Division, fell 3–1 and left Kemper with their tails between their legs. The Kings outshot Kansas City, 36–27, but the Scouts grabbed a 3–0 lead on goals by Rota, Paiement, and Powis. "We didn't play as good as we can, and they played well," said Kings coach Bob Pulford, rather succinctly.[120]

The Scouts returned to K.C. for some home cooking before boarding a plane headed to Chicago, where the second-place Black Hawks were waiting. Little did the Scouts know, the Hawks were waiting in the comfort of their own homes and not at Chicago Stadium for the opening faceoff. A terrible blizzard pounded the Windy City, forcing the Scouts' plane to be rerouted to Indianapolis. From there the team boarded a bus, unaware that the game had already been postponed. As the bus got mired in a traffic jam in Chicago, Jean-Guy Lagace thought he would have a little fun and chat up the people in the neighboring cars, also unable to move. When he jokingly asked one female motorist if she was going to the game, she responded that it had been postponed. Lagace informed the rest of the team that they were heading to an empty arena, and someone on the bus wondered aloud whether the Scouts would win by forfeit if the Black Hawks failed to show up. They should have been so lucky. Somehow, enough hotel rooms were found to accommodate everyone despite the dastardly weather. The game was played the next day, April 3, and the Scouts lost, 6–4.[121]

The last game of the season, a close 3–2 loss to St. Louis, dropped the Scouts' record to a sorry 15–54–11, but compared to the abysmal 8–67–5 mark put up by Washington, the season had been a moderate success despite some dark clouds looming over the horizon.

Bottom Line

The defense crew wasn't great, but the 328 goals it allowed was still better than Minnesota, Detroit, and Washington. The Scouts' biggest problem was their popgun offense, which produced a pathetic 184 goals, just three more than Washington. Guy Charron, however, who scored 42 points in 51 games after arriving from Detroit he was acquired from Detroit, was an absolute steal. Simon Nolet met all expectations set out for him in the summer, leading the team with 58 points. He and Wilf Paiement led the way with 26 goals. Fred Shero may have given up on Nolet, but by season's end even the legendary Flyers coach was impressed by Nolet's evolution. "He seems to be more of a leader now," he said after one Flyers-Scouts tilt. "He never was before. It's done him a lot of good as a person. Some people surprise you when they're put under real stress. All of a sudden he's had to prove himself."[122]

Nolet's reputation had improved so much that Cup contenders Montreal, and even Philadelphia, asked the Scouts what it would take to acquire him, but Sid Abel refused to part with his captain. The Scouts' Booster Club voted Nolet the club's MVP, and the Kansas City hockey writers chapter nominated him for the Bill Masterton Trophy, awarded to the player who best exemplifies the qualities of perseverance and sportsmanship, but he lost out to Buffalo's Don Luce.

The offense got a little thin after the Scouts' top four, although several players enjoyed career years. Dave Hudson scored nine goals and added a personal-best 32 assists. Ed Gilbert scored 16 goals and 22 assists. Robin Burns finished with 18 goals and 15 assists. Randy Rota scored 15 goals and added 18 assists. Lynn Powis had 11 goals and 20 assists.

In goal, Denis Herron proved more than capable of handling the number one job. His 4–13–4 record and 3.75 goals-against average were not all that impressive, but his .896 save percentage after his trade from Pittsburgh put him just behind the NHL's most elite goaltenders, yet still ahead of solid veterans Gary Smith, Ed Johnston, Gilles Gilbert, Gilles Villemure, and Doug Favell, all of whom played for playoff-bound teams.

Peter McDuffe performed well as the de facto number one goalie, protecting the cage a team-high 36 times, and finishing the year 7–25–4 with a 4.23 goals-against average and .883 save percentage.

Financial Woes

As year one wound down, more and more rumors swirled concerning the Scouts' financial outlook, and there were many reasons for concern. First of all, the Michel Plasse trade smacked of financial desperation. He was an excellent young goalie playing tremendous hockey for an expansion team still finding its identity. Plasse wanted a six-figure deal, but Abel refused to sign him to such a lengthy pact. Almost immediately, people began to wonder why the Scouts gave up on their number one goalie so quickly. Second, when Alan Eagleson, the executive director of the NHL Players' Association, not to mention Wilf Paiement's agent, publicly stated that he was worried that his clients playing for Pittsburgh and Kansas City might not get paid, it sent up warning flares. Luckily, no Scouts players missed a paycheck, but as time would tell, the public's concerns were indeed valid.

The Scouts were owned by so many different people, and most of them were small business owners with limited resources. Everyone started out with dollar signs in their eyes, especially after witnessing the 14,000-plus crowd at the first game at Kemper, but when attendance plummeted in November, the one-percent investors, few of whom had deep pockets, were unwilling or unable to invest more dough. Ed Thompson did his best to downplay the situation, claiming the Scouts had many partners "who would like a bigger share. We're very well capitalized. There's no problem whatsoever," which couldn't have been further from the truth.

Another distressing sign was that the Scouts violated league rules by traveling to other cities on game days in order to save money on meals and hotels. "I think that's a ridiculous assumption on your part," Thompson retorted defensively to the *Hockey News*' Jay Greenberg before explaining that the St. Louis Blues had flown into Kansas City the same day they were scheduled to play the Scouts. "Does that mean they're in financial trouble? What for? To save a few dollars on a hotel, that doesn't mean anything."[123]

Thompson may have been putting on a brave face, but the Scouts' financial issues were real, due in part to a lack of fan support. After opening night's crowd of 14,758, fewer and fewer fans showed up at Kemper to watch the Scouts struggle. "What I would like to know," Thompson asked two months after the Scouts' November 2 home debut, "Where have they been since?" At that point, the Scouts had played just eight home games, and attendance never improved in the ensuing 32. "The experienced clubs tell us during the latter part of December attendance picks up," Thompson said, but crowds remained ominously sparse. Nevertheless, Thompson remained optimistic that the trend would change because this downturn in fortune was just part of an expansion team's expected progression to money-making juggernaut. "Naturally, we would like to have capacity crowds," said Thompson. "But other franchises at this stage of the game were drawing 3,000 to 4,000."[124,125]

Why did the Scouts have such a hard time attracting fans? It could have had something to do with competition from the NBA's Kansas City Kings, the fact that pro and college football were both in full swing, and the Scouts' ten home games in November, which may have overwhelmed the neophyte fans. "I think our schedule hurt us," Thompson opined. "There were too many times we had three games in one week. People just can't afford to come that often."[126] Or maybe it was simply because hockey was not indigenous to the American Midwest, and it was just a tough sell in football country. Ticket prices were also more expensive than they had been when Kansas City was a minor-league hockey town. If the Scouts had managed to get more Saturday home games, the club might have made a little money. The Scouts had but ten Saturday home games, which were attended by an average of 10,501 fans, a figure in line with what the Washington Capitals drew at Capital Centre.

A little more effort in promoting the Scouts would have helped a great deal as well. "We just didn't have the time before, with the arena problems we had," Thompson explained in what could be considered an extremely poor excuse for the Scouts' shoddy pre-season promotional strategies. Yes, the people running the Scouts were newbies at building a hockey franchise in a football town. They should have known that some potential fans probably couldn't distinguish a hockey puck from a urinal puck. "We've had people call and want to know whether you have to wear a coat to the game," Thompson said. "They don't know whether the games were inside or outside."[127] These people clearly needed to be first enticed and then educated, but early on, the Scouts refused to have promotional events such as Ladies' Night, and the Scouts didn't organize puck and stick giveaways like every other team did regularly. It was only after management realized that simply dropping a hockey team in a new arena was not enough to draw fans, that special promotional events and giveaways were organized.

If there was any silver lining to the dark cloud hovering over Kemper Arena, it was that talent-wise the Scouts were miles ahead of their counterparts in D.C. The Scouts won more games than Washington, and they got blown out a lot less too, losing only six games by more than five goals. Why the Capitals struggled so much more when they plucked players from the same talent pool is probably due to better scouting by the Scouts, and Baz Bastien played a big part in assessing the motley crew of has-beens and washouts leading up to the expansion draft. "We really had a good book on the guys in the minor leagues," said Bastien. "Then, Sid really did a job on the National Leaguers. We had a heckuva list. The homework was really well done. That was the biggest satisfaction in the thing. We were spending a lot of money on these guys, and there was the fear we would get there and end up with nothing."[128]

By trading away Plasse for Herron and Lagace, and spare parts Crashley, Snell, and Giroux for Charron, the Scouts added three quality players and upgraded their scoring and defense while giving up very little. The fact that Sid Abel could make such improvements without having quality assets to trade said something about his skills as a general manager and assessor of talent.

With a little luck, a few more good trades, and a first-round draft pick ready to make a splash in the big league, the Scouts had as good a chance as any to make a major jump in the standings. "We'll be better next year," captain Nolet predicted. "And better the next year, too. These things take time, but we'll do it."[129]

The Bottom Line on Year One of the Scouts-Capitals Era

The famous expression, "A chain is only as strong as its weakest link," was never truer than in 1974–1975; the NHL was arguably at its lowest point in years, and it was arguably due to the inclusion of the Scouts and Capitals. In the 1986 book *The Klein and Reif Hockey Compendium*, hockey statisticians Jeff Klein and Karl-Eric Reif claim, "there is evidence that this expansion was the one that definitely shouldn't have been undertaken." Klein and Reif devised a mathematical formula that allowed them to more accurately compare the plus-minus records of all NHL players. The details of their mathematical formula are unimportant here. What is important is how much the Capitals' and Scouts' inclusion in the NHL drastically changed the game itself. "With this laff-riot Wayne & Shuster pairing donating the gift of 9–0 victories to just about every club that played them, plus ratings around the league soared; the twentieth man on the plus list the previous year had a +16.4 rating, but this year the twentieth man has a +21.8 mark."[130]

By December 1974, less than three months into the NHL's fourth expansion phase, there were already plenty of grumblings that this expansion was the one that would set professional hockey back. The *Chicago Tribune*'s Bob Verdi suggested that the best Christmas gift the Washington Capitals and Kansas City Scouts could receive was "more games between each other. Like about 80."[131]

In 1974–1975, a whopping 92 points separated the 113-point first-overall triumvirate of Montreal, Philadelphia and Buffalo from last-place Washington. There were several other teams who finished far below .500 as well: Detroit, Minnesota, California, and Kansas City all finished with fewer than 60 points. Had it not been for Washington and Kansas City, many of those clubs, if they had been lucky, would have languished somewhere in the 45–50-point range. The moribund Stars, Wings, and Seals looked like Stanley Cup contenders against the Capitals and Scouts, compiling a 19–8–2 record.

From 1973–1974 to 1974–1975 the league's goals-per-game average rose from 6.39 to 6.85, the highest since 1944–1945, when the NHL had one significant similarity to the mid–1970s: the talent pool was no more than a tiny puddle. In 1944–1945, the NHL could blame World War II for poaching many of its top players. In 1974–1975, the NHL could blame both itself for expanding too quickly but also the WHA for doing the same, forcing professional teams to depend on minor-leaguers to fill roster spots created by yet another round of expansion.[132]

Needless to say, opponents were merciless. Winning 8–0 or 9–1 was never enough; teams felt compelled to reach double digits and set a new franchise record. A hat-trick was unacceptable when a fourth goal could be had with little effort. Bill Mikkelson remembered how going to Philadelphia, Boston, or Montreal was "almost like facing an all-star team," and that these powerhouses treated a game against Washington as "a night off" which they would "use to pad their bonuses."[133]

Consider the fact that *half* of the NHL's 18 teams set post-expansion franchise records for goals scored per game, and in some cases, these increases were significant. For example, Buffalo scored a team-record 3.29 goals per game in 1972–1973, but in 1974–1975, scored 4.43 goals per game. The New York Islanders, who were anything but a powerhouse their first two years in the league, scored just 2.33 goals per game in 1973–1974, but when there were two new punching bags added to the league, they scored 3.30 goals per game. Pittsburgh, another team that was not renowned for its offensive prowess, scored a team-record 3.29 goals per game in 1972–1973; two years later, it was a whopping 4.08 per game. St. Louis, like Pittsburgh, had always been a rather quiet team in the offensive zone, and their team record for goals per game was a paltry 2.99, set in 1972–1973, but in 1974–1975, that record was upped to 3.36. One also can't ignore the Vancouver Canucks, who emerged from inconsequence to win the Smythe Division title. They scored a team-record 2.99 goals per game in 1972–1973 but upped that mark to 3.39 in 1974–1975.

There were also six teams who allowed more goals per game in 1974–1975 than in any other season since the start of the expansion era. Minnesota saw the largest single-season jump, going from a team-worst 3.55 goals-against average in 1968–1969 to a distressing 4.26 average in 1974–1975. The New York Rangers went from a high of 3.22 goals-against average in 1973–1974 to 3.45 the following season. The Toronto Maple Leafs went from 3.58 goals-against per game in 1972–1973 to 3.86 in 1974–1975.

All those increases in scoring most definitely point to sloppy defensive play, which is expected after an expansion draft cuts deep into every team's roster. With the WHA gearing up for its fourth season, there would be yet again 32 professional teams competing tooth and nail to sign the best hockey talent in the world. Yet again, there wouldn't be enough of it to go around, but at least the poor souls languishing in Kansas City and Washington would have something to look forward to in the end: an unexpected and much welcomed trip to the other side of the world.

Period 3

•• 6 ••

The Washington Capitals, 1975–76

There is no doubt that the 1974 expansion had a negative impact on the NHL. The league's non-stop expansion had badly diluted the sport, and the poor quality of play was reflected in the league's attendance, porous defensive play, and non-stop clutching and grabbing. Before the Capitals and Scouts played their first games, Stan Fischler wrote:

> Quality was the first victim of expansion, and as a result veteran spectators in the six established NHL cities began staying away from the arenas in droves.
>
> But somehow the NHL managed to replace the empties. In new hockey cities such as Atlanta, the league was catering to a fan whose only previous connection with ice had been in highballs. The question remained: Just how much expansion-dilution could big-league hockey sustain before even nonsavvy fans began turning away?[1]

That answer would come soon enough, as by the end of the season, several teams looked to pull up stakes.

The *Toronto Star*'s sports editor stated that the NHL's outlook was "dreadful" and that more "dull, meaningless contests can be expected in the immediate future than ever before."[2] The Capitals and Scouts were involved in more lopsided games than could be counted on one's fingers and toes. In fact, the Scouts lost six games by six goals or more, while the Caps lost by at least six goals 17 times. The Scouts allowed at least eight goals in a game four times. The Capitals gave up at least eight goals on 16 occasions. In seven of those games, the opposition cranked Washington for ten goals or more. Games against Washington and Kansas City were essentially meaningless and not exactly a hot ticket. Sure enough, attendance plummeted in several cities throughout the last half of the 1970s as the gap widened between the haves and have-nots. The good news was that the Scouts were not last in the NHL in attendance—that "honor" went to the California Golden Seals for the eighth year in a row, thanks to a league-low average of 6,172. The bad news was that the Scouts' average attendance of 7,356 was *second*-worst. In fact, no other NHL team drew less than 10,000 though the Capitals came dangerously close to that mark averaging just 10,004.

One could argue that the addition of the Capitals, in particular, had a major effect on the Norris Division. Perhaps it was because Washington played its division rivals six times each that those teams showed tremendous improvement over the course of the season. The Canadiens improved 14 points over their 1973–1974 finish and the Penguins jumped 24 points, while the Kings leapt into second place thanks to a 27-point improvement. The dysfunctional Red Wings actually dropped ten points, but still managed to beat the Capitals *five* times.

"If we don't get too many injuries; if we play to our potential, we can finish last," said Milt Schmidt.[3] And that, in a nutshell, is where the Washington Capitals stood entering season two. There wasn't much Schmidt could do to improve his team except make small moves he hoped would add up to a major impact: a shrewd draft pick here, a crafty scouting hire there, maybe an unheralded free agent signing in the off-season. He had no choice but to ride out the storm and hope to survive with a roof over his head. "It wasn't easy to get personnel," he admitted many years later. "I never even tried to trade because I didn't have anybody to trade."[4] Despite Schmidt's claim that he did little on the trade front, he made quite a few important deals in the final half of 1974–1975, and while the Caps came out on the winning end of most of those trades, none of them made much of an impact on the team's overall record.

The only truly valuable chip Schmidt had was the first-overall pick in the Amateur Draft, which as any good general manager knows, should never be traded unless the price is just right. In fact, just one year earlier, as the Capitals were gearing up for the draft, Schmidt was quoted as saying he "would be very leery" about trading away a first-round pick, especially if it was the number one choice overall. Schmidt went so far as to suggest that the NHL forbid teams from trading away their first-round picks because, in his opinion, "The whole idea of the draft [was] thrown out when that [happened]."[5]

It turns out, when one's team wins eight games over the course of a season, beliefs can change, and No. 1 picks *can* move. Philadelphia dangled fourth-line center Bill Clement, their own first-round pick, and prospect Don McLean in front of Schmidt, and the Washington GM took the bait. "Bill Clement," promised Schmidt, "will be a star on the Washington team for years to come. He will be a leader."[6]

Clement wasn't the most talented Flyer, but he possessed strong defensive skills and was an excellent penalty killer with a deft scoring touch. Flyers coach Fred Shero thought highly of Clement, even calling him and Rick MacLeish the two best skaters on the Flyers. He was also a world-class impressionist. He regularly made bus rides and plane trips more tolerable thanks to his excellent mimicry of Shero, Bobby Clarke, and goalie Bernie Parent (complete with a facemask).

On a team less stacked than Philadelphia, Clement surely would have received more ice time, so his 21 goals and 37 points in 1974–1975 definitely showed potential. Since the 1975 pool of junior league graduates was again considered devoid of can't-miss prospects,[7] the Caps rolled the dice on Clement. "He is a young player with championship experience who should be a winner for years to come," Schmidt explained.[8]

Clement was disappointed to be leaving the two-time defending champs, but he also relished the opportunity to become a star in his own right in Washington. "It is what makes this deal worthwhile," Clement explained as he tried to look on the bright side of hockey's equivalent of a terminal brain cancer diagnosis. He admitted he was "not overjoyed" about joining the worst team in the history of professional hockey, but that upon further reflection, he felt "far more positive."

"I have a new job," he said. "I want to get at it."[9]

To have any chance of moving up in the standings, the Capitals had to jump at the chance to acquire any new talent that showed potential. The June intra-league draft was one of those occasions, and this time around, the Caps, who badly needed right wingers, selected Hartland Monahan from the New York Rangers. When Monahan, who was Hall of Famer Bernie Geoffrion's son-in-law, was drafted by Washington, he had but seven games of NHL experience under his belt, but taking a chance on young players was the best and cheapest way Washington could improve its roster.

Getting Monahan almost didn't happen, though. The intra-league draft, after all, had become rather worthless and boring in recent years. The draft worked this way: every team protected a certain number of players, much like in an expansion draft, and the league's worst teams got the first crack at whoever was exposed. The draft had become so obsolete that teams usually passed up their chance to select one of the unprotected players, who were likely to make zero impact. With little action on the floor once again, Abe Pollin and new team president Peter O'Malley decided to step outside for a bite to eat, but then the Rangers took left wing Dale Lewis from Los Angeles, meaning New York had to expose someone else. That someone was Monahan.

The 24-year-old Monahan would play the best hockey of his career in D.C., and he cost the Capitals just $40,000. He became, as the Capitals' 1977–1978 media guide put it, the team's "number one goodwill ambassador…. If there was a charitable benefit or hockey clinic, Hartland was there and his outgoing, relaxed manner never failed to win friends for the Capitals."[10]

The intra-league draft was indeed a godsend for talent-starved teams like Washington and Kansas City, but by a 14–4 vote, league governors voted against holding another such draft. Monahan holds the distinction of being the last ever player selected in the draft, much to the dismay of New York general manager John Ferguson. "Something must be wrong when you give a guy like that away. It makes you wonder. Damn, it makes you wonder," he said after Monahan scored the first goal in a 5–2 Capitals victory over the Rangers on March 16.[11] The Rangers would have been smart to avoid Dale Lewis and hang on to Monahan. Lewis played just eight games for New York and scored zero points, while Monahan would score 96 points in 156 games with Washington.

As season number two approached, there was the usual front office reshuffling to deal with, but nothing that directly affected the players, management, or coach. First, Abe Pollin stepped down as team president, but remained the club's owner. Pollin felt that by running the Capitals, the Capital Centre, and the Washington Bullets, he was stretching himself too thin and was not able to give the hockey team the attention it needed, Pollin named Peter O'Malley, a partner in the law firm of Shipley, O'Malley, and Miles, and a member of the Capital Centre board of directors, as the club's new president. Lefty McFadden was promoted to assistant to the president.

One post that remained unchanged was the one behind the bench. There were reports during the off-season that no one had showed interest in the job, which the Capitals denied. The Caps wouldn't find their man until the dying days of 1975, so for the meantime, Schmidt remained coach and GM. He made it clear, however, that whoever took over the coaching reigns would be "damn aggressive on and off the ice" and that he couldn't "let the players talk back to him" like they had done to Anderson, something that "griped the hell" out of Schmidt. In the meantime, Schmidt promised to bring that aggression behind the bench. "If a player talks to Milt Schmidt—even today—like that, he'd better be ready to step outside to fight," he said.[12]

A Couple of Jokers and an Ace

The Caps began year two with optimism. After all, they couldn't get any worse. They were also starting training camp with a much deeper roster than one year earlier. The only everyday player to sign with the WHA over the summer was the hard-working Bill Lesuk, who went to Winnipeg, and for less money to boot, to be closer to his ailing parents.

Leading scorer Tommy Williams was back as the team's number one right wing, although Schmidt was hoping Williams could slide over to the center position. Bill Clement was expected to take charge offensively as another top center, while Ron Lalonde was comfortably positioned as the number three pivot and number one face-off specialist. If there was one position where the Capitals had an embarrassment of riches, it was down the middle, but Nelson Pyatt, for one, fully expected to stick with the Capitals after his impressive showing the previous year. "Yes, I expected to play regularly," he later admitted. "But I didn't want to look cocky, just hard-working."[13]

The other forward positions were another ball of wax altogether. At right wing, there was Jack Egers, whose talents were never in doubt, but he had missed all but 14 games due to a back injury. After he experienced back spasms in training camp, there were no guarantees that year two would be any different. There was also Stan Gilbertson, normally a left wing, who had impressed in his short stint near the end of the season playing right wing on Williams' line. Gilbertson was also starting a two-year contract with the expectation that more offense would be forthcoming.

Unfortunately, Egers and Gilbertson got on Schmidt's shit list after the pair got caught keeping beer in the bathtub of their hotel room, where they were hosting after-workout parties with the boys. They got into a verbal altercation with Schmidt, which resulted in three-game suspensions for both.

Mike Lampman remembered one incident from training camp which may have been the one that got Egers and Gilbertson suspended, and it originated from one Garnet "Ace" Bailey's hotel room. "Ace and I roomed together [during the 1975–1976] Capitals training camp.... We all liked Ace," Lampman said, trying his hardest not to laugh at the story he was recounting over the phone from his home in Hawaii.

> He was a real character. As the training camp went on, Ace decided that our room was going to be the cocktail barroom after the two-a-day practices in training camp. But it was made clear by the GM, Milt Schmidt, and Jimmy Anderson that alcohol was not allowed in the rooms. Well, Ace decided that the only place he could put alcohol, and not have it found, was in the toilet tank. Sure enough nobody ever looked there, not even the maids. And over

a short period of time after our two-a-day practices, all the guys ended up drinking in our room. And Ace made sure the liquor flowed. After a short time, Milt and Jimmy wondered where everyone was since no one was in the hotel or neighborhood bars. There was a knock on our door and in came Milt and Jimmy to take stock of who was going to be fined for breaking the training camp rules. It was hearing the knock on the door that Ace jumped in the bathroom shower and pulled the curtain. Oddly enough, Milt never thought to pull the curtain back. At about that time, Jack Egers decided that he had had enough of Jimmy and Milt jumping into this to ruin the good time everyone was having. Jack proceeded to chase both Jimmy and Milt out of our room and back to their rooms. We all got fined … except Ace. Jack got a token one-day suspension and a larger fine. But it was a good team building thing that came to an end.

It is unknown whether Gilbertson was suspended because of his role in the same incident, but he believed the time off had a positive effect on his health. "I usually tire in camp," he explained, "but right after those three days I felt stronger."[14] The asthma attacks that had hindered him in Oakland subsided to the point where he only needed to take a pill every night rather than get a weekly injection. Nevertheless, the asthma still affected his stamina once in a while.

After Gilbertson and Egers, there was nothing but inexperience at right wing. John Paddock had played but a handful of exhibition games, Hartland Monahan had seven NHL games on his resume, Tony White had just five games, and Ron Anderson injured his knee during training camp and never played another NHL game. On the left side, prospects were even scarier. Mike Marson and Ace Bailey were both assured spots, but after them there were a lot of question marks. Many forwards would be shifted from one position to another just to cobble a roster that was barely competitive.

Yvon Labre and Jack Lynch were the Capitals' number one defense pairing. "I'm beginning to mature as a defenceman," Lynch said at the time. "It takes defencemen longer, you know. This was my best year by far and I give a lot of the credit to Yvan [sic] Labre, my partner. We complement each other very well."[15]

Of course, the Caps' X factor, the element that could truly make the team competitive, was the swashbuckling, but oft-injured Greg Joly. "My main goal," he declared, "is to play a full 80-game schedule. You know, the way things have gone, I haven't even been able to get into what I'd call good shape."[16] Joly had played just 44 games and scored a whopping one goal and seven assists to go along with a plus/minus rating of -69, second worst on the club. In one game against Toronto, Joly was on the ice for three goals early in the game, and Jimmy Anderson immediately benched his prized defenseman because "he wasn't working hard enough." He added that since Joly was "making the money he [was], he'd better put out."[17]

The Capitals had put enormous pressure on young Joly's shoulders, something he never should have been burdened with. To expect a teenager to lead an expansion franchise to glory is outrageous, but Joly harbors no ill will towards the team that drafted him. "I'm not blaming them at all," he said many years later, "because in all fairness to them, I did not play very good."[18] Fans, however, seemed to understand the enormous pressure Joly was under. In an article in the May 1975 *Hockey Digest*, one fan defended the young defenseman: "You get hurt a little and you get gun shy, and you do a few stupid things. You have to give him room for awhile."[19] Had this fan been running the Washington Capitals, perhaps we would be talking today about Greg Joly, NHL All-Star, and not Greg Joly, first-round bust.

The 1975–1976 season started off well enough for Joly. He registered three assists in his first five games, and in two of those games he was +1, a rarity for a Caps defenseman, but the good times were fleeting. He went pointless in 18 straight games from November to March, in part because he was always nursing some sort of injury. He injured his Achilles tendon in training camp, then on December 5 against Buffalo, his right skate hit a groove in the ice and he injured his knee, costing him 36 games.

The heroic Ron Low was unquestionably the Caps' number one goalie, but he would soon be joined by 24-year-old Bernie Wolfe, who would duke it out with the zero-wins-for-his-Capitals-career Michel Belhumeur for the back-up position.

If Only These Games Counted

The Caps played the Scouts twice early in the exhibition schedule, and once again, their expansion cousins' old superiority complex reared its ugly head. The Scouts gave defense prospect Terry McDonald a chance to prove himself, and he looked pretty good in the two wins versus Washington, but Sid Abel didn't want pre-season success to go to the kid's head. "Remember, it's only been two exhibition games against Washington," Abel said rather dismissively. "He looked good, but wait until we play St. Louis. Things get faster and he may not know where he is out there."[20]

Despite starting the pre-season with three straight losses, the Capitals finished with a (gasp!) .500 record: four wins, four losses and one tie, including a five-game unbeaten streak! Tony White and Bob Gryp led the team with six points apiece, while Marson, Monahan, and Williams each scored five.

The pre-season was filled with shocking moments, including a September 23 contest in which the Caps stunned Buffalo 3–1 while using three different rookie goalies: Grant Cole, Garth Malarchuk, and Bernie Wolfe. The next time the teams met a few days later, the Caps fell behind 4–0 after just nine minutes of play only to stage an unexpected comeback before eventually losing 5–4. A few days earlier, on. The Caps also trounced Detroit, 8–4, and earned a comeback 4–3 win over the defending Cup champs from Philly. Of course, Bobby Clarke, Bill Barber, Bernie Parent, and a few others were absent, which bothered some in the Washington organization. "Stuff like this you expect in exhibition games at a small rink in Canada somewhere," said a Capital Centre spokesman. "but it's really bush pulling something like this in a league city."[21]

Washington also defeated Toronto, 4–1, on September 28 in London, Ontario, despite being bombed with 57 shots, but what most people remember from the game is the second-period bench-clearing brawl that was triggered when the Leafs' Dave Dunn speared Mike Marson in the face and cut him near his left eye. Dunn and Marson had dropped the mitts in the first period, and in the second frame, when Dunn finished serving an unrelated penalty, he struck Marson. Marson swung his stick at Dunn in retaliation, but Darryl Sittler thwarted the assault with his own stick (and according to some newspaper accounts, with his left arm), which in turn caused Marson's twig to shatter. Sittler charged at Marson, and players on both benches rushed out onto the ice. Sittler was eventually handed a double minor penalty and a game misconduct, while Dunn received five minutes for spearing. Marson was not only ejected from the game, he was also suspended for the Capitals' regular season opener.

The Caps would have enjoyed a six-game unbeaten streak had they not blown it in their final pre-season game. The Blues were visiting D.C., and ran into some penalty trouble and surrendered power-play goals to Bailey, Egers, and Pyatt. Down 3–1, Bob Gassoff was serving another penalty when Jerry Butler grabbed a loose puck in front of his own net, skated end to end, and slipped the disc past Belhumeur. The tide had turned, and the Blues reeled off another four goals, including a second shorthanded marker in the third period, to skate off with a 6–3 win.

If Only These Games Didn't Count

All in all, despite the meltdown versus St. Louis, the Capitals had reasons to feel optimistic, but so does every other team before opening night. For some of those teams, it takes a few weeks for Stanley Cup aspirations to evaporate, but for the Caps, it was a matter of days. As depressing as their 1–15–2 start had been the previous year, the 1975–1976 Caps got off to an arguably worse start, not winning their first game until October 26, their tenth game of the season. Seventeen of their first 28 games were on the road, the Capitals' very definition of Hell on Earth.

Although victories would remain elusive, scores would be much closer than they had been in year one, not that the Caps earned more respect along the way. For instance, in the season opener the Pittsburgh Penguins started goaltender Gord Laxton, who had *zero* games of NHL experience, over veterans Gary Inness and Michel Plasse. The rookie looked impressive in his debut, blocking 26 Washington shots while his teammates took care of business at the other end. As the Pens worked a 4-on-3 power play in the first five minutes of the game, Dave Burrows scored, followed by a Vic Hadfield marker early in the second frame.

Greg Joly and Tony White scored in the dying minutes of the period to help the Capitals mount a comeback, but from then on, nothing else would beat Laxton. Colin Campbell scored the eventual game-winner 5:48 into the third period, and Syl Apps iced the game with a power play goal at 18:36.

The Capitals followed up the 4–2 opening night loss with another spirited effort against Philadelphia on October 9. Despite being outshot, 50–28, Washington gave the Flyers a run for their money, losing a close 5–4 contest. Six days later, the 105-point Los Angeles Kings narrowly beat the Caps, 4–3, and the 113-point Buffalo Sabres, who had run roughshod over Washington in almost all their previous meetings, could only squeak out a 5–4 win.

Another close game, one that actually resulted in a point in the standings, took place on October 17 versus California. A shade under 8,000 fans attended the Seals' home opener, which saw Dave Hrechkosy open the scoring at 16:45. Greg Joly evened the score less than two minutes later, and former Seals Hartland Monahan and Stan

Gilbertson put Washington up, 3–1, in a 62-second span in the second period. It looked promising for the Caps to pick up the duke, but with just 5:29 left in the frame, Jim Neilson scored a power play goal.

Penalties would end up costing the Capitals dearly on this night. Willy Brossart went off for tripping, and then Yvon Labre and the Seals' Wayne King were penalized for roughing, so the teams played most of the final minutes at 4-on-3. Michel Belhumeur could taste his first victory in a Capitals uniform, but with just 1:13 left to play, rookie Gary Holt dashed the poor goaltender's hopes. "I saw the center zone open," Holt said about his first NHL goal. "Jim [Neilson] fired me the puck and I lunged at it, knocked it off the defenseman's stick and it went in. I just poked at it, and it caught the goalie by surprise. He reached down, but it was just a little too late."[22]

As the Capitals sat at 0–6–1, the Kansas City Scouts, who had been cruising through a much easier schedule to that point, were showing some spunk thus far, 1–2–1 coming into their game with Washington on October 22. As in the earlier game against the Seals, the Caps had victory in their midst, but let it slip away twice.

Bill McKenzie looked great in goal for Kansas City, stopping a couple of close-range shots, but partly because Washington's shooters couldn't get enough wood on the puck. Overall, the Caps managed just 20 shots on McKenzie, while allowing just 20 themselves, a team-record low for shots against. That being said, the Caps looked flat, neglecting to play the body and missing passes throughout the game.

Tommy Williams scored just 1:05 into the contest, but the Scouts fought back thanks to a goal by Dave Hudson at 8:06. Williams scored again 50 seconds later to make the score 2–1 Washington, but Gary Croteau tied the game near the end of the period. Wilf Paiement put Kansas City ahead in the second period, and Croteau scored an empty-netter in the last minute of the game to give the Scouts a 4–2 win. The hard-luck Michel Belhumeur was tagged with yet another loss.

Burning Up the Road

On October 26, the Chicago Black Hawks were coming off a 4–0 victory over Kansas City on their way back to the Windy City. The Capitals, of course, had just one road win to their credit since entering the NHL, but on this night, the hockey gods finally stood on Washington's side.

Down 2–0, Hartland Monahan scored his second goal of the season 7:11 into the second period, and Tony White scored his third just 0:24 later to knot the game at 2–2. Cliff Koroll and Stan Gilbertson traded goals in a 15-second span later in the period before White scored another to give Washington a 4–3 lead heading into the second intermission.

In the third period, Pyatt scored an unassisted goal to put Washington ahead by two, but the Black Hawks kept sending wave after wave of attackers at Ron Low, who brilliantly stopped 48 shots, while his counterpart Tony Esposito handled just 17. The Hawks clawed their way back on goals by Dale Tallon and Darcy Rota, and it seemed like it was only a matter of time before the dam would finally break and wash the Capitals right out of Chicago Stadium, but a crazy thing happened ... the Capitals resisted. Tony White, drafted 161st overall by Washington in 1974, completed his hat trick just 1:15 after Rota had tied the game, and Gilbertson, who was off to his best ever start, scored his seventh goal at 18:18 to ice the shocking 7–5 win for Washington.

"You would think that a team with our record would get discouraged," said Schmidt. "It's got to be frustrating, but the club's morale is good. If I had thought they didn't care, I would have left a long time ago."

Another positive the Capitals could draw from in those early weeks of the season was that their first road win occurred in October rather than March. "It's been a tough road, but we're going to make it," said Hartland Monahan.[23] In fact, when the Caps beat Kansas City in their own rink just four days after defeating Chicago, it not only seemed like they were going to make it, but also that Hell had frozen over; the Caps had more wins on the road (two), than at home (zero).

"I thought we caught a very tired hockey team," said Schmidt. The Scouts had just come back from a one-game road trip to Minnesota, while the Caps were patiently waiting for them to return home. "Since they figured to be a little more tired," Schmidt explained, "our plan was to go in after them and send two men in after the puck." The plan worked; Washington led 3–0 by the game's mid-point on goals by Williams, Egers, and Monahan. Robin Burns cut into the Capitals' lead at 15:59 of the middle frame, but Marson restored the three-goal cushion with his second of the season in the dying minutes of the period. Washington outscored K.C., 2–1, in the third period to make the final score 6–2.

Bep Guidolin was livid after the game. "I don't have any comment on that game," he said. "There is nothing to say about a game like that."[24]

The Caps celebrated their road win in a way that was becoming a sort-of team tradition. "So I played in Kansas City and we won, 6–2," said goaltender Bernie Wolfe, "and it was my first NHL game and the [third] road win in Capitals' history. It was kind of exciting. We picked up a garbage can and put a Stanley Cup label on it. The guys paraded it around the dressing room. That's the closest I've come to a Stanley Cup."[25]

Wolfe carved himself out an important role with the Capitals, supplanting Michel Belhumeur as the club's back-up goaltender, but as Ron Low suffered through a rash of injuries and ailments, Wolfe was given his fair share of starts. Scout Billy Taylor first noticed Wolfe as the young man was tending goal in a college hockey tournament. After watching Wolfe for just two periods, Taylor called NHL headquarters and asked to have the goaltender's name added to the Capitals' negotiation list. "Never know who might beat you out," said Taylor to explain his sudden burst of scouting enthusiasm.[26]

The Capitals signed Wolfe to a contract October 1, 1974, but that first season Wolfe plied his trade in Richmond with the Capitals' other prospects. Before long, Low went down with an injury and Wolfe was ordered to meet the Capitals in Los Angeles for their October 28 game. Belhumeur got the assignment that night and lost, 6–0, so Wolfe got the start the next time out in Kansas City. He won his first game but wouldn't win another until late January. Wolfe was not too discouraged, however, and he accepted the challenge of the bigger and better shooters the NHL offered. "They're lots more accurate up here," he would later say. "They find those corners. Milt wants me to stay up more, and I'm trying to. I'll try anything that will improve my game. But I've played my [scrambling] style for 15 years and the change can't come overnight. Tony Esposito does it that way, and he's pretty successful. And there's Dave Reece and Wayne Stephenson."[27]

One Team's Losses Are Everyone Else's Gain

With their second road win of the season, it seemed as though the Caps were finally getting a few breaks. Perhaps management was feeling a bit cocky when it guaranteed the Capitals would beat the far-superior L.A. Kings on November 5. If the Capitals lost or tied the game, every fan in attendance would receive a free ticket to a future home game. The Kings had finished the previous season at 42–17–21, and again this season they were on a bit of a roll, including that 6–0 whooping a week earlier so, in all likelihood, "Guaranteed Win" night would end badly. While the game was close, the Caps still ended up on the losing end of a 3–1 score, and 12,527 fans got free ducats. The Caps played well, and could have come away with a tie, but in the third frame, with the score 2–1, L.A., Stan Gilbertson's goal was called back because Jack Lynch was in the crease. The video replay indicated, however, that Lynch had been pushed in.

The Capitals did not win another game until, surprisingly enough, those same L.A. Kings paid another visit to D.C. on November 26. The Caps were closing in on a dubious team record: a winless month. Tony White beat Rogie Vachon for his eighth goal 0:20 into the contest, the fastest Washington goal from the opening face-off. Gilbertson scored his 11th goal at 0:56 to set another team record for fastest two Washington goals. The Kings never recovered from the Capitals' sudden offensive splurge. Greg Joly scored a shorthanded goal at 18:48, but Marcel Dionne returned the favor 13 seconds later to make it 3–1 Washington. Nelson Pyatt added his seventh goal at 2:49 of the second period, and Ron Lalonde scored his first, another shorthanded goal at 4:02, to put the Caps up, 5–1.

The dogged Bill Clement, who had scored three times in his first seven games, found himself in a 13-game goalless slump, but when he rang a backhander off the crossbar, it flopped into the net. White added his second of the evening with less than three minutes to play to give Washington a shocking 7–2 win. The five-goal margin was the largest yet in a Capitals win.

The Capitals' lucky streak lasted exactly 60 minutes before they went on a winless streak for the ages. Between November 29 and January 23, the Capitals' record was, believe it or not, 0–22–3. Twenty-five games without a win set a new NHL record which, fortunately for the Capitals, would be broken by someone else before the 1975–1976 season ended, but more on that later.

Injuries began piling up at an alarming rate and at a time when the team needed all hands on deck. Low, for instance, couldn't stay out of sick bay. It all started rather innocuously when Toronto's Lanny McDonald's stick struck Low in the cheek, but

Low's health problems soon got much worse. He injured his knee when he got caught underneath a pile of bodies in a goal crease scramble and missed two weeks. When Low returned, Atlanta's Tom Lysiak unleashed a shot so hard that when it hit the Caps' number one goalie in the head, it ripped the mask right off him and left him with a 12-inch cut. In his stead, Bernie Wolfe asserted himself as the team's number one goaltender.

Ace Bailey separated his shoulder, which put him on the injured list until December. The injury did, however, give 25-year-old Mike Lampman an opportunity to prove himself. Lampman had been an expansion draft pick but did not suit up for the Caps their first season. He played just three games in November before returning to Baltimore, but he would play a significant role in the conclusion of the Capitals' season.

The Capitals' schedule didn't get much easier as the calendar flipped over from November to December. In fact, the team would play six games in eight nights, and the opponents in the first game were not exactly pushovers. The Caps' old nemeses from Buffalo paid a visit to D.C. on December 3, but the Capitals scored four times in the second period to take a 4–3 lead against the 1975 Stanley Cup finalists. The Sabres' Jerry Korab took matters into his own hands and released a howitzer from 55 feet out that eluded Wolfe six minutes into the third period. Wolfe was outstanding, however, making 37 saves overall to preserve a 4–4 tie with one of the best teams in the league.

The following night, the Capitals embarked upon a four-game road trip that would take them to Boston, Montreal, New York, and Atlanta. On December 4, Washington held the Bruins off the scoresheet for two periods despite being outshot, 28–11. Former Bruin Ace Bailey, fully recovered from his injury, scored the only goal of the first 40 minutes, and the Capitals stood a chance at pulling off a monumental upset, but the Bruins tightened up their game in the third period, outshooting Washington, 15–2, and scoring three times. Bailey scored again in the frame, but the rest of the Capitals couldn't get their offense into gear, and the game ended 3–2, but the fact that the Capitals struck fear in the eyes of the mighty Bruins showed that the second-year club was not completely up a certain feces-filled creek without a paddle. "We almost pulled it off," said Schmidt. "Almost. We just didn't have enough. That was the most I could have asked from them. We don't quite have enough experience."

For nearly pulling off the impossible, Schmidt earned high praise from Bruins coach Don Cherry. "Milt Schmidt had them playing the way they had to play to beat us," Cherry said. "You just hang on and hope your goalie is hot."[28]

The Bruins were an excellent team, yes, but the star-studded Montreal Canadiens of 1975–1976 were truly special. The Habs were coming off a couple of so-so campaigns, but this season would be a new beginning for the storied franchise. They would lose just 11 games all season and rack up an astonishing 127 points en route to their first of four straight Stanley Cups. Seven of their players would finish the year with more points than the Capitals' leading scorer. Despite the long odds, the Caps' made a game out of it for the first 37 minutes, holding the Habs to a 3–3 score, but that's when it all went to Hell. Montreal scored six straight goals to take the game, 9–3, bombing Bernie Wolfe with 54 shots, while Washington matched the measly 13 shots they had mustered against Boston.

Fresh Blood

The rest of the Capitals' road trip yielded two more losses, 5–2 to the Rangers and 7–1 to the Flames, dropping Washington to a dismal 3–22–3. Season two clearly was not progressing the way everyone in the organization had hoped. There were a few bright spots here and there, such as the play of Stan Gilbertson and rookies Bernie Wolfe, Hartland Monahan, and Tony White, but the team just wasn't winning, so Schmidt pulled the trigger on a big trade to shake the team up. Gilbertson was off to the best start of his career with 13 goals and 14 assists in 31 games, playing on a line with Tommy Williams and Ace Bailey (then Ron Lalonde after Bailey went down with a separated shoulder), but he was dealt to Pittsburgh for Harvey "Too Tall" Bennett, who was not exactly setting the world on fire with his three goals and three assists in 25 games.

Schmidt trading his leading scorer was indeed a curious move since the pop-gun Washingtonians needed all the offensive help they could get, but Gilbertson was viewed as somewhat of a trouble-maker. His surprising offensive splurge was likely an anomaly considering he had never breached the 20-goal mark in four previous NHL seasons, so Schmidt dealt Gilbertson while his value was sky high. Unfortunately for Gilbertson, while he was employed by the Penguins, he was involved in a serious car accident in the summer of 1977 that ultimately ended his career. Gilbertson swerved off the road, trying to avoid a car barreling down on him in his lane, and although he was lucky to survive the crash, his leg suffered irreparable nerve damage, forcing doctors to amputate above the knee.

Despite his rough start to the season, Bennett came from good hockey stock. His brother Curt was already a star with Atlanta, and their younger brother Bill was a 6'5", 235 lb. left wing who was on the verge of signing with Boston. Their father, Harvey Sr., had been a goaltender with the Bruins back in 1944–1945. The junior Bennett did not get the opportunity to prove himself, often seeing his linemates get shuffled around or playing at left wing, which was not his natural position. "Harvey may be at left wing for us, at least for awhile, but we think his best spot is center," Lefty McFadden explained after the trade, but the Caps' coach had other ideas. Milt Schmidt asked Bennett if he had ever played right wing, and when Bennett replied in the negative, Schmidt responded, "well you might be playing it tonight."[29] It wasn't an ideal situation for Bennett, but he thrived after arriving in Washington, scoring 12 goals in 49 games.

What made the Cranston, Rhode Island native attractive to the Caps was his size, all 6'4" and 215 pounds of him. Moving Bennett out of the way was akin to hoping to knock over a redwood. McFadden made no illusions as to why Bennett was acquired: "He was the toughest forward in the [International League]. And that's what we're looking for: toughness up front…. We have a strong guy, a fairly decent skater, who plays good defense. We think that we can make him an offensive threat."[30]

Schmidt was not done wheeling and dealing. He also acquired right wing Bob Sirois from Philadelphia, and he cost the Caps relatively little, just future considerations, which later became defenseman John Paddock. Sirois, who was born and raised in Montreal, had just three games of NHL experience but had scored 72 goals and 153 points in his last season in the QMJHL. McFadden had coveted him for a while: "I have seen this kid maybe 40 times and he is always somewhere close to the net.... A real smart hockey player, Sirois is tough to knock off his feet—he can take a check."[31] Sirois was not known for being particularly aggressive, which was practically a sin in 1975 Philadelphia, but Washington was more than willing to give him a chance if it meant a few more goals on the scoreboard.

Sirois could have wilted knowing he was leaving the Stanley Cup champs for the Norris Division chumps, but he relished the opportunity to prove himself in Washington. "No question that being with the Philly organization helped my hockey," he said. "But it was time to move on. I'd been waiting long enough for my chance. I'm better off in Washington than with the farm team in Richmond."[32] The Capitals quickly realized they had a keeper. In one Capitals media guide, Sirois was described as a "fluid, graceful skater" who could make "the opposition's defensemen look as if they had their skate laces tied together. His maneuverability, combined with a natural stickhandling talent, made him a continual offensive threat."[33]

Sirois and Bennett would both make positive contributions before long, but the Capitals' winless streak continued unabated. On December 17 against Boston, the Capitals managed a team-record 39 shots on goal but still lost, 3–2. Two nights later, in front of a sell-out home crowd of 18,130, the Caps lost, 7–5, to the fearsome Philadelphia Flyers. "Close but no cigar," Schmidt said after the Philadelphia game. "I have to give the Caps bouquets for the way they handled themselves, the way they worked against the Stanley Cup champions." In reality, the Flyers were in full control of the game despite the close score. Bernie Wolfe was heroic in facing 54 shots, while his counterpart, Wayne Stephenson, faced but 22.

Former Flyer Bill Clement drew first blood with his ninth goal at 3:57, but Bill Barber tied the game 4:21 later. Sirois scored his first goal of the season a little over a minute later, but sniper Rick MacLeish responded with his 14th goal at 13:19. Despite the 2–2 score, the Flyers outshot Washington, 23–3.

In the second period, it was more back-and-forth scoring and more acrobatics from Wolfe, who faced another 18 shots and gave his team a chance to win. Ace Bailey made it 3–2 at 2:35, and on a power play shortly afterward Greg Joly slapped the puck from the point, and Harvey Bennett tipped it past Stephenson to shockingly put Washington up by two goals before eight minutes had elapsed. "The point man was mine," Bobby Clarke lamented. "I got caught way in. If I had been in position, I could have blocked the shot."

The Flyers were not about to let Washington steal an important two points and roared back on goals from Clarke, Reggie Leach, and Rick MacLeish, but Blair Stewart proved the Capitals had moxie and tied the game with just 14 seconds left in the second period.

There was no reason for the Caps to have a chance at pulling out a win or a tie, but with one period left, the score was 5–5. "They were getting the breaks," said Flyers coach Fred Shero. "It was lucky we didn't have 15,000 fans against us here. Coming back after we got behind by two goals would have been tough."[34]

Reality soon set in as Barber scored his second goal of the night early in the third period. The score remained 6–5 until 17:11, when MacLeish remembered how earlier in the game he had aimed at a corner of the net and Wolfe kicked it away. This time, MacLeish iced the game with his hat-trick goal, a shot that pierced Wolfe's five-hole just as the goaltender was going down to close it up. "I was disappointed with that goal," said Wolfe. "I was tired. Never got set up right. If that one doesn't get by me, we're still in the game."

When Wolfe was asked after the game if he thought he'd like to be somewhere else instead of being pelted with a shot a minute, he answered that he was "glad to be in the NHL, and ... glad to be with Washington."[35] There are no confirmed reports of this, but after the Caps' next game, he may have thought about asking local newspapers for a retraction as the winless streak raged on.

Rock Bottom

The lowest point of the streak, if not in the franchise's short history, was undoubtedly December 21, 1975, when the Sabres gave their fans an early Christmas present: a warm red light that bathed the entire Memorial Auditorium with a seemingly eternal glow.

The Sabres had started the year winning 17 of their first 22 games, which was already six more wins than the Caps had recorded in their entire history, but in the last ten games, the Sabres had gone a miserable 2–5–3, so tensions were mounting in Buffalo. With back-to-back games against Washington and Kansas City, however, there was a better than average chance some of the pressure would be relieved.

It was obvious early on that this would not be a banner night for the Capitals; they didn't get a shot on goal for the first 12 minutes. Overall, they were outshot, 50–15, and 22–2 in the third period. Buffalo got off to a 2–0 lead in the first period on goals by Gilbert Perreault and Fred Stanfield, but the Capitals hung in. In the second period, Tony White cut the Sabres' lead in half with his 11th goal of the season just 0:23 in, but Rick Martin and Don Luce each responded within two minutes. The Sabres continued to apply pressure and finished the frame up, 6–2. That's when the game got out of control.

Craig Ramsay scored early in the third period to make it 7–2, Martin completed his hat-trick, and finally Perreault notched his second goal at 6:06. A little over a minute later, Danny Gare increased the Sabres' lead to 10–2, and Luce upped the score to 11–2. The Sabres weren't done either. Not by a long shot. At 9:38, Martin ripped home his fourth of the evening, and it seemed the Sabres had completed their onslaught, but at 16:32, Peter McNab made it 13–2, and at 18:11 Stanfield fired home Buffalo's 14th goal. The eight goals and 23 total points scored in the third period, not to mention the 40 total points scored in the game, were all NHL records for one team. In the end, Martin, Ramsay, Perreault, Stanfield, Gare, and Luce each scored at least four points.

As for the Caps, Low was tagged for ten goals on 36 shots, while Wolfe allowed four on 14 shots in 12 minutes of ice time.

"I feel very sorry for Washington, that we took out our frustrations on them," said Sabres bench boss Floyd Smith. "But thank God they [goals] went in tonight. You like to see that when your team is struggling like we were. We really needed this game."

"It was one of the first nights in a month that the guys were all enthusiastic," said Martin, in what could have been the understatement of the century.[36]

Jack Lynch was asked if he remembered the 14–2 pasting. One would think that such a soul-crushing defeat would stick in one's craw, but the game didn't register with Lynch at all. "To be honest with you, I could not reflect on that game, and I'm sorry to say that, but I really couldn't," he said. "But I think the reason for that was that that was just one of many bad games. It was nothing for us to lose 8–2." In Lynch's estimation, there was another, far more embarrassing loss the Capitals suffered. "We had a pre-season game where we lost like 10-something against the farm club of the Philadelphia Flyers, the Maine Mariners.... That game sort of impacted me more than the 14–2 game."

The Caps returned home on Boxing Day to take on Minnesota, yet another "Guaranteed Win" night, and the Caps were feeling generous once again. The overall effort was far better than the one they had given in Buffalo, but a 1–1 draw still wasn't a win, and more Caps fans walked away with a belated Christmas present.

Goodbye, Uncle Miltie

The Capitals' increasingly embarrassing and morbidly fascinating winless streak got so bad that Milt Schmidt resigned as coach and general manager. Players had asked captain Bill Clement to talk to Schmidt about his decision, hoping he would reconsider, but Schmidt had made up his mind. No matter which way one looked at it, things just weren't working out. As Washington's general manager, Schmidt's record was 11–95–10, which translates to an abysmal .138 winning percentage.

Schmidt's resignation came on the heels of a humiliating 6–0 drubbing at the hands of the Montreal Canadiens in D.C on December 29. He had told the players before the Montreal game that it would be his last with Washington. He also indicated that the Caps' excruciating 14–2 loss to Buffalo was a decisive factor in his resignation. "All-in-all, perhaps a change is for the best and it would be a shot in the arm if someone else did take over," Schmidt said at a brief news conference.

Players were understandably upset to see Schmidt go despite the fact that the team wasn't winning. "The man gave me my first chance," said Yvon Labre. "If it hadn't been for him, I might never have played in the NHL. I love the man." Greg Joly described Schmidt as "a real coach, a real man and a teacher. I'm going to miss him more than I could possibly say."[37]

"He was a real gentleman," remembered Ron Lalonde. "He had a vast history in the game, with Boston. He certainly drew respect from everybody."

One could argue, however, that after winning just three of 36 games, a change behind the bench was necessary. The Capitals were an unholy mess, and the dressing room culture was not at all conducive to winning. The lousy attitude that had infected so many players had permeated since the beginning of the team's first season. One anonymous player admitted that players took advantage of Schmidt. Many were out of shape and not at all interested in turning the team around and improving morale. "We knew we were going to get our asses clobbered every night, so no one wanted to work," the player said. "He couldn't handle the club, and it showed."[38]

Even though there wasn't much talent available in the expansion draft, Schmidt was ultimately responsible for the choices that were made. It was his decision to go with youth rather than experience, and it was he who called the shots at two unsuccessful Amateur Drafts.

"He obviously didn't really want to be coaching behind the bench, but he really didn't have a choice at that point," said Ron Lalonde. "He was a good guy. He looked out for his team.... The fans loved him. The owners loved him. He was well-liked in that area. I think, in the end, he just felt he was too old for this nonsense and let someone else take over."

In to replace Schmidt as general manager was 51-year-old Max McNab. He had played three years with the Detroit Red Wings starting in 1947–1948 and was a member of their Stanley Cup–winning team in 1950, but a back injury put a premature end to his NHL career. Undaunted, he moved on to the Western League's New Westminster Royals, where for seven seasons he averaged just under a point per game and won the league's MVP Award in 1955. After hanging up his skates, he became the minor-league San Francisco Seals' first coach, leading the expansion outfit to the playoffs. Following a stint in Vancouver, McNab was named the coach, general manager, and eventually vice-president of the San Diego Gulls, where he remained until the league's demise in 1974. When the WHL went belly-up, McNab became the president of the Central Hockey League until he made the move up to the NHL. The CHL later named its playoff MVP trophy after McNab.

Goodbye, Country Club ... Hello, Drumlines?

McNab promoted 40-year-old Dayton Gems head coach Tom McVie to the Capitals' bench, and his arrival was a breath of fresh air. Under the hard-nosed McVie, life would never be the same for the soft, discipline-challenged Caps. "He was unlike any NHL coach I ever had," remembered Ron Lalonde. "He had this rough, deep, growly voice.... He didn't make a lot of friends and couldn't care less, but he started getting some effort and some talent to come forward. He was very hard to know. He didn't fraternize with the players. He wanted to keep that harsh, rough image. I think as I got to know him after hockey, I realized there was another side to him.... He was great for me as a player, and I appreciated him as a coach."

McVie wasted no team imposing his will on his players. According to Ira Lacher in the January 1978 issue of *Action Sports Hockey*, "the Richard Nixon Saturday Night Massacre, another fabled housecleaning in another part of town, look[ed] like a feather-dusting by comparison."[39]

Bernie Wolfe spoke fondly of McVie. "When [McVie] was brought in for the first game, he said, 'Gentlemen, this country club is officially closed,' and we started doing two-a-days in the middle of the season … and doing push-ups on the ice in the morning skate…. It was night and day, but maybe that's what we needed. We didn't play much better, but we definitely were in shape."

"We had a room down by the dressing room," remembered Ron Lalonde.

> It was like a pool table and a couple of fridges with beer in it. Injured players would be down there before the game and then in between periods. We'd be in the dressing room getting dressed and you'd hear guys laughing and there would be more guys in there than there was getting dressed to get out for the game, and I know Tommy McVie, the first game he came to coach and he's giving us his pre-game talk, and he hears all this racket going on next door in the rec room, he put in a rule that if you're injured you don't come anywhere near the dressing room. You come up before the game for treatment, and you come up in the press box. He closed off that room, which I thought was a great move…. That wasn't the right motivation for the guys who were trying.

On one road trip to Minnesota, the team plane didn't land until 10:30 p.m., but that didn't stop McVie from calling a midnight practice, which predictably resulted in a 7–3 loss the next night. Sacrificing two points was necessary if it meant gaining several more in the long run. Practices were always a serious matter to McVie, and players would undergo them in full equipment. "Burn the sweatsuit," he was heard saying once.[40]

God forbid you were even a second late for practice! According to Jack Lynch, one of McVie's favorite adages was "If you're five minutes early, you're already ten minutes late." Players were expected to arrive at the practice rink in Fort Dupont, in downtown Washington, at least one hour early so they could go through their weight training first. In the blue-collar McVie's opinion, if suburbanites could trudge to work through early morning rush hour traffic every day and walk through their office doors by 8 o'clock, so could hockey players. To catch any stragglers, McVie would lock the dressing room doors exactly one hour before anyone took to the ice. One time Blair Stewart was nowhere to be found as the deadline came and went, so the doors shut like a safe at the bank. A few minutes later, there was a knock on the door. Stewart was fined a day's pay and an additional $500, a hefty sum indeed.

Tommy McVie meant business. One time Greg Joly strained himself so much during practice that he threw up from exhaustion, but he still had just enough energy to weakly spit out his feelings. "You're sick," he said to McVie, who later told Joly that on days when no practice was scheduled, he sat in his hotel room "lighting matches and burning [his] arms." McVie could never quite ascertain whether Joly understood that he was actually kidding.

Burned biceps or not, the Caps' new coach cracked a whip unlike any coach in the pro ranks, and he was actually referred to as "Simon," in reference to the villainous slave-owner from Harriet Beecher Stowe's *Uncle Tom's Cabin*.[41] Jack Lynch remembered:

> When Tommy McVie came in we outworked every team we played and lost … and they used to laugh at us when we'd have our warm-ups, our game-day skates. We would work harder in our game-day skates than the other team that came into our building. They'd sit there and watch us practice and were shaking their heads … here we are doing wind sprints, doing everything they would normally do on their off days for practice, we were doing on a game

day … and because we were bad, [McVie] resigned himself to the fact that "OK, this is what I've got to work with, but one thing's for sure, we're not gonna get outworked."

"A lot of people asked me why I would take a job with a team like that," McVie told broadcaster Dick Irvin for the latter's book, *Behind the Bench*. "My answer was that the Montreal Canadiens had Scotty Bowman coaching them and they hadn't asked me to replace him. Nobody else asked me to take any other job in the NHL. I'm the one guy walking around who has coached three expansion teams and can actually carry on a half-decent conversation. Anyone who's coached as many as two is usually with Jack Nicholson in the cuckoo's nest."[42]

McVie instituted a more defensive style of play over the "catch-as-catch-can" style of play that had prevailed since Day One. The players learned that skating and checking would be the order of the day. McVie demanded that no matter where the puck was on the ice, two men were required to chase after it. His philosophy was that the Caps were a young team with energy to burn, and that they would not be in danger of tiring out from a little extra effort. He believed that if a team was hungry enough and forechecked relentlessly, the other team would make mistakes and turn over the puck.[43]

McVie also implemented a novel motivational tool he hoped would inspire the players: martial music, whose wonders McVie had discovered by happenstance. The fitness fanatic was running laps one day while a high school marching band was practicing outside. McVie noticed that he had run his best ever time as the music

Coach Tom McVie made a huge impact on the Capitals immediately upon his arrival, insisting that his players become more disciplined and get in tip-top shape. Here he is signing a stick for a young fan at a banquet concluding the 1975–1976 season (Ron Lalonde collection).

wafted through the air, so he thought his players could also benefit from the rhythmic drumming. "It motivates guys hearing all those drums and bugles," McVie claimed. "In the minors it worked so well we blew the other team out in the first period for 15 straight games."[44]

Players practically killed themselves laughing when McVie introduced them to the sounds of drumlines, but it didn't take long for everyone to change their tune. Ron Lalonde remembered the martial music having a positive effect:

> He had somebody he knew that had a marching band, and he went and recorded [them], and before the game, maybe ten minutes before we were going on the ice, he would come in and blast this marching music.
>
> Some of the guys were complaining and they'd be mimicking it. After a while, you realize all of a sudden your feet are moving and you're getting revved up, and by the time you hit the ice you're already pumped up and ready to go, and that became a tradition. We played this marching music before every game.... It was just a little thing, but he was trying to find an edge to make us better, and I think it worked.

McVie made it his mission to toughen up his troops, who had been coasting for a season and a half. Personally, he was perpetually fit, and he would never ask his players to do anything physical that he wasn't prepared or able to do himself. To do away officially with the old country-club attitude that had poisoned the team, McVie made sure the players got into playing shape right away and instituted daily weigh-ins. McVie even confidently claimed that tipping the scales was not even necessary. "I can tell by looking if a guy's a few ounces overweight," he said.[45] After McVie got through with his new troops, there wouldn't be a lot of fatsos in the lineup. In fact, after about three weeks, the players had lost a combined total of about 100 pounds.

Mike Lampman had never made much of a dent with the Vancouver Canucks and St. Louis Blues, his two previous NHL teams, and to that point he had played just three games for Washington, but under McVie, he thrived:

> I remember these double-digit losses.... I remember we had an away game in Philadelphia and Tommy McVie stood outside the bus looking at all the players when they boarded to see who had a look of disdain on their face with the loss or the look of "I don't care," and that was Tommy.
>
> I liked Tommy as a coach. He and I meshed nicely, and you start looking at my development of my career in Washington, it was because of Tommy McVie. He bought into my style of play, and I had better results with him than I ever had with the team.... He was a basic nuts-and-bolts guy.

Jack Lynch, like many of his teammates, bought what McVie was selling, and in the end he was a positive influence. "He was the Pied Piper," said Lynch. "I would have gone through the wall for him."

In late January, while the Capitals were in Vancouver for a game against the Canucks, McVie planned two pre-dawn practices, and the shuttle-bus driver was scheduled to arrive at the team's hotel at 5:15 a.m. sharp. One of the two days, the driver failed to show up, which surprised McVie because he certainly hadn't called the bus company to cancel anything. The players denied calling the company themselves, but their smiles gave them away. McVie should have immediately suspected that the team's resident shit-disturber was at the epicenter of the mystery.

In a 2019 interview, Ron Lalonde told the story of the aborted early-morning practice:

> Tommy McVie ... had a hard time getting ice time to practice, and finally, through some of his contacts, got ice, and it was at five in the morning, or some ungodly time, he arranged for a bus, and he made sure we all got wake-up calls, and we all come down to the lobby.... Ace Bailey had phoned the bus company and canceled the bus, and here we are all downstairs waiting. [McVie] was so mad. He was livid that the bus company didn't show up, but he didn't realize that Ace Bailey had canceled it.[46]

Undeterred, McVie managed to get his troops to the rink for that early-morning skate. Jack Lynch remembers that day well:

> We'd just played the night before ... we played terribly and [McVie] was upset.... Somebody in Vancouver was able to search out ice time and ... the minor hockey kids were coming in for their regular Saturday when we were leaving the building in our equipment. Parents [were] standing around in awe that an NHL team would practice at that time of the morning. I remember that like it was yesterday.... It was like we had just barely got to bed and we were getting up, and it seems to me we had to get dressed at the Pacific Coliseum, then go to practice and then come back to the Pacific Coliseum in our equipment.... I do recall there being a delay of some sort.... A lot of guys were really ticked off, I mean, were very upset. The union and everything in the National Hockey League ... that would never happen today, but back then it did.

The affable Bailey was always up to something, although McVie was probably unaware of most of Ace's shenanigans. "There was another time," recalled Mike Lampman, "we were all in a bar [Fonzarelli's] after curfew ... so McVie shows up at the bar at the curfew time, and there's a dozen of us in there. Ace somehow saw McVie come in the bar to take stock of who was there, and he hopped over the bar and hid. Tommy McVie missed a bunch of us, including me. We all went home out the back door and the evening was over for us, but that was Ace being the character that he was."

Beaten by a Phone

Wins didn't come right away under McVie, but he pointed the team in the right direction. The new bench boss admitted that he worked the players so hard that the resulting fatigue may have cost the team a win or two, and that the first half of January was "the hardest working 15 days of [his] life." He knew, however, that for the Caps to move forward and shake the "loser" label, he had no choice but to instill a hard-working, blue-collar approach.[47]

McVie made his NHL coaching debut New Year's Eve, 1975, against Detroit, and the Capitals did what they did best ... they lost, this time by a 4–0 score. What was unusual about the game was that McVie was outduelled by a phone (yup), so it was a historic evening for many reasons.

Detroit's general manager and interim coach, Alex Delvecchio, decided that he could better assess his team perched high above in the press box and ring up assistant coach Billy Dea when he had something important to communicate, much like Commissioner Gordon dialing up Bruce Wayne. Seriously. The phone Delvecchio used was red, like the one that resided in Wayne Manor. Equipment manager Dan Olesevich answered calls and relayed the information to Dea.

Acting out the most repeated scene in the history of the 1960s *Batman* TV series turned out to be a stroke of genius as the Wings looked outstanding. Former Cap Mike Bloom drew first blood at 10:21 of the first period, and he scored the game's final goal in the dying minutes of the game. In between, the Wings' Nick Libett and Bill Hogaboam also scored to make sure the Capitals would be unable to mount a comeback.

One small hiccup occurred during a ten-minute span when Olesevich left the phone off the hook, but judging by the final score, Dea managed to get by. "And the phone I had, I was answering public relations department questions," admitted Delvecchio. "We had a baby sitter call to request the parents return home."[48]

On January 2, the Caps played to a somewhat better result, but still not what they were looking for. With the Golden Seals riding a five-game losing streak themselves, something had to give, but as usual it was the Caps who were caught in the middle of a storm of pucks, as California rang up a team-record 51 shots on Ron Low and Bernie Wolfe. The game was a wild affair that saw several breakaways, lots of goals, and 68 penalty minutes. The Seals' newly acquired Wayne Merrick scored the opening goal at 0:39, but Greg Joly scored his sixth goal unassisted less than seven minutes later. Tony White put Washington up, 2–1, with his 12th goal of the season, but that's when the game took a turn for the worse.

The Seals dominated the second period, scoring four consecutive times on efforts from Gary Sabourin, Merrick, Jim Pappin, and Bob Girard. By the time Nelson Pyatt answered back with 1:19 left in the frame, the final result was no longer in doubt. California's Al MacAdam scored another unassisted goal at 3:27 of the third period to make it 6–3. Greg Joly and Blair Stewart scored third-period goals for Washington to keep the score close, but every time the Capitals scored, the Seals responded. Merrick set a Seals record with six points, including three goals, in California's 8–5 win.

When the Capitals suffered their 100th all-time defeat on January 8 against St. Louis, they had played a grand total of 121 games, and had managed just 11 wins. What did Tommy McVie have to say about the less-than-momentous achievement? "I'd rather find out my wife was cheating on me than to have to keep on losing like this," he said. "At least I could tell my wife to cut it out."[49]

As though setting a record for fastest 100 losses wasn't enough, the very day the Capitals' all-time loss total ticked over to triple digits, Greg Joly went down with an injury yet again, this time when a tumble into the boards caused a hairline fracture of his right ankle that would cost him 26 games. "Last year was a bad year for everybody," Joly admitted. "This year started off good. Before my injury things were comin' easier. But I've had to start all over."[50] When Joly returned, he was not in the best of shape, and he lost all his momentum.

After falling in St. Louis, the Capitals had revenge on their minds as the Seals travelled to D.C. on January 9, but a 5–0 humiliation in front of their home crowd left McVie fuming. "There's not much I could say after a game like that," he said, "but I at least had the nerve to come out."[51]

On January 11, the Capitals took on the Boston Bruins in D.C., and as had become the norm, they lost again, their eighth straight game, which extended their overall winless streak to 21, tying the NHL record. Despite the debacle that had been Washington's first NHL season, the 1975–1976 Caps' 3–34–5 record was actually the worst mark at this point by *any* team in *any* NHL season. If they continued at this pace, they would finish the season with just *five* wins.

Tommy Williams, who had been with the Caps since day one, would unfortunately never get the opportunity to leave the game a winner. He got off to a great start, scoring 12 points in his first 11 games, and he even came close to netting a couple of hat-tricks, but he also

Hard-luck Greg Joly was more known for his frequent injuries than his on-ice exploits. The Capitals rushed Joly to the NHL before he was ready (Doug McLatchy collection).

went into a tailspin with just one point during a 12-game stretch in December. He played his last NHL game December 21, finishing the night -5 in that 14–2 travesty versus Buffalo. The Caps waived their all-time leading scorer (79 points in 107 games) out of the league, leaving him with a bitter taste in his mouth. He directed scathing comments towards his former teammates. "It's a good thing the Caps don't have to play the Russians," he said, referring to the Central Red Army and Soviet Wings outfits that had been running roughshod over NHL opposition during their North American exhibition tour. "Those guys would score 20 goals, maybe 30 against the Caps, and I'm not trying to be funny," Williams continued.

Tommy McVie thought his team could benefit from watching two of the world's greatest collections of hockey players perform against each other, and he made it mandatory for everyone to attend a 7–7 contest featuring the two visiting Soviet clubs at Capital Centre. "We can learn from them," he said to reporters after his Capitals' afternoon practice. His strategy couldn't have come at a better time. The Caps were truly in dire straits after losing their first seven games under McVie's watch. McVie hated losing, and he admitted that all the losing made him "sick to [his] stomach."[52]

Game number 22 of the winless streak was against Montreal, which was always a guaranteed loss, but the Capitals kept the game close, losing just 3–2. Perhaps the Capitals were inspired by the Russians' performance, but a loss was still a loss, and the Caps now had the winless streak record all to themselves. Washington would go on to lose 12 straight games, which would bring the winless skid up to 25, a total of 58 days without a duke, but those dubious streaks were about to come to an end.

Hell Freezes Over

The Caps' turnaround began when they acquired center Gerry Meehan. In the January 1978 issue of *Action Sports Hockey*, the soft-spoken and articulate Meehan was described as being "well versed in hockey's flesh market, having toiled with six different big league clubs" during his seven-year NHL career.[53] Meehan had been a good NHL scorer since cracking the lineup of the expansion Buffalo Sabres in 1970. After getting little ice time with Toronto and Philadelphia in 1968–1969, Meehan scored 24 goals and 55 points in his first season in Buffalo, and he continued at a 45–60-point rhythm year after year. After being traded to Vancouver with Mike Robitaille in October 1974 for Jocelyn Guevremont and Bryan McSheffrey, Meehan found himself struggling for the first time in years. Before the season was over, he was shipped off to Atlanta, where he briefly regained his scoring touch, but by the middle of 1975–1976, Meehan was traded once again, with defenseman Jean Lemieux and a first-round draft pick (originally belonging to Buffalo), to Washington.

Meehan was a perfect fit, scoring five goals in his first seven games with Washington, and he finished the campaign scoring 31 points in 32 games, mostly on a line with Blair Stewart and Harvey Bennett. Coincidentally or not, the Capitals started winning games.

Lemieux, a Northern Quebec product from Noranda, added some skill and a much-needed right-hand shot to the Capitals' blue line corps. Although he would play just 64 career games with Washington, he scored 13 goals, an impressive total for a defenseman. He was originally drafted in the third round by the Flames in 1972, and he enjoyed a nice, 10-goal, 42-point rookie season in minor-league Omaha. The following year, Lemieux played just 32 games for Atlanta and tallied three goals and five assists, but in 1974–1975, his first full NHL season, he managed three goals and 24 assists. In 1975–1976, Lemieux upped his goal total to four and picked up nine assists in 33 games, which was about as much as any defenseman had managed in Washington, but as a Capital, his offensive totals would increase significantly.

Considering what the Caps had given up to land Bill Clement, it was shocking Max McNab would send Washington's captain to Atlanta after just 42 games. Clement had scored 10 goals and 17 assists, which put him near the team lead, but now just two months after his arrival, he was gone. In a curious bit of trivia, Clement was about to join his *third* team in three days! On January 20, Clement participated in the league's All-Star Game as a member of the Wales Conference, the following day he was in uniform for Washington as the Caps took on the Islanders on Long Island, but on January 22 he was on his way to Philadelphia to join the visiting Flames.

I don't know how I made it through the third game because I'd been up half the night after the All-Star Game. And then after the game in Washington I didn't get traded [until the next day]. They worked me out. I stayed up late with the guys in Washington. They wanted to hear about the All-Star Game. I hardly had any sleep. Tommy McVie killed us in practice the next day and then said, "Max McNab wants to see you." And I get on the phone with Cliff Fletcher [Atlanta's GM] after [Washington] traded me and he says, "We need you in Philadelphia tonight." I was like, "You're bleeping kidding me? I can hardly even lift my arms." And I went back to Philly and played that night. And we got smoked, I think 7–2, and I slept for a day and a half.[54]

The trade was a real downer for Tony White, the plucky left winger from Newfoundland who had found instant chemistry with Clement, scoring 16 goals and 12 assists in 47 games.

Billy was quite a centreman for moving the puck. He was aggressive and a great forechecker. And he played very strong defensively, so playing with him, you got a few more opportunities than you probably would have playing with other people. He had a lot to do with my success. I had a tendency to sniff out the holes, and he was able to get the puck to me. We had Hartland Monahan on the other wing, and Hartland was a pretty good skater who could shoot too. So between the three of us, we chipped away and chipped away, and I didn't have a bad year.[55]

The dust had barely settled on the stunning trade when the 17–23–5 New York Rangers, struggling through their worst season in a decade, travelled to Landover, looking for an easy two points that would keep them in the Patrick Division playoff picture. The Rangers could not have picked a more inopportune time to catch the injury bug, going into the game without regular defensemen Doug Jarrett and Ron Harris as well as winger Bill Collins. Goalie Dunc Wilson had just had his appendix removed, but gamely soldiered on and took his spot in the net.

Jean Lemieux made his Washington debut on this night, which was handy since Greg Joly was injured and would be out of the lineup until March 12. Meehan was not in the lineup, so the Capitals were forced to play with just ten forwards because Mike Lampman was nursing injured knee ligaments. Blair Stewart and Bob Paradise were just returning from leg injuries of their own.

During the warm-up, an errant puck smacked Willie Brossart in the face, which he said he was fine with if it meant finally winning a game. Who knew that Brossart's bruised kisser would end up being the Capitals' good luck charm?

The Rangers' Bill Fairbairn took a slashing penalty at 2:26 of the opening period, so the Washington power play got to work early, and Lemieux made his presence felt quickly. The defenseman unleashed a blast from the right point, and the puck sailed over Wilson's shoulder and rippled the twine to give the Caps a 1–0 lead. By the midway point of the game, Washington led 3–0 on two more goals by Ron Lalonde and Nelson Pyatt, but that simply served to wake the slumbering Rangers. Steve Vickers scored his 20th goal just 56 seconds after Pyatt's seemingly backbreaking goal, and Rick Middleton and Wayne Dillon followed with goals of their own before the second stanza was over.

Phil Esposito put the Rangers in front 4:05 into the third period, but the Caps found another gear as time dwindled. Bob Sirois potted his fourth goal at 11:06, and Tony White scored off a rebound less than two minutes later to put Washington ahead, 5–4. Ace Bailey then stuck the knife further into the Rangers' backs with his seventh goal at 16:58. Middleton helped New York rally once again by scoring with less than two minutes to play, but Bailey scored an empty-netter with seconds remaining to seal the Capitals' 7–5 win, ending the longest winless streak in league history, and finally earning Tommy McVie his first NHL win after 11 straight defeats.

What followed the win could be called total jubilation. According to Milton Richman of United Press International, "one TV channel in Washington led off its nightly news program with the heart-stopping announcement: The Capitals won a game! Stay tuned for further details."

Players hugged and celebrated the momentous victory even though the Rangers' days of contending for the Stanley Cup were long gone. The Capitals would take the victory anyway, thank you very much! Some fans even gave the Caps a standing ovation, something which must have taken the players aback as this was not a customary reaction for fans of this team. One inebriated fan leaned over the boards and jubilantly exclaimed to everyone who could hear him, "Hey, we're number 17!"[56]

As the Capitals basked in the afterglow of victory, poor Willie Brossart just couldn't catch a break. While he got the win in exchange for sacrificing his face, he wouldn't be so lucky his next time out. During an 8–2 thrashing in Pittsburgh to start a season-longest seven-game road trip, Pierre Larouche nicked Brossart just below the eye, and Brossart got demoted to Richmond, never to return to the NHL.

After that 8–2 drubbing on January 24, the Caps settled down, first losing a close 2–0 decision to Los Angeles on the 27th, and defeating the Golden Seals, 4–2, in Oakland on the 28th, giving Washington three road wins on the season versus just two at home. Against the Seals the Caps were down, 2–1, in the final frame but quickly scored three times in 2:35 to overtake the pesky Pacific Blue sextet. Bernie Wolfe finally broke his personal 16-game winless skid, making the win doubly sweet for him. Of the Capitals' four all-time road wins, two had come in Oakland, where the green, plastic Coliseum Arena garbage can players had once hoisted over their heads as a makeshift Stanley Cup was still collecting refuse.

As the Capitals trudged across the continent, scrounging for whatever points they could get, games remained close for the most part. On January 30, Vancouver defeated Washington, 4–2, followed by a maddening 4–4 tie in Toronto. One Leafs goal went in off Gerry Meehan's knee, and another score happened because Yvon Labre failed to clear a puck that had landed near his skates. A third goal occurred while Tony White and Jack Lynch were in the penalty box. Despite all the bad luck, the resilient Caps surprisingly held a 4–3 lead late in the third period, but Tiger Williams tied the game with just 1:20 to play.

Believe it or not, after playing in Vancouver and then Toronto, the Capitals jetted back West to face Kansas City and lost 5–1, before turning the plane around yet again towards Chicago, where the Caps fell, 4–2. Back in D.C., the Caps pulled off a 2–2 tie with Los Angeles but were shut out by St. Louis three nights later.

If there was one thing the Caps needed to give themselves a confidence boost and put an end to their six-game winless streak, it was a visit from the Detroit Red Wings. Yvon Labre, the team's new captain, considered the game the best the

Capitals had ever played. "In the two years we've been playing, this was the best feeling this team has ever had," he said.

"We came out to the third period with confidence that we could win. Once we got those two quick goals, the team really started to fly," Labre said.[57] The goals he was referring to were Jean Lemieux's seventh at 3:01 and Nels Pyatt's 22nd eight seconds later. Pyatt's goal put Washington up 5–4, and they never looked back. Harvey Bennett scored at 7:38 to give Washington a two-goal lead, and Ron Lalonde rippled the back of the net at 14:06 to give the Caps a three-goal cushion. Detroit's J. P. Leblanc whittled the gap to two goals, but Gerry Meehan finished the Caps' third-period onslaught with his 14th goal, an empty-netter, at 19:18 as Washington took the game, 8–5.

"Our conditioning program is beginning to show," said Tommy McVie after the game. "This team could have played four periods of hockey and won."[58]

One victory, however, proved little. These were still the Washington Capitals, and if they were consistent in one area, it was inconsistency. The Caps followed up their tremendous victory with a flop against Toronto, a 5–1 loss on February 16, before heading to Madison Square Garden for a date with the Rangers. Of course, the last time the teams met, the Caps came out on top with a 7–5 win. That would not be the case this time around.

The Capitals got off to a great start, drawing first blood 59 seconds after the opening face-off, but things went downhill fast soon after. Wayne Dillon and Ron Greschner scored within four minutes to put New York up 2–1, and Steve Vickers, whose name would end up on the scoresheet seven times before the night was over, picked up an assist on each goal. Vickers scored two goals and added two helpers in the second period alone.

After 40 minutes, the Rangers led 7–3, but it would get much worse in the third period. Pat Hickey made it 8–3 at 1:13, so it didn't really matter that Jack Lynch scored on a power play some eight minutes later. Rick Middleton, Vickers, and Hickey all scored in the final eight minutes to deliver the Rangers an 11–4 win. Not only did Vickers finish the game with seven points, but Rod Gilbert also had a goal and four assists, while Wayne Dillon and Phil Esposito both scored a goal and added three assists.

While Yvon Labre had seemingly scored to put the Capitals up 3–2, the goal was disallowed because the horn sounded to signal the end of the first period. McVie wasn't looking for excuses, however. "I believe hard work and talent will win for you," said McVie. "That goal wasn't the reason we got beat. We got beat because we didn't work. Toward the end of the game I was only going with the guys who wanted to try. I only had two lines that wanted to, so I played them more."[59]

Patsies No More

For the next little while, the Capitals became a much more competitive team, the 11–4 loss to New York notwithstanding. The Caps returned home for a four-game stretch, and all signs pointed to a very rough ride since the Islanders, Flyers, Bruins, and Black Hawks were next on the docket. The first game, against New York on February 22, was, as expected, a one-sided loss. The Islanders' record was 30–17–12, while Washington was dead last in the NHL, so the 4–0 final score in favor of New York surprised no one.

Two days later, however, the Caps gave the Flyers all they could handle. Philadelphia's all-star goalie, Bernie Parent, was making his season debut after a ten-month layoff following surgery to fix a pinched nerve in his neck. The Caps took advantage of a shaky Parent and jumped out to a 3–0 lead. "We certainly didn't help him like we should have," said Flyers captain Bobby Clarke. "We let the game get too wide open which made his job tougher." Twenty-four seconds after Hartland Monahan scored Washington's third goal at 12:48, Flyers ruffian Dave "The Hammer" Schultz responded with his stick rather than his fists. Orest Kindrachuk scored on a power play at 17:41, and the Flyers were in the driver's seat once again.

In the third period, there was a 10-minute delay due to a power outage at Capital Centre. Shortly afterward, Gary Dornhoefer knotted the game, 3–3, and Reggie Leach added his 44th goal to give the Flyers the lead. The Capitals tested the Flyers' mettle by tying the game 0:52 later on a goal by rookie defenseman Pete Scamurra, and Bob Sirois put Washington up, 5–4, with his eighth goal just three minutes later. The defending champs were not about to let the Washington Capitals snatch two points from them, however, and Tom Bladon tied the game on a deflected shot from the side boards with less than six minutes remaining.

It was a "moral victory" to tie the Flyers, said Tommy McVie. "Of course I would have been happy with a win, but I'll settle for the tie. We played a mighty powerful outfit and skated with them all the way."[60]

Three days later, the Capitals displayed their new-found confidence and refused to give in to the mighty Boston Bruins. The Caps were outshot, 17–3, in the first period, and after Gregg Sheppard, Ken Hodge, and Andre Savard put Boston up, 3–0, midway through the second period, it seemed unlikely that Washington would gain any points in the standings, but Ron Lalonde and Harvey Bennett each scored in the dying minutes, narrowing the gap to 3–2. "After the first period," McVie said, "we matched them stride for stride and were stronger at the end. We're outworking other teams." Sirois scored on the power play for the third time in two games at 3:11 of the final stanza, and the Capitals miraculously wrangled a 3–3 tie against one of the league's top clubs.

McVie, who was never content with less than two points gained, told the media afterwards that he would "never be satisfied until [the Capitals were] winning on a regular basis."[61] The coach certainly had reason to be pacified, however. Since ending their 25-game winless streak, the Caps had gone 4–9–4, an unprecedented stretch of success for this team.

In their following game, versus Chicago, the Caps stunned the Smythe Division frontrunners, 4–1, thanks in part to two more goals by the surging Gerry Meehan. The win gave Washington its first-ever three-game undefeated streak. It was also the Capitals' eighth victory, achieved in just 65 games rather than the 80 it had taken the year before. Sure, it wasn't much of an accomplishment, but considering the sad state of affairs just five weeks earlier, eight wins was a big deal. As usual, however, McVie

Believe it or not, the photograph of this happy bunch was taken March 24, 1976, immediately following a 7–3 loss at the Detroit Olympia (Ron Lalonde collection).

was not resting on his laurels; he was always on the lookout for improvement. "I'm happy with the game," he said. "But the team did make some fundamental mistakes which if we don't correct them, it will cost us in the future."[62]

After four losses in a row on the road, the Capitals set a new single-season record for wins against the same New York Rangers who had humiliated them, 11–4, a month earlier. McVie was proud to point out after the 5–2 upset on March 16 that his team could "skate with any club" and "outhustle everybody." The Rangers directed 38 shots at Ron Low, and even though the Capitals "were getting knocked down," as McVie put it, they "kept on getting right back up."[63]

The Soda Truck Game

Despite back-to-back 7–3 pastings at the hands of Pittsburgh and Toronto on March 19–20, McVie felt confident his team could trounce the visiting Scouts, who were having problems of their own. While the Capitals had endured an excruciating 25-game winless streak, the Scouts were nipping at their heels with a 19-game skein of their own. The Capitals' brass, perhaps high from the good vibes during their recent stretch of good fortune, promoted their March 23 game against Kansas City as "Guaranteed Win Night." If the Caps failed to win this game, fans could redeem their ticket stubs for a free pass to see Washington take on Montreal in the season finale. McVie took it upon himself to add a little fuel to the fire by belittling the moribund Scouts. "Lose to those guys and I'll quit, and some of our players ought to consider going back to Canada to drive a taxi or a soda truck."

McVie should have resisted the urge to flap his gums. Despite the Capitals' recent improved output, they were still dead last with a paltry 27 points compared to Kansas City's 35. It should also be noted that the Scouts had won two of three games versus Washington, so it wasn't as though the Capitals had dominated their expansion cousins.

The Scouts were more than ready to teach the Capitals a lesson in humility, jumping out to a 4–0 lead on goals by Robin Burns, Chuck Arnason, Dennis Patterson, and Craig Patrick. The goals by Patterson and Patrick were scored just 17 seconds apart, chasing Ron Low from the game. Ace Bailey and Tony White scored to narrow Kansas City's lead to 4–2, but Arnason added his 20th goal to put the Scouts back in the driver's seat.

With the Caps trailing 5–2 to start the third period, McVie's words looked to have had a detrimental effect on his players, but in the end they came through and saved their coach from the unemployment line. Bob Sirois scored his tenth goal at 2:14, and Blair Stewart and Jack Lynch each tallied to set a Capitals team record for fastest three goals (two minutes, 18 seconds). The Capitals may not have won the game, but they salvaged some pride in clawing their way back to a 5–5 draw.

For the beleaguered Scouts, it was their 20th straight game without a win. The Caps' Jack Lynch remembered the Scouts' Steve Durbano exclaiming afterward that "Not even Jesus Christ and all the disciples could save this team."

After the game McVie (kinda) recognized the error of his ways, realizing he shouldn't have belittled his opponents. "It was my fault," he said. "I think I put too much pressure on my players. Me and my big mouth, coupled with a Guaranteed Win Night, had us pretty tight for a while." Without missing a beat, however, McVie still boasted that his Caps "showed what [they] were made of the way [they] came back," and that the Caps were "a better hockey club than Kansas City at this point."[64]

"If they're better, how come they didn't win and had to come from behind?" asked an amused Eddie Bush, K.C.'s recently hired coach. "Tommy makes a lot of rash statements, and sometimes he has a lot of backing up to do. And, the employment situation is tough enough without having guys back driving taxis."

One person who wouldn't need to look for a job elsewhere was McVie. "Thank God, I didn't have to make a decision," he joked about his pre-game condition to resign if the Caps lost. Reporters asked him what he would have done had the Capitals lost. "You'll never know," he responded, and no one ever did.[65]

The Coca-Cola Bottlers' Cup

"Guaranteed Win Night" also just happened to be attended by a half-dozen Japanese guests who were busy preparing for the Capitals' and Scouts' "NHL Japan" series set for mid-April. Newspapers had reported since early March that negotiations were ongoing to send the two basement dwellers to Japan, but nothing was confirmed until the 12th, when the Japan National Hockey League announced that the Scouts and Capitals would play each other in a four-game exhibition series from April 14–18. The first two games would take place in Sapporo, the site of the 1972 Winter Olympics, and the last two games would take place in Tokyo.

The reasons for organizing the NHL Japan series are shrouded in mystery, but according to a short piece penned by Morton S. Hodgson, Jr., the president and representative director of Coca-Cola Japan, "in commemoration of the [American bicentennial and Coca-Cola's 90th anniversary, Coca-Cola was] sponsoring the 'Coca-Cola Bottlers' Cup Pro Ice Hockey Series' to be played by two exciting NHL teams from America, the birthplace of Coca-Cola and of professional ice hockey."[66]

Jack Lynch remembers that when the players got wind of the post-season exhibition tour they got "really excited about it to the point where even guys that ... were sort of going back and forth from Richmond to the Caps, it gave them motivation to make sure that they were on the team that was going to make this trip to Japan, and I remember several of the guys being absolutely ecstatic—they were sort of borderline, as I said—got the word that they were part of the team going over.... I remember getting word that we were going, I was over the moon. I thought, 'This is gonna be just absolutely awesome, and it was."

Japanese promoters, representing a newspaper and a TV network, initially approached the league about sending two representatives to participate in the exhibition tour, and they couldn't have cared less who participated in the NHL Japan series as long as they could skate and shoot a puck. Any North American team of professional caliber was guaranteed to be the very best club Japanese fans had ever witnessed.

The event was sponsored by Coca Cola Japan, which was American-owned. It was expected that this series would be an ingenious and creative way to promote Coca Cola, which was starting to feel some pressure from its soft drink competitors. Six of its 17 bottling franchises pooled together $400,000 to cover, among other expenses, the players' meals, hotel rooms, fares, and gifts. Simply put, had it not been for Coke's money, the series never would have taken place. The series championship trophy, the Coca-Cola Bottlers' Cup, would take on the name of the event's sponsors.

A few other companies also played a big role in getting the series to happen. Video Promotions organized the actual event, *Nikkan Sports*, a daily sports newspaper, was responsible for publicity, and the American Embassy also lent its support for the event. L.A. Kings general manager Jake Milford acted as a liaison between the league and the Japanese representatives, since the overseas organizations had many business ties with the California media capital.

There was some initial hesitation on the Scouts' and Capitals' part. The players loved the idea of taking a trip to Japan to have a little fun after a depressing regular season, but the NHL Players' Association fretted over the lack of preparation time, and team managers were less than keen on arranging for what was nothing more than an exhibition series. There was so much dilly-dallying in K.C. and D.C. that Coca Cola Japan almost pulled the plug on the whole event, but Video Promotions managed to convince everyone that this series could work. Figuring it would be easier to speak to the potential tour participants directly, the sponsors asked

Clarence Campbell for his blessing. Max McNab represented Washington, and Baz Bastien represented Kansas City. The Kings' John Bealey, who was familiar with international travel, helped work out some of the kinks, and before long, the Japan adventure was on.

Campbell wanted to make sure a few ground rules were set before any NHL players touched down in Sapporo. For one thing, neither team would be allowed reinforcements, unlike what the Rangers did in 1959 when they added Bobby Hull, Ed Litzenberger, Eric Nesterenko, and Pierre Pilote of the Chicago Black Hawks to help them take on the Boston Bruins in a 23-game barnstorming tour of Europe. Although a few star play-

This now-rare decal was prominently featured in promotional SWAG for the NHL Japan series (Robin Burns collection).

ers from non-playoff teams would have certainly improved the overall quality of the Scouts' and Capitals' rosters, Campbell feared these ringers would question the authority of the teams' managers and coaches, which, in an exotic locale like Japan, could mean players enjoying the nightlife a little too much and leading to a potential public relations disaster.

In order to stifle player rowdiness on what was likely going to be the longest road trip of their lives, Campbell insisted that the players' wives and girlfriends be invited as well. The *Toronto Star*'s Milt Dunnell couldn't help take a little jab at Campbell's condition, saying that the league president was "going out of his way to make sure these poor chaps, who have spent six months of futility on skates, get absolutely no respite from the monotony of hockey."

Considering that each team would be allowed to bring 25 people, plus one guest each, as well as three NHL officials—Jimmy Christison, Ryan Bozak, and Malcolm Ashford—Japanese promoters would be on the hook for a lot of yen. Campbell, for one, was surprised the promoters hadn't shied away when they found out the league would be sending not only non-playoff clubs, but the two worst clubs it had to offer, and that these two teams would require such a large entourage. When the NHL sent the Bruins and Rangers to Europe, the promoter apparently lost a ton of money, so everyone was hoping to avoid another financial fiasco. "These overseas trips have to be carefully planned," Campbell warned. "The last time two of our teams went to Europe for an exhibition tour, it could have been a disaster if our money had not been arranged in advance."[67]

The decision to send the dregs of the NHL to Japan for the purpose of stirring interest in hockey was predictably met with snickers. Bill Davidson of the *Brandon Sun* had this to say about the tour: "Ah so, it's a nostalgia kick: Kansas City Scouts and Washington Capitals are going to play four exhibition games against each other in Japan as part of the U.S. Bicentennial celebrations. Yes, it could set hockey back at least 200 years."[68]

Milt Dunnell joked that saying the Japanese were "hungry" for hockey was actually an understatement, and that it was "closer to being a famine."[69]

The *Medicine Hat News*' Pete Mossey had this amusing take on the tour:

> The U.S. State Department hasn't always received top marks for intelligence, so it's not surprising they are sending Kansas City Scouts and Washington Capitals to Japan for a series of exhibition games ... sending these two clubs on a Japan tour, to build up the image of the NHL, makes as much sense as having the Broad Street Bullies ... represent the NHL at a meeting of the Mothers For Clean Hockey Society.[70]

Jim Taylor of the *Vancouver Sun* was particularly nasty towards the Capitals and Scouts in his sports column: "The last time the U.S. shipped two bombs to Japan it ended a war. This time it could start one." Taylor questioned the logic behind the series, something most media members had been doing since it was announced. He wondered how the U.S. State Department could "launch missiles to destroy half the world in two minutes, get the entire Air Force up in five, but it needs two months to get airline reservations for 38 guys." He also wondered why no one thought of sending two of the NHL playoffs' first-round losers over to Japan instead of "Two fugitives from What's My Line?"[71]

Ouch.

And those were some of the nicer comments Taylor wrote about the NHL's unlikeliest ambassadors.

Earning Respect

The final four games of the regular season were a testament to just how inconsistent the Capitals could be. First, they pulled off a solid 5–3 win over Detroit on March 30, evening the teams' season series at 3–3. The Red Wings were not exactly championship material, but the Philadelphia Flyers certainly were, and when they met the Capitals on April 1, they made sure everyone was aware of that fact. The Flyers were hoping for a serious test before beginning their quest for a third straight Stanley Cup, but the Capitals disagreed and instead let Philly outshoot them, 62–23. "A game like this does nothing for us," said Bobby Clarke. "How can it? After they were down four or five goals, you knew they weren't going to come back." Fred Shero kept sending out the high-octane Leach-Clarke-Barber line in the third period, even though the game, for all intents and purposes, was over. The final score: 11–2.

Overall, it was a pitiful effort from the Capitals. "The Caps, who are 10–58–10, fell down a lot," wrote the *Wilmington News Journal*'s Gary Mullinax. Three times their goalie saved the puck from being knocked in by his own teammates.

"The goalie, Ron Low, said afterwards his team got out of its game plan. Right."[72] He was in the crease for all 62 Flyers shots.

Two nights later, however, the Capitals rebounded and defeated the playoff-bound Pittsburgh Penguins, 5–4, even though the Pens outshot Washington, 52–27. Low got the nod in goal once again, meaning he faced a preposterous 114 shots over two games! Somehow, he managed to survive both onslaughts. "A combination of the Pens polite play and referee Ron Wicks boys-will-be-boys philosophy left the Capitals without a power play for an entire game for the first time," wrote the *Hockey News*' Ron Weber. "It wasn't needed. Ace Bailey caromed in the winner off his skate."[73]

Beating Pittsburgh was one thing, but beating the NHL point leaders from Montreal was quite another, and they were the last team on Washington's schedule before heading over to Japan. This was the game where anyone who was in attendance for the "Guaranteed Win Night" fiasco against Kansas City could have a seat free of charge. On this night, the Capitals' chances of winning were subatomically tiny. If ever there was a guaranteed win in the cards, it was to be Montreal's as the Canadiens had lost as many games all year as the Capitals had won (11). In the end, the Habs' win wasn't as guaranteed as expected, and the sellout crowd of 18,130 was in fact treated to a great contest.

It took 36:18 for the Habs to break the scoreless deadlock. Steve Shutt took a shot some 20 feet in front of the Washington net and beat Bernie Wolfe. Shutt's goal should have spelled the end for the Capitals, but instead, they fought back on a goal by Tony White, who deflected a right-point shot by Yvon Labre, just 1:14 later. As the second period wound down, the Canadiens were on a power play, and Shutt scored his 45th goal of the season as players piled into Wolfe's crease.

The Capitals got a power play of their own after defenseman John van Boxmeer was nabbed for hooking. Hartland Monahan scored his 17th goal on assists from Rick Bragnalo and Gerry Meehan, and suddenly the Caps were back in the game. With less than nine minutes remaining in the game, hell froze over as the Capitals stunningly took a lead on the vaunted Habs. Rick Bragnalo, standing behind goalie Michel Larocque's net, picked up his third assist of the night as he feathered a pass to Mike Lampman, who shot the puck to the left of the goaltender and into the cage.

The Habs desperately needed to salvage their pride, and as was usually the case, they found a way to take control of the game when they needed to do so immediately. With just 2:17 remaining, Yvon Lambert scored his 17th goal, and just seconds later, Guy Lafleur came through with his 56th. Suddenly, it was 4–3, Montreal. McVie pulled Wolfe with a minute and a half left, hoping for a miracle, but the Habs held on for the win.

"By all means. That last game showed [effort]," McVie stated proudly. "We didn't roll over and die. Other than three or four times we weren't outworked." McVie also believed his players "finally got some pride. Everybody from fans to the receptionist to the bus driver noticed the difference."[74]

At the Capitals Fan Club's end-of-season banquet, Bernie Wolfe was named the team's Most Valuable Player, and Yvon Labre was named Most Popular Capital, which was earned due to his strong work ethic and commitment to keeping the opposition honest. Labre led the Capitals in penalty minutes with 146 even though he was far from the club's best fighter. He was even named to a Philadelphia newspaper's "hardest tryers" team, so his hustle was also noticed outside of D.C. He was also the Capitals' nominee for the Bill Masterton Trophy, which is awarded to the player who best exemplifies the qualities of perseverance, sportsmanship, and dedication to hockey. Another award winner was Ron Lalonde who picked up the Capitals' Unsung Hero award.

Greg Joly picked up the Most Promising Player award, although he still had a long way to go to justify his lofty draft position. He would end 1975–1976 with eight goals and 17 assists, but got into just 54 games. He became the first Capitals defender to score twice in one game, which he accomplished January 2 in an 8–5 loss to California. During that same month, the *Hockey News*' Ron Weber declared that the 21-year-old "still [wasn't] a big hit man in front of his own goalie—and probably never [would] be. But this side of Bobby Orr, he [could] stickhandle with any blueliner and [had] become a true quarterback in moving the team down the ice.

"He [lost] the puck now and then but only because he [had] it so often."[75]

Tommy McVie also showed a side of himself his players had never seen before. "When Tommy came in," Jack Lynch recalled, "he was such a driving influence on us we thought he had no sense of humour and little did we know … when we

Tommy McVie always felt at home in front of a microphone, including here at the 1975–1976 year-end banquet organized by the Capitals' Fan Club. Next to McVie is Ed Randall, then-president of the Fan Club. He sat near the visitors' blue line at just about every home game and, to get the players' attention, he would yell into a megaphone that hung around his neck (Ron Lalonde collection).

had our end of season banquet and get-together he stood up and was like a one-man comedy show, and we were on the floor."

With their second-half resurgence, the Capitals had proven they belonged in the NHL, but McVie admitted he still didn't feel completely fulfilled. "You know me. I'm not satisfied. We did make some headway, but I'm surely not happy."[76] There was only one thing that would bring McVie satisfaction, but since the Stanley Cup was out of the Capitals' reach, the Coca-Cola Bottlers' Cup would do just fine.

7

The Kansas City Scouts, 1975–76

The Kansas City Scouts and Washington Capitals won a grand total of 23 games between them their first season, and the rest of the NHL just stood there with mouths agape and fingers pointing. Both the Capitals and Scouts had publicly pleaded for help, but all cries fell on deaf ears. If anything, it seemed as though the league and its member teams had lost whatever enthusiasm they once had for the latest round of expansion. In the early weeks of Kansas City's second NHL season, Bep Guidolin expressed his anger and disappointment in the league for not providing his team with the horses to keep them in the race. "They're all brothers in the National Hockey League until it comes time to help you in the team," he exclaimed. "Then they're not brothers anymore. Now they're 'enemies.' They don't want to help you because if they do help you, you're going to beat them."[1]

Guidolin predicted that if the NHL provided the Scouts and Capitals with better talent, the entire league would come away winners. Like Milt Schmidt had done earlier, Guidolin practically begged the NHL's stronger teams to give up some of the players warming benches in the minors, believing this boost in talent would help the Scouts draw fans both at home and on the road. "But they're keeping these players just sitting there," he opined. "These kids want to play. Now if they don't play, they go to the WHA. That doesn't sound reasonable to me.… I think they should expose these players. Let's make a deal for them. Let's get a little bit of parity going and in two or three years we'll fill the buildings, and also our own building."[2] In a way, Guidolin predicted what would eventually happen with the Vegas Golden Knights some 40 years later, when the NHL provided them with some players with potential. The entire NHL benefited from the publicity generated by the Knights' unexpected run to the Stanley Cup final. Unfortunately, it took the NHL years to fully understand the logic of building strong expansion clubs, so the disparity between the Scouts and Capitals and the rest of the league continued unabated.

The Winds of Change Blow into K.C.

Aside from their awful 0–8–1 start and 2–18–4 crawl to the finish line, the Scouts' first NHL season was not all that bad by expansion standards, but it wasn't one for the ages either. "There were nights," Baz Bastien admitted, "when all I could do was just pray the clock would run down."³ Changes were going to be made as there were lots of holes in the roster, and just because some players filled a role in season one, it did not mean they were guaranteed a spot in season two.

One major problem that needed to be rectified was the Scouts' lack of grit. As a team, the Scouts accumulated just 744 penalty minutes, by far the lowest mark in the league. Only one Scout, Wilf Paiement, had over 100 penalty minutes (101 to be exact), the 54th-highest mark in the league. Paiement's toughness was greatly appreciated, but as the Scouts' most talented player, he couldn't be expected to drop the gloves in defense of more passive teammates and risk breaking a hand in the process. Besides, he was also the team's youngest player, so it was odd asking the baby of the bunch to stick up for hardened veterans. On the opposite end of the penalty spectrum, the NHL leaders, the Philadelphia Flyers, had picked up *1,969* penalty minutes and were led by Dave "The Hammer" Schultz and his unfathomable *472*. There were *six* Flyers who had more penalty minutes than anyone on the Scouts. Not only were the Flyers setting records for penalty minutes, but so were most other teams, so Sid Abel needed to bulk up his crew in a hurry.

With the number two pick in the Amateur Draft, the Scouts selected 6′, 195-pound left winger "Mean" Barry Dean, who had registered seasons of 208, 213, and 159 penalty minutes with Medicine Hat of the Western Canada

Ed Gilbert (#24) and Wilf Paiement (#9) celebrate a goal on the cover of the Scouts' second-year media guide (author's personal collection).

Hockey League, not to mention 40 goals and 115 points his final junior season. Drafting Dean addressed two of the Scouts' biggest needs: toughness and a bigger presence at left wing. Kansas City scouting director Jon Choyce noted that Dean was "not a real great skater," but that he was "tough" and could protect the puck "long enough to make a play with it" rather than just dump it off to someone in a panic.

Dean was also drafted by the WHA's Edmonton Oilers, but the odds of landing Dean seemed in Kansas City's favor. "I feel more strongly towards the NHL," he said. "It's too cold here [referring to Medicine Hat]. I want to get away. I've seen enough cold."[4] Perhaps the Oilers saw the writing on the wall and figured if they traded Dean to a warmer city, they would at least get something in return, so they dealt him to the Phoenix Roadrunners, where he would play the entire 1975–1976 season.

With their second pick, 20th overall, the Scouts selected 5'9", 190-pound left wing Don Cairns from the WCHL's Victoria Cougars. Like Dean, Cairns had some offensive skill, but it was his 214 penalty minutes in 68 games that drew the most attention. Cairns failed to deliver the goods, however, as in seven career games with the Scouts, he drew zero penalties, so if the Scouts hoped to get tougher, they would have to consider the trade market.

Sid Abel made two summer deals that gave the Scouts some much-needed depth, but provided little in the form of toughness. On June 18, 1975, Abel sent Lynn Powis and a second-round pick to St. Louis for Denis Dupere and Craig Patrick, both former 20-goal scorers. Hall of Famer Lynn Patrick was Craig's father, and his grandfather was the legendary Lester Patrick, one of the Hall's earliest inductees. "Really," Abel continued, "he's the kind of kid you would be proud to have for your own son."[5] Patrick was expected to become the Scouts' third-line right winger behind Simon Nolet and Wilf Paiement.

In acquiring Dupere, the Scouts were hoping he could fill the void Dean had been expected to fill. The prospect of adding a winger who just a few months earlier had represented Washington at the All-Star Game was certainly mouth-watering for a talent-starved team like the Scouts. Dupere automatically became the Scouts' number one left wing, ahead of Gary Croteau, Robin Burns, Randy Rota, and Norm Dube. While the trade, in theory, gave the Scouts more scoring depth, things didn't work out quite as well as they had hoped.

Dupere performed well in exhibition games, especially with Guy Charron and Simon Nolet skating on his line. In the regular-season opener against the Islanders, Dupere made a nice pass from behind the net to set up Charron for the Scouts' only goal, but disaster struck the newest Scout just days later.

"He told me he thought the clock fell on him," Nolet reported Dupere saying after Dupere and goalie Bill McKenzie ran into each other during a skating drill the first week of the season.[6] McKenzie suffered nothing more than a sore left shoulder, but Dupere broke his collarbone and wouldn't return to the lineup until January 1. In the 42 games Dupere played after his return, he scored just six goals and seven assists, and never quite rediscovered his form. The deal worked out well for the Blues, however, as they used the Scouts' 20th overall pick to select Brian Sutter, who would score 636 points in 779 career games in the Gateway City.

As the regular season got under way, Abel dealt Rich Lemieux to Atlanta for right wing Fred "Buster" Harvey, who had enjoyed a few good years with Minnesota, including a 21-goal, 55-point campaign in 1972–1973, and a 44-point season with the Flames in 1974–1975, a total which would have put him second in Scouts scoring.

Dupere's injury issues notwithstanding, the Scouts' forward depth had been improved, but the blue line was another matter. For one thing, the bizarre Brent Hughes contract situation that had been simmering since the previous training camp needed to be resolved, and the Scouts were not likely to come out of it unscathed. Hughes had played out the final year of the pact he signed with Philadelphia three years earlier, and he had already signed a three-year contract with San Diego Mariners of the WHA which would take effect starting in 1975–1976. Hughes had been arguably Kansas City's best defenseman, and the Scouts did not want to lose him, but there wasn't much they could do. Their best hope was that the Mariners' attendance and arena issues would force their sinking ship to capsize, forcing Hughes to return to the NHL, but Hughes's attorney assured him the WHA club was going to remain operational.

Hughes was one of the major reasons the Scouts' defense had held up reasonably well their first season, so his departure hurt. Jean-Guy Lagace had also been a valuable addition to the team, so much so that when he went down with an injury in the second half of the season, holes were exposed on defense. Larry Johnston played the last bit of the season with a bum wrist and was therefore not as effective as he could have been. Dennis Patterson, Claude Houde, and Jim McElmury were not exactly household names either, but they put up a few points.

Defenseman Mike Baumgartner had showed some potential, but he never fully recovered from a Dennis Kearns shot that hit him in the left eye during a game against Vancouver on December 14, 1974. "I tried playing some softball around here last summer," Baumgartner said from his home in Minnesota. "I couldn't hit the ball and I tried to play first base, but it was tough following the throws."

Abel believed Baumgartner would be ready for training camp, but the defenseman struggled playing hockey as much as he did baseball. "I had trouble following the puck and stickhandling. I believe the doctors wanted to tell me not to play before camp started, but I wanted to play." Baumgartner was sent to Springfield, but in his first game there he suffered a broken nose, which got him thinking that perhaps his hockey career had run its course. "There's a scar in the back of my eye that's changing all the time," he explained. "My sight isn't as good as it was six months ago and it won't get any better."[7]

With Baumgartner's career up in the air, Abel got on the horn to convince free agent defenseman Larry Hornung, formerly of the WHA's Winnipeg Jets, to sign with Kansas City. Abel had acquired the rights to Hornung a year earlier when Bob Bourne was dealt to the Islanders, and now that Hornung's contract was up, Abel moved in. Unfortunately, Hornung had no interest in moving south. "My family is settled here," the defenseman said. "It just wasn't feasible to make the move for the same amount of money."[8]

Having failed to secure a deal with Hornung, Abel saw ominous clouds hovering over his defense squad. "If we're going to make the playoffs, all of the defensemen we have now will have to play to the top of anyone's expectation," he said. Even with a healthy Lagace and Johnston, the Scouts' defense was shaky. The Scouts had little in the way of trade bait, and what bait they did have, they did not want to part with. "The hardest thing about dealing for a defenseman or anyone," Abel admitted, "is that a team doesn't want a player back in his place—unless it's a Paiement or a guy they'd take in a minute. They want No. 1 draft picks and we're not trading those."[9]

Abel then looked toward Detroit and acquired 36-year-old former all-star Gary Bergman and goaltending prospect Bill McKenzie in exchange for Glen Burdon and Peter McDuffe. Giving up McDuffe, who had proven to be a solid netminder for a weak expansion team, was indeed a steep price, but players of Bergman's caliber rarely became available. Besides, Denis Herron was more than capable of handling the number one job in net.

As the Scouts' media guide put it, when Bergman was acquired, "the Scouts defense took an immediate jump on the credibility scale."[10] He was a solid, rushing defenseman who could act as a role model to the Scouts' young defensemen. The 30 points and 105 penalty minutes he had accumulated in 1974–1975 were both more than any Scouts defenseman's.

"He was always above average when it came to skating, penalty-killing, work on the power play, and making sound decisions with the puck," wrote Nathaniel Oliver of *The Hockey Writers* website. Add in his robust and physical nature as a defender, and there was not an avenue to his game that Bergman did not have covered. In many ways, Gary Bergman was *the* prototypical defenseman."[11]

Bergman had been in the league since 1964, was a member of Team Canada in the 1972 Summit Series, and played in the 1973 All-Star Game. He was also a downright good guy, having won the 1973 Charlie Conacher Humanitarian Award for his work with crippled children and adults. The only downside in acquiring Bergman was that he was firmly in the twilight of his career and could call it a career at any moment. In fact, he had thought about quitting when he was told of the trade, but the Scouts' players and management convinced him to attend training camp.

Bergman still had the will and the desire to compete, but his body was beginning to betray him. "Training camp has really been tough," he candidly admitted. "It's been tearing up my rear. I can go for 30 seconds, then boom, that's it." Bep Guidolin knew his newest defenseman's body was becoming creaky, so he insisted that Bergman prepare himself at his own pace and not kill himself trying to compete with the youngsters in the line-up. Bergman was a great influence on the Scouts, and his veteran leadership was sorely needed on a team lacking experience and poise. "I like everything he's doing now," said Guidolin. "He's settling us down in our own end, and we hope what he's doing will rub off on the kids."[12]

As for Bill McKenzie, he had struggled to win many games with Detroit in 1974–1975, but that was partly because the Wings were hardly better than Kansas City. That said, his inflated 4.70 goals-against average and 1–9–2 record were not terribly comforting. McKenzie was a quick and aggressive goaltender who was working towards a Master's Degree in physical education from Ohio State University.

There had also been rumors over the summer that Abel was toying with acquiring free agent Red Wings superstar Marcel Dionne. Of course, this being 1975, there was no such thing as true free agency, so teams who signed a free agent were required to send a player of equal value to the player's former team. Still, Abel felt confident he could pull off the trick even though the Scouts boasted no one who approached Dionne's stratosphere. Furthermore, league rules prohibited teams from trading recent first-round picks, so Wilf Paiement was off the table, but the Scouts had an abundance of future draft picks, including likely top-ten selections in the next several drafts.

Convincing Ed Thompson to relinquish some precious dough to sign Dionne was the biggest hurdle. Dionne was fresh off a breakout 121-point season and was not going to come cheap, but Abel was undeterred. "I've been in contact with Alan Eagleson, Dionne's agent," he said. "I know St. Louis and the Rangers are strong in the bidding, but I've told them we're interested and not to do anything until they talk to us. It might take awhile. Dionne has all summer to shop for the best offer. It's a nice position to be in."[13] In the end, the young French-Canadian star signed with Los Angeles, where he would score 1,307 points in 921 games.

There were also rumors that 40-year-old free agent Norm Ullman was offered a chance to sign with Kansas City, but the future Hall of Famer chose to sign with Edmonton of the WHA. Even though Ullman had scored but nine goals and 26 assists, his experience and skill would have been of tremendous value to the Scouts.

Shaking Off the Expansion Label

The Scouts entered 1975–1976 with an improved roster. They had a reliable and experienced, albeit banged-up, new number one defenseman in Bergman, and three recent 20-goal scorers, Dupere, Patrick, and Harvey, who could hopefully repeat their past performances and compliment the talents of Nolet, Paiement, and Charron. By all indications, the Scouts were looking to shake off the expansion label and move up in the standings. "It's time to pull up our socks and become an NHL club," said Guidolin during training camp.[14] Guidolin's goal for year two was quite simple: make the playoffs, a goal that was not so far-fetched in the terribly weak Smythe Division.

The Scouts got a scare during the pre-season as Paiement injured his leg, but the 19-year-old brushed off the mishap. "The doctor doesn't really know what it is," Paiement said. "I think I pulled the Achilles tendon just a little bit." Losing Paiement was a potential nightmare for the Scouts. "I don't want to take a chance with him," Guidolin said. "He's a kid who wants to play. You know how they are—they'll tell you anything.... When I see one of our big guys get hurt, it scares me. I cringe." Paiement's doctor gave the young star the go-ahead to play in a 4–2 exhibition win against the Blues, but it turned out his injury troubles were far from over.

The Scouts surprised the NHL by storming out to a 3–1–2 mark in the exhibition schedule, but it shouldn't have been all that surprising considering that two of those wins were against Washington, and the other win and one tie were against the lackluster St. Louis Blues. Gary Croteau led with Scouts with four goals, indicating he was ready to put his poor eight-goal 1974–75 season behind him. Despite the excellent pre-season results, Sid Abel had some concerns. "Even though we've won," said Abel, "there've been spots I haven't been pleased with. We played an exceptional opening game against Washington. Since then we've played just well enough in spots to win."[15]

When the season got officially underway on October 8, the Scouts showed some early promise, tying the Islanders 1–1, but the opening-night crowd of less than 7,000 was an ominous warning of hard times ahead. They defeated Vancouver, the reigning Smythe Division champs, 4–2, three nights later. Despite losses to St. Louis and Atlanta which dropped the Scouts to 1–2–1, they still had every reason to be pleased with themselves although eight of their nine goals scored were by the line of Randy Rota, Guy Charron, and Simon Nolet. Bep Guidolin could see he had a strong first unit, so he left it intact while shuffling everyone else around. "Randy's not big, but he's showing us he'll come back and check," the coach said. That line's making things happen. If you've watched the others closely, there's been one guy coming out with the puck and he's been by himself. They're not coming out together. They've got to start communicating."[16]

Charron, in particular, was enjoying a sweet start to the season, and his star was soaring high. He began the season with 11 goals in his first 19 games, and he also strung together six straight games with at least one goal, despite playing on one of the league's lowest-scoring teams. The Red Wings had given up on him because he was supposedly soft in the corners and weak defensively, but Charron worked with a vengeance to kill his poor reputation. "He's winning faceoffs and carrying the puck well," Guidolin said. "[The Red Wings] say he didn't hit. Well, I've seen him be hit and hit back since he came here."

In fact, Charron had been brought up as a defensive specialist who could kill penalties and play on a checking line, but one year with the Nova Scotia Voyageurs, Montreal's farm team, he began scoring goals and was consequently expected to continue doing so. He was rarely asked to take on a defensive role with either the Canadiens or the Red Wings. "I went to Detroit and I guess they thought of me as a goal-scorer, so they didn't put me on a defensive line," Charron explained.[17] The way he was racking up points in Kansas City, it was hard to imagine Charron ever seeing time on a checking line again.

The Washington Capitals, on the other hand, were suffering through another miserable early-season stretch, and since this was the most hard-luck franchise the NHL had ever seen, ending their own seven-game winless streak just was not in the cards. The Scouts travelled to Washington on October 22, hoping to climb back up to the .500 mark.

Tommy Williams put the Caps out in front just a minute and a half into the game, but the reliable Dave Hudson tied it up halfway through the period. Williams, the Capitals' biggest gun the previous year, scored another goal to put Washington up, 2–1, but Croteau responded with his first before the buzzer sounded. Paiement gave K.C. a 3–2 lead in the second period, and Croteau iced what was a contender for dullest game of the year[18] with his second goal with less than one minute remaining.

For the Scouts to defeat their expansion cousins was certainly satisfying, but it paled in comparison to the feeling they got from defeating the Boston Bruins at the legendary Gardens the following night. The Bruins controlled the pace of the game, outshooting the Scouts, 37–17, but it was the Scouts who took a 1–0 lead at 7:08 of the second period on a goal by Simon Nolet. The Bruins stormed back in the third period thanks to a couple of goals by John Bucyk, which should have been enough to kayo the Scouts, but Buster Harvey evened the score with less than five minutes to play. Had the injured Bobby Orr been in the lineup, it likely would have made a difference, but no one can know for sure. What is known, however, is that with just 1:56 remaining, Guy Charron scored the game-winner, and the Scouts were now officially above .500 on the road for the first time ever.

Of course, this being an expansion team in its second season, the joy of beating a team of All-Stars was short-lived. After falling, 3–0, to Toronto at Maple Leaf Gardens on November 1, a date with the 8–1–2 Philadelphia Flyers the following night did not bode well for the Scouts, especially after the Flyers manhandled Boston, 8–1, less than 24 hours earlier.

Flyers captain Bobby Clarke drew first blood at 5:19, scoring a short-handed goal on a pass from linemate Bill Barber. Orest Kindrachuk then made it 2–0 with 0:42 left in the frame.

Things didn't get much better in the second period. "Freddie [Shero] came in after the first period and asked us why we weren't hitting," said Flyers pugilist Dave Schultz. "He said we have to play the same against Kansas City as we did against Boston last night. He didn't say anything after the second period." Bill McKenzie faced 23 shots in the middle period, and the Flyers scored six goals, including four in a span of three and a half minutes. The last was scored by Gary Dornhoefer, who drolly quipped after the game: "I thought we had the game in hand when I scored that big goal."

Mel Bridgman scored the only two goals of the third period to complete the onslaught, a 10–0 Flyers win, in which the victors outshot the losers, 51–19. "They don't give you a thing," said Nolet, who knew the Bullies' style all too well. "No matter what the score they check the [expletive deleted] out of you." Bep Guidolin also shared some negative comments after the game, but his colorful choice of language forced newspapers to keep them off the sports pages.[19]

After the game, the Scouts' fifth consecutive loss, the players just sat at their dressing room stalls for about 15 minutes, depressed about the embarrassing defeat. "It's just the humiliation of a night like this," said Bergman. "The harder we work, the worse things seem to go wrong."

"What can we do?" Robin Burns asked. "That's the question everyone's asking."[20]

The Scouts had scored just 18 goals in 11 games, and they had been shut out in four of their last five outings. The team's one productive line—Rota, Charron, and Nolet—suddenly couldn't find the back of the net.

"I tried to help them all I could," reasoned Fred Shero. "I used four lines no matter what the situation. I didn't even tell my players not to take stupid penalties." To add salt to the wound, Shero also said he believed the Scouts "seemed better last year.... Maybe they were tired."[21]

Despite the devastating loss, the Scouts rebounded, beating California, 3–2, and upping their record to 4–7–1 in the process. Perhaps they were motivated by captain Nolet playing in the game despite battling the flu and a 103-degree temperature. Wilf Paiement, however, was still stuck on one goal since the season opener.

At one point in the game, Charron intercepted a pass at the Seals' blue line and fed the puck to Paiement, who found himself all alone in front of goalie Gary Simmons. Paiement skated to within about ten feet of Simmons, shot, and watched the puck trickle weekly to the right of the goal. The Scouts' feisty sophomore slammed his stick against the glass in disgust. "I was just so damn mad," he later said. "I want to play good. I hate to play when I play bad.... I'm not relaxed like I was last year. I can't sleep." As the *Hockey News*'s Ken Rudnick put it, Paiement "was fighting the puck and the puck was winning."

The good news was that Paiement hadn't lost any of the cockiness he had displayed in his rookie season. "I'll pop a few goals so quick, they won't know what hit them.... If I start popping goals, we'll make the playoffs. I've only missed 'em once in my life and that was last season."[22]

The rest of November was a lot tougher because it included a seven-game Eastern road trip. "A horse show. That's what's in our building now. Those people are more interested in a horse show than hockey," Guidolin complained. "That's what happens in a city-owned building."[23]

The trek began on November 12 in Atlanta, where the Flames were still recovering from a slow start to the season. Because the Rangers were enduring their worst campaign in years, the Flames were actually six points ahead of New York in the Patrick Division playoff race. Rey Comeau broke the scoreless tie at 8:20 of the second period, and the game remained 1–0 until 1:45 of the third, when Curt Bennett gave Atlanta a two-goal lead. At the 6:33 mark of the final frame, Pat Quinn picked up a penalty for high-sticking at the same time Randy Manery was handed two minutes for tripping. Charron took advantage of the 5-on-3 situation by notching his sixth goal just as Quinn and Manery were about to exit the penalty box. That was as close as the Scouts got, finding themselves on the losing end of a 2–1 score.

The Scouts were probably hoping that a date the following night with the 3-10-3 Red Wings would be the perfect way to rebound from a tough loss. The Scouts got a lucky break 0:29 into the game as rookie Dennis Polonich was twice reprimanded, once for charging and once for high-sticking, and like the previous night against Atlanta, Charron capitalized. Later in the period, Polonich made up for his gaffe by scoring his first two NHL goals. The Scouts tried to dig themselves out of their hole, but the Wings kept piling on more dirt. Dan Maloney scored a pair of goals in the second period to put Detroit up, 4–1, before Paiement finally scored his second of the season, beating recently acquired Ed Giacomin with less than three minutes to play in the period.

Michel Bergeron briefly restored the Wings' three-goal lead ten minutes into the final period, but Buster Harvey responded 0:25 later to close the gap to two goals once again. Guidolin pulled Bill McKenzie in the final minute, hoping to tie it up, but Walt McKechnie iced the game with an empty-netter to give Detroit a 6–3 win.

Since the start of the season, the Scouts' pop-gun attack had cost them more than a few games because the Kansas City goaltending was nothing short of spectacular on most nights. The Scouts had scored just 30 goals—more than a quarter off the stick of Charron—in 16 games, and it is hard to win consistently scoring fewer than two goals a game. On November 19, however, the Scouts' shooters often found the net.

The 4–10–2 Scouts, after suffering a 4–2 defeat in Boston, were in the midst of a four-game winless streak. Next on the agenda was the New York Rangers, who were unbeaten in three games. The Scouts were so geared to get this one started that Dennis Patterson opened the scoring just 44 seconds in, and Ed Gilbert added a goal of his own six minutes later to put the Rangers in a deep hole. Pete Stemkowski responded 3:32 into the second period, but Gilbert scored again exactly six minutes later. Dave Hudson seemed to put the game out of reach very early in the third period, but the Rangers' Rick Middleton made the score 4–2 on a power play 2:36 later. Charron scored his ninth goal of the season at 11:36, which should have sealed he victory for Kansas City, but Stemkowski and Carol Vadnais potted goals to put the Scouts' once-sure victory in doubt … for 53 seconds. Patterson scored his second goal of the season at 17:12, and the Scouts notched a 6–4 win, their first-ever versus the Rangers. Rangers goaltender Dunc Wilson faced just 35 shots compared to Denis Herron's 46, but despite the lighter workload, Wilson got very little help from his defense. It was the Scouts' first six-goal effort since they lost a 7–6 heartbreaker to Montreal nearly a year to the day earlier. "It was our best game of the year," Bep Guidolin boasted.[24]

On November 23, the Scouts road show continued in Buffalo, which was always bad news because by the mid–1970s, the Adams Division–leading Sabres and their French Connection Line were scoring so regularly that goalies had sunburns on their necks. As was the norm, the Sabres struck early. Don Luce, mired in a 12-game scoreless streak, tucked home his first goal by beating Bill McKenzie on a wraparound from behind the Kansas City net. Randy Rota knotted the game at aces at 8:09, taking a pass from Buster Harvey and hammering the puck past goalie Gerry Desjardins, so all seemed well again until Craig Ramsay restored the Sabres' one-goal lead.

In the second period, the Sabres did what they did best: score bushels of goals. First, Danny Gare rippled the twine with his 16th just 0:21 in, followed by singles from Luce, Peter McNab, and light-scoring Bill Hajt. The line of Luce-Ramsay-Gare combined for nine points on the night, while the French Connection was surprisingly quiet, not picking up a single point despite firing 16 of the Sabres' 46 total shots. With the Sabres up 6–1, Craig Patrick finally broke a season-long scoring drought with a goal at 18:09 on assists from Wilf Paiement and Guy Charron, but it was far too little, far too late.

The Scouts limped into St. Louis for the first game of a home-and-home series on November 26 with a 1–5 record on their road trip. Garry Unger opened the scoring at 9:33 of the first period, but that lead was erased in the second frame as Simon Nolet scored his fifth goal and 16th point, and the slumping Paiement scored his third goal on a power play with just 1:34 remaining. The Kansas City lead didn't last long, however, as Unger took charge early in the third period, scoring 37 seconds after the opening face-off and completing his hat-trick at 6:51.

With a little under nine minutes remaining in the contest, St. Louis's Bob Gassoff and the Scouts' Paiement dropped their mitts in the Blues' zone and fought all the way to the penalty box. Larry Johnston jumped in and was promptly ejected for being the third man in the fight. Paiement was given two minutes for roughing and a ten-minute gross misconduct penalty, while Gassoff was given five for fighting and another ten as well. All three were out for the rest of the game, but the Scouts found themselves on the power play.

The Blues led, 3–2, with less than five minutes remaining, but Derek Sanderson's slashing penalty at 15:32 helped put the kibosh on any hopes St. Louis had of winning. On the man advantage, Nolet fed the puck to Ed Gilbert, who ripped a 15-foot shot past Gilles Gratton to tie the game, 3–3.

It was a nice end to a difficult road trip, and it seemed to motivate the Scouts, who went on a decent 6–9–1 stretch, which, for a second-year team, was akin to a 15-game winning streak. "Just say we came of age on the road trip," Guidolin said, and he wasn't kidding as the Scouts started making serious inroads on a playoff spot.

Much of the talk after the game revolved around Johnston's third-period game misconduct for getting involved in the Paiement-Gassoff scuffle. Johnston received an automatic $100 fine, but Guidolin was not going to let his defenseman pay it. "That's one fine we're going to pay and you can quote me on that," the coach said. "We had a meeting with the players and we told them we're not going to pay for stupid penalties, but [jumping in to defend Paiement] wasn't a stupid penalty."[25]

Simon Nolet turned 34 on November 23, but the team didn't celebrate their captain's big day until after the tie in St. Louis and the end of their seven-game road trip. St. Louis was hit by a snowstorm the day of the game, closing the airport until noon the next day, so the team opted to charter a bus that would take everyone back to K.C. in about four hours. The team had been on the road for 16 days, so one more night sleeping in a hotel was no one's idea of a good time. However, good times were certainly had on that rented bus, as the players shared two cakes and probably a few pops. The team arrived home at 3:30 a.m. Thanksgiving morning, but everyone was ready to play the Blues in the return engagement that night.

The Blues, on the other hand, licked their wounds and made the short trip to Kansas City seeking revenge. After a scoreless first period, the Scouts suddenly turned into the Montreal Canadiens and rammed home three goals in 9:32. Paiement scored his fourth goal 40 seconds into the middle period, followed by a Germain Gagnon power-play goal at 6:52. Gary Bergman then took a pass from Robin Burns and pumped home an easy six-foot shot past goaltender Ed Johnston to give Kansas City a 3–0 lead. The Blues stormed back on goals from Unger and Ted Irvine within a span of 2:17, but it was too little, too late as the Scouts preserved their one-goal lead and skated off with a 3–2 win.

After a 5–3 loss to the sorry Detroit Red Wings, the Scouts travelled to Chicago to take on the Smythe Division-leading Chicago Black Hawks, who had gone an impressive 13 games without a loss. What was incredible about the Hawks' undefeated streak was that they had tied their last three games and seven of their last ten!

The Hawks certainly tried their best to avoid tying yet another game, drawing first blood 1:35 after the opening face-off and outshooting the Scouts, 40–22, yet it still wasn't enough. The Scouts kept the Hawks off the scoresheet the rest of the way, and Paiement notched his sixth goal at 9:40 of the third period to earn the Scouts a

1–1 tie. Believe it or not, the Hawks also tied their next game against Pittsburgh three nights later, giving them an unbelievable five stalemates in a row and eight in their last nine games!

Cutting a Wilf Loose

"To say that we are improved over last year is the understatement of the year," Bep Guidolin said after the Chicago game. "While we have been playing good hockey, we have not been winning and have not been scoring at the rate we should. We just came off a 17-day road trip which, while taking a lot out of us, showed that we are capable of beating some good teams."[26]

Despite Guidolin's gushing, when the 6–13–4 Scouts hosted the Habs in K.C. on December 3, no one would have predicted the Scouts would put up much of a fight. Coming into the game, the Habs were 18–4–3 and had won their last six games. Nevertheless, after 20 minutes, the Scouts took a 3–0 lead on the shell-shocked Canadiens on goals from Burns, Patrick and Paiement. The ultra-skilled Habs could never truly be counted out of a game, however, and they pressured Herron throughout the second stanza. Pucks eventually started hitting the target, and the Scouts could see victory slipping away. Steve Shutt scored on the power play at 7:03, followed by Yvon Lambert's 14th at 13:14 to close the gap to 3–2, but 16 seconds after the Habs' second goal, Burns tallied to put the Scouts up by a pair. Yvan Cournoyer scored 2:16 later to make it 4–3, but Paiement responded at 18:10 to restore Kansas City's two-goal lead.

Montreal back-up goaltender Michel Larocque had started the game, but after he allowed five goals on 15 shots, Ken Dryden came in for the third period. The Habs continued to pressure Herron, and Lambert broke through with his second goal of the night at 1:24 to narrow the Scouts' lead to 5–4, but Jacques Lemaire took a penalty just past the halfway point of the period, giving the Scouts the man advantage. Paiement scored his third of the night to give K.C. another two-goal lead, not to mention a piece of Scouts history. Robin Burns remembered Paiement's hat-trick well because it cost his own wife a luxurious prize:

> I got two goals and Wilf Paiement had two goals, and the first hat-trick in Kansas City's history would be presented a mink coat, so I scored two, Wilf scored two, and I hit the crossbar and missed it, and Wilf went on and tucked it in and he got the hat-trick, so after the game my wife kinda went, "Well, that was really nice. Thanks very much," and so Wilf had his girlfriend Sue down there and she became his wife.... Wilf, two weeks later shows up with this full-length mink coat made for himself. We all pissed our pants laughing. Well, as time goes by, I saw Wilf years later and he said, "You shoulda won that mink coat because it ended up costing me about $20,000." He had to buy his wife a new mink coat years later, so what goes around comes around.

Jacques Lemaire made up for his ill-timed penalty with his ninth goal of the season at 16:30, setting up a nerve-racking final few minutes, but 6–5 was as close as the Canadiens got despite outshooting the Scouts, 42–25. The win was an incredible accomplishment for the young franchise; the Habs would lose just 11 games all year.

"What a night," Paiement exclaimed. "I'm really happy. It's really great getting three against Montreal because hardly anyone does that." Habs head coach Scotty Bowman accepted the blame for the embarrassing loss. "Chalk this one up to me," he said. "I changed goaltenders when we'd won six straight. There was no reason to take Kenny out. I was trying to be a nice guy and it cost us."[27]

For former Canadiens farmhand Robin Burns, the victory was extra special.

> We grew up with the Original Six, so when you played against an Original Six team, you just seemed to—I don't know what it was—you dug down deep and you just seemed to play at a higher level, and I think they might have played at a little lower level.... I grew up in the Montreal organization, so I played with or against 90 percent of that team, so stepping on that ice was quite a thrill.... To beat them, that was something else.... That was our Stanley Cup.... We caught them on a night that they were flat.... Scotty Bowman, he was absolutely livid, and I did see him. It felt good to put two goals in against 'em.

Abel Gambles Again

The Scouts, while well below the .500 mark, were actually still in contention for a playoff spot in the weak Smythe Division. To help push the Scouts over the top, Sid Abel added more depth by acquiring Germain Gagnon, who had scored 51 points in 1974–1975, off waivers from Chicago. Abel made an intriguing move on December 9, 1975, acquiring the talented Henry Boucha from Minnesota for a 1978 second-round pick. Boucha, an Ojibwa from Warroad, Minnesota, had starred on the 1972 silver-medal winning American Olympic team, and had spent two-and-a-half seasons in Detroit, scoring 14 and 19 goals in a limited role. Boucha also had some flair, something the Scouts needed to boost attendance. This being the early 1970s, Boucha had started letting his hair grow, which eventually became a problem since it got into his eyes. He broke with NHL tradition and started wearing a headband during games, and much to his surprise, the look became his trademark. Boucha is sporting his famous headband on his one and only Kansas City Scouts card from the 1976–1977 O-Pee-Chee set.

Minnesota had thought so highly of Boucha that they sent Detroit Danny Grant, one of the all-time great North Stars (five seasons of 29 goals or more, and the 1969 Calder Trophy as NHL Rookie of the Year). Grant went on to score 50 goals his first year in Michigan, so even though Boucha scored a respectable 15 goals in 51 games, the trade looked one-sided.

Could Boucha have put up numbers close to Grant's? We'll never know for sure, because on January 4, 1975, against Boston, Boucha was sucker-punched by fourth-liner Dave Forbes. The two had been needling each other throughout the game, and they eventually squared off. Boucha scored the decision in the fight, which upset Forbes, so when he saw a chance to get even, he took it. When Boucha wasn't looking, Forbes punched him in the right eye while the butt end of his stick was jutting ever so slightly out of his glove, fracturing Boucha's orbital bone.

Boucha was out of the lineup until February 22, but he should have been out longer. The Stars rushed him back into action before he was ready, and he struggled to regain his form. At the end of the season, Boucha became a free agent as he hadn't negotiated a new contract before his injury. He signed with the Minnesota Fighting

Saints of the WHA, who had long coveted him, and he rebounded well with 35 points in 36 games. Before long, players began hearing rumors of the Saints shaky financial situation, and when Boucha discovered that his contract had never been guaranteed, he signed with Kansas City. Sid Abel was more than willing to gamble on the 24-year-old continuing to produce at his prolific WHA pace, and early on, the gamble paid off as Boucha scored three points in his first three games with Kansas City.

In the meantime, the good times kept coming for Kansas City in the weeks leading up to Christmas. The Scouts promptly beat Pittsburgh 3–2 at Kemper on December 9, Bep Guidolin's 50th birthday. Guidolin said afterwards that Denis Herron had done a "helluva job" keeping the high-octane Penguins offense to just two goals. "They've got every line that can score. They can score 10 goals."

As they had done a week earlier against Montreal, the Scouts got off to a great start, leading 2–0 after 40 minutes on goals by Randy Rota and Simon Nolet. The Scouts hadn't been terribly consistent since the start of the season, but there were a few breaks, which often happens when things are going one's way. For instance, Pittsburgh's Vic Hadfield seemingly scored to make it 2–1, but officially, the shot rang off the post. "It hit the net," Hadfield argued. "The linesman said it was in. [Referee] Alf Lejeune said he didn't see it."[28]

Jean-Guy Lagace scored a short-handed goal on Michel Plasse 3:24 into the third period to put K.C. up, 3–0, and further plunge the dagger into the Penguins' collective hearts. "That sure isn't something I practice, but I thought all the time that I would fake him and shoot a backhander," the Scouts' defenseman said. "I faked and he went down. Still I was lucky. I just got it inside the post."[29] The Penguins woke up shortly afterwards. Pierre Larouche scored on the power play just 0:39 later, and Jean Pronovost scored his 19th goal at 19:44, but it was too little, too late, and the Scouts skated away with the win.

After losses to Minnesota, Montreal, and Atlanta between December 11 and 16, the Scouts won two in a row for just the fourth time in franchise history. The first of those wins was against the struggling Vancouver Canucks, who one season earlier won the Smythe Division pennant. This year, at 10–13–5, they were barely ahead of the 8–18–4 Scouts. Guy Charron scored twice for Kansas City in a 6–5 victory, and he would have registered a hat-trick if not for a shot that hit the goal post. The missed shot cost Charron's wife a mink coat like Wilf Paiement had taken home weeks earlier. "Well, I've got two sleeves of it, anyway," he said after the game.[30] Gary Croteau and Simon Nolet also scored twice each to help the Scouts move to within three points of Vancouver and St. Louis, who jointly held second place in the division.

"That's the most ice I've ever had in the NHL," said a pleased Charron, who had been on fire ever since coming to Kansas City a year earlier. "But I'm not complaining. I rode the plank for too many years."[31]

Two nights later, the Detroit Red Wings, who had gone 10–11–1 since starting the season a miserable 0–7–3, travelled to Kemper, hoping to keep their playoff hopes alive, but the Scouts were playing like they had a purpose, and they had no intention of rolling over. As in most of their recent wins, the Scouts got off to a good start, and after 20 minutes they led, 1–0, on Craig Patrick's fifth goal. Croteau scored 52 seconds into the second stanza to put Kansas City up by two, and the Scouts were off and running. Michel Bergeron's marker whittled the gap to 2–1, but the Wings couldn't sneak another puck past the sizzling Denis Herron. Charron scored his 15th goal on assists from Paiement and Patrick just over two minutes later, and Paiement scored his 12th on an assist from Charron at 19:07 to give the Scouts a 4–1 win in front of a meager crowd of 6,733.

For once, the Scouts did not need an offensive outburst to win the game, because the defense held up nicely when they had the lead. "The defense played super and the forwards came back," said Herron. "It was one of our best games this year." Instead of selfishly looking for more offensive glory, the Scouts held back and played responsible hockey, holding the Wings to just eight third period shots. "We played the best positional hockey we've played in a while," said Bep Guidolin. "It was good, solid hockey.... When a defenseman went in deep, a forward backed him up. That's what I love to see—everybody playing hard and playing unselfish hockey."[32]

And then everything went to hell in a hand basket....

The Streak, part one

The 10–18–4 Scouts were easily on pace to surpass the 15 wins and 41 points they racked up their first season. There was no reason to think the Scouts were about to embark upon perhaps the worst 48-game stretch of any NHL team ever. The Scouts fell 5–1 to Toronto on December 20, but no one rang any alarm bells. Then they lost, 5–1, to Buffalo December 23, but life went on. Interestingly, Baz Bastien handled the coaching duties in the latter contest as Bep Guidolin stayed behind due to an illness in his family. To this day, the NHL does not recognize Bastien's one and only game behind the bench and still credits Guidolin with the loss.

After a three-day break, Guidolin returned to the team, but the Scouts performed no better for him than they did for Bastien. The L.A. Kings creamed the Scouts, 9–4, in Los Angeles on December 27, but the Scouts rebounded with a 3–1 win in Oakland the following night. The victory over the Seals gave the Scouts a record of 11–21–4, which wasn't great, but because they were playing in the sad Smythe Division, they were just one point behind third-place St. Louis. In reality, the season was all but over.

Ironically, despite having a far superior record to Washington, the Scouts were getting far less attention than their expansion cousins. People tend to have a morbid fascination with futility, and the Caps had that market cornered. As 1975 came to a close, the Scouts were hitting their all-time peak. Meanwhile, the Caps were hitting rock bottom; Milt Schmidt was replaced as coach and general manager, and Washington's 3–28–5 record put them behind their pathetic year one pace.

The Scouts, on the other hand, had flown under the radar all year and kept surprising opponents. Guy Charron was sailing along effortlessly with 38 points in 35 games, and the rejuvenated Wilf Paiement was on pace to crush his rookie marks, thanks to 14 goals and 15 assists in 36 games. The rest of the team wasn't scoring much, but the defense was playing reasonably well behind the still-effective Gary Bergman. Denis Herron was one of the busiest goalies in the league, yet he carried a respectable 3.34 goals-against average into January. "He deserves to be on the [mid-season Campbell Conference] All-Star team," Bep Guidolin gushed to one beat writer. "Vote for him."[33] Even opposing players and coaches noticed the impact Herron had on his team. "I haven't seen anybody better this season," said Canadiens coach Scotty Bowman.

"He keeps getting better and better," said Islanders goalie Glenn Resch. "No telling how good he'd be with a contender."[34]

Yes, the Scouts' rise up the standings was noteworthy, but a cynic will tell you that a team can't depend on a hot goaltender and a couple of sizzling scorers forever. It was only a matter of time before the rest of league caught on to the sneaky Scouts. The victory over the Seals in late December was the last one the Scouts savored before a very dark cloud gathered over Kansas City. One loss followed another, and another, and another as the Scouts set a dubious franchise record of 14 consecutive losses. "People didn't take us serious," believed Robin Burns, "but then I think a lot of teams coming in said, 'Hey, this team is 11–21–4, they're not 24–2–4 or something like that. I think as fast as we got going … the wheels fell off the bus and we couldn't right the ship."

Teams caught on fast that if they peppered the Scouts' goaltenders with enough shots, the dam would eventually break. One of the most embarrassing defeats during the streak was an awful 8–1 thrashing at the hands of the New York Islanders. Jude Drouin scored his first career hat-trick, and he admitted it was "exciting" but that he wished "it had come against a better team."[35] Not long after, the Scouts were crushed, 8–4, by the Rangers, drubbed 8–3 by the Red Wings, and slaughtered 7–1 by the Flyers. Even the putrid Minnesota North Stars managed to pump nine goals past Bill McKenzie on January 28, despite taking just 28 shots.

It didn't take long for the streak to grate on the nerves of Bep Guidolin, even affecting his desire to go out for a beer after a tough game. "Hell, I have to go home to my apartment and look at the walls and brood," he complained. "I'm afraid to show up in the Arena Club or someplace else where they know me. They all come up to me and say, 'you know what you really need?' And I'd say, 'hell, yes, I know what I really need, I'm the coach ain't I?'"[36]

At one point during the season, someone asked Guidolin, "Has this been a nightmare?" His response? "You gotta sleep before you can have nightmares."[37]

Let the "Demolition Durby" Begin!

Hoping to reverse the worrisome trend, Sid Abel dialed up Pittsburgh general manager Wren Blair and acquired offensive-minded Chuck Arnason, who had scored 26 goals and 58 points the previous year, but who had struggled to find the net this season. He would wake up quickly in Kansas City.

"He's got a very hard shot," said Denis Herron, who had played with Arnason in Pittsburgh. "I used to hate seeing him at practice. Now I've got him here."[38]

"I'm not a finesse guy," Arnason admitted. "If I don't blow it by the goalie it won't go. I just blast it." Arnason developed his mighty shot in his youth by pelting his neighbor's garage door with pucks until the door couldn't take it anymore and collapsed. "My dad had to buy a new door," Arnason recalled.[39]

Arnason starred in Flin Flon, Manitoba, with the legendary junior league Bombers, scoring 79 goals and 83 assists in 1970–1971, but graduating to the Montreal Canadiens, who drafted him 7th overall that year, proved difficult. He scored 54 points in 58 games with the AHL's Nova Scotia Voyageurs and won the Calder Cup, and according to Arnason, "Mr. Pollock said I'd be up after that. They called me up for awhile but they never had anything to do with me," so off Arnason went to Pittsburgh, where he enjoyed some success. But when the 1975–1976 season began, he mysteriously found himself riding the pine.[40]

The cost to Kansas City was Ed Gilbert, who had scored but four goals and eight assists this season, and 34-year-old captain Simon Nolet, who had 10 goals and 15 assists in 41 games. The teams also swapped 1976 first-round picks, which with Pittsburgh likely going to finish far ahead of Kansas City in the standings, was a bad move by Abel.

In the same trade, the Scouts also addressed one of their primary needs: toughness. After a 4–2 loss to Philadelphia on New Year's Day, Guidolin fumed about how the Flyers were just a "bunch of hatchets." He added that what the Scouts needed was "a couple of guys in here to do the same thing…. We ought to bring in a couple of butchers who can't even skate, but just swing their sticks at everybody in the league and try to chop their heads off."[41]

Instead of bringing up a couple of butchers, Abel acquired just one: the most notorious, bat-shit-crazy, one-man gang skating in the North American pros. One could have politely called the ferocious 6'1", 210-pound Steve Durbano a proverbial loose cannon, if that loose cannon was in fact a ballistic missile launcher with a wonky trigger. He had been christened with a few nicknames during his big-league career, notably the cute "Demolition Durby" and the not-so-cute "Mental Case." The latter nickname best explained the problem with Durbano: he was almost impossible to control and had many self-destructive tendencies, notably a volatile temper and substance abuse issues that would plague him his entire life. Nevertheless, Guidolin was not worried. "He's not a goon," the coach said. "He's a good kid, a good hockey player. He gets upset with himself sometimes and that disrupts his playing ability."[42]

The *Manhattan* (KS) *Mercury*'s Dave Wright argued that having a renowned pugilist in the line-up was paramount. "The name of the game is still goals, of course, but lacking that, which the Scouts still do, dull moments are fewer are [*sic*] farther between if you've got a good goon or two around," he explained.

Fans had started craving blood rather than goals and finesse plays. According to Wright, one night when Wilf Paiement made a nice move against a Toronto defenseman and ripped a good hard shot at the net which was stopped by the goaltender, the crowd responded with "light applause" followed by "groans," but when Durbano pasted a Leaf into the boards a few seconds later, "the crowd roar[ed] its approval of the defenseman's cave-man approach."[43] This is the muck hockey had devolved into by 1976.

"He was a crazy guy," former NHL and WHA player Cam Connor once recalled on his podcast *View from the Penalty Box*,

It's like Muhammad Ali used to say. He said, nobody's afraid of a tough guy, but everybody's afraid of a crazy man. And I'll be honest with you, I didn't want to fight this guy; I think I could have beat him up, but I know that if I beat him up, the rest of my life when I played against him, you gotta look over your shoulder because he's gonna get you back, and he was somebody that I perceived that would spear you in the face, hit you over the head, crosscheck you across the neck from behind.[44]

Stan Fischler wrote extensively about Durbano in his book, *Hockey's Toughest Ten*. He believed that "when it [came] to Durbano, opinions [varied] as widely as the width of the Mississippi River."

According to *Toronto Star* columnist Milt Dunnell, Durbano was "described as vicious, vindictive, hot-tempered and irresponsible.'" Others, according to Fischler, described Durbano as "friendly, soft-spoken and self-analytical."[45]

Durbano's junior career was littered with violent outbursts which in retrospect were warning signs of what his professional career would become. As a 17-year-old junior, Durbano started heckling a timekeeper and punched a police officer who had the nerve to interfere in his business. Durbano was slapped with a $50,000 suit which was later dismissed, but more trouble lay ahead.

Steve's father, Nick, had once been a scout for the New York Rangers, and he owned the OHA's Hamilton Red Wings. "The trouble with the Durbanos," said *Toronto Star*'s sports editor Jim Proudfoot, "is that they are cursed with volcanic tempers, which so far have obscured the many good things of which they are both capable."[46]

A good example of how frightening that "volcanic temper" could be occurred the evening of January 19, 1973, in Atlanta while Durbano was toiling with St. Louis. He had been out of the Blues' lineup for nearly two months with mononucleosis, and this was his first game back. The West Division was extremely competitive, and it was incredibly rough thanks to outfits like the Flyers and Blues, who employed brawlers and goons like they were going out of style. The Blues have often been accused of indirectly birthing the Broad Street Bullies of the mid–1970s, because toughies like the Plager brothers, Bill, Bob, and Barclay, ran roughshod over the once-passive Flyers in the early days of expansion. The latter two Plagers were still around in 1972 when Durbano joined the Blues to complete what was arguably the most fearsome defense crew in hockey.

The Flames, on the other hand, were anything but aggressive, with the exception of a few players but not goaltender Phil Myre, though he was the Flame at the epicenter of a massive donnybrook in the third period. "Durbano pushed me out of the crease while a shot was being taken," Myre said. "I just wanted to show him he couldn't intimidate me, but I didn't intend to hit him in the head." Intentional or not, that hit to the head was enough to send Durbano into orbit. Durbano was bleeding badly from the head, but that didn't stop him from charging at Myre like an enraged bull staring down a red cape. Atlanta's Bob Paradise stepped in to stop Durbano, and the tension on the ice subsided ... for a few minutes.[47]

Paradise and teammate Jacques Richard were busy brushing away abandoned gloves and sticks, preparing for play to resume, and Myre busied himself smoothing the ice in his crease when Durbano lived up to his not-so-cute nickname. Everyone thought Durbano had left the ice for repairs, but there was no way he would let Myre go back to stopping pucks. "I figured," Durbano said, "that this might be my only chance for revenge, so I went after Myre." Trainers told the guard watching the gate that Durbano needed to get back onto the ice, so the guard obliged, which in retrospect was not the brightest move.

Veteran reporter Jim Huber vividly described the scene. "The following split seconds will be indelibly transcribed for years to come on the crowd's mind," he wrote. "It keeps coming back in terrifying slow motion. A crime is being committed and an arena full of witnesses watches on in stillness. The door to the ice opens. A St. Louis player, his face torn with anger, slowly steps onto the surface." Durbano skated towards Myre with just one mission in mind: run over his assailant and beat him to a bloody pulp. Durby charged at the unsuspecting goaltender and rammed him into the steel goal frame. The two fell over, and Durbano started punching away while the other players tried to break up the melee. "We should have hit Durbano over the head with a stick when he came out like that," said Flame Pat Quinn. "That would have controlled him."[48]

Durbano's behavior improved little, if at all, with Pittsburgh. The 1974–1975 pre-season was an interesting period in his career and a microcosm of the self-destructive behavior that would later destroy his life. During a chippy pre-season affair with the WHA's Cleveland Crusaders, four fights had already taken place before Durbano went bananas. Just after the fourth skirmish, Durbano was skating off to the Pens' dressing room when he drilled the Crusaders' Gerry Pinder with a clean right hand. The Crusaders did not take this offense lightly, so they spilled out onto the ice, followed by the entire Penguins bench. Not only did fights break out everywhere on the ice, they broke out in the stands as well. Cleveland coach John Hanna pulled his club off the ice with 4:38 left, giving the Penguins a rare forfeit win, not that it really mattered at that point since the Pens already had a 5–2 lead. Durbano received a $300 fine from Clarence Campbell, but here's the kicker: Durbano was playing even though he had already received a two-game suspension, which would only kick in during the regular season, for yet another boneheaded move he pulled on September 25 against, of all teams, Kansas City.

In this assault on his future team, Durbano took exception to the Scouts' Gary Coalter, so Durbano swung his stick at Coalter's neck. Luckily, Coalter was moving at that moment, so the stick missed its target, but Campbell suspended Durbano because of his obvious intent to injure.

Durbano practically forced his way out of Pittsburgh, not necessarily because of his questionable on-ice antics, but because he had also had a run-in with coach Marc Boileau. During the third period of one game, Durbano retreated to the dressing room and did not return, so Boileau responded by refusing to use Durbano in future games. The Penguins decided to unload Durbano and be done with him, but the fans were upset to see their folk hero leave, booing Boileau mercilessly in the Penguins' next game. Boileau, already on thin ice due to the Penguins' lackluster record, was fired a week later.

"Everybody on this team's going to be a little braver with him out there on the ice now," said an absolutely giddy Bep Guidolin, who firmly believed that adding some muscle to the Scouts was the medicine that would cure them of all their woes.[49]

To this day, Durbano holds the NHL record for most penalty minutes per game (5.1) among players who have accumulated at least 1,000 career minutes in the box. That said, when he was focused, the guy could actually play hockey. He had a good shot, and he even totaled 21 points (and 231 penalty minutes) in 49 games for St. Louis in 1972–1973. He had also been a first-round pick of the Rangers in 1971, so he was, at one time, highly regarded.

Despite his volatile nature, many teammates had kind words to say about Durbano. They often describe the man they called "Durbo" as someone who was kind and compassionate, but who strayed from the righteous path and let his demons get the better of him. Denis Herron, in particular, knew Durbano well, having been his roommate for a time. "They came to see me, and they asked me if I mind to have [sic] Steve Durbano as a roommate. I said, I don't mind…. Steve Durbano was a gentleman, polite, was incredible as a roommate. It was interesting that the image he showed in the NHL and the image that he showed as a person [were different]…. I think he made some bad choices in his life, but honestly, with me … the guy was a gentleman. If he wanted to do something in the room, he asked me first."

Paul Gardner was selected by the Scouts in the 1976 Amateur Draft, and Durbano took the youngster under his wing during his rookie NHL season. Durbano and Gardner's brother, Dave, had once been teammates on the OHA's Toronto Marlboros, and as a favor to the elder brother, Durbano made sure Paul's transition to the big league would be smooth.

In the end, however, the addition of Arnason and Durbano did little to change the Scouts' fortunes. In fact, things got worse. With the Scouts' playoff hopes quickly evaporating, and the losing streak looking like it was never going to end, Abel sent Buster Harvey to the Red Wings for Phil Roberto in what was essentially a trade of two expendable players who had not displayed enough hustle. The trade occurred just before the opening faceoff of an 8–3 pasting courtesy of those aforementioned Wings, so at least one team was happy hours after the deal.

Dan Maloney scored a shorthanded goal at 2:11 of the first period, followed by markers from Michel Bergeron and another shortie from Bill Hogaboam to close out the frame. Nick Libett and Rick Lapointe scored goals within 33 seconds of each other to make the score 5–0, and the game was not even half over. Arnason scored his eighth goal on a power play not long after, but Lapointe restored the Wings' five-goal lead on another power play. Detroit coach Alex Delvecchio must have been thrilled with the Wings' special teams, as Terry Harper potted another with the man advantage with just 0:42 left in the second period.

Wilf Paiement's lip had been sliced for nine stitches courtesy of a Bryan Watson high stick earlier in the game, but Paiement provided the Scouts with a goal in the third period and an assist on Arnason's power play marker. Maloney and Arnason exchanged goals in the third period, but by that point the result was never in doubt. The light-scoring Lapointe scored two goals and two assists for the victors, whose eight goals were a season high.

"We have no excuses for our loss," said Bep Guidolin before promptly making an excuse for the Scouts' loss. "We have so many new players it takes awhile to adjust to skating styles."[50]

The Toronto Maple Leafs were a little more charitable on January 15, only beating the Scouts 6–4, but a loss was still a loss. "Toronto just played better than we did tonight," Guidolin said afterward. "But I'll tell you one thing. We've made some good trades and we're a better hockey team." In reality, the game wasn't close at all.

The Leafs held a 6–2 advantage after 40 minutes, so the Scouts' attempt at a third period comeback was futile. Paiement scored his 18th goal on a five-minute power play at 15:51 as the Leafs' Dave Dunn sat in the penalty box for high-sticking. Arnason scored his second of the evening 0:58 later on the same power play to make the score look respectable.

"We won't get settled for about a month, I guess," Guidolin continued. "And that will probably be too late for this year. But listen, we're in a lot better shape for next year. I like the guys we've got now and they want to work to win."[51]

Guidolin's tune would soon change.

The coach's frustrations had been simmering for a while, but there was a full-on eruption on January 20. "I'm sick and tired of the media making excuses for guys making $90,000," Guidolin griped. "A guy's going bad and he says I don't communicate. I communicate with these guys nine months a year and it still doesn't reach them."[52]

Robin Burns was making only about $70,000, but that didn't mean he and Guidolin always saw eye to eye. In a 2007 interview with John Meagher of the *Montreal Gazette*, Burns said that Guidolin was "absolutely horrendous as a coach" and that he did not teach his players much. "A practice would literally consist of: 'Okay guys, twice around the rink to your right, line up and do some 3-on-2s, 2-on-1s, 1-on-1s, line up at the blue line and take some slapshots at the goalie, then work on what you need to work on, guys, and see ya.'"[53]

Burns may have had a point. In November, Guidolin had an interesting explanation for why the Scouts' power play was so inept. "We don't have the kind of team that we can work on the power play," he said, sounding like he had given up ever trying to teach his team anything. "I just put my best five guys out there, guys who can score goals. If you have a guy like Bobby Orr on the point, then you have a power play. Then you can work on things."[54]

Guidolin vs. Johnston

As the streak continued, Larry Johnston became the unwanted center of attention and the target of Guidolin's ire. Guidolin curiously claimed he had been dissatisfied with Johnston's play since the start of the season, although newspapers had quoted him praising his defenseman several times in the previous months. The *Hockey News*' Ken Rudnick also claimed, in the magazine's January 16, 1976, edition that the Scouts' "steadiest defenseman in recent weeks [was] Larry Johnston."[55] What drove Guidolin bonkers was Johnston breaking curfew after the 8–3 massacre against Detroit, so he scratched Johnston from the lineup for the Scouts' next game against Toronto.

Guidolin's disciplinary act did not sit well with many players. Everyone was already frustrated with the losing streak, and the loss to Detroit was embarrassing. There were rumors that many players had lost their confidence in Guidolin. Exacerbating the issue was the belief that Guidolin was a poor communicator who couldn't juggle lines properly. He believed that if he got too close to his players, it would just make it more difficult for everyone whenever he had to hand players tickets to the minors or send them packing for good. "Their job is to play hockey, not have a church social with me," Guidolin ranted. "I didn't talk to Bobby Orr in Boston, so who do they think they are…. I was more nice to them than tough. How many times could I have caught those guys out late? You couldn't count that high."[56]

Guidolin appointed a player to collect fines from anyone who admitted breaking curfew, and in the end, seven guilty souls stepped forward, but Guidolin still blamed Johnston for instigating a small mutiny. He wanted to banish the defenseman to Springfield to "teach him a lesson," but Sid Abel was unwilling to go that far, so Johnston remained a Scout. Despite publically praising Johnston's play earlier in the season, Guidolin did an about-face and claimed he in fact did *not* like Johnston's playing style, and that he "never thought he was a good hockey player" but that he

Larry Johnston was a tough as nails defenseman who ran afoul of Bep Guidolin one night in Detroit in January 1976 (Robin Burns collection).

had "nothing against the guy personally."⁵⁷ Considering the venomous rants Guidolin unleashed at Johnston through the print media that January, that last assertion was hard to believe.

Johnston, on the other hand, thought Guidolin was making him a scapegoat for the Scouts' lengthy losing streak. "I'm taking the heat for everybody," the defenseman said. "Why me?"⁵⁸ The comments upset Guidolin to no end, so he gave Abel an ultimatum: either send Johnston to the AHL, or Abel could find himself a new coach.

Unfortunately for Guidolin, Abel thought very highly of Johnston. Abel met with the players, but Guidolin was not in attendance. The general manager indicated that Johnston was staying put, but that he had no intention of replacing Guidolin either. Abel could feel the losing streak grating on everyone's nerves, and that all the little issues that had been simmering since the start of the season had come to a boil. According to Abel, the team's problems were openly discussed that day, and at the end of the closed-door meeting, the players were motivated to get on with the season. "The mood of the team is excellent," Abel chirped to the local media, but it wasn't really.⁵⁹ New team captain Guy Charron said all the right things when he was interviewed soon after and indicated that everyone had let bygones be bygones, but change was definitely afoot.⁶⁰

Despite the airing of grievances, Guidolin stood firm in his threat to resign if Johnston wasn't demoted. "I thought the [players'] reaction was good but Bep didn't feel it was to his liking," Abel said. "After about an hour delay after I first talked to him, he notified me he wouldn't be behind the bench tonight." Abel asked Guidolin to reconsider, but the Scouts' prideful coach stood firm.⁶¹ The general manager stated that Guidolin said "he would never come into [the Scouts'] dressing room again."⁶² And just like that, Bep Guidolin was out, but he took one final parting shot before trudging off. He explained that he had been looking for support to show that he was indeed running the show, but that he "didn't get it."

"I felt the player was more important than me because he has more support than me.... [Johnston] pushed my back against the wall until I was forced to resign. He's the king of the team. If he's the Bobby Orr of the team I'm glad I resigned. If they're depending on Larry Johnston to get them into the playoffs they're in trouble."⁶³

Johnston, however, chose to remain silent on the matter. "I don't want to say anything," he said. "I feel I'm a better man for it."⁶⁴

Guidolin felt the players had played hard during the early days of the streak, but that they had eased off the gas a little and then just seemed to have given up. "I'd look at them when they got two goals down and it looked like they'd lost their wife," he said.⁶⁵

Henry Boucha found it particularly difficult dealing with the constant losing during his brief tenure in Kansas. "Guys getting used to losing, that's a cancer ... people not really caring and just kind of finishing out the year and getting it over with," he explained. The feeling of hopelessness was palpable. Boucha, whose entire tenure in K.C. coincided with the team's second-half debacle, described playing for the Scouts as "like there were four players out there compared to five, most of the time."

Un-Abel to Make Heads Nor Tails

For the next three games after Bep Guidolin's sudden departure, Sid Abel took over behind the bench, but the result was the same as the previous nine games: all losses. In his first game, against St. Louis, it was obvious Abel was not going to last long as Scouts coach. "It has been a long time," he admitted. "I lost my voice. I was really afraid I'd have too many men on the ice or something. One time we didn't have enough. I had Arnason at right wing and Charron at center—they both came off at the same time and we didn't have enough players."[66]

On the positive side, Abel placed Dave Hudson on a line with Phil Roberto and Gary Croteau, and the trio played solid defense while scoring 14 points in their first six games together. The new partnership gave everyone involved a boost. After 46 games, Croteau had scored just 11 points. Roberto had arrived in K.C. out of shape and had scored just a single point in his first four games. Hudson, meanwhile, had played with a variety of linemates, which may have contributed to his underwhelming first half (14 points in 45 games). After the trio started playing together, Croteau scored 22 points in his last 35 games, Roberto finished the year with 21 points in 33 games, and Hudson scored 17 points in 29 games. Despite the line's success, few wins came of out it.

On January 23, Bill Oleschuk, playing in his first NHL game, replaced Denis Herron, who was hospitalized with a kidney stone caused by his excessive consumption of protein-laced milkshakes. Herron had hoped that downing an obscene number of milky beverages would help him gain weight, but in the end the shakes only had an adverse effect on the goaltender's health. The 20-year-old Oleschuk was up to the task as he faced a whopping 52 shots from the California Golden Seals, 24 in the first period alone. Both marks were Seals records, but Oleschuk was outstanding. "I was nervous," he admitted. "There was pressure because I wanted to play well. Maybe there wouldn't have been as much if the team was winning." As usual, the Scouts lost, this time 4–1, and the losing streak reached 11 games.

"He played a good game," Abel said about Oleschuk. "As far as initial saves went, he was excellent. But he got in trouble with rebounds.... As soon as he learns that he's not going to be a bad kid."[67] The Scouts could have helped out their rookie netminder with more goal support, but only Croteau found the back of the net at 6:49 of the second period, making the score 2–1, California. Just four minutes later, Bob Stewart put the Seals back up by two, and Dennis Maruk put the cherry on the sundae with a final goal at 19:27.

Abel made it clear that he never had any desire to coach the Scouts long-term, so after three games behind the bench he hired Eddie Bush, the team's *fourth* coach in the last month, to finish out the season. If all went well, there was the possibility that Bush would return behind the bench in October. "We'll just cross that bridge when we come to it," the new coach said. Despite the heavy odds against turning the Scouts around, Bush had every intention of making an impact with his new club. "If everybody pulls their weight around here we should be okay," he said. "I'm not used to being around losers and I don't want to get used to it."[68]

Bush, a former Red Wing who played 26 games with the team during World

War II, had accrued more than 20 years experience as a coach, but only in the junior leagues, and unfortunately, it showed. "Eddie Bush was just there to complete the year and nothing else," said Denis Herron. Henry Boucha described Bush as "nonchalant" and said that he "really wasn't a great motivator."

> He knew the writing was on the wall, that the team was probably going to fold at the end of the year, so we just basically went through the motions and got through that year.... He didn't have a lot of advice.... He's the one who came up and said, "There's no more dough in K.C. M.O." and we just all kind of felt that ... we were probably going to be sold. We weren't drawing well. There were 5,000 people in the stands at times, and it just wasn't a good place to play.

Robin Burns agreed that Bush was not the right fit for this team. "When you're sitting there and he's having you skate full speed to the red line, dive on your stomach; they'd call it the Henri Richard ... he had drills that were unbelievable, and so you go from a Bep Guidolin, who coached in the Stanley Cup, had quality teams, and then Eddie Bush ... he was certainly old school.... You're working so hard to end this streak and it just seemed to be endless." According to Burns, Gary Bergman grew so frustrated doing stomach rolls on the ice that he skated over to him and told him he would sooner retire than continue with the amateurish practices.[69]

Some days, it was Bush who wished Burns would retire.

> At the time I was working for Lange skates.... In the summer time, I was one of the ones who was developing this new molded skate, and I had worked with them for a couple of summers so I could take a mold of a guy's foot, send it in, and then skates would be there within a couple of days, so I ended up getting, oh I guess, ten guys were wearing the skates by the time we ended up going to Japan.... I gave the puck away or something like that, and Eddie Bush turned around and said, "Burnsie, maybe you should just stick with selling skates and quit hockey." Little did he know how bang on he was.... I went on to not only stick with Lange skates, I went on to start a skate company called Micron with another guy I know and Italian backers.

Some sort of higher power may have been sending Bush a sign when a daylong snowstorm prevented him from landing in Chicago to watch Abel and the Scouts take on the Black Hawks, so he made his NHL debut January 28 in Minnesota. Bush would have been wise to stay home; the North Stars creamed the listless Scouts, 9–3. "I'm not going to get discouraged or downhearted," Bush said after the game. "I've got to work with them. That's what I'm here for."

"This was actually my first look at the team other than one practice," he continued. "Maybe it's a good way to see them."[70]

This losing streak had seemingly taken on a life of its own. If there was one razor-thin silver lining, it was that after 49 games, the 11–34–4 Scouts were still light years ahead of the 4–40–5 Capitals, not that this fact made anyone terribly happy in the Kansas City dressing room. The Scouts rode what had become a 13-game losing streak into Pittsburgh on January 29 for the first half of a home-and-home series. Despite looking dreadfully tired from their disastrous road trip, the Scouts took a 1–0 lead thanks to a two-on-one completed by former Penguin Robin Burns. The lead lasted all of 2:15, until Vic Hadfield beat Herron. Hadfield's goal seemed to deflate the Scouts as the Penguins outshot them, 15–3, in the second period and took a 5–1 lead.

Former Scout Ed Gilbert scored a funny goal in the third period by jamming his stick at the puck at the same time Herron was falling on it, making the score 6–1. Denis Dupere scored in much the same way a little later by nudging a loose puck that goaltender Gary Inness thought he had frozen, but it didn't matter much since the Scouts were still down by four, and as close as they were going to get to tying the game.

According to *Pittsburgh Post-Gazette* sportswriter Bob Whitley, the Penguins played "as if they were beating a dead horse—with very little enthusiasm." He bemoaned the fact that even though former Penguins Chuck Arnason and Steve Durbano were back visiting, albeit in foreign uniforms, it did not "lend much to the morbid atmosphere that prevailed. A sparse crowd of 8,360 came expecting a killing and a killing they got, without much resistance from the apparently weary Scouts." Whitley added that if Hunter F. Thompson had driven across the country with the Scouts, he could have written "Fear and Loathing in the National Hockey League in less time than it takes the woe-begotten Scouts to give up six or seven goals."[71]

The two teams met again in Kansas City two nights later before a season-high crowd of 12,741. Many of those in attendance were surely there to take in a free post-game concert by young country music star Tanya Tucker. The Scouts didn't do much in the first period, letting the Penguins outshoot them, 11–5, but the game remained scoreless after 20 minutes. Wilf Paiement scored his 19th goal 0:35 into the second period, and the 1–0 lead stood for almost nine minutes before Syl Apps responded. Paiement tipped Gary Bergman's point shot past Michel Plasse less than three minutes later for his 20th goal, and the Scouts escaped the second period with a 2–1 lead.

Jean Pronovost deflected a Ron Stackhouse point shot and shuffled the puck past Denis Herron at 1:54 of the final frame to tie the score at 2–2, and Rick Kehoe seemed to hammer home the final nail in the Scouts' coffin with his 17th goal at 4:42. But unlike recent games, the Scouts found some resiliency and fought back. Arnason scored his 12th goal just four minutes later, and he followed that up with another tally at 11:45 to put Kansas City up, 4–3. Victory was within reach until light-scoring Lew Morrison tied the game with less than four minutes to play. The end result was a tough pill to swallow, but the Scouts couldn't complain too much since their 14-game losing streak had just come to an end. "That was probably our best-played game from start to finish," said Paiement. "We had been losing so long, everybody just decided to give 120 per cent."[72] That said, even though one streak came to an end, another continued: 15 straight games without a *win*.

The Blues came to Kansas City on February 4, but all they could muster was a 3–3 draw, and the Scouts had suddenly gone two games in a row without a loss. And then the unbelievable happened … the Scouts actually won! The victory was against the 5-42-6 Washington Capitals, but in the record books, a win is a win, and the Scouts' 16-game winless streak was mercifully over.

Kansas City got off to a great start as Gary Croteau scored his 11th goal 47 seconds after the opening face-off as the Caps' Yvon Labre sat in the penalty box for roughing. The score remained 1–0 until Jack Lynch tied the game at 15:25, but the Capitals didn't pose much of a threat the rest of the way. The Scouts put the game away with a three-goal flurry in a span of 4:13 in the second period. Charron, Burns, and Paiement each picked up singles to give Kansas City a 4–1 lead after 40 minutes. With the game out of reach, Bergman scored his fourth goal of the season with assists going to Craig Patrick and Guy Charron. Steve Durbano picked up two assists and Denis Herron made 32 saves in the impressive 5–1 win, Eddie Bush's first in the NHL. It would also be his last.

When the Scouts tied the Islanders, 2–2, on February 12, Bush could smile knowing he was behind the bench for what became a team record four-game undefeated streak. Sure, three of the four games were draws, but at least that meant points in the standings, and the ship finally seemed righted, except it really wasn't. Not even close.

To say the 1975–1976 Scouts were streaky is an understatement. They are the only team that can lay claim to a professional sports record that may never be equaled: three consecutive team record streaks in a row. Pay close attention for a minute. First, the Scouts set a team record for most *losses* in a row (14); then they set a record for most games in a row *without a loss* (4). What was the third streak, you ask? Well, the Scouts would also end up setting a new record *winless* streak from February 12 to April 4, but no one could have possibly expected it to be a sequence so incredibly awful, the Scouts' players likely reminisced about the good old days when they went just 16 games without a duke.

The Streak, Part Two

As the Scouts put the most miserable period of their history behind them and embarked upon an unlikely four-game undefeated streak, they began arguably the most miserable period of any team in history, which was not limited to problems on the ice, but off the ice as well. President Ed Thompson publicly stated the team was in a "crisis situation" and that it would not remain in Kansas City unless it sold 8,000 season tickets for the 1976–1977 season. That was a pretty tall order considering the Scouts had sold about 5,000 season tickets their first year, but only 4,100 their second season. In their first 16 home games, the Scouts drew just 117,378 fans, 7,456 less than in the same number of games a year earlier. It was reported in the March 19 edition of the *Maryville Daily Forum* that "season-ticket sales are up approximately $100" and "most of the new orders are from individuals."[73]

"We felt it would be a four to five year operation for us to reach a break-even point." Thompson explained, "but we didn't anticipate the lack of attendance in Kansas City which we have faced and the rise in player's [sic] salaries. I am not saying we are not willing to lose but there comes a time when an economic judgment has to take place."[74]

The Scouts were one of the worst-attended teams in the league, with figures hovering around the 6,100 mark per game in February, but the biggest issue for Thompson was indeed salaries. The average NHL salary was a little over $30,000 when K.C. was awarded an NHL franchise. No one knew at the time what impact the WHA would have on professional hockey. No one expected the new league to survive its first season, let alone turn the NHL on its ear with its ridiculous contract offers.

Thompson claimed that two years later, the average NHL salary was about three times what it had been in 1972. "We had a little cash-flow problem because of that," Thompson admitted.[75] As a result, the Scouts were expected to lose about $1 million for the season, which was especially problematic since they were not owned by some rich mogul with money to burn. The Scouts were owned by about 30 local investors, none so wealthy he was willing to absorb substantial losses. Twice over the course of the season, these small-time owners had been asked to fork over a little dough to keep the team afloat, but Thompson learned quickly that their generosity had limits. Thompson had expected the team to close in on the break-even point, maybe even turn a small profit, but with the team unable to expand its fan base and salaries continuing to rise, not to mention the fact that the Scouts still owed about $4.8 million of their $6 million expansion fee, and that they still owed the St. Louis Blues a cool million in territorial rights, fears for the worst were indeed justified.

Of course, Kansas City had every reason to want the Scouts to remain in town. If the Scouts left, the city would lose the high rental fees the team paid out over 40 home dates at Kemper; there were not nearly enough rock concerts and evangelical events to fill all those potential voids on the calendar, so Thompson pleaded with city officials and local businessmen to help the Scouts with a season ticket drive. "We had asked them for help earlier," Thompson said. "but the city didn't respond because it wasn't on a crisis basis.... If the business community and city want the Scouts to stay, they will get out and get the job done. They did it before for football and baseball."[76] It didn't help matters that at the same time Thompson was pleading for help, there were reports he had received a salary increase of several thousand dollars a year, but Thompson refused to comment on the matter. "The Scouts are losing about a million dollars a year," he said. "What my salary is or what it was raised to is nobody's business, and it certainly isn't the problem. I'm not going to comment."[77]

NHL president Clarence Campbell affirmed that the league would not wave its magic wand and make the Scouts' financial problems disappear. "We just can't do it," he told the *Kansas City Star*'s Steve Marantz in February. "We don't have the resources to do it. If the Scouts are beyond their capabilities, they will have to reorganize." Campbell also indicated that the league could assume some of the Scouts' debts and keep the team solvent, if it ever declared bankruptcy. The president also brought up the prospect of relocating the franchise, an unpleasant thought which had been repeatedly popping up elsewhere in the league, and which would stubbornly persist in newspaper articles about professional hockey for the rest of the decade.[78]

On the ice, the news was not much better as the Scouts continued to struggle despite putting an end to their ignominious 14-game losing streak. After tying the Islanders 2–2 February 12, a huge accomplishment considering the talent on that team, the Scouts fell, 5–4, to Chicago on Valentines' Day, 5–1 to the Rangers the day after, and 6–1 to the surging Penguins on February 17.

Things didn't get any easier as the Boston Bruins rolled into town. Ken Hodge staked Boston to a 1–0 lead on an opening period power play, and the closest the Scouts came to tying the score was clanking a couple of pucks off the goalposts. Charron took one of those shots, but he came through for Kansas City late in the second frame. As the Bruins were crashing the Kansas City net, goalie Bill McKenzie dished the puck over to Paiement, who fired the puck up the middle to Charron, who was breaking out towards center ice. The Scouts' star split the Bruins' defense of Brad Park and Dallas Smith, and beat Gerry Cheevers on a 20-foot shot to the goaltender's left side.

In the third period, Phil Roberto gave Kansas City a quick 2–1 lead, but Smith and Jean Ratelle scored two quick goals 70 seconds apart, which should have been enough to finish off the Scouts. But at 12:18, Arnason tied the score 3–3 when he lifted a shot over Cheevers, who was sliding towards him at the right circle, but the final score just extended the Scouts' newest winless streak to five games. As an interesting side note, the contest was the first head-to-head confrontation between Henry Boucha and Dave Forbes since the latter viciously attacked Boucha over a year earlier, but there were no retaliatory attacks of any kind.

Two nights later the Atlanta Flames, on a nine-game road losing streak themselves, visited Kemper, so something had to give, and unfortunately it was the Flames' skein that came to an end with a 3–1 victory. On February 22, the Scouts' winless streak reached seven games as Minnesota blitzed K.C., 6–3. It was also Wilf Paiement's last game of the season, as he was forced out of the lineup due to calcium deposits that had developed in his right thigh. After a terribly slow start that saw him score just two points in his first 12 games, Paiement corrected his season trajectory, notching 41 points in his next 45 games, but now he would be out until the NHL Japan series.

On February 25, the first-overall Montreal Canadiens landed in K.C. looking for an easy two points, but Denis Herron played out of his mind, stopping each and every shot the Habs launched at him over two periods. The Scouts held on to a miraculous 1–0 lead until 3:56 of the third frame, when Yvan Cournoyer scored on a rebound to tie the game. The Habs poured it on, not wanting to let another game against Kansas City slip away. Yvon Lambert scored his 27th goal at 11:34, and Doug Jarvis put the game out of reach at 17:38 to secure Montreal's 3–1 win. Herron could not be blamed for the loss as his teammates were badly outshot, 36–17, and 15–4 in the final frame. "I've never seen anyone stop so many of them in one game this year," said Montreal coach Scotty Bowman. "A lot of them were pointblank [sic]."[79]

The following night against the Islanders, the Scouts followed the same recipe for disaster: take a lead on a powerhouse, depend on the goalie to make a lot of huge saves, then watch victory slip away. This time the Scouts were outshot, 41–17, yet had taken a 1–0 lead on a second-period goal by Randy Rota, and went up 2–0 in the third period on Gary Croteau's 13th. Then everything fell apart. Chuck Arnason took a hooking penalty at 2:58, and the Islanders scored eight seconds later. Four minutes after that, Lorne Henning tied the game at 2–2, which is how the score ended up, extending the Scouts' winless streak to nine games.

Even though Herron—and for that matter every other Kansas City goaltender—had failed to register a single shutout in nearly two seasons, Eddie Bush was quick to praise his young goalie for keeping the Scouts in games when they had been clearly outclassed. "Herron's been playing great," he said. "He's just had a few bad breaks. Last night Montreal scored two flukey goals and tonight Henning's goal shouldn't have been allowed because of a high stick, but the ref didn't call it. You can't play much better when you have four periods of shutout hockey against these two teams."[80]

Hockey historian Andrew Podnieks once described Kansas City as "the home of the goal against and the capital of the loss." By the end of the 1975–1976 season, it was indeed true.[81] March was not exactly a happy time to be a professional hockey player in K.C., and there were many reasons to shed tears and pull out one's hair. Since Christmas, the Scouts had won just one game, against the equally sad Washington Capitals, and Kansas City's playoff hopes had completely evaporated. Attendance was lousy.

Ed Thompson met with Jay Moore, the owner of the WHA's Cleveland Crusaders, but nothing came of it, although the fact that Thompson met with an owner from another league indicated that some foul plot was afoot and the possibility that the Scouts could be sold. Crusaders players responded to the rumors by wearing black armbands in a game against the Cincinnati Stingers to show their displeasure with Moore.

The Scouts' financial situation was so dire, there were rumors the Scouts would be unable to meet their March 15 payroll, so they made a formal request to the NHL to loan them $400,000 so they could finish out the season. Of course, the NHL was not just going to cut the Scouts a check, no questions asked. After all, the league had already spent a fortune propping up the ailing California Golden Seals and Pittsburgh Penguins. According to the *Kansas City Times*, supporting the Seals cost the league in the neighborhood of $11 million before the team was sold to San Francisco hotelier Melvin Swig in the summer of 1975. The NHL had absolutely no interest in heading down that road again, especially since there were rumors of several other teams hurting financially. The last thing Clarence Campbell wanted was to set a precedent by handing the Scouts a large sum of money and then having to deal with other owners desperately looking for a handout.[82] Professional hockey was not exactly a booming industry in 1976, and many of those who had once gleefully lined up to purchase a team were now looking to unload their money pits.

To avoid embarrassment, especially in the heat of the current war for supremacy with the WHA, the NHL granted the Scouts a $300,000 loan (the Scouts would be responsible for covering expenses in excess of that $300,000) to help them finish the season, even though Campbell had said a week earlier that the league would not "commit one nickel to them" and prop up yet another wheezing franchise. "If the Scouts fold," he said, "we have an emergency plan ready to help us finish the schedule."[83] Campbell clearly didn't give a damn whether or not Kansas City continued to host a hockey team, and he was fully ready to leave the Scouts' corpse behind as the rest of the league soldiered on. He also said that the league's policy was "no gifts, no loans, no co-signing," but he also gave the Scouts a glimmer of hope by stating that "[p]erhaps this [would] change" the following day when the league planned to announce its decision. Luckily for Thompson, the NHL was in a charitable mood.

According to the terms of the agreement, the Scouts needed to do one of three things before April 25: find new partners who would invest money in the team; sell the team to a local buyer; or relocate the franchise. "The total appearances of the league are best served by the arrangement," Campbell explained in one of the most mind-numbingly dull quotes ever uttered. "The league's overall position has been strengthened by the agreement."

The news of the loan made the front page of the *Kansas City Star*. Thompson couldn't have been happier, and he saw this turn of events as a "great vote of confidence" which "reaffirm[ed] the league's faith both in the present ownership and in Kansas City as a town for a hockey franchise" and showed "how important it [was] to keep [the Scouts'] season ticket drive on a positive approach."[84]

Ah yes, the season ticket drive....

When the news of the NHL's loan dropped, someone at the press conference asked Thompson who was in charge of getting those season tickets sold. In a very telling sign that this franchise was not on the most stable footing management-wise, Thompson said *he wasn't sure who was in charge*! Was it the president of the Chamber of Commerce or some local construction magnate who had once been the chairman of the Jackson County Sports Authority? Who knew? "It wasn't long before someone called those two men and discovered that, no, they were not heading the ticket drive," wrote Steve Marantz in the April 2 edition of the *Hockey News*. "It turned out there was no chairman, and it further turned out that the ticket drive was floundering for want of leadership and organization."[85]

If anyone had any idea how many season tickets had been sold to that point, you would think the Scouts' *president* would have a ballpark idea, but Thompson admitted that no one in the Scouts office, including himself, had even a clue how many season tickets had been purchased. "It became apparent that nobody in the Scouts office was interested enough to shepherd their own life-or-death effort," wrote Marantz.[86] The *Hockey News*' Kansas City correspondent eventually deduced that just "120 new tickets had been sold, leaving the Scouts 3,880 short of their April 15 goal of 8,000. That's assuming the 4,000 ticket holders renew."[87]

Thompson was frustrated that more wasn't being done to help the Scouts. "All I've heard are excuses from the mayor and most of the businessmen," he said, oblivious to the fact that the Scouts had done relatively little themselves to sell tickets. Thompson believed everyone was telling him that his goal of selling 8,000 season tickets was nothing more than a pipe dream, but the face of the Scouts' ownership ground could only gripe that he couldn't see "any effort by the mayor" or anyone else to push ducats onto fans. Thompson was nearing the end of his rope, and his frustrations were beginning to get the better of him.

Mayor Charles Wheeler, Jr., held a press conference to address the growing need to keep the Scouts in town, but all Thompson could retain from the gathering was that Wheeler supposedly believed the Scouts ownership was unstable and needed an infusion of capital. "There are a lot of people who have more money, but that doesn't mean they are willing to commit more cash than we have," said Thompson. "We don't need to apologize for anything.... I've kind of turned my cheek for the last time.... I'm not going to be a political football over this deal." Thompson ended his rant by wondering out loud how many tickets the Scouts could have sold with a "legitimate effort," but that they would "never know" for sure and that they were "entitled to an all-out effort" which they were not getting despite an endless series of pleas since the start of the calendar year.[88]

Despite the temporary end to the Scouts' financial plight, the team still had to deal with their horrendous second-half slide, which saw them go from being a whisker out of the playoffs to miles away from every other competitor in their division. Next on the schedule: the dreaded Philadelphia Flyers.

If ever the Scouts were going to beat Philadelphia to end the winless streak, March 7 was the night. Sure, the Flyers had not lost in 18 games, but Bernie Parent was making his Spectrum debut after missing most of the season due to a pinched nerve in his neck. He was likely a little rusty, and the Scouts could have taken advantage, but it was the Flyers who peppered Denis Herron with a 51-shot barrage, while the Scouts managed just 23 on Parent, including a whopping 10 through two periods. The Flyers were up 3–0 after 40 minutes, and they were in full control when Jean-Guy Lagace scored on a low shot that found the right side of the net. In the end, all that goal did was ruin Parent's shutout as the Flyers romped to an easy 4–1 win.

The Scouts should have also taken advantage of the exhausted Vancouver Canucks on March 10, but the end result was again disappointing. Vancouver was returning home after a grueling seven-game road trip, and this first game back would be the Canucks' fourth in five nights. The *Vancouver Sun*'s Archie McDonald described the Canucks' trip as "the kind of scheduling the Marquis de Sade would have approved," so two points were definitely ripe for the Scouts' taking.[89] Nevertheless, the Canucks dominated the first period and skated rings around their guests. Chuck Arnason gave K.C. a 1–0 lead, but Bobby Lalonde stole the puck from Larry Johnston near Herron's net and sneaked it past the goal line with just two seconds remaining in the frame. Rick Blight and Chris Oddleifson each potted a goal in the second period to put Vancouver up by two. Despite the Canucks' fatigue, they managed a whopping 45 shots on Herron, just the rotten-cherry-on-the-dropped-sundae-festering-under-the-sun-in-a-Dairy-Queen-parking-lot this winless streak had become.

Three nights after the debacle in Vancouver, the Scouts travelled to St. Louis on the way back to Kansas City, but the Blues took a 5–3 decision that officially eliminated the Scouts from playoff contention, and officially freed them up to face Washington in Japan in April.

With absolutely nothing left to play for, the Scouts laid another egg March 16 against Chicago. "I'd have to say this was one of the most disappointing games we've had since I became coach," said Eddie Bush.[90] The Hawks were in a dogfight with Vancouver for the Smythe Division crown, and even though Cliff Koroll admitted it was tough to stay motivated playing against a doormat expansion team, the game was of vital importance, and he scored a hat trick. He opened the scoring at 15:11 of the first, then got lucky as his 50-foot shot bounced past Herron and into the net. Alain Daigle put the Hawks up by three with a power play goal at 5:12 of the second period, but Dave Hudson cut the lead to 3–1 just 0:16 later. Koroll scored his third goal at 12:15, and Pit Martin potted another shortly after to put the game out of reach. Guy Charron notched his team-record 27th goal just 30 seconds into the final period, but Ivan Boldirev restored Chicago's four-goal lead. Even though the Scouts outshot the Hawks, 35–27, the 17th-ranked expansionists fell, 6–3, and extended their winless streak to 16 games.

The schedule didn't get any easier as the Boston Bruins were next in line to take down the Scouts, but early in the contest, it certainly seemed as though the Bruins were doing everything in their power to end the Scouts' streak. Dave Hudson scored his 11th goal just 42 seconds after the opening faceoff, and Gary Croteau doubled the Scouts' lead in the dying minutes of the first period.

And then everything fell apart … again.

The Bruins showed why they were leading the Adams Division when they tied the score with a couple of goals 24 seconds apart in the second period. Jean Ratelle scored on a rebound after Bill McKenzie stopped Bobby Schmautz, and Hank Nowak caught a pass from Wayne Cashman and backhanded the puck past the Scouts' goalie. Gregg Sheppard hammered a 35-foot shot past McKenzie to put the Bruins up by a goal, and they never looked back. It just wasn't the Scouts' night. Gary Bergman claimed Don Marcotte had knocked him down near McKenzie, which allowed Terry O'Reilly to slip the puck past the goal line, but to no avail. Rubbing more salt in the wound, Ratelle scored his second goal on the ensuing power play to seal the 5–2 Boston win.

The Scouts had had plenty of opportunities to end their winless streak, but failed every time. Since the less-than-overwhelming California Golden Seals were visiting Kemper next, there was a chance the streak would mercifully expire. The Scouts must have been shocked to take the ice in front of a team-record 16,219 fans. "I was really concerned about playing well that game," said Charron. "Playing in front of all those people every game you'd go nuts."[91] Of course, there was a reason for such a large crowd for a game against the lowly Seals: $2 tickets! Naturally, those who had already paid as much as $8 for their tickets were furious to hear about the Scouts' last-minute promotion.

The crowd certainly aroused the Scouts early on as Randy Rota scored his 11th goal at 3:41 of the opening period on assists from Guy Charron and Steve Durbano, and then Gary Croteau scored his 15th at 8:59 to put K.C. up by two. The game seemed ripe for the taking, and the Scouts held on to their 2–0 lead until 12:51 of the third period, when California's Bob Girard scored on a 15-foot shot that beat Denis Herron on his left glove side. As was now Scouts tradition, the roof caved in once again 1:37 later as Larry Johnston flubbed a clearing attempt, Jim Moxey dished the puck over to an open Fred Ahern standing in front of the net, and he potted his 15th goal to tie the game 2–2, which is how it ended.

At this point, the Scouts' second ridiculous winless streak in three months was becoming morbidly fascinating. "I look at the games that we were in close and really competitive and maybe a stupid penalty here, a stupid penalty there, or something," recalled Robin Burns. "Winning breeds winning, and losing breeds losing. It just seems that we would steal defeat from the jaws of victory so many times it was almost like a joke, and then sometimes you get into the latter part of a hockey game, and you're winning 2–1, and you're saying, 'Oh my God, we're actually winning,' and then you'd end up losing it 3–2, so it was a difficult time for sure."

As the Scouts continued to find new ways to lose, Burns found plenty of creative ways to describe the team's woes. "An entanglement of troubles," he said before blurting out a few more one-liners. "A spontaneous nurturing of the fruits of disappointment," he uttered, before hitting the nail one last time: "A demented departure from the reality of hockey."[92] The Scouts' once-promising season had turned into an absolute farce. After such a collapse of epic proportions coupled with the direst financial forecast possible, there really was nothing the players could do but laugh at their miserable lot in life. A series of punch lines and giggles were all that were left as the team went through the motions to close out the season. Oddly enough, as the Scouts were plunging towards their nadir, the once-laughable Washington Capitals were winning a few here and there. The Capitals' coaching change had done wonders, while the Scouts' new coach barely made an impact at all.

On March 21, the Scouts put up a comically awful *eight* shots versus Buffalo. The heroic Denis Herron performed his magic, as usual, and held the Sabres to just three goals on 37 shots. He must have wondered what higher power had it in for him, because the Scouts not only performed poorly in front of him, they also had two goals disallowed.

"That's what happens when you're an expansion team," he exclaimed after game officials posted on the scoreboard that the Scouts had taken two shots in the third period before taking them both away. "What are they trying to do? Humiliate us? They took the shots off to make it look like we didn't have any in the third period. Isn't that great for a big league town?" The Scouts weren't any happier when a controversial Brian Spencer goal counted. Spencer himself even thought it was a phantom goal. "When I looked at the replay, I saw it wasn't in, but this makes up for assists and goals I had in the past that weren't counted," he said after the game.[93] Steve Durbano was so disgusted by his team's effort that he declared the Scouts the worst team he had ever played for, a sentiment which did not change decades later any time he was interviewed about his NHL career.

Durbano also lived up to his not-so-cute nickname once again. The Sabres' Lee Fogolin was looking to make a name for himself, so he jumped an unsuspecting Durbano and landed a couple of good shots on the Scouts' resident goon. Well, that turned out to be one hell of a mistake. The kid was safely in the penalty box while Durbano was at the Kansas City bench getting a sip of H_2O. Suddenly, Durbano beelined it toward Fogolin like an enraged bull rushing at a matador, and he threw a water bottle the youngster's way before skating back to his own bench, mission accomplished.

The Sabres didn't take too kindly to Durbano's gesture and leaped over the boards to get at the Scouts' pugilist. "I thought I was going to die," recalled Henry Boucha. "I dropped my gloves and stick and skated out there to try to stop some of the guys, and all of a sudden everyone just stopped. They just stood there looking into the corner. When I turned around, there was Durbo, standing in the corner with two hands on his stick, swinging it like a baseball bat. They all knew how crazy he was and nobody from the Buffalo team wanted anything to do with that." The referees finally reached the rabid wolverine and led him off the ice as fans threw just about everything they had bought at the concession stand at Durbano, who finished the game with 21 penalty minutes and earned himself a two-game suspension.[94]

"Things have got to get better in the days ahead," Bush remarked after the Buffalo game.[95] Unfortunately, things got worse. Poor Denis Herron may have endured the most difficult three-game stretch of games in the history of professional goaltending. Over a personal four-day stretch of hell from March 27 to 30, Herron faced 59 shots from Montreal, 53 from the New York Rangers, and 52 from Los Angeles.

Robin Burns remembers the Montreal game, an 8–2 loss in which he had a "ringside seat" for a special milestone moment. For the second year in a row, almost to the day, Guy Lafleur scored his 50th goal of the season while Burns was assigned to check the future Hall of Famer. Burns' father must have had a long memory, since he clearly remembered that his son had developed a penchant for letting Canadiens legends score milestone goals against him. This time, when Lafleur potted his 50th, the elder Burns chided his son: "Congrats ... you did it again."[96]

Against L.A., the Scouts actually got out to a 3–0 lead after just 8:21, and the winless streak appeared on the verge of dying, but as had been the custom all season long, the Scouts blew it. L.A. narrowed the gap to 3–2 before Phil Roberto scored an insurance goal, but no Scouts lead was ever truly safe. With the score tied at 5–5, Gary Croteau put K.C. up by one to give the Scouts some hope, but the vastly superior Kings scored three times in the final frame to win the goal-fest, 8–6. Gary Bergman picked up two assists on the night, the final multi-point game of his illustrious career.

"No matter what you say about this, it's awful," said a downtrodden Eddie Bush. "I'll tell you, it's tough. I'm just ... just frustrated now. It's a good thing there's two kinds of luck," Bush added. "Otherwise, we wouldn't have any."[97]

The most memorable part of the evening, however, was a wing-ding between the Kings' Dave Hutchison and the Scouts' Steve Durbano. The two hotheads let their emotions get the best of them and started jawing at each other at center ice. Hutchison was said to have knocked Durbano's helmet off, snatched his toupee, placed it on his stick, and sent it back Durbo's way. Well, off into orbit Durbano went once again in what would become his last official appearance at Kemper. When he arrived in the penalty box, Durbano grabbed some pucks in a bucket and launched them at pretty much anyone who wasn't either a Scout or a Scouts fan. He got the toss, but no way that was going to stop him from tossing Eddie Bush's practice pylons onto the ice. With nothing left to throw onto the ice, off came his skates and onto the frozen surface they landed. Durbano's ballistic behavior resulted in another 19 minutes in penalties.[98]

As disappointing as it was for the Scouts to see their miserable winless streak so close to ending that they could taste it, if you think things got any easier, think again as Herron withstood a 43-shot barrage from L.A. on April 3, which of course resulted in another loss. In the final game of the regular season, Herron faced a relatively normal 35 shots against Vancouver, but the Scouts still lost, 5–2. The season-ender brought the Scouts' hellish winless streak to an abominable 27 games, a brand new NHL record!

Robin Burns recalled one not-so-memorable moment that pretty much summed up the Scouts' entire second half. "A young fan ... he was yelling, 'Robin, Robin, a puck!' So I flipped the puck over the boards ... and didn't the kid miss it, hit him right in the head, and he ended up with about four or five stitches. It was just one of those stupid memorable moments when you end up going, 'Holy shit, you know things are going bad when you're flipping a puck to a fan, and the kid misses it, hits him in the forehead and bang!'"

The following fact is almost too unbelievable to be true, but in the last 44 games of the season, the Scouts won only *once*, and while many would call that a collapse of absolutely Biblical proportions, Denis Herron disagreed when he was asked what happened to cause the team to fall apart so dramatically. "I don't think it was that much of a collapse as much as the teams were a little better than us.... It's pretty much from the All-Star Game all the way down to the end of the season, and what happened is teams started to push a little bit harder for the playoffs and probably, of those 44 games, we came close quite a few times … maybe luck, or stuff like that didn't go our way, but I don't think it was a collapse really."

Officially, the Scouts' winless streak came to a merciful end at 27 games, because there were no more games to lose on the schedule. Unofficially, the streak was still kicking, screaming, and making a scene as the Scouts prepared for their historic tour of Japan.

Robin Burns: "The team photo was taken as a memento. KC that year [1975–1976] never took a team photo, so we all got together for the shot" (Ron Lalonde collection).

OVERTIME

•• 8 ••

The Coca-Cola Bottlers' Cup

Nineteen seventy-six truly was a unique period in hockey history. Consider the fact that two NHL teams' owners, general managers, and players *all* agreed that playing in Japan *for fun,* in what players would later learn was a spectacularly inappropriate and precarious setting, would be totally acceptable. Today, there is no way the NHL would send one, let alone two of its franchises to Japan to play an exhibition series for no other reason other than to put on a good show. General managers and team owners would have absolutely no interest in risking their millionaire meal tickets' health and safety to play in a series where there was nothing to gain but a small brass trophy. Sending players to the Olympic Games, a tournament which generates millions of dollars, is never a sure thing, so the Coca-Cola Cup would have absolutely no chance of existing in the 21st century. Besides, after witnessing the 2018–2019 St. Louis Blues climb out of last place at the All-Star break, qualify for the playoffs, and then win the Stanley Cup, the NHL could never definitively confirm any particular teams for an overseas series. There would be just too much risk of plans falling apart. There simply would not be enough time to promote and prepare for the event.

In 1976, however, conditions were just perfect for an NHL invasion of Japan.

"I think [the NHL] just wanted to float a trial balloon and just see, because some people said that Japanese hockey was starting to come on," said Robin Burns about the NHL's decision to send the Scouts and Capitals to Japan to compete against each other in a four-game exhibition series for something called the Coca-Cola Bottlers' Cup. Some newspapers reported that the event was organized "as an expression of goodwill marking the U.S. bicentennial."[1]

When Bernie Wolfe was asked in 2019 why the NHL Japan series was organized in the first place, he said:

> It had to do with introducing hockey to Japan. I don't believe that there had been any games there, and even though we weren't the Montreal Canadiens or the Philadelphia Flyers, we were still NHL players that would have the speed of the game and the finesse, and our skating ability would impress the Japanese to no end, and get them kind of excited about possibilities of hockey coming to Japan. I think it was a safe choice having us go, but I think whoever they sent—you got to remember this is the NHL, they weren't sending a pee-wee hockey team—they were sending NHLers to a place that had never seen a NHL game.... We would be putting on a very impressive show.

Many wondered why the league would bother sending teams to Japan in the first place. After all, what exactly could the NHL gain in its efforts to promote the game in a land where hockey was about as foreign as Martian apple pie? Like many of the league's decisions in the 1970s, it may have revolved around the WHA, or more importantly, the notion of thwarting the rival league, which kept talking about expanding beyond North America. In the end, the WHA never followed through on those plans, but at the time, anything seemed possible.

In the years leading up to the NHL Japan Series, many popular North American and European sports had made their way to the Land of the Rising Sun. There were not only the 1964 Tokyo Summer Olympics and the 1972 Sapporo Winter Games, but also English soccer events, Australian rugby matches, Major League Baseball barnstorming tours, NBA-ABA All-Star exhibition games, and American

The NHL Japan series generated much excitement in Tokyo (Ron Lalonde collection).

college All-Star games. Now it was hockey's turn to take center stage. Lee Kavetski of *Pacific Stars & Stripes* wrote at the time that, "Ice hockey [had] seen a marked surge in popularity and participation among Japanese high school, college and semi-pro industrial teams in recent years. But this will be the first opportunity for Japanese rink fans—and American military and civilian personnel stationed in the area, too—to see the NHL professional glitter game."[2]

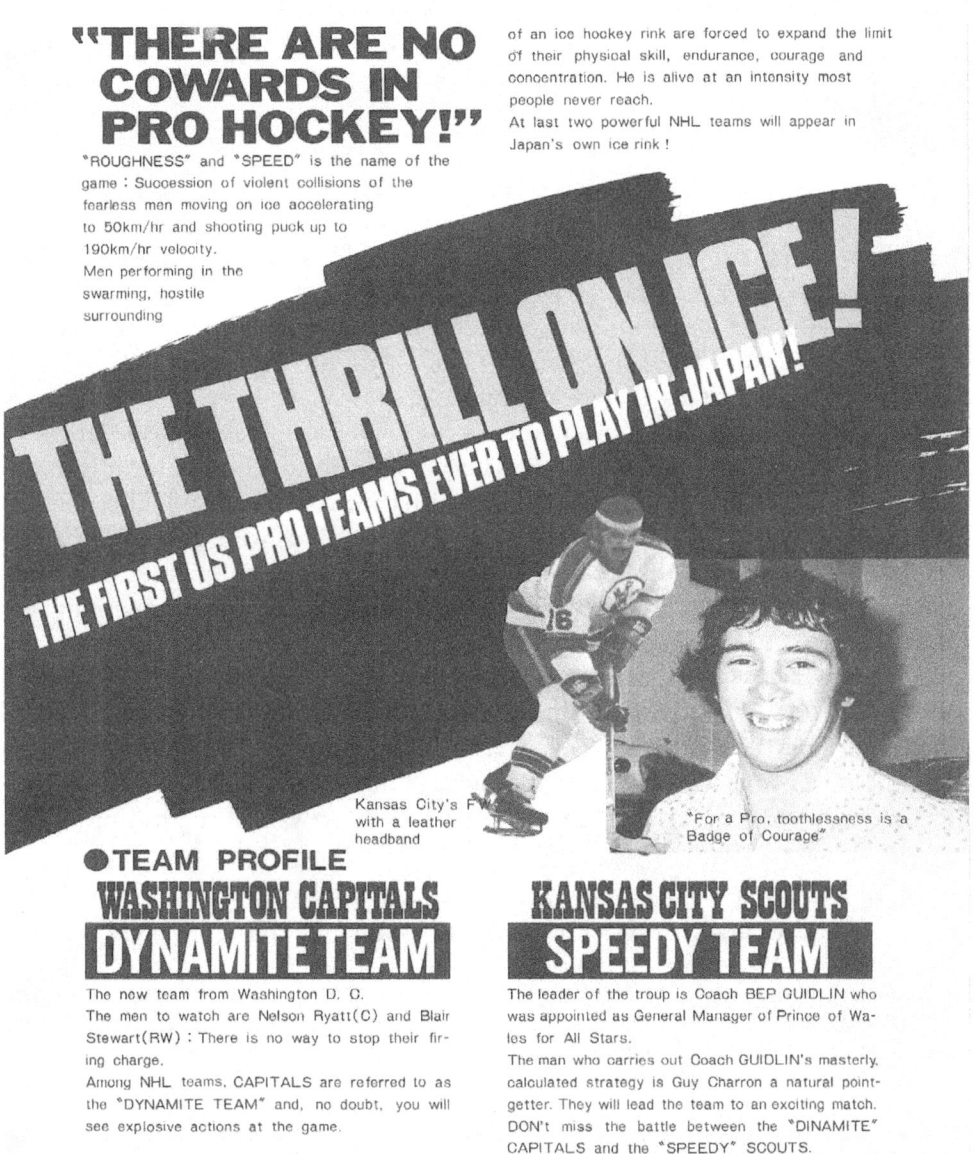

The rhetoric included in the advertising for the NHL Japan series placed much emphasis on the grit, speed, and flash of professional hockey players (Ron Lalonde collection).

On the surface, the idea of sending two of the worst teams in NHL history to promote the sport overseas made no sense. Surely, the league could have sent better ambassadors to Japan, but the NHL's reasoning did in fact make sense. The last thing the NHL wanted was to see weeks of planning and preparation go down the toilet because one of the series participants got hot at the wrong time and qualified for the playoffs. Thankfully, the league figured correctly that both cellar-dwellers would be mathematically eliminated from playoff contention by January, so no one ended up with egg on their face. It stands to reason that if the Scouts, who were 11–21–4 on December 28, and were just one point out of a playoff spot, had played at the same pace just a few weeks longer, the NHL could never have found an opponent for the Washington Capitals, and the Coca-Cola Cup series would never have happened.

Opposing Philosophies

At a pre-series press conference, Eddie Bush joked that this four-game set was "the Japanese version of the Stanley Cup."[3] Tommy McVie, however, certainly bought into the notion that there was a huge prize awaiting his players at the end of the series. Make no mistake, the demanding McVie fully expected his players to capture the Coca-Cola Cup. Before the series began, he admitted he would be "very, very unhappy if [the Capitals didn't] win all four with the Scouts."[4] Despite the wonderful accommodations and the holiday atmosphere, the Capitals were going to work hard every day. "Right up until we left from Washington," said Ron Lalonde, "we continued to practice even though our season was over. We flew out to L.A. the night before and practised in the L.A. Forum before flying from L.A. to Japan."

On their way to Japan, the Capitals had a three-hour layover in Hawaii because the plane just ahead of them had blown a wheel on the runway. Wolfe remembered the team got "a little bit wasted" at the bar, which infuriated McVie. In fact, he was so unimpressed by his team's loosey-goosey behavior that as soon as the Caps landed in Japan, he called a practice. "I'm not sure if Tommy was trying to impress anybody," Wolfe said.

> But there were just a whole bunch of Japanese reporters and fans leaning over the boards with their cameras, and I remember the workout was so hard, a couple of our players actually puked right over the boards on cameras the Japanese reporters were holding.
>
> We were proud to represent Washington. We wanted to win. Tommy McVie took this as serious as a playoff game or a regular-season game. This was definitely not a vacation. He practiced us really hard. We had curfews. He expected a lot from us on the ice. In no way was this a fun trip.

Wolfe then corrected himself. "Well, it turned out we enjoyed ourselves, but Tommy McVie didn't look at this as a vacation."

According to Denis Herron, the atmosphere in the Scouts' camp was far different. "At that point, you had [Tommy McVie], and he was arrogant, and 'We're gonna beat you guys...,' and we said, 'We're not gonna go if we're not going for fun. We're going to go give you a good show, but we're not going there to compete. We just did that all year, and we're going to go there to have a good time, and they finally agreed to that ... we competed well, but [were] less intense than Washington."

While the Scouts may not have made themselves throw up over winning an exhibition series like the Capitals did, according to Robin Burns, they did not coast through the games. "We played with intensity," he said. "It wasn't like an All-Star Game, you know what I mean? There was hitting. There was fights. It was excellent hockey." The Scouts simply viewed this once-in-a-lifetime opportunity differently from their Washington counterparts. "The Capitals, it was like they were going for the Stanley Cup," Burns remembered. "We went one day to visit a beer factory the day of a game, but the Washington players were not allowed to go; they were in to have an afternoon nap and [get] ready for the game. We took advantage of sight-seeing as well as socializing with the people." Would the Scouts' relaxed attitude rouse them from their funk and lead them to victory, or would the Caps' intense training regimen pay off? It was time for Bush's and McVie's opposing philosophies to collide.

Praised and Pampered

To say the teams and their wives were spoiled by their Japanese hosts would be an understatement. Wolfe remembers the warm reception that awaited when the Caps' plane touched down in Japan. "When we got off the plane, it said, 'Welcome Washington Capitals: Team of beautiful women and brave men,' and my wife laughed because here she's almost seven months pregnant, and after fifteen hours on a plane, she said she looked anything but beautiful."[5]

"I've never been treated like this in my life," said McVie at a lavish reception two days before the opening game.[6] He then broke one of his false teeth on an hors d'oeuvre, so not everything went perfectly.

The Caps and Scouts may have been laughingstocks back home, but make no mistake, in Japan they were treated like champions. "Yes, they are the two bottom teams in the league," said Jack Sakazaki, a highly-placed executive for Video Promotions, "but it doesn't matter because they are so much above the standards of everyone else playing here."[7]

Promoters were very excited to host the two North American teams almost no one in Japan had ever seen or read about. Since the sport of hockey was unknown to most, advertisers had to go out of their way to hyperbolize the speed, toughness, and overall greatness of professional players. In one ad promoting the series, the Capitals were referred to as "Dynamite Team" and it was written that "no doubt, you will see explosive actions at the game." As for the Scouts, they were referred to as "Speedy Team." There were other unintentionally funny lines all over this ad, such as "There are no cowards in pro hockey!" and "For a Pro, toothlessness is a Badge of Courage." The ad also explained that "Men performing in the swarming, hostile surrounding of an ice hockey rink are forced to expand of their physical skill, endurance, courage and concentration. He is alive at an intensity most people never reach."[8]

The event cost a reported $400,000, and the Coca-Cola Bottling Company

Robin Burns: "This little girl liked my jacket and came over with an orange as a gift. I'm sure someone most likely sent her over for a picture. This took place at one of the banquets given in our honour" (Robin Burns collection).

reportedly forked over about 75 per cent of that total. Players from both squads would receive $1,250 for participating plus a $45 per diem, and all expenses would be paid. During the Tokyo portion of the tour, everyone stayed at the first-rate New Otani Hotel, whose exterior was used as the headquarters of the nefarious Osato Chemicals in the 1967 James Bond movie *You Only Live Twice*. During their stay, the players took in sumo wrestling, a traditional dinner at a grill house, and a Kabuki theater production. The wives and girlfriends were taken on a tour of Kyoto and passed the time shopping and getting manicures at the hotel. "Some girls never left the hotel when they found they could get such bargains in facials, manicures and getting their hair done," said Mike Lampman's wife, Robin.[9]

The players were free to do as they pleased in their spare time, but McVie kept his troops on a tight leash. Jack Lynch remembered the Japan trip fondly, but he also recalled not having all that much down time, mainly due to the task at hand: beating the Scouts. "There really wasn't a whole lot in terms of touring or that kind of thing.... The wives had a chance to do that, so they would organize events for the wives, but ... we were focused on winning, so our practice time might have been 11 o'clock in the morning, and Tommy always practiced for an hour and a half, two hours. By the time that was over, your day was shot in terms of any extracurricular activities."

When the Caps managed to find a bit of free time, the culture shock sometimes made it difficult to adapt to their new surroundings. Bernie Wolfe spent a lot of his time with his wife, but she didn't have an easy time adjusting to Japan. "My wife was pregnant, and not doing well being able to hold down a lot of food," he said. "I remember spending an afternoon looking for food that she might be able to eat and keep down, and she saw an American club sandwich on the menu, so we bought it and when she took a bite of it she looked at it, and rather than turkey it was raw fish. That made her want to vomit. She then ordered strawberries, which she was able to eat, but three strawberries were $8 back then, which was a lot of money."

Wolfe also remembered the unusual procedure one needed to follow when ordering in a restaurant. "In restaurants, when you went to eat, they had a display of each of the meals in a big glass counter so what you would do is before you sat down you would take a look at the glass counter and pick which meal you wanted because you wouldn't have been able to explain it to the server because of the language barrier."

Going to the grocery store also proved a challenge. "No one spoke English in Japan in those days," recalled Wolfe. "I remember going to a supermarket and ... all I was asking for was butter, and no one could understand what I was saying, but then I met a woman from France who was in the store, and I'm able to speak French because I grew up in Montreal, and I asked her and she pointed to me that it was in a different area ... their butter is in a tin can, almost like a sardine can; not like what we're used to in Canada and the United States."

Game One: Wednesday, April 14, 1976

The series opened at 6:30 p.m. at the Tsukisamu ice rink in Sapporo, the site of the 1972 Winter Olympics, in front of 4,500 fans. "The arena was really chilly," remembered Mike Lampman. "It almost reminded you of your childhood days in some of the old arenas." Even though shivering was an inconvenience fans would have to endure to witness their first NHL game, tickets weren't discounted in the least. In fact, some cost up to $26 apiece, no chump change in 1976.

In the first period, during a goal-mouth scramble in front of Denis Herron, the Caps took a 2–1 lead on a goal by Mike Marson. At 12:17, Bob Sirois made it 3–1 on an assist from Pete Scamurra. Washington beat Herron twice more in the second frame, while Guy Charron scored once on Wolfe. The Caps sat back on their 5–2 lead in the third period, boring the fans and disappointing McVie. With 23 seconds left in the game, one Caps' player yelled out, "Pearly gates!" referring to the string of pearls each player on the winning team would receive.[10]

Sirois was the biggest star of the lackluster series opener, scoring two goals and picking up an assist. Playing on an Olympic-size rink that was 15 feet wider than NHL ice surfaces agreed with the swift French Canadian. "Skating is my best point and the wide rink really gave me room," he said. Rick Bragnalo and Tony White also scored singles for Washington, while Gary Bergman picked up the first Kansas City goal in the opening frame.

According to a game description in the *Washington Post*, both teams looked groggy and listless, leaving many fans disappointed. "I expected more fighting and blood," lamented 47-year-old Keisuke Atarashi, likely because promoters had promised fans violence in order to draw a larger crowd.[11] One Japanese reporter explained that NHL players' "business is kicking, fighting and bloodshed," leading many naïve fans to believe hockey was essentially *Rollerball* on ice.[12] Later in the series, a flustered television commentator had to explain to viewers why no one had been badly injured yet, a comment that would surely lead to a firestorm of criticism on *Twitter* today.

The Japanese were not your typical hockey fanatics, and Sapporo's crowds were anything but ordinary. McVie described the atmosphere in Sapporo as if "they'd put 5,000 mannequins in the seats."[13] Hartland Monahan compared the Sapporo crowd to "a morgue."[14] According to Ron Lalonde, the fans in Sapporo "were really quiet. They were almost polite. You'd hear clapping like at a play or something … polite applause."

Bernie Wolfe also remembers the crowds being extremely respectful. "The Japanese people are very polite, and so they don't boo and they don't cheer. Back then anyways. So it was quiet, but it was sold out. The place was packed. But you could hear a pin drop, so when a puck hit the boards, or anything like that, there was a huge echo."

According to Robin Burns, 95 per cent of the fans in Japan were "shirt-and-tie businessmen, and we'd score a goal and it was like 'OHHHHH!' or there'd be a number of hard hits … and it was just mild applause." For these competitors, who were used to hearing angry, testosterone-fuelled fans shouting obscenities about the players' sexual orientation or their mothers' fictional bedroom history, this four-game exhibition tour was certainly an eye-opening experience.

Fans also had trouble grasping the subtleties of the game. "I remember, on occasion," remembered Mike Lampman, "when the puck would go into the stands, they would politely throw it back." In fact, many, if not all professional Japanese baseball teams forbid fans from keeping foul balls, so it is likely the fans believed this custom was also observed in hockey. While Japanese spectators may have craved blood like the animals who populated the Philadelphia Spectrum, they had much more sophisticated arena culinary tastes than the average fan, choosing sake and noodle soup over beer and hot dogs.

Game Two: Thursday, April 15, 1976

As the Scouts and Capitals were gearing up for game two, trouble was brewing back in Kansas City. The season-ticket drive had as much momentum as a World War I tank driving through No Man's Land, and the dying Scouts lay entangled in barbed wire, begging to be saved. The $300,000 loan from the NHL had all but evaporated, forcing Ed Thompson to lay off members of the front office, including Sid Abel and Baz Bastien. "It was depressing," admitted the team's president.[15] It was looking very likely that the next three games would be the last to feature players wearing the Scouts' blue, red, and yellow.

Game one had been a relative disappointment, so promoters and club officials were relieved when both teams brought their "A" game for the second contest. Steve Durbano, in particular, made quite an impression on those in attendance. With Washington up, 3–1, the Scouts' resident goon skated through the Caps' defense to narrow the gap to a single goal and prove he was able to play good hockey when the mood struck him. That mood didn't last long. Durbano later drew a hooking penalty, then picked up another two minutes for angrily slapping the puck, breaking his stick, and hurling the lumber at the referee. The crowd stood silent until a Kansas City wife yelled out, "You stupid referee!" which made everyone laugh.[16]

Ron Low got his first start of the series for Washington, and he played a solid game, but he almost didn't see it through to the end. He was knocked hard into a goal post, and he needed the help of team physician Arthur Holmes to get back onto his skates.

In the third period, the Caps scored three times, including two power-play goals in a 42-second span, to give them a 6–2 win and extend the Scouts' miserable winless streak to an unofficial 29 games. For the win, the Caps skated off with cassette tape recorders. Gerry Meehan scored twice for the victors, while Sirois, White, Lampman and Lemieux scored singles. Jean-Guy Lagace scored the other Kansas City goal.

The Scouts knew that down 2–0 in the series, their backs were against the wall, but they still talked tough. "We have 24 hours to rest our aches and pains and we haven't started to fight yet," said Gary Croteau. "We're going to win that third game in Tokyo."[17]

Jim McElmury (#2) and Harvey Bennett (#27) in action as photographers snap a few shots during game 3 of the NHL Japan series (Robin Burns collection).

The players had put on a great show. One Sapporo television director was "dancing at the end of his microphone lead," according to the *Washington Post*'s John Saar. Young boys crowded the glass, hoping to get a stick or an autograph. "We skated better and hit harder," said Meehan. "We are not just going through the motions. We are here to win."[18]

Fans also witnessed their first NHL fight, courtesy of Washington's Blair Stewart and Kansas City's Larry Johnston, a spectacle which left those in attendance dead silent. It was an understandable reaction as one woman in the crowd pointed out, "We are not accustomed to seeing the foreigners fighting in public."[19] Were fans suddenly offended now that the promise of violence had been delivered? On the contrary, according to Ron Lalonde, "they would giggle. It was funny to them to see hockey players fighting on the ice." For ornery Canadians to fight on the ice should not have been surprising to anyone who read the press releases leading up to the series. In fact, in one press release translated into English, it was claimed that Canadians often "learn to fight on the ice before they fight on the street, when they are little."

These burly professional hockey players could not have looked more alien to the average Japanese spectator. The *Washington Post*'s John Saar described the players as having "cut glamorous piratical images." These dashing, swashbuckling, bloodthirsty foreign pirates were invading Japan to provide its people with a breathtaking, violent, and athletic demonstration the likes of which they had never seen. TV cameras and newspaper photographers could not get over the lack of teeth in the players' mouths, not to mention the scars on many of their faces. On one broadcast, according to Saar, "viewers had a dentist's eye view of Caps' winger Hart Monahan's missing teeth. 'I told them they got knocked out in a fight with my wife,'" Monahan joked.

Players looked menacingly huge, yet they were so swift on their skates that they left university players attending one practice at a loss for words. "They are so … dynamic," said one awestruck 19-year-old. It was almost unfathomable that the Scouts and Capitals were actually the two *worst* teams in professional hockey. "I can't believe it," said Akenichi Tsuchida, a former player himself and a passionate supporter of the game. "They are so strong [and] powerful."[20]

"One of the other funny things was the Japanese people were enthralled with the fact that hockey players had no teeth," said Ron Lalonde. "The reporters, after the game, they'd come in with their cameras and they wanted the players to take their teeth out and get a picture taken, and they thought that was hilarious." Even the intense Tommy McVie let his guard down ever-so-briefly and showed a side of himself even his players had rarely, if ever, seen. "The first and only time we ever saw anything where he would let his character come through … he took his teeth out," remembered Ron Lalonde. "He could [take] a puck and put it in his mouth, and the first time he did it was in Japan in our series, in the bus. He was happy we had won, and somebody egged him on or something, and we've got some pictures of him, but that was the first time I saw a lighter side of Tom McVie."

Reporters were also fascinated by how two teams could beat the hell out of each other on the ice yet socialize afterwards. "I was working with Lange skates," remembered Robin Burns, "and we had a distributor in Japan, and he took us all out to a sumo wrestler's restaurant, and I took three, four guys on my team, and I took [Jack Lynch and Yvon Labre] on the Capitals team that I played with in Hershey."

One reporter asked Yvon Labre how the players could possibly accept staying at the same hotel and socializing like old friends before skating onto the ice and beating the hell out of each other. "It's all part of our job. That's what we get paid for," Labre responded. "We don't want to hurt anybody; we just want to make a good living." The reporters looked at Labre quizzically, hoping for a more satisfying answer, but they got none, so they went to Gary Croteau. "A lot of us have played together on other teams and are good friends," he said before explaining that competition trumped friendship and that players could not accept "letting the other man take money out of your pockets. There's no friendship on the ice."[21]

McVie's opinion on fraternization was about as blunt as an anvil landing on Wile E. Coyote's head. "There was a lot of guys that players on each team knew pretty well, and they would fraternize a bit," recalled Ron Lalonde, "but McVie, he didn't support that at all.... The one thing you didn't [do] during a warm-up, especially on an NHL rink was, you didn't turn around in warm-up and start talking to the other team. Tommy McVie was real old school and these guys are taking money and bread out of your pocket. If you want to talk to those guys, do it outside of the rink; don't do it in front of the fans."

So that's what Robin Burns did with a few of his friends on the Capitals. Hockey players had always kept their personal and professional lives separate, but by the 1970s, they began fraternizing much more openly. In the long run, this type of fraternizing led to greater bonds between players and helped them gain power over team owners.

Game Three: Saturday, April 17, 1976

After Ron Lalonde was interviewed about his experiences competing for the Coca-Cola Cup, he sent me a scan of a promotional poster for the games in Tokyo. The poster hailed the NHL Japan series as "the biggest sports event of 1976" with a "rocketing puck at speed of 190km/hr … that's professional." Lalonde also mailed me a rare "Coca-Cola Bottlers' Cup Pro Ice Hockey Series" program, which contained several sections educating the average Japanese spectator, many of whom had never seen a hockey game. Lalonde also provided me with a translation of most of the program, although the origins of this document are unknown. The translation may not be totally accurate, but it does provide insight into how the Japanese perceived professional hockey players. Here are a few snippets, mistakes and all, from the program's translation:

- "The ice hockey is the fastest field game."
- "When they wear colour uniform, it is just like a light exposure."
- "Bobby Jull the famous in NHL has a record of puck speed of 190 kph. literally the speed of light."[22]
- "Many players say quite often, after the game, in the change room. What is the symbol of ice hockey? What? Players have false teeth! The Japanese might

- laugh about it, but in Canada and the States, more dareing players have spaces between their teeth."
- "Crash on the ice—it is the most attractive and high light of professional hockey. Players take their teeth out before they change in their change room. Some stern faces have marks on the foreheads. But when they take their teeth out, these same faces change funny faces. Even when they are excited and playing body check, their faces seem to have a slight smile because of the absence of their teeth. First thing after the game they put their teeth in. They are so excited and quite often they forget where they put their teeth, or put in someone else's teeth. Each time this happens, they say 'Where is my teeth?'"
- "Hockey game sometimes develop to group wrestling or boxing, and make observers excited."

The Scouts and Capitals had made quite an impression on the Japanese press and spectators. That much was obvious despite the challenges presented by English. While the original game program, written almost exclusively in Japanese, was printed before a single game had been played, the translated document was released either during or after the series, as it includes references to the teams' respective styles of play, and how it impressed fans in attendance. "After the recovery from long tired trip in the second game, they showed us a very active play. You know they are professional when you watch their speed. We saw that the Capitals attacks straight but the Scouts have very skillful side passes. However both teams had very skillful defence and offense. Many players say 'We aren't professional, if we can't make the observers happy.' They surely play hockey for people who observe and enjoy." In the end, it didn't really matter that a few words were mangled; the Japanese spoke the language of hockey after all!

After a successful foray into Northern Japan, the players travelled south to Tokyo for games three and four. "Tokyo was a big, busy city," explained Bernie Wolfe. "Sapporo was cold; there was snow on the ground. It was dark, kind of dingy, you know, with the mountains … very different from Tokyo…. People were elegantly dressed in Tokyo, but very basically dressed in Sapporo … workmen-like, working-type clothes in Sapporo. I'm sure it's changed completely, but in 1976 that's what it was like."

"City-wise, Sapporo was not as clean," recalled Denis Herron, "because I remember when I went to Tokyo, I said, 'Oh my God, it is so clean here.' You took a cab, you could eat on the floor of the car, it was so clean. Everybody was wearing a mask because of pollution … and everybody wore blue corduroy suits. That's what I remember from Japan."

"Climate wise, Sapporo, that's the north, and it was more like winter, so it was much cooler. They had some experience with hockey," remembered Ron Lalonde. "Tokyo, it seemed hockey [was] out of place. Huge city with main streets. I remember the big sort of news was McDonald's had opened up a store in Tokyo, but they were soy burgers. Meat was hard to come by in Japan, and so we all had to go and try a hamburger from Japan, but it wasn't the most tasty we'd ever had."

Fans in both cities looked and acted very differently as well. "Tokyo was a little

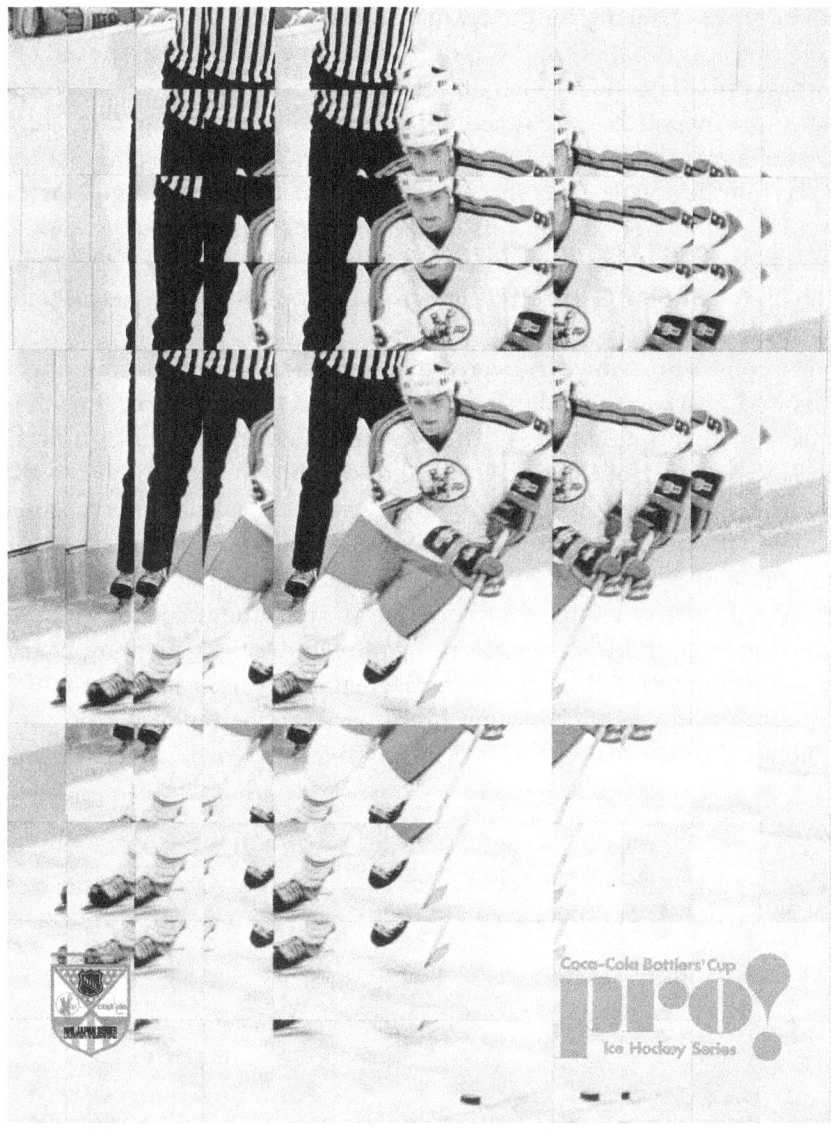

This dizzying Coca-Cola Cup program is definitely a product of its time, and it is now a rare collector's item (Ron Lalonde collection).

more uptight," said Robin Burns. "Sapporo might have been a little looser; the fans were a little looser." They were also very respectful of others' personal property, as Burns recalled in the same interview. "Steve Durbano, he left his wallet on a boot tray, and on the way to the rink he realized it. He went back in a cab, and sure enough his wallet was still sitting on that boot tray. They never touched it."

After a one-day layoff, the series resumed at Tokyo's National Yoyogi Stadium. A crowd of 9,200, bolstered by many North American fans, attended the 6 p.m. contest. The atmosphere at the rink was far different than in Sapporo. A U.S. Army brass band played in the stands, and on the sidelines there were cheerleaders, decked out in Coca-Cola-sponsored uniforms, from a nearby American school. Around the rink were banners cheering on the teams. In the middle was the very benign "Go, Teams Go," flanked by Scouts and Capitals logos on each end. On the left of the banner were the words "Hit'M Hard Scouts!" in red letters on a white background, while on the right was the much more racially insensitive "Scalp'M Capitals!" in white letters on a blue background. The red carpet was laid out for the players, and a huge table displaying the geisha dolls that would be awarded to that night's winners was placed right next to where the players exited the dressing room to head out onto the ice. Players from each team were introduced in numerical order, and much like at the annual NHL All-Star Game, the players skated out onto the ice and saluted their adoring fans.

Playing conditions, however, were beyond farcical. The rink contained all sorts of hazards and quirks that today's NHLPA would never accept. For one thing, a sheet of ice was installed *on top of* the Olympic swimming pool. In fact, in photos of the Tokyo games, one can see several diving boards hovering above the net at one end of the improvised rink. The slushy ice surface was not exactly conducive to a smooth, free-flowing NHL game. "It was wet," said Yvon Labre after game three. "Swimming pool ice. That kind of soft ice slows down the game. You just can't carry the puck." The ice was so awful and rough that the puck bounced around awkwardly. When Labre was told there was a swimming pool under the rink floor, he responded, "Thank God we didn't fall through. It was wet enough on the ice."[23]

The poor lighting created another nightmare for goaltenders, who could barely see the puck speeding at their heads. Making matters worse, there was no glass or

The Scouts and Capitals all lined up after being introduced just prior to game 3 in Tokyo (Robin Burns collection).

screen behind the net, but rather fishing nets, to protect fans. Wolfe remembers it as being "sort of like a boomerang.... The net would go back and then throw the puck forward again, so you also had to be careful on a high shot that you didn't get hit in the back of the head on a rebound."

Wolfe remembers Chuck Arnason giving him trouble due to the lethal combination of his nasty slap shot and fishing-net-topped boards. "He could really shoot the puck and the lighting was very bad, and he shot them high, so.... I was always kind of nervous about him ripping one and not being able to see it, and I know a couple of times he hit high ones off that netting and then the puck would just ricochet off that and you would never know where it [was] going. You had as much concern when it came off the netting, of hitting you in the back of the head as when he shot it hitting you in the front of the head, so I remember Chuck Arnason was very tough."

The boards themselves were also a little shorter than normal, and with no plexiglass at the ends of the rink, players risked flying overboard if they were checked at just the right angle, but that wasn't the players' only issue. "There was nothing really holding [the boards] back other than some cement blocks all around," explained Ron Lalonde, "so when you hit it, there was lots of give to it, but beyond the boards there was more ice."

"The side boards were, golly, they were just kind of like nailed on, and they were rickety ... if you tried to check a player into the boards, I really think the boards

Steve Durbano leads the Scouts onto the ice for game 3 in Tokyo. Behind him are Gary Bergman, Larry Johnston, and Chuck Arnason. Note the table to the players' left and the geisha dolls that were awarded to the winner of the game (Robin Burns collection).

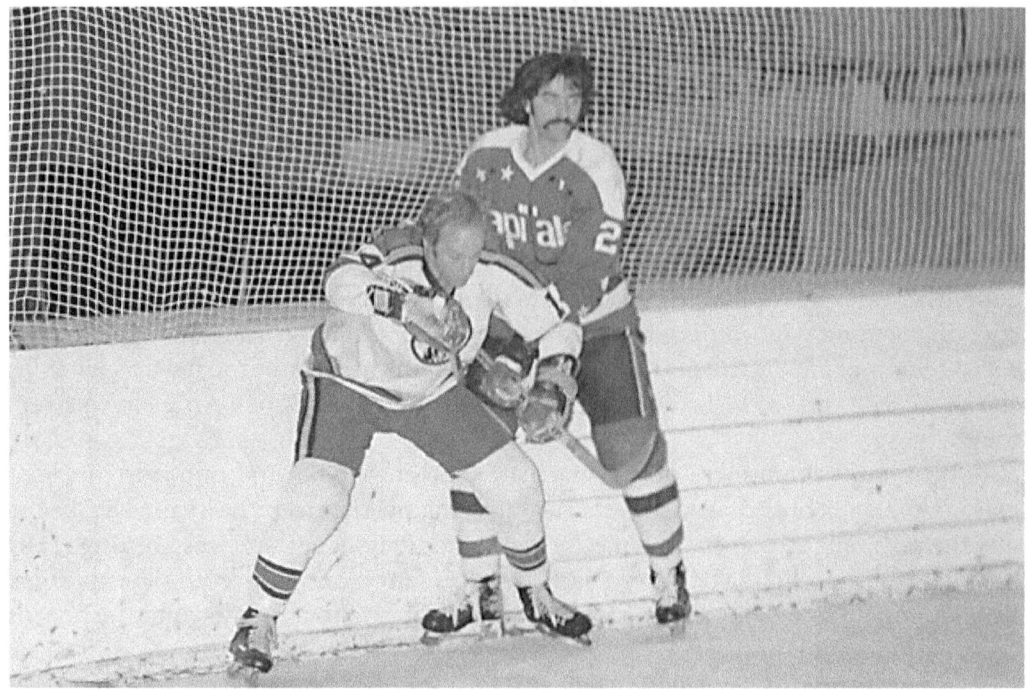

The Scouts' Craig Patrick battles in the corner with the Caps' Mike Lampman in game 3. Note the questionable quality of the boards behind them (Robin Burns collection).

would have come falling down," recalled Mike Lampman. "The ice was mediocre, and the facility itself was subpar, and dangerous, actually, so you know, it was really kind of understood on both sides that we weren't going to check each other into the boards, because the boards may just not stand up."

Some players took advantage of the abnormal playing conditions to entertain others. Ace Bailey, for instance, was once benched for half a period for some unknown infraction, so to prove to McVie that he was motivated and badly wanted to get back into the game, Bailey started doing starts-and-stops behind the bench. "Tom McVie was going crazy; he was so upset," remembered Robin Burns. "We yelled over to Ace and said, 'What are you doin'?' and he said, 'I'm trying to work up a two-beer thirst!'" Burns laughed, recollecting how Bailey was skating like a madman behind the bench.

Ron Lalonde had never heard the story before, but when I recounted the yarn Burns had spun for me, he had a good chuckle too. Everyone loved Ace Bailey, and teammates and opponents all had their favorite tales. "It sounds like it was a farce, but it wasn't a farce," explained Burns. "Anybody that knew Ace Bailey would appreciate that story, and by just saying that story, people would say, 'Well, that was Ace. That was the type of guy he was.'"

One could tell the players were starting to enjoy themselves during this tour, and the humorous quips and offbeat shenanigans were omnipresent. For instance, Tokyo got a good glimpse of North American hockey as Blair Stewart squared off with Steve Durbano in the first period of game three. Stewart dropped the mitts

8. The Coca-Cola Bottlers' Cup 225

Top and bottom: In what might have been a world first, the Capitals and Scouts fought *on* a swimming pool. Note the diving board in the background. The main combatants are Jean-Guy Lagace and Blair Stewart (#23) (middle). Robin Burns (#13) and Harvey Bennett (#27) are on the left. Ron Lalonde (#22) and Denis Dupere (#15) are on the right. "We were all just dancing," said Burns (Robin Burns collection).

again later in the period, this time with Jean-Guy Lagace. After the game, Durbano delivered the best, and in his case, the most tongue-in-cheek quote of the night: "Ah, really, we're all lovers, not fighters."[24]

Early in game three, Arnason found himself skating in alone on Wolfe, and the hard-shooting Scout let a point-blank shot rip, but Wolfe skated out a few yards to cut down the angle and blocked it. Greg Joly put Washington up, 1–0, early on assists from Bob Sirois and Tony White, and Mike Lampman scored at 9:30 to give the Caps a two-goal lead. Robin Burns scored at 16:15 to give the Scouts some life, and at 1:06 of the second stanza, Randy Rota made it 2–2, but the Scouts followed the pattern of games one and two. "They get a lead, we catch up and then they score again," said Durbano. "We can't keep coming back. Psychologically we slow down."[25] McVie's intense training schedule was paying off as the Caps always played their best hockey as the final buzzer drew closer.

The most amazing goal of the series may have come in the second period off Tony White's twig. According to Ron Weber of the *Hockey News*, White "gave a deke here, a move there and slid the puck past Denis Herron in a superb effort" to put Washington up, 3–2.[26] Harvey Bennett and Blair Stewart each scored in the second frame to give the Caps a commanding 5–2 lead. Lampman scored his second goal of the game at 18:22 of the third, and Washington clinched the Coca-Cola Cup with another impressive 6–2 victory. "Skating and passing well," wrote Weber, "and keeping continuous pressure on the Scouts at both ends of the ice, the Capitals had played their best game in Asia."[27]

Dave Hudson takes a face-off in the neutral zone during game 3 as Mike Lampman (#21) and Phil Roberto (#27) look on (Robin Burns collection).

Rick Bragnalo (#18) has his eyes on the prize. Gary Bergman (#5), Larry Johnston (#6) and Guy Charron (with the captain's C) are the Scouts in the photograph (Robin Burns collection).

These strange-looking North Americans were making quite an impression on Japan, and many odd questions were directed their way. Wolfe, who won his second game of the series and had gained a bit of a following by this time, was taken aback by one local reporter who asked, "They say you used to be a big playboy?" Wolfe, who admittedly has never been anything of the sort, smartly dodged the dicey situation. "I am married and my wife is with me. It must be a misprint," he responded.[28]

Media coverage was more limited in Sapporo than in Tokyo, therefore no game summaries have been found in newspapers of the era for games 1 and 2.

Game Three Summary

Washington	2	3	1–6
Kansas City	1	1	0–2

First period—1. WSH, Joly (White, Sirois) 6:30; 2. WSH, Lampman (Lalonde) 9:08; 3. KC, Burns (Roberto, Dupere) 16:15. Penalties: Bergman 2:16, Stewart 3:25, Burns 4:30, Durbano (major) 8:15, Stewart (major) 8:15, Bennett 9:02, Burns 17:21, Lagace (major) 17:21, Stewart (major) 17:21, Bennett 17:21.

Second period—4. KC, Rota (Charron, Patterson) 1:06; 5. WSH, White (Lynch) 8:21; 6. WSH, Bennett (Lemieux, Stewart) 10:03; 7. WSH, Stewart (Lynch, Lemieux) 14:46. Penalties: Stewart 5:17, Lampman 15:19.

Third period—8. WSH, Lampman (unassisted) 18:21. Penalties: Stewart 8:04.

Shots on goal:

Washington	8	11	10–29
Kansas City	11	6	8–25

Goaltenders: WSH, Wolfe; KC, Herron
Attendance: 9,200

Game Four: Sunday, April 18, 1976

After losing the first three games of the series, the Scouts entered game four shrouded in uncertainty and insecurity. Due to the dismal attendance figures that had plagued the Scouts since early in year one, not to mention the team's inability to sell enough season tickets to make it worthwhile to remain in Kansas City, rumors suggested the team would be contracted if a new owner couldn't be found. Both Sid Abel and Baz Bastien had been laid off with the rest of the Scouts' office staff because the team had run out of money and were in default of the $300,000 loan from the league. Abel was on vacation when he was dismissed, while Bastien was in Japan with the rest of the club. Abel ended up back in Detroit, where he became a popular TV and radio game analyst. Bastien was not out of work long as he accepted the assistant general manager position with the Pittsburgh Penguins.

If the Scouts wanted to end what had become a 30-game winless skid, game four was a do-or-die situation to say the least, but there were other reasons for them to be motivated. "The wives were getting a little pissed off because all the Washington wives were getting the gifts," joked Burns.

On a more serious note, the players also learned that Gary Bergman planned on retiring at the conclusion of the series. "We were on the ice the day of the game, the warm-up," Burns said, "and someone said something to Bergy, and he said, 'Well, this is it. This is my last NHL game,' and everybody was a little bit shocked, but I think everybody that night said, 'We've got to put in an unbelievable effort.'" Despite the players' shock, there had been signs all season long that Bergman's retirement was inevitable. Playing in Kansas City had been taxing on his family, who were used to him playing in one city (Detroit) for ten of his 11 NHL seasons. "We were talking on the phone and my son started crying because he missed me," Bergman said earlier in the season. "Then my eyes started filling up. I told him to put his mother on the phone and I said, 'Janie, get him a plane ticket and send him down here.'" Nine-year-old Blake spent a few days visiting his Dad in Kansas City.

Health was also a great concern for Bergman as his 37-year-old body struggled to keep up with the younger players who were getting bigger and faster every year. Back in October, in the final game of the pre-season, he bruised his left knee; later in the season, he suffered a severe cut on the left side of his face, which required plastic surgery. If all that wasn't bad enough, Bergman also bruised his right elbow and forearm one night against Chicago. Most notably, he strained his right knee against Atlanta in November, and as he spent time with his wife and four children while undergoing treatment in Detroit, he contemplated retirement. "I think anyone

This photograph was taken during the warm-up before game 4 in Tokyo, Gary Bergman's last NHL game. Next to Bergman (on the left) is Larry Johnston (Robin Burns collection).

would feel that way when they're home and see their kids again," he said. "Plus, you don't want to get into that injury syndrome. I've had a lot of nagging things. And at my age, that's what they are—nagging…. My behind's dragging at the end of a game."[29] Bergman's teammates definitely owed it to the veteran defenseman to give it their all since he himself had played injured the entire series; Bergman had broken a toe in game one but played in every game thereafter.

Game four began at 1:30 p.m. Tokyo time and was broadcast throughout Japan as what the *Washington Post*'s John Saar called "a quaint parody of the Stanley Cup playoffs."[30] Randy Rota opened the scoring at 18:55 of the first period on assists from Croteau and Charron. Craig Patrick put Kansas City up 2–0 at 7:19 of the second period. Mike Lampman responded for Washington with his series-leading fourth goal at 10:37, but the Scouts' Jim McElmury followed that up with his first goal at 13:16. Croteau beat Ron Low at 18:12 on assists from Rota and Charron to give the Scouts a 4–1 lead. John Saar described the Caps' play as "lethargic" and similar to being "pushed around the ice like a car with a dead battery."[31]

Washington came out strong in the final period as Jean Lemieux beat Herron just 3:15 in. Otherwise, Herron performed marvelously, "making diving, kicking saves that brought roars from the Japanese and American fans," wrote Lee Kavetski of *Pacific Stars and Stripes,* Herron was particularly strong during the final two minutes, when the Scouts had two players in the penalty box, but in the end, the Capitals' efforts were futile.[32]

With the 4–2 series-closing win, the Scouts not only salvaged some pride, but

Trainer Dale Graham stands next to back-up goaltender Bill McKenzie, resting on the Scouts' bench during game 4. Other players, from left to right, are Robin Burns (#13), Wilf Paiement (#9), Denis Dupere (#15) and Dave Hudson (#11). At the feet of the crouching Craig Patrick (#14) can be seen one of many cement blocks holding the rickety boards in place (Robin Burns collection).

they ended their 30-game winless streak and took home ladies wrist watches as a reward. The win, however, held greater meaning to the players than simply ending what had become the longest winless streak, unofficial or otherwise, in NHL history. "When [Bergman] told us in Japan that he was retiring," Burns said. "He said, 'One hundred percent, this is my last game,' so that's why it made it very emotional, and that's why we certainly busted our ass that last game to win it. I mean, it broke the streak, but it also was a far greater meaning to that last game....

"After the game I hugged Berg and said, 'Hey, it's nice that you're going out a winner,' or 'That one's for you,' something like that."

If one reads the many season previews for the 1976–1977 season, Bergman's name appears on the team roster, as if the team was hoping to coax him out of retirement, but in the end, Bergman stood firm in his decision to hang up his blades.

Tommy McVie chalked up the Caps' dismal game four performance to being "hockeyed out," and he believed the Scouts had extra incentive in trying to avoid the embarrassment of a series sweep. Overall, however, McVie was pleased with the result of the NHL Japan series, saying "it's been a very successful trip for us. We've won three games, outscored them, outplayed them in 10 out of 12 periods and dominated the series." Players on both teams were quick to credit McVie for the Capitals' sudden improvement, and how this series win would point the Capitals in the right direction for the 1976–1977 season.[33] Yes, the Coca-Cola Cup was a minor championship in the grand scheme of things, but it was in fact the Washington Capitals' first real team success, and it finally gave the players a reason to hold their heads, maybe not *high* in the proverbial sense, but at least waist high.

Game Four Summary

Kansas City	1	3	0–4
Washington	0	1	1–2

First period—1. KC, Rota (Patrick, Charron) 18:55. Penalties: Johnston 5:31, Durbano 6:04, Sirois 9:16, Lalonde 12:40, Labre 17:58.

Second period—2. KC, Patrick (Rota, Charron) 7:19; 3. WSH, Lampman (Meehan, Lalonde) 10:37; 4. KC, McElmury (Roberto, Hudson) 13:16; 5. KC, Croteau (Bergman, Charron) 18:12. Penalties: Bennett 0:45, Bergman 0:45, Johnston 4:15, Bragnalo 4:48, Labre 16:38, Scamurra 17:20.

Third period—6. WSH, Lemieux (Bragnalo) 3:15. Penalties: Bennett 0:13, Durbano 2:54, White 15:36, Rota 17:54, Johnston 17:54, Patterson 18:03.

Shots on goal:

Kansas City	14	11	8–33
Washington	8	6	9–23

Goaltenders: KC, Herron; WSH, Low.
Attendance: 9,300.

"They didn't work as hard as we did," believed Wolfe. "Eddie Bush, he was more like probably Milt Schmidt. He probably wasn't pushing the guys nearly as hard as McVie was pushing us. So, were they ready? They definitely were better rested than we were, but I think we had maybe a little better team than Kansas City, and we won, so maybe all that hard work paid out, but after playing 80 games, we didn't really have to be pushed that hard…. Whatever it was, we won three out of four, so Tommy's way was better."

"We really didn't take it as serious as we should have," admitted Robin Burns. That said, the teams played competitive hockey and did not coast through the four games. "I thought everybody worked really hard, and the shots were just as hard," recalled Wolfe. "No one eased up. There was hitting. There was [sic] slap shots…. So I think everything was about the same. I don't know if anybody really busted their back side, but I would believe that Kansas City wanted to win all four games, as I know we wanted to win all four games."

At the conclusion of game four, the teams lined up and shook hands, and there was a short on-ice ceremony where the Capitals received the Coca-Cola Bottlers' Cup. After the trophy presentation, the teams retired to their dressing rooms to indulge in some complimentary bottles of Coke.

"The Washington Capitals have discovered, at last, what they've been doing wrong—playing on the wrong continent," wrote Ron Weber in a *Hockey News* article celebrating the Capitals' moment of triumph. "They are now acknowledged to be the best hockey team to ply their trade in Japan," Weber continued. He admitted that the honor would be considered small potatoes in NHL hubs such as Montreal or Boston, but that Washington would "take the honor, saying thank you, very much."[34]

When a Japanese reporter asked Blair Stewart what he planned on doing during the summer, he answered, "Drinking." Stewart then corrected himself, and said, "I mean ... traveling and relaxing."[35]

Stewart may have let the cat out of the bag with his "drinking" comment. The Capitals and Scouts spent five days in Hawaii at the NHL's expense, but before taking off, the Kansas City players had themselves one last blowout bash. "The new Otani was a plush, plush, plush hotel," Robin Burns remembered fondly, "and we had quite a party after that night; it was called the 'Sayonara Banquet,' and we all had bought a bottle of booze, and we had one floor, so we had a party on that one floor."

Today, the NHL Japan series is often derided because the 1975–1976 Capitals and Scouts are both considered to be among the worst hockey teams ever produced. The honest truth is that the negative opinions of the series are completely unfounded. By all means, the series was an overwhelming success in spite of it being contested by two teams that had combined for 23 wins that season. If anything, the Capitals and Scouts left their Japanese hosts feeling satisfied and even thirsty for more NHL hockey. Coca-Cola actually turned a profit on the series, though how much was never disclosed. Some K.C. and D.C. players even considered playing in Japan after they found out they could make a decent living there. It was reported in the May 21, 1976, edition of the *Hockey News* that some North American players earned between $20,000 and $35,000 a year in Japan. While those numbers were significantly less

Baz Bastien and Robin Burns enjoying a laugh at the hotel (Robin Burns collection).

than what the NHL and WHA were offering, it was a comfortable salary, and it was more than what the minor leagues were offering at the time. For some players, it could have meant better job security, not to mention a major increase in ice time and the possibility of playing for a winning club. Considering that the Scouts were on the verge of collapse, Japan was not out of the realm of possibility for many players, but in the end, no one signed a contract.

In the *Hockey News*, series correspondent Mel Tsuji wrote that the spectacle was "only fair" and that the two clubs were sometimes "lethargic" and "disorganized." Tsuji did concede, however, that "the occasional bursts of speed, the hard shooting and the half dozen or so fights that broke out on the tour more than satisfied a crowd usually accustomed to the tamer styles of Japanese hockey."[36] The Japanese treated the Scouts and Capitals like champions, a first-time experience for either of the NHL's bottom-feeders. In a weird way, and for a very brief time, they were arguably the most celebrated hockey teams in the world even though the NHL and WHA playoffs were well underway and neither the Scouts nor the Capitals were anywhere close to competing for a world championship.

The NHL Japan series was such a success that Video Promotions' Jack Sakazaki said shortly afterward that he was already negotiating a deal with the California Golden Seals and Los Angeles Kings to travel West for a fall series. A Capitals press release announcing the team's triumph stated the Coca-Cola Bottlers' Cup would become an annual event. The success of the series prompted Eddie Bush to envisage a bright future for hockey in Japan. "They sure go for baseball here. I imagine in time, the Japanese will go for pro hockey. This tour ... this is how it all starts."[37]

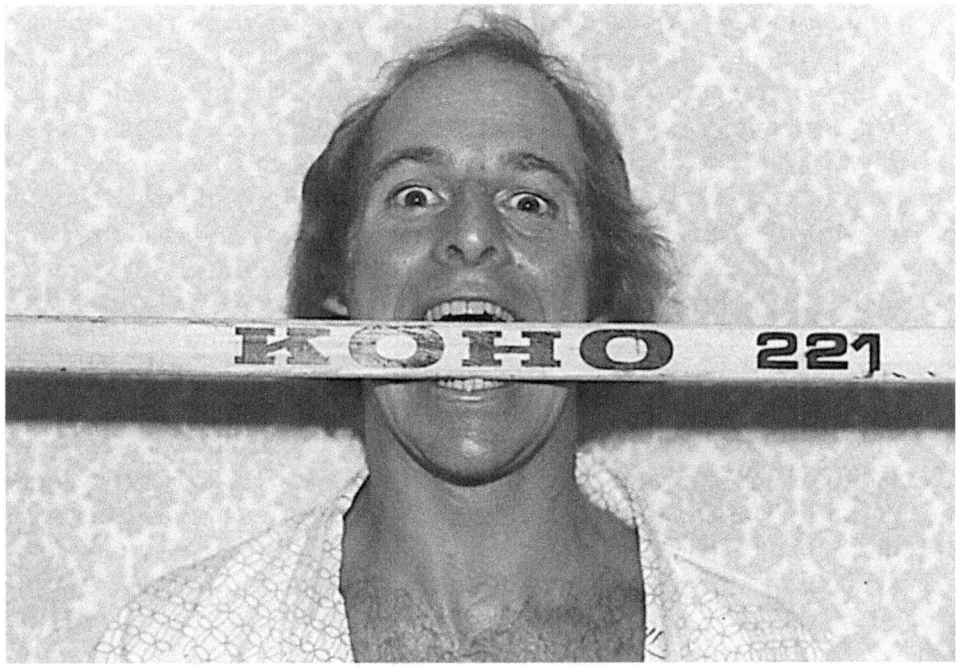

Craig Patrick doing his very best to promote the durability of KOHO brand hockey sticks (Robin Burns collection).

Tommy McVie had nothing but kind words for the teams' gracious hosts, and like many who participated in the event, he hinted at future exhibition games. "The Japanese went out of their way with gracious hospitality," McVie said. "There's nothing I can think of they haven't done for us."[38]

Despite the hopeful tidings, the NHL Japan series was a one-and-done event. The fall series between L.A. and California never came to fruition, but that might have been because the Seals were having financial problems and were on the verge of pulling up stakes and moving to Cleveland. Had the Seals' future been a bit more secure, could there have been a chance we would be talking today about the Coca-Cola Bottlers' Cup as a popular, annual event? An optimist would say "sure," but a realist would point out that there would have been far too many hurdles to clear for that to happen.

It is unlikely that another series like the Coca-Cola Cup will ever take place again. Times have changed, and the game has become much more complicated. "Such an event is quite a few steps down from the NHL participating in the Olympics," believes Mike Lampman. "The teams aren't making anything. Having their players compete, they are risking their marquee players getting hurt; that could affect the following season, and these games don't go on the record in any way." That said, money drives the world, so you can guarantee that if the NHL ever finds a way to make a little coin by sending teams overseas at the conclusion of the regular season, sponsors will be lined up around the block to plaster their name on a championship trophy. There is a better-than-average chance, however, that those games will not be played on an Olympic swimming pool. That darn Players' Association is always getting in the way of a fun little tale.

Of course, this exceptional event took a unique set of circumstances to become reality in the first place. It was indeed the perfect storm, a truly appropriate term to describe the two years leading up to the Coca-Cola Cup tournament. The damage to both reputations and careers was devastating. Poor Jimmy Anderson never coached another NHL team, and neither did Bep Guidolin. Milt Schmidt and Sid Abel were never given another chance at building a team. Kansas City is still wondering when the NHL will give them a second chance. Somehow, Abe Pollin and the Capitals managed to survive the storm despite the humblest of beginnings.

Had the NHL not expanded to Washington and Kansas City in 1974 for the purpose of spiting the WHA, the NHL would not have had two teams so awful to make it possible to send them halfway around the world for the goodwill series. Had the WHA not dangled large contracts to the best 18-year-old junior players, the Capitals and Scouts would have been able to draft prospects from a far deeper talent pool, making them so much more competitive. Had the NHL-WHA war not decimated the talent pool of the professional ranks, the expansion draft would have provided the Caps and Scouts with far better players. Had European players been more accepted in North America, Washington and Kansas City could have strengthened their rosters enough to avoid falling so far off the playoff grid that the NHL never could have guaranteed their participation in the post-season series.

Yes, the NHL Japan series was a nice event, and it produced so many wonderful memories for those who participated in it, but it was a product of its time.

•• 9 ••

Aftermath

While the Capitals' 11–59–10 record was easily the worst in the league, there were plenty of reasons to feel optimistic for the future. They were one of the best conditioned teams in the NHL, and they had a good young core, notably goaltenders Ron Low and Bernie Wolfe, and forwards Tony White, Nelson Pyatt, and Hartland Monahan. Nevertheless, many jokes were still thrown their way. In the January 1978 issue of *Action Sports Hockey*, Ira Lacher wrote that "cockeyed optimists, and fans with long lifelines, were predicting that, given the Caps' rate of improvement, they might possibly be a playoff team in, say 2020," but in reality the Caps were already a much better team in April 1977 than they had been in October 1976.[1] They had won eight games in the second half of 1975–1976, and blowout losses became the exception rather than the norm.

With those eight wins under his belt, Tommy McVie was the winningest coach in franchise history. He had instilled a winning attitude in his players, and they were more than ready to conquer the Scouts in Japan. Coming back to D.C. with that peewee-style trophy was a matter of pride, and it may have been the catalyst to one of the all-time greatest single-season improvements in sports history.

"You've got to admire some of these fellows, the way they keep slugging," said McVie. "It could get pretty discouraging because we've got so very, very far to go. But I can't complain about the way these people put out. They're real pros.

"Every little thing helps. When we won that exhibition series in Japan, even though it was against Kansas City, it had to help. It gave my guys just a bit of confidence, a feeling that everything they do isn't totally in vain."[2]

"Tommy McVie being a new coach," said Mike Lampman, "it was my opinion he treated [the NHL Japan series] almost like the first four games of the following season ... that these were important games not to be taken likely, and we were going to put out, and we did."

The 1976–1977 Capitals surged from 32 points to 64, helping McVie finish second in voting for the Jack Adams Award for coach of the year. Of course, Montreal's Scotty Bowman, who led the Habs to a 60-win season, was pretty much guaranteed to win it, but McVie's achievement was remarkable nonetheless. "I have a simple philosophy," McVie explained during his first full season as Capitals coach. "If you don't want to get beat at anything, you won't. That's all there is to it. That's what I told these guys at camp last September."

During the summer, the team travelled to the University of Ottawa for extensive physical testing. Players, as well as McVie himself, were each assigned their own conditioning program. "I felt it would help the cause if I went through the tests and had a program, too.

"Each player had his own master program of conditioning which he guarded the way a football player guards his playbook. Much of the program was designed to increase stamina and endurance."

Mike Lampman loved playing for McVie since the coach gave the Capitals exactly what they needed: discipline and a better level of fitness. "Tommy came in with a real no-nonsense attitude," Lampman remembered. "You know, that we were going to work harder getting in shape, and Tommy's was a real blue-collar approach because it started with training camp … we had to be able to run a six-minute mile, do 100 sit-ups, and I think 75 or 100 push-ups, and this was a test that you had to take at the beginning of training camp."

Jack Lynch remembered how during the Caps' first training camp under McVie, players were not only expected to run a mile in five minutes and 45 seconds or better, but that they were also expected to do so in 100-degree weather in the Dayton Arena parking lot! If you puked, too bad. If you missed the 5:45 cutoff, too bad. On you went to coach McVie's shit list. It was a real wake-up call for the Caps, many of whom, as Lynch put it, ran "like Clydesdales." Hartland Monahan was a strongly built player, but he may have been one of the Clydesdales Lynch was referring to, as he once admitted, "Running absolutely kills me." McVie was unfazed by his player's health concern, responding that "Monahan had better be prepared to die."[3]

McVie had his guys believing in themselves for the first time since the team came into existence. "It's almost like 20 brothers playing on the same team," he said, pride evident in his every word, but what McVie had accomplished went beyond simple brotherhood; the Capitals ceased being intimidated by their more talented opponents. Sure, they still took a licking once in a while, but they got back up and begged for more.[4]

McVie also stressed the importance of accurate passing to generate more goals, an issue that had always plagued the team. The coach even kept statistics on how many passes were completed, which in the pre–Internet, pre-iPad days, was either a complete fabrication meant to impress gullible sports readers or the most painstaking statistical compilation of the era. However, that doesn't mean McVie's teaching style was reminiscent of an average Tony Robbins presentation. "Because of my passing drills and my yelling, screaming and shouting we went from 45 percent completed passes to 80 percent," the coach said, but something must have worked because the Capitals made major gains in year three.[5]

Another big reason for the Caps' sudden turnaround was the acquisition of former Scout Guy Charron, who had played out his option in Kansas City and become a free agent. McVie couldn't have been happier to have Charron in the Capitals' fold. "Guy is my kind of guy," the coach said. "He has performed better than any of us expected. He's a class guy who has provided us with character and leadership as well as production." That production translated to an impressive 36 goals and 82 points and an appearance in the All-Star Game. If Charron had had a choice, however, he would have remained with the Scouts, but Kansas City did not make a satisfactory contract offer to their all-time leading scorer. When it became clear Charron was not going to sign for less than he was worth, he signed a deal with Washington. "Guy seemed to be one of the only Kansas City players that cared in that [Coca-Cola Cup] series," said McVie. "I told Max to get him, and we traded a darn good hockey player to get him."[6]

Of course, this being 1976, "free agents" were not exactly free. If a player chose to sign with a new team, that team was required to surrender a player of equal value, hence the reason why free-agent, 26-goal scorer Nelson Pyatt was sent packing. Pyatt had led the team in goals and ended the season as the Capitals' all-time leading goal scorer (32) and second-leading point scorer (59). The centerman also finished sixth in the NHL in goals and points (49) by a rookie. Nevertheless, he had experienced a very turbulent season. When the Capitals struggled early on, he flourished, but when the Caps started winning around February, he struggled due in part to a nasty flu bug that greatly affected his play. Opponents eventually figured out that Pyatt liked to deke players to the right, so he was shifted to right wing, and Rick Bragnalo took Pyatt's old spot at center. Pyatt's -56 mark was also the club's worst, and was second-worst in the league behind the -61 of Kansas City's Larry Johnston.

Despite the marked improvement in the Capitals' offense and overall defensive play, there were a few stinkers here and there, notably April 2 in Montreal, where the defending Stanley Cup champs put on a hockey clinic for the ages. Bernie Wolfe got the start in goal for Washington, and he tried in vain to withstand the barrage of pucks that was customary on any trip to Montreal. On this night, the Habs blitzed Wolfe for three goals before the game was even five minutes old. Ron Low spelled Wolfe soon after, and the Caps calmed down somewhat. McVie should have just let Low finish the game as it simply wasn't Wolfe's night, but as the coach had done repeatedly throughout the season, he switched his goalies just for the sake of switching them.[7] After Low allowed just one goal on 25 shots, McVie sent Wolfe back into the net. It was not McVie's finest coaching decision. The Habs torched Wolfe for four more goals (including Steve Shutt's 59th goal which set a new league record for left wings) in the first 3:04 of the third period, and the rout was on. After giving up seven goals on just 14 shots (and 11:15 of ice time), Wolfe was mercifully pulled again in favor of Low, but by this point Low had lost his magic touch and allowed another trio of goals to bring the final score to a humiliating 11–0. The only thing more frustrating than the double-digit drubbing was that the Caps had the, ahem, "privilege" of repeating the night all over again 24 hours later when the Canadiens visited D.C.

The hockey gods, however, had other plans.

Low manned the crease in this, the season finale for both teams, and early on it seemed like those in attendance at Capital Centre would get a glimpse of what their team had endured in Montreal. Guy Lafleur opened the scoring at 4:21, but instead of folding, the Caps hung in as Bill Riley, the Caps' rookie-of-the-year, scored his 13th goal at 11:01. Steve Shutt notched his 60th seven minutes later, but that was it offensively for Montreal. The Caps outshot the Habs, 25–19, and refused to give in to the superior Canadiens. McVie pulled Low in the dying seconds of the game, pressing for the equalizer, but "Bunny" Larocque barred the door, and the game ended 2–1.

The legendary Canadiens, perpetually riding on a fluffy cloud high above the rest of the NHL mortals, took notice of the lowly Capitals, who had spent 60 minutes punching well above their weight class and nearly securing a point. Jack Lynch remembered the aftermath of the April 3 contest vividly and recalled the memorable interaction that occurred in the minutes following the final buzzer.

> It was just one of those things that at the end of the game, for some reason, they stayed on the ice as we were sort of acknowledging the crowd or whatever, and they engaged with us…. I went up to Guy Lafleur, and I put my hand on his stick and I said, "Can I have that?" and he said, "Sure" and gave me his stick, and I thanked him, and the biggest mistake I made was not getting him to sign it for me, but I got the stick, and Ken Dryden was just ahead of him, and I went to him, and I asked him could I have his goalie stick, and he said the same thing, "Sure," and so I come off the ice with my stick and two others…. When I went to the dressing room I actually sat in my stall with the sticks and waited…. I was worried that somebody was going to steal the sticks out of my locker, so I stayed in my stall until everybody had left the dressing room, and then I went and showered knowing that when I came back those two sticks would be there, and those two sticks are down in my basement right now.

By 1977–1978, however, the Capitals returned to the style of play that had defined the franchise its first two years. McVie's motivational magic had worn off, and the Caps sank to a horrendous 17–49–14 record, just three points up on last-place Minnesota. McVie was fired before the start of the 1978–1979 regular season, but he latched on to the Winnipeg Jets of the WHA before the end of the year and led them to the rebel league's final Avco Cup championship.

Some members of the Coca-Cola Cup winners remained productive during the Caps' downturn, including Guy Charron, who scored 38 goals and 73 points, and Bob Sirois, who finished second on the team with 61 points. For the most part, however, McVie's original marching-band connoisseurs disappeared. Ron Low was traded to Detroit before the 1977–1978 season. Greg Joly didn't even make it to year three and never got to experience the Capitals' turnaround or their subsequent return to dreadfulness. Mike Marson never fit into McVie's system and was eventually traded. Bernie Wolfe ran into injury issues and lost his status as a number one goalie. Mike Lampman suffered a career-ending spinal injury just as his career was starting to take off. Jack Lynch badly injured his knee in a collision with Vancouver's Hilliard Graves and was never the same. Injuries eventually caught up with Yvon Labre as well, and his playing time was reduced to just a handful of games. Young defensemen like Rick Green and Robert Picard, drafted in the 1976 and 1977 Amateur Drafts, were expected to lead the Caps to the playoffs, but in the end both disappointed and were traded away. All that was left in Washington were a few aging veterans and young prospects with a limited upside. The Capitals would not play their first playoff game until 1983.

Ace Bailey was among the many players who took a step back in the Capitals' fourth season. He played just 40 games and scored only seven goals before finding himself in Edmonton of the WHA the next year. In the Alberta capital, he was asked to mentor a young Wayne Gretzky, then in his first professional season. Their friendship would last a lifetime, which was tragically cut short on September 11, 2001. Bailey was working for the Los Angeles Kings, and he and amateur scout Mark Bavis had just visited their AHL affiliate in Manchester, New Hampshire. Both were aboard United Airlines Flight 175, which took off from Boston heading back to L.A.

when the plane was hijacked and flown into the South Tower of the World Trade Center in New York. "He was a happy-go-lucky, wonderful human being that died tragically, unfortunately in 9/11," said the Scouts' Robin Burns.

Just about everyone who ever played with Ace Bailey has at least one good yarn about him, and it usually involves some sort of shenanigan he caused. Ace Bailey was proud to be known as the dressing room cut-up, and he took even greater pride in almost never getting caught for the shit he pulled. Despite his many skills, Ace Bailey is most fondly remembered for the person he was, his visits to Boston area children's hospitals while he played for the Bruins, and the impact he made on his many teammates over the years. "We all enjoyed Ace…. He was a great teammate," remembered roommate Mike Lampman. "He was one of the guys that would drop the gloves to defend a teammate. I remember him fighting Tiger Williams and Ace was clearly overmatched … but take Tiger on he did. Ace was one of the guys who was a good teammate when the times got tough, and there were a lot of tough times."

Condition Critical

With the 1975–1976 regular season drawing to a close, the Scouts' primary concern was selling 8,000 season tickets for the following season. The Scouts had averaged 7,892 fans for the year, which was better than the 7,356 of the year before, but still not nearly enough to make the team solvent. Kansas City mayor Charles Wheeler, Jr. took it upon himself to lead a season-ticket drive to keep the Scouts in town. Clarence Campbell hoped the Scouts would "continue to operate and ultimately, flourish in Kansas City," as he wrote in a letter to Wheeler.

"The next move is up to the Scouts management," Wheeler said. "I've assembled the committee [to sell season tickets] and we're ready."[8]

Rumors had circulated for months that Ed Thompson was looking to unload the Scouts, which would leave them wide open for relocation. Carl Scheer, Jr., of the American Basketball Association's Denver Nuggets was believed to be interested in diversifying his sports portfolio, but because the ABA was on its last legs itself and was on the verge of merging with the NBA, purchasing the Scouts was a headache he declined to take on.

An even wilder rumor had the Scouts being purchased by a group led by Toronto entrepreneur Ted Tobias, who had once tried to put a WHA team in nearby Hamilton, Ontario. In March 1976, rumor mills stated that the Scouts would be moved to Toronto, and then, if all went according to plan, the great Bobby Orr, of all people, who was set to become a free agent on June 1, would be offered a contract and an ownership stake in the team. The only thing holding Tobias back, other than common sense and a realization that this was a ludicrous plan, was that the WHA's Toronto Toros had yet to decide whether they would remain there or move elsewhere for the 1976–1977 season.[9] Needless to say, neither the Scouts nor any other struggling NHL team moved to Toronto, even though the Toros packed their bags for Birmingham, Alabama.

A rumor that made much more sense was that the NBA's Kansas City Kings were considering purchasing the Scouts. Kings general manager Joe Axelson admitted the team was "interested to a certain extent" but that he hadn't "heard anything new in three weeks." One of the Kings' primary owners, H. Paul Rosenberg, said the Kings had "a continuing interest."[10]

By the end of April, the Kings "made a proposal to the Scouts dependent on both parties resolving certain conditions satisfactory to each. The proposal consist[ed] of the Scouts effecting settlements with certain creditors and the Kings assuming liabilities with respect to others and [was] conditioned upon this and proper financing," said a statement by Wheeler after a meeting between the Kings' and Scouts' respective presidents and legal counsels.[11]

The sticky part of the deal was what to do about the Scouts' liabilities, somewhere in the neighborhood of $7 million, no chump change in 1976. Most of that $7 million was owed to the NHL in expansion fees, not to mention the $300,000 loan the league had granted the Scouts in March, $138,000 in rent, and $44,000 in arena user fees. The Scouts also owed the St. Louis Blues $800,000 for encroaching on their territorial rights. The Kings' owners were hoping that in exchange for rescuing the Scouts, the NHL would cut them some slack and reduce the amount owed.[12]

On May 4, a tentative deal was reached, but shortly afterward the Scouts' lease at Kemper Arena was renegotiated. For the first two years of the lease, the Scouts would pay the city six percent of its net gross receipts (which included ticket sales and television rights proceeds) up to a maximum of $200,000, which would go towards rent. In years three and four, the Scouts would pay eight percent with no maximum rent. In the fifth year, that percentage would increase one more point. For the last 23 years of the lease, the Scouts would fork over 12.5 percent of receipts, and the minimum rent paid would increase to $260,000.[13]

It seemed as though the Scouts would live to see another day, but a plot twist suddenly emerged. Robert Margolin, a Kings director and attorney, wanted to include a new clause in the 28-year lease that would allow the new owners to move the Scouts if the club's financial losses exceeded $250,000 in one year or $75,000 or more in two of three years preceding the year in which the idea of moving the franchise came up. The Kings would pay the city a penalty of $130,000, but they would not be liable for any other damages. Considering that the Scouts had reportedly lost $5 million in their two years of operation, losing a mere $250,000 in one year was not just a realistic possibility, but a likely scenario.

The last-minute swerve smacked of cold feet or perhaps an underlying desire to move the team to another location once a better deal could be found. Councilman Richard Berkley believed the clause was an "easy out" giving no one—not the city, nor the taxpayers, nor the arena bond holders—any protection. Assistant city attorney Richard Ward and city manager Robert Kipp believed that adding this new clause was inconsistent with the rest of the lease, meaning it would have to be renegotiated. Joe Serviss, who was the chairman of the city council finance and audit committee, was terribly disappointed by the turn of events and refused to endorse anything. "I think we will have to stand by the lease we have negotiated," he told Margolin. "We have come a long way since we started on this. I think this is a lease you can live with."

Margolin had put the Scouts and Kansas City in a real bind. He told the committee the lease needed to be adopted immediately because the Kings were scheduled to meet with the NHL's finance committee three days later and with league officials the following day. "I cannot stand up in Chicago Tuesday and tell the N.H.L. I haven't got a lease," Margolin said. "I don't think I can go back to the group and recommend the purchase without this clause."

Kipp was not at all surprised by the last minute gun to the head. The Kings had tried these dirty pool tactics before and had been successful in getting what they wanted, but this time their strategy failed.[14]

The lease was predictably voted down. Joe Axelson explained afterwards that purchasing a team that had lost $5 million since it played its first game was a huge risk which would make any potential owner "extremely cautious." He added that the Kings "understandably would not risk the substantial investment and credit involved unless free to dispose of the franchise in the event of significant losses resulting from the community's failure to support the team."[15]

On one hand, Serviss was not bitter about the sudden turn of events. "They did a good job of trying to save hockey for Kansas City," he said of the Kings owners. "It was a valiant effort…. There is no use trying to point blame. I hope everybody leaves this with a decent taste in his mouth." As for the Kings, they were smarting from Kipp's earlier "raids" comment. Rosenberg played the old "community-first" card by insisting that he and the Kings acted out of civic pride and tried their best to save the Scouts, but in the end "got kicked in the teeth."

"We'll concentrate on running our basketball team."

And just like that, the Scouts were on life support once again. "Unless somebody comes out of the woodwork, the league will decide that there will be no hockey in Kansas City," said Thompson.[16]

An opinion piece in the *Kansas City Times* explained the potential fallout of losing the Scouts: "Kansas City … can survive without major league hockey. But the failure of the 2-year-old enterprise would represent a hurtful loss of stature for a city which is just now beginning to enjoy national acclaim for its vitality, leadership and quality of life. On the more tangible side, the taxpayers face a loss of nearly half a million dollars a year if Kemper arena loses the prime tenant for which it was built."[17] The Scouts had 40 nights a year booked for games, and it was estimated that the team generated around $575,000 from rent, users' fees, concessions, and parking.

The situation was so dire that the NHL even considered dissolving the franchise altogether rather than moving it elsewhere, even though such a drastic (and embarrassing) move had not been made since World War II. There was also the question of what to do with the Scouts' players. It was possible they would all become free agents if the Scouts folded, but there was also a chance they would become property of the 17 other clubs, since the Scouts had not paid back the $300,000 loan they received from the NHL. In order to begin contraction proceedings, the league was required to send the Scouts a complaint sheet, which stated that the franchise had not yet paid its league dues and had not repaid the loan. The Scouts' roster was frozen until the situation was resolved, although the Scouts participated in the June 1 Amateur Draft.

There was one small ray of hope, however, in the form of Mayor Wheeler, who indicated he was still trying to sell enough season tickets to reach $1 million and was hoping to find a few investors with deep enough pockets to scrounge up another $2 million to keep the Scouts afloat.[18] The league gave him 10 days, but as the ten-day extension came closer and closer to its conclusion, no progress had been made. "I can't see anything on the horizon," said William Clarkson, Wheeler's liaison with the city's business community. "I don't know what could happen now unless some members of the business community stepped in on purely a civic basis and took over the team in a caretaker role, but that would be a big gamble and there is no indication that it will happen."[19]

Wheeler and Clarkson even announced that they were now willing to live with an escape clause if it meant saving the Scouts, but by this time the Kansas City Kings' ownership group had mixed feelings about going ahead with the purchase. Wheeler personally phoned the Kings and asked them to reconsider buying the Scouts, but they declined.[20] The NHL gave the Scouts until June 7 to find a new owner or else the team would be no more.

Even though the Scouts no longer employed a general manager nor an assistant general manager, there were whispers that an anonymous investor was interested in buying the NHL's out-of-control dumpster fire, but that this person wished to remain anonymous until the sale was complete. Local clothier Gene Novorr, who had been a part of the Scouts' original ownership group, claimed that "This particular person said not to worry about the financing." Novorr said he felt "90 per cent certain" that the Scouts were saved, and that two days earlier, he had "felt just the opposite."[21]

"The banks have made it clear that they would be 100 per cent behind us, and the city has been very helpful. I can't see one hitch right now," said Novorr a few days later.

The NHL granted the Scouts yet another extension, this time to June 25, to get their affairs in order and come up with a plan to refinance the team, or else the club would be dissolved. The team had no choice but to move fast too, since several of its top players' contracts had already expired. Guy Charron, Denis Herron, Craig Patrick, Chuck Arnason, Jean-Guy Lagace, and Gary Bergman had all become free agents. "We hope they'll hold off making any move until our reorganization iscomplete [sic]," Novorr said.[22] However, Novorr had no idea that other plans were afoot.

As June gave way to July, a group lead by oil magnate Jack Vickers and former New York Knicks star Bud Palmer expressed an interest in purchasing the Scouts and moving them to Denver, Colorado. When told of the news, Novorr called it a "shock," saying that he had "never even heard of them being interested" and that if any discussions had been taking place, he "was not told about it." He also lamented that he and his group were "so close to keeping [the Scouts] here it's pitiful" and that they had done "six months' work in three weeks."[23]

Palmer had originally tried to buy the California Golden Seals and move them to Denver, but in the end, Seals owner Mel Swig decided to relocate the club to Cleveland. The Denver area, therefore, was still available, as was the luxurious new McNichols Arena. Palmer indicated that his group had offered "$5 million-plus" for the Scouts. "We have a pretty strong group of investors who are interested," he said. "We want to get this resolved by the end of next week at the latest."[24]

In the meantime, Novorr and his group scrambled to find the money to save hockey in Kansas City, but in the end, after months of waffling, the NHL finally put its foot down and told everyone that if a move to Denver was not formally agreed upon by Palmer's group, the Scouts would be contracted from the league. "I told [Novorr's group] the league had signed an agreement with [Denver]," said the NHL's attorney, John Ziegler. "I told them time had run out on Kansas City."

Novorr was understandably upset after putting up a valiant yet losing effort to save hockey for Kansas City. "I feel terrible hockey has left Kansas City," he said. "We made a bonafide offer. I don't think the league ever considered our offer entirely."[25] Novorr honestly believed hockey could have survived in Kansas City had the club done more to put itself out there in the community and connect with the fans, and had the NHL done more to provide the club with better players. "The fans aren't at all responsible," he said. "Look, we lost a ton of dough—$5,000,000 in two seasons—but the fans were never educated about hockey and we weren't able to put a team on the ice that was capable of playing in the Central Hockey League."[26]

One fan who was probably quite disappointed, not to mention surprised, to find out the Scouts were no more, was Gary Bryan, whom the *Kansas City Times*' Jay Greenberg described as "either strange in his fanaticism or congratulated for his foresight." Bryan worked for a Saudi Arabian airlines firm. In December 1973, almost 11 months before the first puck drop, Bryan bought three season tickets for the Scouts' first *three seasons,* presuming that tickets would eventually become such a hot commodity he either wouldn't be able to acquire or afford them. The most mind-boggling part of Bryan's overenthusiastic purchase was that he was not even going to be *on the same continent* to watch a single game the first two seasons; he was being transferred back to Saudi Arabia and wasn't expected back until 1976–1977, so he planned on handing his tickets over to a couple of friends while he was out of the country. Of course, decades before the Internet became a reality, Mr. Bryan must have been shocked to find out upon his return to North American that his beloved-yet-never-even-seen Kansas City Scouts had packed their bags and moved to Denver to become the Colorado Rockies.[27]

Welcome to Rocky Hockey

"When I look back, the whole formula for the Scouts was right," Robin Burns asserted in a 2019 interview. "It's just someone forgot to turn on the stove. Every ingredient was in the pot. Everything certainly could have worked so, so very well, and it's just unfortunate." Burns pointed out in a 2007 interview with John Meagher of the *Montreal Gazette* that the Scouts had an excellent core consisting of Simon Nolet, Guy Charron, Wilf Paiement, and Denis Herron, but "good teams find ways to win and bad teams find ways to lose." The Scouts would often hold the lead in the third period, but "the puck would bounce in, followed by a comedy of errors."[28]

Burns did not make the move to Denver with the rest of the Scouts. He did not fit into the Rockies' plans, so they planned to send him to the minors. Burns was just 29 years old, but with three young children who had never had the opportunity to grow in one city for any great length of time, he decided to settle his contract. Luckily for him, Scouts part-owners George Schurr and Bob Fisher knew Bud Palmer's partner Jack Vickers well, so Burns was bought out at 95 cents on the dollar. Burns received a few enticing offers from the WHA, but fearing he was becoming a journeyman, he chose another, more profitable and personally satisfying route.

Since hockey players were not paid the kind of money today's NHL players earn, Burns had to work a summer job to make ends meet. While at Lange Skates, he helped develop the company's innovative plastic skate design. He went on to become the president of Micron, another skate company, where he got the idea for a polycarbonate face mask. He was playing pick-up hockey when he got hit in the face, and he realized there had to be a way to protect hockey players' mugs. Before long, ITECH made the face mask *the* must-have piece of hockey equipment for children and adults, and it became the third-largest hockey equipment manufacturer on the planet.

Burns studied polycarbonates and worked on perfecting a face shield that would not shatter upon impact, indeed a high-tech, almost unfathomable idea at the time. He visited a company called Leader on the South Shore of Montreal and, with the help of one of their engineers and a designer, they came up with the first face shield. The product seemed promising, but that did not mean everyone thought it was a great idea ... at first. "Dr. Tom Pashby at the Canadian Standards Association [CSA], he said he would never approve of a piece of glass in front of anyone's face. He was the father of helmets and the wire cage, which was fairly new. I said I could prove it was more protective than a wire cage.... Seven years later, he was a firm believer and my greatest asset in the world. He became a driving force."[29]

Burns' success in the business world has allowed him to become a philanthropist as well, including founding Procure Walk of Courage, an organization that raises awareness for prostate cancer, with Father John Walsh. He also made a sizable donation to Concordia University in Montreal, and in return the hockey Stingers named their penalty box after him. Another passion of his is Youth for Christ, which provides meals for disadvantaged kids in the Montreal region. Burns may not have been able to "score into the Grand Canyon" when he played, but he has scored big-time outside of hockey despite only a high-school education.[30]

Every now and again Burns receives an autograph request, which he is more than happy to fulfill. Unlike most professional hockey players, he *literally* has just a single bubble gum card to his name, as his moniker is the *only* thing O-Pee-Chee printed correctly on the front. The action shot actually features teammate Bryan Lefley standing in front of the Kansas City net. Burns himself is nowhere to be found on the cardboard slab. "And to think you work all your life to get on an NHL bubble gum card," he chuckled.[31] Turns out O-Pee-Chee got the last laugh on the clown prince of the Kansas City Scouts, but Burns has absolutely no regrets. "I had quite a day, Maggie Muffins!" he told me at the end of our phone interview in 2019. Quite a day, indeed.

Unbeknownst to Burns at the time, an exciting future lay ahead for him, but the future looked bleak for the wobbly Colorado Rockies. Other than Wilf Paiement, there was little reason for optimism. Guy Charron was gone, and so was rock-solid Denis Herron. Rockies general manager Ray Miron let Herron become a free agent, so the Scouts' star goaltender signed with Pittsburgh, who surrendered goalie Michel Plasse, winger Simon Nolet, and defenseman Colin Campbell as compensation, as per the free agency rules of the day.

The move to Denver may have solved the franchise's financial problems, but it also created a great deal of uncertainty. "NHL moguls dilly-dallied an unconscionably long time before deciding the fate of the Kansas City Scouts, leaving the new people in Denver far too little time to begin setting up an efficient front office operation," wrote the *Hockey News*' Frank Brown in the magazine's annual yearbook. "This is a team that couldn't sell tickets in its original home, was easily the league's weakest franchise last season, and by mid–August didn't even have a coach." In fact, in that same yearbook, the Rockies did not even have a logo featured in the team's round-up, unlike the transplanted California Golden Seals, who had a beautiful brand new "Cleveland Barons" logo to show off. "The shift achieved nothing, except to save some jobs," Brown concluded.[32] The shift did, however, spare the NHL the shame of folding a franchise just two years into operation, something that would have made the league seem all too similar to the cash-strapped, disorganized WHA.

According to Brown, "The defense needs a transfusion, with ancient Gary Bergman over the hill. Steve Durbano has violent moments, but is really not that good a defender. Dennis Patterson is a fringe major leaguer, at best. Up front, Colorado inherits bodies who have seemingly made a career of hanging on with expansion and cellar clubs," notably the former Golden Seal Craig Patrick, former Islander Dave Hudson, ex–Red Wing Phil Roberto, and the unfortunate Denis Dupere, who in the two previous years, had bounced around from Toronto to Washington to St. Louis to Kansas City to his final NHL home, Denver.[33]

By the end of that initial campaign slinging pucks in the Rocky Mountain state, Ray Miron had done his best to wipe out all traces of Scouts DNA. A few players, notably Wilf Paiement, Gary Croteau, Dave Hudson, Jim McElmury, Denis Dupere, and Chuck Arnason, were retained, but Henry Boucha, Steve Durbano, Phil Roberto, Larry Johnston, Randy Rota, and Roger Lemelin played just a handful of games before being traded or released. The club now belonged to Paiement and Nelson Pyatt, young draftee Paul Gardner, and prodigal son Barry Dean, back in the NHL after the Phoenix Roadrunners closed up shop.

In late August, the Rockies hired 47-year-old Johnny Wilson, formerly of Detroit, who had a .538 winning percentage under his tutelage despite never qualifying for the playoffs. Wilson was a popular "player's coach" wherever he landed, but even he couldn't save the Rockies from finishing dead last in the Smythe Division with a 20–45–14 record. The Rockies continued the Scouts' ignominious tradition of collapsing in spectacular fashion in the second half of seasons. Before long, the term "Rocky Hockey" was coined to promote the sport to locals, but it was used by players to describe the up-and-down feeling they got from playing in Denver for too long.

Taking the Scouts and Rockies' collective eight-year history into consideration, they are arguably the all-time worst second-half team in any sport, ever. In 1974–1975, the Scouts started the year 13–36–7 but finished 2–18–4. The next year, there was that dreadful one-win-in-44-games finish. When the Scouts moved to Denver, the Rockies started 19–31–10, but finished 1–15–4. The 1977–1978 Rockies looked like they were taking major steps forward thanks to a pretty impressive collection of scorers. They started the year 8–12–6, but finished a mediocre 11–28–15, yet they still qualified for the playoffs because the Smythe Division housed one of the worst collections of teams in NHL history, *three* of which actually finished with fewer points than the Rockies' 59, the highwater mark of their dismal six-year stint in Denver. Predictably, the Rockies were swept in the preliminary round by the Philadelphia Flyers.

By the end of that season, only a handful of Scouts remained with the Rockies, notably the dependable Gary Croteau, who eventually earned the team captaincy. He was never the most talented player on the roster, but through hard work, he enjoyed the only two 20-goal seasons of his career in Colorado, and with 390 games under his belt, he was the longest-tenured player selected by either the Scouts or Capitals in the 1974 expansion draft.

Dave Hudson remained another steady performer in Colorado until retiring at the end of 1977–1978, but he had a great future ahead of him. In 1993, he founded ColorMark, a Dallas-Fort Worth printing company that now generates over $20 million a year.

Goaltenders Michel Plasse and the Bills (McKenzie and Oleschuk) stuck around until the end of the decade, with Plasse getting the majority of the starts, and none of them succeeding at stealing enough games to make the Rockies competitive.

And then there was Wilf Paiement, whose star shone brighter than anyone else in Denver. As a Rockie, he became everything the Scouts had hoped he would become, setting several franchise records. In 1976–1977, he scored 41 goals and 81 points, and the following year he notched 36 goals and 87 points. On October 25, 1978, however, Paiement put a permanent black mark on his otherwise stellar career. The 1–4–1 Rockies were in Detroit that night, and the Wings' superpest, Dennis Polonich, started mouthing off to Paiement. The Rockies' All-Star retaliated with a vicious swing of lumber that landed right in Polonich's face, causing severe lacerations, a broken nose, and a concussion. Polonich had proven to be a pugnacious but effective player in his three full NHL seasons, but after the attack he was never the same. He later sued Paiement for the injuries and received an $850,000 settlement in 1982. Paiement was suspended 15 games, the second-longest suspension in NHL history to that point, and the Rockies went a miserable 3–9–3 during that span. On a much less controversial note, Paiement was the last player not named "Gretzky" to wear number 99 in an NHL game, which he did during his tenure with the Toronto Maple Leafs in the early 1980s, long before the "99" became sacred.

The less said about the 42-point disaster that was 1978–1979, the better, but when Don Cherry took over the Rockies' bench in 1979–1980, things began looking up ever so slightly. The Rockies went 12–21–3 in their first 36 games, which was not great, but far better than the 7–27–10 they went the rest of the year. The collapse was even greater in 1980–1981: a three-game winning streak to start the year, a .500 record for the first 22 games, and a 14–19–6 mark at the 36-game mark, but an awful 8–26–7 finish. The Rockies' final season, 1981–1982, was hardly better, and attendance remained low, so the team uprooted itself and settled in East Rutherford, New Jersey, where they went on to win three Stanley Cups as the Devils.

Whatever Happened to the Coca-Cola Cup?

While the Coca-Cola Cup never became an annual event, its story does not end with the Caps' triumph. The monetary value of the Coca-Cola Cup may be negligible, but the trophy's half-century journey is a priceless tale. In 2013, during the interview process for my original article on the Coca-Cola Cup, it dawned on me that not one Washington player had the foggiest idea what happened to the trophy they had captured. It wasn't until decades later that Mike Vogel, a senior writer for the Capitals, stumbled upon it. "Found that trophy in a storage closet years ago.... I'm sure it's still around somewhere, but I have no idea where," he wrote to me in an email. "In hockey, if it's not the Stanley Cup it's pretty worthless.... It's probably in an office or a closet somewhere, or maybe someone took it home to use as a flower pot."[34] He snapped a few pictures of it at the time, proving the Cup's existence, which left me feeling satisfied that the trophy was taken back to Washington and not left to rust at the Yoyogi Olympic swimming pool, but disappointed that it had gone AWOL.

When I wrote to Vogel in 2020 to tell him about my plan to turn the original article into a book, he informed me that the Cup had resurfaced and that it rested in the office of Capitals director of hockey operations Kris Wagner. I wrote to Wagner to find out what exactly had happened to the legendary trophy. He told me that after the Cup was awarded to the Capitals, it made its way back to Landover, where it resided at Capital Centre for two decades. As the Capitals were preparing to move into the new downtown MCI Center around 1997, Capital Centre was doomed to fall victim to a barrage of dynamite and wrecking balls. Before the building came down, however, director of operations George Parr visited the site to look for anything interesting that may have been left behind. Had it not been for him, the whereabouts of the Coca-Cola Cup would have remained a mystery for the ages.

The Coca-Cola Cup had been displayed in one of the bars in the Capital Centre concourse. When Parr brought the huge, mysterious trophy back to the office, everyone was absolutely baffled as to what it was and what it represented. Since when had the Capitals played a game, let alone *won* anything in Japan? When Ted Leonsis bought the Capitals in the late 1990s and the team's annex offices were moved a few blocks away, it quickly became apparent that there was little storage space in the new digs, so the Coca-Cola Cup was stashed in whatever nook, cranny, or broom closet had just enough space to accommodate it. Not long after, the trophy was rediscovered once again, but rather than let it collect dust in some dark corner of the Capitals' administrative offices, employees awarded it to the team's annual bubble hockey champions. Known as the "Bubble Boy" event of the Capitals' annual holiday party, it pitted teams of two against each other until only one was left standing, and the winners would receive the mysterious Cup with a brand-new, scotch-taped label over the original engraved brass plaque gracing the base of the trophy. The hockey operations department one day realized that the team was being somewhat disrespectful to the trophy and what it once meant to the players who had captured it, so when their offices were moved from downtown to Arlington, Virginia, the Cup was stashed in Wagner's office, where he continues to collect rare Capitals artifacts and memorabilia. The Coca-Cola Bottlers' Cup remains safe and sound to this day, next to the last pair of goalie pads former Vezina Trophy winner Braden Holtby wore in D.C. Sure, the brass on the trophy is now a tad tarnished and there may still be the odd piece of scotch tape on it, but otherwise the Coca-Cola Cup is in great shape.

There was once talk about having the Coca-Cola Cup refurbished and given a proper space to be celebrated, but in the end, it was decided not to display it to the public, for much the same reason the Capitals never displayed the Presidents' trophies and Wales Conference trophies they had also won. After all, the team's ultimate goal had always been to win the Stanley Cup. Now that the Capitals have a very impressive trophy case including said Stanley Cup, it makes sense to show off the very first championship the team won, but those plans have yet to be realized. Perhaps one day, the quirky little Japanese trophy will see the light of day and cause a new generation of Capitals fans to wonder: "What in the world is the Coca-Cola Bottlers' Cup?"

Compared to the Stanley Cup playoffs, the Coca-Cola Cup series seems trivial, yet the players interviewed for this book were all delighted to reminisce about their once-in-a-lifetime adventure, so I'm sure they will be happy to hear that the little trophy almost no one remembers having seen in the first place still holds a special place in the Capitals organization.

For the Scouts, however, even though they lost the series, and the ladies wrist watches they took home for winning game four have probably all been lost to the sands of time, the tournament was also significant. "I think we were trailblazers," said Burns. "You look back at it and you go 'Wow, that was a unique trip, a one-of-a-kind trip,' It was an incredible adventure

To this day, the Coca-Cola Bottlers' Cup remains a long-forgotten symbol of pro hockey supremacy in Japan. While it has a certain peewee tournament look, the story behind it is Hall of Fame–worthy. No Washington player interviewed for this book could remember what happened to the trophy after the NHL Japan series (courtesy Patrick McDermott).

for everybody … little did we know it would be the last game the Scouts would play."

For the triumphant Capitals, the Coca-Cola Cup became a symbol of legitimacy in a sport that had thoroughly embarrassed them since day one. The trophy itself was inconsequential; the real prize was the pride the players had gained and the memories they had made. "It was an incredible once-in-a-lifetime trip…. Wonderful memories," defenseman Jack Lynch wrote to me back in 2014.

Even if the Coca-Cola Cup's place in the history of the Washington Capitals is as a symbol of bubble hockey supremacy at the team's headquarters, it will always remain a noteworthy trophy. If anything, it is a delightful memento commemorating a bizarre, but unforgettable chapter in international hockey history, and it never would have happened had the two years previous to the NHL Japan series played out just a little differently.

Appendix: Statistics

1974–1975

Team Statistics

	Overall	PTS	WIN%	GF	GA	GPG	GAA	PIM
Kansas City	15–54–11	41	.256	184	328	2.30	4.10	726
Washington	8–67–5	21	.131	181	446	2.26	5.58	1071

Home, Away, and Divisional Records

	Home	Away	Campbell	Wales	Patrick	Smythe	Adams	Norris
Kansas City	12–20–8	3–34–3	6–32–6	9–22–5	1–16–3	5–16–3	4–9–3	5–13–2
Washington	7–28–5	1–39–0	3–30–3	5–37–2	1–13–2	2–17–1	3–16–1	2–21–1

Special Teams

	PPG	PPO	PP%	PPGA	PPOA	PK%	SHG	SHGA
Kansas City	57	351	16.24	53	233	77.25	6	6
Washington	48	372	12.90	94	328	71.34	8	18

Shots

	SF	SC%	SA	SV%	SO	SOA
Kansas City	2223	8.3	2805	.883	0	13
Washington	1845	9.8	3064	.854	1	12

1975–1976

Team Statistics

	Overall	PTS	WIN%	GF	GA	GPG	GAA	PIM
Kansas City	12–56–12	36	.225	190	351	2.38	4.39	968
Washington	11–59–10	32	.200	224	394	2.80	4.93	943

Home, Away, and Divisional Records

	Home	Away	Campbell	Wales	Patrick	Smythe	Adams	Norris
Kansas City	8–24–8	4–32–4	4–34–6	8–22–6	1–16–3	3–18–3	3–9–4	5–13–2
Washington	6–26–8	5–33–2	5–27–4	6–32–6	2–13–1	3–14–3	1–15–4	5–17–2

Special Teams

	PP	PPO	PP%	PPGA	PPOA	PK%	SHG	SHGA
Kansas City	46	352	13.07	80	295	72.88	2	17
Washington	53	375	14.13	64	252	74.60	2	3

Shots

	SF	SC%	SA	SV%	SO	SOA
Kansas City	2192	8.7	2894	.879	0	5
Washington	1953	11.5	2955	.867	0	9

GA—goals against
GAA—goals against average
GF—goals for
GPG—goals per game
PIM—penalties in minutes
PK%—penalty-killing percentage
PP%—power-play scoring percentage
PPG—power-play goals
PPGA—power-play goals against
PPO—power-play opportunities
PPOA—power-play opportunities against

PTS—points
SA—shots against
SC%—scoring percentage
SF—shots for
SHG—shorthanded goals
SHGA—shorthanded goals against
SO—shutouts for
SOA—shutouts against
SV%—save percentage
WIN%—winning percentage

1974–1975 Kansas City Scouts Scoring and Goaltending Statistics

Player	Pos	GP	G	A	PTS	+/-	PIM	EVG	PPG	SHG	GWG	EVA	PPA	SHA	S	S%
Simon Nolet	RW	72	26	32	58	-52	30	13	11	2	2	14	18	0	196	13.3
Guy Charron	LW	51	13	29	42	-41	21	9	4	0	0	16	13	0	157	8.3
Dave Hudson	C	70	9	32	41	-19	27	7	2	0	1	22	9	1	115	7.8
Wilf Paiement	RW	78	26	13	39	-42	101	20	6	0	3	11	2	0	195	13.3
Ed Gilbert	C	80	16	22	38	-45	14	5	9	2	0	16	6	0	190	8.4
Robin Burns	LW	71	18	15	33	-40	70	11	7	0	1	10	5	0	126	14.3
Randy Rota	LW	80	15	18	33	-38	30	12	3	0	0	16	2	0	182	8.2
Lynn Powis	C	73	11	20	31	-54	19	8	3	0	0	8	12	0	149	7.4
Rich Lemieux	C	79	10	20	30	-35	64	7	3	0	1	14	6	0	131	7.6
Jim McElmury	D	78	5	17	22	-47	25	4	1	0	1	9	8	0	136	3.7
Gary Croteau	LW	77	8	11	19	-36	16	7	0	1	1	6	3	2	136	5.9
Brent Hughes	D	66	1	18	19	-52	43	1	0	0	0	13	5	0	80	1.3
Norm Dube	LW	56	8	10	18	-12	54	6	2	0	1	9	1	0	78	10.3
Jean-Guy Lagace	D	19	2	9	11	-20	22	0	2	0	0	3	6	0	40	5
Bart Crashley	D	27	3	6	9	-16	10	2	1	0	1	3	3	0	39	7.7
Claude Houde	D	34	3	4	7	-31	20	1	2	0	1	3	1	0	41	7.3
Larry Johnston	D	16	0	7	7	-17	10	0	0	0	0	6	1	0	13	0

Appendix: Statistics 253

Player	Pos	GP	G	A	PTS	+/-	PIM	EVG	PPG	SHG	GWG	EVA	PPA	SHA	S	S%
Gary Coalter	RW	30	2	4	6	-8	2	2	0	0	1	4	0	0	20	10
Dennis Patterson	D	66	1	5	6	-56	39	1	0	0	0	5	0	0	53	1.9
Larry Giroux	D	21	0	6	6	-20	24	0	0	0	0	4	2	0	27	0
Butch Deadmarsh	LW	20	3	2	5	-5	19	2	1	0	1	1	0	1	32	9.4
Ted Snell	RW	29	3	2	5	-8	8	2	0	1	0	2	0	0	25	12
Bryan Lefley	D	29	0	3	3	-24	6	0	0	0	0	2	0	1	14	0
Doug Buhr	LW	6	0	2	2	0	4	0	0	0	0	2	0	0	3	0
Glen Burdon	C	11	0	2	2	-3	0	0	0	0	0	2	0	0	2	0
Chris Evans	D	2	0	2	2	-1	2	0	0	0	0	0	2	0	4	0
Ken Murray	D	8	0	2	2	3	14	0	0	0	0	2	0	0	5	0
Doug Horbul	LW	4	1	0	1	-3	2	1	0	0	0	0	0	0	5	20
Roger Lemelin	D	8	0	1	1	-9	6	0	0	0	0	1	0	0	4	0
Peter McDuffe	G	36	0	1	1	0	0	0	0	0	0	1	0	0	0	
Mike Baumgartner	D	17	0	0	0	-9	0	0	0	0	0	0	0	0	13	0
Mike Boland	D	1	0	0	0	0	0	0	0	0	0	0	0	0	0	
Hugh Harvey	C	8	0	0	0	-2	2	0	0	0	0	0	0	0	5	0
Henry Lehvonen	D	4	0	0	0	4	0	0	0	0	0	0	0	0	2	0
John Wright	C	4	0	0	0	-3	2	0	0	0	0	0	0	0	5	0
Denis Herron	G	22	0	0	0	0	2	0	0	0	0	1	0	0	0	
Michel Plasse	G	24	0	0	0	0	18	0	0	0	0	1	0	0	0	
Team Total		80	184	315	499	---	726	121	57	6	15	207	105	5	2223	8.3

Goalie Stats

Player	GP	W	L	T/O	GA	SA	SV	SV%	GAA	SO	MIN
Peter McDuffe	36	7	25	4	148	1262	1114	0.883	4.23	0	2098
Denis Herron	22	4	13	4	80	767	687	0.896	3.75	0	1279
Michel Plasse	24	4	16	3	96	773	677	0.876	4.06	0	1420
Team Total		15	54	11	324	2802	2478	0.884	4.05	0	4797

1974–1975 Washington Capitals Scoring and Goaltending Statistics

Player	Pos	GP	G	A	PTS	+/-	PIM	EVA	PPG	SHG	GWG	EVA	PPA	SHA	S	S%
Tommy Williams	C	73	22	36	58	-69	12	13	7	2	1	23	13	0	135	16.3
Denis Dupere	LW	53	20	15	35	-43	8	12	8	0	0	9	6	0	133	15
Mike Marson	LW	76	16	12	28	-65	59	11	5	0	2	16	7	0	91	17.6
Yvon Labre	D	76	4	23	27	-54	182	4	0	0	0	17	6	0	71	5.6
Ron Lalonde	C	50	12	14	26	-40	27	7	4	1	1	10	2	2	67	17.9
Mike Bloom	RW	67	7	19	26	-54	84	7	0	0	0	15	4	0	88	8
Dave Kryskow	LW	51	9	15	24	-29	83	7	1	1	0	12	3	0	99	9.1

Appendix: Statistics

Player	Pos	GP	G	A	PTS	+/-	PIM	EVA	PPG	SHG	GWG	EVA	PPA	SHA	S	S%
Doug Mohns	D	75	2	19	21	-54	54	1	1	0	0	11	7	1	82	2.4
Bill Lesuk	LW	79	8	11	19	-33	77	5	1	2	0	8	2	1	119	6.7
Stan Gilbertson	LW	25	11	7	18	-37	12	9	2	0	1	4	3	0	65	16.9
Ace Bailey	LW	22	4	13	17	-29	8	3	1	0	0	7	5	1	46	8.7
Ron Anderson	RW	28	9	7	16	-20	8	5	4	0	0	7	0	0	43	20.9
Steve Atkinson	RW	46	11	4	15	-25	8	6	3	2	0	2	2	0	92	12
Pete Laframboise	C	45	5	10	15	-36	22	5	0	0	0	8	2	0	86	5.8
Bob Gryp	LW	27	5	8	13	-24	21	5	0	0	0	5	3	0	43	11.6
Bruce Cowick	RW	65	5	6	11	-43	41	5	0	0	0	5	1	0	73	6.8
Gord Smith	D	63	3	8	11	-60	56	1	2	0	0	7	1	0	58	5.2
Gord Brooks	RW	38	1	10	11	-19	25	0	1	0	0	7	3	0	80	1.3
Nelson Pyatt	C	16	6	4	10	-13	21	6	0	0	1	1	3	0	33	18.2
Jim Hrycuik	C	21	5	5	10	-12	12	4	1	0	0	2	2	1	29	17.2
Bill Mikkelson	D	59	3	7	10	-82	52	0	3	0	0	6	1	0	47	6.4
Paul Nicholson	LW	39	4	5	9	-29	7	4	0	0	1	5	0	0	46	8.7
Greg Joly	D	44	1	7	8	-69	44	0	1	0	0	4	3	0	73	1.4
Jack Lynch	D	20	1	5	6	-54	16	1	0	0	0	1	4	0	28	3.6
Jack Egers	RW	14	3	2	5	-14	8	2	1	0	1	1	1	0	21	14.3
Lew Morrison	RW	18	0	4	4	-14	6	0	0	0	0	4	0	0	21	0
Ron Jones	D	19	1	1	2	-13	16	0	1	0	0	1	0	0	13	7.7
Michel Belhumeur	G	35	0	2	2	0	10	0	0	0	0	2	0	0	0	0.0
Tony White	LW	5	0	2	2	0	0	0	0	0	0	2	0	0	8	0
Willie Brossart	D	12	1	0	1	-13	14	1	0	0	0	0	0	0	12	8.3
Larry Fullan	LW	4	1	0	1	-2	0	0	1	0	0	0	0	0	5	20
Blair Stewart	C	2	1	0	1	-2	2	1	0	0	0	0	0	0	4	25
Murray Anderson	D	40	0	1	1	-40	68	0	0	0	0	1	0	0	23	0
John Adams	G	8	0	0	0	0	2	0	0	0	0	0	0	0	0	0
Ron Low	G	48	0	0	0	0	4	0	0	0	0	0	0	0	0	0
Joe Lundrigan	D	3	0	0	0	-3	2	0	0	0	0	0	0	0	2	0
Andre Peloffy	C	9	0	0	0	-8	0	0	0	0	0	0	0	0	7	0
Bill Riley	RW	1	0	0	0	-1	0	0	0	0	0	0	0	0	0	0
Rod Seiling	D	1	0	0	0	0	0	0	0	0	0	0	0	0	2	0
Team Total		80	181	282	463	---	1071	125	48	8	8	195	81	6	1845	9.8

Goalie Stats

Player	GP	W	L	T/O	GA	SA	SV	SV%	GAA	SO	MIN
Ron Low	48	8	36	2	235	1622	1387	0.855	5.45	1	2587
John Adams	8	0	7	0	46	275	229	0.833	6.90	0	400
Michel Belhumeur	35	0	24	3	162	1165	1003	0.861	5.37	0	1810
Team Total	80	8	67	5	443	3062	2619	0.855	5.54	1	4797

Appendix: Statistics 255

1975–1976 Kansas City Scouts Scoring and Goaltending Statistics

Player	Pos	GP	G	A	PTS	+/-	PIM	EVG	PPG	SHG	GWG	EVA	PPA	SHA	S	S%
Guy Charron	C	78	27	44	71	-51	12	18	9	0	4	33	11	0	226	11.9
Wilf Paiement	RW	57	21	22	43	-37	121	17	4	0	3	14	8	0	178	11.8
Gary Bergman	D	75	5	33	38	-52	82	4	1	0	1	19	14	0	125	4
Craig Patrick	RW	80	17	18	35	-24	14	13	3	1	0	16	2	0	143	11.9
Gary Croteau	LW	79	19	14	33	-24	12	15	4	0	1	10	4	0	139	13.7
Robin Burns	LW	78	13	18	31	-40	37	11	2	0	0	14	4	0	145	9
Dave Hudson	C	74	11	20	31	-28	12	9	2	0	0	17	3	0	114	9.6
Randy Rota	LW	71	12	14	26	-39	14	10	2	0	1	13	1	0	146	8.2
Simon Nolet	RW	41	10	15	25	-9	16	8	2	0	1	8	7	0	123	8.1
Chuck Arnason	RW	39	14	10	24	-35	21	9	5	0	0	7	3	0	122	11.5
Phil Roberto	RW	37	7	15	22	-11	42	4	3	0	0	11	4	0	89	7.9
Dennis Patterson	D	69	5	16	21	-28	28	5	0	0	0	13	3	0	76	6.6
Buster Harvey	RW	39	5	12	17	-31	6	5	0	0	0	10	2	0	76	6.6
Denis Dupere	LW	43	6	8	14	-7	16	4	2	0	0	8	0	0	37	16.2
Jean-Guy Lagace	D	69	3	10	13	-35	108	1	1	1	1	5	5	0	75	4
Ed Gilbert	C	41	4	8	12	-29	8	3	1	0	0	6	2	0	74	5.4
Larry Johnston	D	72	2	10	12	-65	112	1	1	0	0	5	5	0	77	2.6
Steve Durbano	D	37	1	11	12	-30	209	1	0	0	0	8	3	0	65	1.5
Henry Boucha	C	28	4	7	11	-13	14	2	2	0	0	4	3	0	42	9.5
Germain Gagnon	LW	31	1	9	10	-14	6	0	1	0	0	8	1	0	30	3.3
Jim McElmury	D	38	2	6	8	-14	6	1	1	0	0	3	3	0	43	4.7
Hugh Harvey	C	10	1	1	2	-5	2	1	0	0	0	0	1	0	11	9.1
Claude Houde	D	25	0	2	2	-13	20	0	0	0	0	2	0	0	16	0
Ken Murray	D	23	0	2	2	-2	24	0	0	0	0	2	0	0	12	0
Terry McDonald	D	8	0	1	1	-5	6	0	0	0	0	0	1	0	4	0
Bill McKenzie	G	22	0	1	1	0	4	0	0	0	0	1	0	0	0	0.0
Don Cairns	LW	7	0	0	0	-1	0	0	0	0	0	0	0	0	2	0
Norm Dube	LW	1	0	0	0	0	0	0	0	0	0	0	0	0	0	
Denis Herron	G	64	0	0	0	0	16	0	0	0	0	0	0	0	0	0
Roger Lemelin	D	11	0	0	0	-1	0	0	0	0	0	0	0	0	1	0
Rich Lemieux	C	2	0	0	0	0	0	0	0	0	0	0	0	0	1	0
Bill Oleschuk	G	1	0	0	0	0	0	0	0	0	0	0	0	0	0	0
Team Total		80	190	327	517	---	968	142	46	2	12	237	90	0	2192	8.7

Goalie Stats

Player	GP	W	L	T/O	GA	SA	SV	SV%	GAA	SO	MIN
Denis Herron	64	11	39	11	243	2211	1968	0.890	4.04	0	3611
Bill McKenzie	22	1	16	1	97	624	527	0.845	5.20	0	1119
Bill Oleschuk	1	0	1	0	4	52	48	0.923	4.00	0	60
Team Total	**80**	**12**	**56**	**12**	**344**	**2887**	**2543**	**0.881**	**4.31**	**0**	**4790**

1975–1976 Washington Capitals Scoring and Goaltending Statistics

Player	Pos	GP	G	A	PTS	+/-	PIM	EVG	PPG	SHG	GWG	EVA	PPA	SHA	S	S%
Nelson Pyatt	C	77	26	23	49	-57	14	21	5	0	0	16	7	0	151	17.2
Hartland Monahan	RW	80	17	29	46	-49	35	15	2	0	2	23	6	0	142	12
Tony White	LW	80	25	17	42	-41	56	18	7	0	2	13	4	0	166	15.1
Ace Bailey	LW	67	13	19	32	-42	75	11	2	0	2	11	8	0	131	9.9
Gerry Meehan	C	32	16	15	31	-7	10	13	3	0	0	10	5	0	80	20
Bob Sirois	RW	43	10	19	29	-33	6	6	4	0	0	12	7	0	109	9.2
Ron Lalonde	C	80	9	19	28	-27	19	6	2	1	0	17	2	0	92	9.8
Stan Gilbertson	LW	31	13	14	27	-26	6	8	5	0	0	8	6	0	62	21
Blair Stewart	LW	74	13	14	27	-52	113	13	0	0	0	12	2	0	88	14.8
Bill Clement	C	46	10	17	27	-30	20	8	2	0	0	12	5	0	95	10.5
Greg Joly	D	54	8	17	25	-47	28	4	3	1	1	10	7	0	81	9.9
Harvey Bennett	C	49	12	10	22	-25	39	11	1	0	1	10	0	0	72	16.7
Jack Lynch	D	79	9	13	22	-52	78	4	5	0	1	8	5	0	126	7.1
Yvon Labre	D	80	2	20	22	-38	146	2	0	0	0	16	4	0	110	1.8
Tommy Williams	RW	34	8	13	21	-34	6	6	2	0	0	7	6	0	39	20.5
Jean Lemieux	D	33	6	14	20	-22	2	1	5	0	1	6	8	0	65	9.2
Mike Lampman	LW	27	7	12	19	-6	28	7	0	0	1	11	1	0	55	12.7
Peter Scamurra	D	58	2	13	15	-38	33	1	1	0	0	13	0	0	49	4.1
Rick Bragnalo	C	19	2	10	12	-4	8	2	0	0	0	4	6	0	28	7.1
Bob Gryp	LW	46	6	5	11	-18	12	6	0	0	0	3	2	0	54	11.1
Mike Marson	LW	57	4	7	11	-18	50	4	0	0	0	5	2	0	35	11.4
Willie Brossart	D	49	0	8	8	-49	40	0	0	0	0	8	0	0	36	0
Bob Paradise	D	48	0	8	8	-41	42	0	0	0	0	8	0	0	26	0
Jack Egers	RW	12	3	3	6	-3	8	1	2	0	0	0	3	0	18	16.7
Gord Smith	D	25	1	2	3	-22	28	0	1	0	0	2	0	0	10	10
John Paddock	RW	8	1	1	2	-5	12	1	0	0	0	1	0	0	5	20
Paul Nicholson	LW	14	0	2	2	-4	9	0	0	0	0	2	0	0	10	0
Gord Lane	D	3	1	0	1	-5	12	0	1	0	0	0	0	0	2	50
Michel Belhumeur	G	7	0	1	1	0	0	0	0	0	0	1	0	0	0	0
Larry Bolonchuk	D	1	0	1	1	-1	0	0	0	0	0	1	0	0	1	0

Appendix: Statistics

Player	Pos	GP	G	A	PTS	+/-	PIM	EVG	PPG	SHG	GWG	EVA	PPA	SHA	S	S%
Brian Kinsella	C	4	0	1	1	-2	0	0	0	0	0	1	0	0	11	0
Ron Jones	D	2	0	0	0	-1	0	0	0	0	0	0	0	0	0	
Ron Low	G	43	0	0	0	0	2	0	0	0	0	0	0	0	0	0
Don McLean	D	9	0	0	0	-3	6	0	0	0	0	0	0	0	4	0
Brian Stapleton	RW	1	0	0	0	-2	0	0	0	0	0	0	0	0	0	
Bernie Wolfe	G	40	0	0	0	0	0	0	0	0	0	0	0	0	0	0
Team Total		80	224	347	571	---	943	169	53	2	11	251	96	0	1953	11.5

Goalie Stats

Player	GP	W	L	T/O	GA	SA	SV	SV%	GAA	SO	MIN
Ron Low	43	6	31	2	208	1420	1212	0.854	5.46	0	2285
Bernie Wolfe	40	5	23	7	148	1300	1152	0.886	4.17	0	2130
Michel Belhumeur	7	0	5	1	32	229	197	0.860	5.11	0	376
Team Total	80	11	59	10	388	2949	2561	0.868	4.86	0	4791

Kansas City Scouts Game-by-Game Summary

1974–1975 Season

Date	Goalies	Opp.	Res.	Score	SF	SA	W–L–T	PTS	Goalie Rec.	Att.
Oct. 9, '74	Plasse	@TOR	L	2–6	28	46	0–1–0	0	Plasse: 0–1–0	16,346
Oct. 12	McDuffe	@NYI	L	2–6	36	29	0–2–0	0	McDuffe: 0–1–0	11,801
Oct. 13	Plasse	@PHI	L	2–3	20	40	0–3–0	0	Plasse: 0–2–0	17,007
Oct. 18	Plasse	@ATL	L	2–4	28	30	0–4–0	0	Plasse: 0–3–0	13,117
Oct. 19	McDuffe	@LA	L	0–3	19	30	0–5–0	0	McDuffe: 0–2–0	14,384
Oct. 23	Plasse	@CAL	T	4–4	27	22	0–5–1	1	Plasse: 0–3–1	5,874
Oct. 25	McDuffe 1 ENG	@VAN	L	3–5	24	44	0–6–1	1	McDuffe: 0–3–0	15,570
Oct. 27	McDuffe	@BOS	L	2–8	26	35	0–7–1	1	McDuffe: 0–4–0	15,004
Nov. 2	Plasse	CHI	L	3–4	35	29	0–8–1	1	Plasse: 0–4–1	14,748
Nov. 3	McDuffe	@WSH	W	5–4	28	25	1–8–1	3	McDuffe: 1–4–0	7,964
Nov. 5	Plasse 1 ENG	PIT	L	3–5	48	35	1–9–1	3	Plasse: 0–5–1	6,642
Nov. 7	McDuffe	VAN	L	4–6	37	27	1–10–1	3	McDuffe: 1–5–0	7,091
Nov. 9	Plasse	BUF	L	1–6	19	45	1–11–1	3	Plasse : 0–6–1	8,515
Nov. 13	Plasse	STL	W	5–3	24	28	2–11–1	5	Plasse: 1–6–1	6,585
Nov. 15	Plasse	NYI	W	4–2	33	26	3–11–1	7	Plasse: 2–6–1	6,741
Nov. 16	Plasse	@MIN	L	1–3	31	31	3–12–1	7	Plasse: 2–7–1	14,549
Nov. 20	Plasse	ATL	L	0–1	25	30	3–13–1	7	Plasse: 2–8–1	6,455
Nov. 22	Plasse	MTL	L	6–7	21	42	3–14–1	7	Plasse: 2–9–1	9,177
Nov. 23	McDuffe	@CHI	L	0–6	16	51	3–15–1	7	McDuffe: 1–6–0	15,050 (est.)
Nov. 26	McDuffe	VAN	W	4–3	23	29	4–15–1	9	McDuffe: 2–6–0	7,355
Nov. 27	McDuffe	@ATL	L	2–4	20	33	4–16–1	9	McDuffe: 2–7–0	12,752
Nov. 30	McDuffe	DET	L	0–1	14	19	4–17–1	9	McDuffe: 2–8–0	9,487

Appendix: Statistics

Date	Goalies	Opp.	Res.	Score	SF	SA	W–L–T	PTS	Goalie Rec.	Att.
Dec. 1	McDuffe	@PHI	L	0–10	22	47	4–18–1	9	McDuffe: 2–9–0	17,007
Dec. 4	McDuffe 14/20 (20:00) Plasse 16/17 (40:00)	@CHI	L	3–7	32	37	4–19–1	9	McDuffe: 2–10–0	13,500 (est.)
Dec. 6	Plasse	PHI	T	3–3	20	30	4–19–2	10	Plasse: 2–9–2	8,971
Dec. 7	Plasse	@NYI	L	1–4	25	35	4–20–2	10	Plasse: 2–10–2	11,929
Dec. 10	Plasse	BOS	L	2–6	29	31	4–21–2	10	Plasse: 2–11–2	8,069
Dec. 12	Plasse	CAL	W	5–3	40	29	5–21–2	12	Plasse: 3–11–2	5,979
Dec. 14	Plasse	VAN	T	2–2	24	39	5–21–3	13	Plasse: 3–11–3	7,057
Dec. 18	Plasse	LA	L	0–6	20	30	5–22–3	13	Plasse: 3–12–3	5,983
Dec. 19	McDuffe	@PIT	T	4–4	24	43	5–22–4	14	McDuffe: 2–10–1	7,047
Dec. 21	Plasse (59:46) 1 ENG	@STL	L	4–6	29	31	5–23–4	14	Plasse: 3–13–3	17,919
Dec. 22	Plasse	NYI	L	2–5	30	34	5–24–4	14	Plasse: 3–14–3	7,726
Dec. 28	Plasse	@MTL	L	2–7	25	37	5–25–4	14	Plasse: 3–15–3	16,825
Dec. 29	McDuffe (59:17)	@NYR	L	1–2	26	32	5–26–4	14	McDuffe: 2–11–1	17,500
Jan. 2, '75	McDuffe	STL	L	1–2	34	28	5–27–4	14	McDuffe: 2–12–1	10,058
Jan. 4	Plasse	DET	W	2–1	34	28	6–27–4	16	Plasse: 4–15–3	8,741
Jan. 6	McDuffe	MIN	W	5–2	31	27	7–27–4	18	McDuffe: 3–12–1	9,047
Jan. 8	Plasse	NYR	L	1–6	36	29	7–28–4	18	Plasse: 4–16–3	8,379
Jan. 11	McDuffe	WSH	W	5–3	33	30	8–28–4	20	McDuffe: 4–12–1	10,467
Jan. 14	McDuffe	PHI	L	4–6	32	40	8–29–4	20	McDuffe: 4–13–1	8,057
Jan. 16	Herron	@DET	L	4–7	28	42	8–30–4	20	Herron: 0–1–0	10,196
Jan. 18	McDuffe	CHI	W	4–1	33	39	9–30–4	22	McDuffe: 5–13–1	11,137
Jan. 19	Herron	@BUF	L	0–5	20	40	9–31–4	22	Herron: 0–2–0	15,863
Jan. 23	Herron	@BOS	W	3–2	19	36	10–31–4	24	Herron: 1–2–0	13,260
Jan. 25	McDuffe	@MIN	L	1–4	39	32	10–32–4	24	McDuffe: 5–14–1	13,205
Jan. 27	Herron	BOS	T	3–3	24	31	10–32–5	25	Herron: 1–2–1	9,657
Jan. 29	McDuffe	ATL	T	4–4	33	43	10–32–6	26	McDuffe: 5–14–2	6,677
Feb. 1	McDuffe (58:59)	MIN	L	2–3	30	22	10–33–6	26	McDuffe: 5–15–2	11,138
Feb. 2	Herron	@BUF	L	1–8	28	58	10–34–6	26	Herron: 1–3–1	15,863
Feb. 4	Herron	CHI	T	3–3	35	34	10–34–7	27	Herron: 1–3–2	7,227
Feb. 6	Herron	TOR	W	3–2	37	28	11–34–7	29	Herron: 2–3–2	7,128
Feb. 7	McDuffe	@STL	L	0–5	25	46	11–35–7	29	McDuffe: 5–16–2	17,754
Feb. 9	McDuffe	@CAL	W	2–1	38	34	12–35–7	31	McDuffe: 6–16–2	4,204
Feb. 11	Herron	@VAN	L	0–4	30	42	12–36–7	31	Herron: 2–4–2	15,570
Feb. 13	Herron	WSH	W	5–1	35	30	13–36–7	33	Herron: 3–4–2	6,873
Feb. 15	McDuffe	CAL	L	0–3	24	45	13–37–7	33	McDuffe: 6–17–2	10,147

Date	Goalies	Opp.	Res.	Score	SF	SA	W–L–T	PTS	Goalie Rec.	Att.
	29/31 (40:00)									
	Herron 13/14 (20:00)									
Feb. 16	Herron	@WSH	L	0–3	32	36	13–38–7	33	Herron: 3–5–2	14,214
Feb. 18	McDuffe	NYR	T	2–2	27	29	13–38–8	34	McDuffe: 6–17–3	7,122
Feb. 20	Herron	MTL	L	3–6	28	42	13–39–8	34	Herron: 3–6–2	8,652
Feb. 23	McDuffe	MIN	W	4–2	33	26	14–39–8	36	McDuffe: 7–17–3	7,819
Feb. 26	Herron	@TOR	L	2–4	26	32	14–40–8	36	Herron: 3–7–2	16,331
Mar. 1	McDuffe	@PHI	L	0–3	16	45	14–41–8	36	McDuffe: 7–18–3	17,007
Mar. 2	Herron	@ATL	L	0–4	26	30	14–42–8	36	Herron: 3–8–2	12,118
Mar. 4	McDuffe	@LA	L	4–7	23	36	14–43–8	36	McDuffe: 7–19–3	9,269
Mar. 5	Herron	PIT	T	4–4	37	32	14–43–9	37	Herron: 3–8–3	8,123
Mar. 7	McDuffe	NYR	L	2–5	29	45	14–44–9	37	McDuffe: 7–20–3	11,123
Mar. 8	Herron	@DET	L	1–5	23	38	14–45–9	37	Herron: 3–9–3	11,011
Mar. 11	McDuffe	@VAN	T	3–3	29	42	14–45–10	38	McDuffe: 7–20–4	15,570
Mar. 14	Herron	@STL	L	1–6	26	36	14–46–10	38	Herron: 3–10–3	18,848
Mar. 16	McDuffe	@PIT	L	3–6	36	38	14–47–10	38	McDuffe: 7–21–4	13,404
Mar. 19	Herron (59:05) 1 ENG	NYI	L	1–3	32	29	14–48–10	38	Herron: 3–11–3	7,732
Mar. 22	McDuffe	BUF	L	2–4	25	47	14–49–10	38	McDuffe: 7–22–4	13,567
Mar. 25	McDuffe (59:32)	@MIN	L	1–2	32	26	14–50–10	38	McDuffe: 7–23–4	11,881
Mar. 26	Herron	TOR	T	2–2	25	32	14–50–11	39	Herron: 3–11–4	8,487
Mar. 29	Herron	@MTL	L	1–4	29	31	14–51–11	39	Herron: 3–12–4	17,703
Mar. 30	McDuffe	@NYR	L	2–8	18	59	14–52–11	39	McDuffe: 7–24–4	17,500
Apr. 1	Herron	LA	W	3–1	27	36	15–52–11	41	Herron: 4–12–4	8,487
Apr. 3	McDuffe	@CHI	L	4–6	27	33	15–53–11	41	McDuffe: 7–25–4	9,000 (est.)
Apr. 6	Herron	STL	L	2–3	26	39	15–54–11	41	Herron: 4–13–4	12,383

Washington Capitals Game-by-Game Summary

1974–1975 Season

Date	Goalies	Opp.	Res.	Score	SF	SA	W–L–T	PTS	Goalie Rec.	Att.
Oct. 9, '74	Low	@NYR	L	3–6	12	43	0–1–0	0	Low: 0–1–0	17,500
Oct. 12	Adams	@MIN	L	0–6	30	31	0–2–0	0	Adams: 0–1–0	14,059
Oct. 15	Low	LA	T	1–1	20	34	0–2–1	1	Low: 0–1–1	8,093
Oct. 17	Low	CHI	W	4–3	25	36	1–2–1	3	Low: 1–1–1	9,471
Oct. 19	Belhumeur (59:01) 1 ENG	@DET	L	4–6	25	32	1–3–1	3	Belhumeur: 0–1–0	13,217

Date	Goalies	Opp.	Res.	Score	SF	SA	W–L–T	PTS	Goalie Rec.	Att.
Oct. 20	Low	NYI	L	0–5	26	28	1–4–1	3	Low: 1–2–1	7,514
Oct. 22	Low	DET	L	0–3	25	35	1–5–1	3	Low: 1–3–1	7,368
Oct. 23	Belhumeur (59:42)	@CHI	L	2–3	12	42	1–6–1	3	Belhumeur: 0–2–0	16,660
Oct. 27	Low	TOR	L	3–4	19	45	1–7–1	3	Low: 1–4–1	10,106
Oct. 31	Belhumeur	MTL	L	0–3	19	29	1–8–1	3	Belhumeur: 0–3–0	8,251
Nov. 3	Low	KC	L	4–5	25	28	1–9–1	3	Low: 1–5–1	7,964
Nov. 7	Low 13/19 (22:26) Belhumeur 18/22 (37:34)	@BOS	L	4–10	28	41	1–10–1	3	Low: 1–6–1	14,715
Nov. 9	Belhumeur	@PHI	L	2–6	27	45	1–11–1	3	Belhumeur: 0–4–0	17,007
Nov. 10	Low 14/19 (25:26) Belhumeur 17/23 (34:34)	MTL	L	1–11	17	42	1–12–1	3	Low: 1–7–1	9,781
Nov. 12	Belhumeur	ATL	T	2–2	27	25	1–12–2	4	Belhumeur: 0–4–1	7,823
Nov. 13	Belhumeur	@ATL	L	3–4	25	41	1–13–2	4	Belhumeur: 0–5–1	11,692
Nov. 16	Low	@PIT	L	1–8	27	42	1–14–2	4	Low: 1–8–1	10,332
Nov. 17	Low 8/11 (25:22) Belhumeur 7/10 (24:38)	PIT	L	0–6	26	21	1–15–2	4	Low: 1–9–1	8,697
Nov. 19	Low	CAL	W	6–4	27	25	2–15–2	6	Low: 2–9–1	7,061
Nov. 20	Low	@BUF	L	3–7	14	50	2–16–2	6	Low: 2–10–1	15,863
Nov. 24	Belhumeur	MIN	T	4–4	36	27	2–16–3	7	Belhumeur: 0–5–2	8,897
Nov. 27	Belhumeur	@MIN	L	4–6	30	34	2–17–3	7	Belhumeur: 0–6–2	13,253
Nov. 30	Low	@TOR	L	1–7	22	45	2–18–3	7	Low: 2–11–1	16,418
Dec. 1	Belhumeur	CAL	L	2–5	21	37	2–19–3	7	Belhumeur: 0–7–2	6,949
Dec. 3	Adams	BUF	L	3–5	29	46	2–20–3	7	Adams: 0–2–0	8,696
Dec. 5	Adams	@BUF	L	2–9	17	45	2–21–3	7	Adams: 0–3–0	15,863
Dec. 7	Belhumeur	@STL	L	2–8	29	60	2–22–3	7	Belhumeur: 0–8–2	17,808
Dec. 8	Belhumeur	STL	L	1–3	23	23	2–23–3	7	Belhumeur: 0–9–2	10,215
Dec. 12	Belhumeur	NYR	T	6–6	30	36	2–23–4	8	Belhumeur: 0–9–3	9,089
Dec. 14	Low 10/15 (20:00)	@BOS	L	1–12	16	48	2–24–4	8	Low: 2–12–1	14,075

Appendix: Statistics   261

Date	Goalies	Opp.	Res.	Score	SF	SA	W-L-T	PTS	Goalie Rec.	Att.
	Belhumeur 26/33 (40:00)									
Dec. 15	Low	TOR	W	3-1	31	26	3-24-4	10	Low: 3-12-1	11,526
Dec. 17	Low	@VAN	L	2-4	27	31	3-25-4	10	Low: 3-13-1	15,570
Dec. 19	Belhumeur	@LA	L	1-4	15	42	3-26-4	10	Belhumeur: 0-10-3	9,229
Dec. 20	Low	@CAL	L	2-5	23	44	3-27-4	10	Low: 3-14-1	3,241
Dec. 22	Low	BUF	L	0-4	27	41	3-28-4	10	Low: 3-15-1	10,205
Dec. 26	Low (59:46) 1 ENG	PHI	L	1-4	20	33	3-29-4	10	Low: 3-16-1	18,130
Dec. 29	Low	NYI	L	0-7	19	30	3-30-4	10	Low: 3-17-1	11,010
Jan. 2, '75	Belhumeur	@NYI	L	2-5	15	46	3-31-4	10	Belhumeur: 0-11-3	14,623
Jan. 4	Low 23/32 (40:00) Belhumeur 14/15 (20:00)	@MTL	L	0-10	17	47	3-32-4	10	Low: 3-18-1	16,451
Jan. 5	Belhumeur	@ATL	L	0-3	20	45	3-33-4	10	Belhumeur: 0-12-3	12,045
Jan. 7	Belhumeur 8/9 (49:42) Low 33/35 (10:18)	BOS	T	3-3	15	44	3-33-5	11	Low: 3-18-2	15,222
Jan. 11	Low	@KC	L	3-5	30	33	3-34-5	11	Low: 3-19-2	10,467
Jan. 12	Low	MTL	L	2-7	18	34	3-35-5	11	Low: 3-20-2	9,081
Jan. 14	Adams	LA	L	2-6	25	43	3-36-5	11	Adams: 0-4-0	8,029
Jan. 16	Low	@PHI	L	0-4	20	40	3-37-5	11	Low: 3-21-2	17,007
Jan. 19	Low	PIT	L	2-3	36	40	3-38-5	11	Low: 3-22-2	10,905
Jan. 23	Low	VAN	L	2-3	22	38	3-39-5	11	Low: 3-23-2	8,950
Jan. 25	Belhumeur	@DET	L	2-5	25	38	3-40-5	11	Belhumeur: 0-13-3	11,217
Jan. 26	Low	DET	W	6-3	23	38	4-40-5	13	Low: 4-23-2	10,425
Jan. 30	Belhumeur	@LA	L	4-6	22	35	4-41-5	13	Belhumeur: 0-14-3	9,764
Feb. 1	Low (59:47)	@VAN	L	2-5	20	34	4-42-5	13	Low: 4-24-2	15,570
Feb. 5	Belhumeur	@CAL	L	1-5	27	42	4-43-5	13	Belhumeur: 0-15-3	2,663
Feb. 8	Low	@NYI	L	1-5	12	46	4-44-5	13	Low: 4-25-2	12,531
Feb. 9	Low	@NYR	L	3-7	27	40	4-45-5	13	Low: 4-26-2	17,500
Feb. 11	Low	NYR	W	7-4	26	28	5-45-5	15	Low: 5-26-2	10,104
Feb. 13	Belhumeur	@KC	L	1-5	30	35	5-46-5	15	Belhumeur: 0-16-3	6,873
Feb. 15	Low 8/12 (9:07)	@STL	L	1-7	18	47	5-47-5	15	Low: 5-27-2	18,328

Appendix: Statistics

Date	Goalies	Opp.	Res.	Score	SF	SA	W–L–T	PTS	Goalie Rec.	Att.
Feb. 16	Belhumeur 32/35 (50:53) Low	KC	W	3–0	36	32	6–47–5	17	Low: 6–27–2	14,214
Feb. 18	Belhumeur	LA	L	1–6	15	43	6–48–5	17	Belhumeur: 0–17–3	9,372
Feb. 21	Low	BUF	L	4–9	23	39	6–49–5	17	Low: 6–28–2	8,075
Feb. 22	Belhumeur	@CHI	L	3–10	15	43	6–50–5	17	Belhumeur: 0–18–3	14,000 (est.)
Feb. 23	Low	STL	L	2–7	23	44	6–51–5	17	Low: 6–29–2	7,932
Feb. 25	Low	CHI	L	2–6	27	24	6–52–5	17	Low: 6–30–2	12,671
Feb. 26	Belhumeur	@PIT	L	1–3	23	45	6–53–5	17	Belhumeur: 0–19–3	11,059
Mar. 1	Low	@TOR	L	4–5	24	49	6–54–5	17	Low: 6–31–2	16,446
Mar. 2	Belhumeur	VAN	L	3–7	22	33	6–55–5	17	Belhumeur: 0–20–3	10,248
Mar. 4	Adams 8/13 (20:00) Low 21/24 (40:00)	BOS	L	0–8	27	37	6–56–5	17	Adams: 0–5–0	13,273
Mar. 7	Belhumeur	@MTL	L	4–8	18	34	6–57–5	17	Belhumeur: 0–21–3	16,852
Mar. 9	Low	TOR	L	2–4	13	41	6–58–5	17	Low: 6–32–2	9,450
Mar. 15	Belhumeur 10/15 (14:45) Low 43/50 (45:15)	@PIT	L	1–12	24	65	6–59–5	17	Belhumeur: 0–22–3	13,404
Mar. 18	Low 25/32 (50:57) Belhumeur 6/6 (9:03)	PHI	L	2–7	17	38	6–60–5	17	Low: 6–33–2	18,130
Mar. 20	Belhumeur	MIN	L	1–5	26	40	6–61–5	17	Belhumeur: 0–23–3	7,620
Mar. 22	Low	@BOS	L	2–8	19	41	6–62–5	17	Low: 6–34–2	15,003
Mar. 23	Belhumeur	ATL	L	0–5	31	45	6–63–5	17	Belhumeur: 0–24–3	10,105
Mar. 26	Adams	@LA	L	1–5	19	43	6–64–5	17	Adams: 0–6–0	10,636
Mar. 28	Low	@CAL	W	5–3	25	20	7–64–5	19	Low: 7–34–2	3,933
Mar. 30	Low	DET	L	5–8	21	35	7–65–5	19	Low: 7–35–2	10,509
Apr. 2	Adams	@DET	L	3–8	31	40	7–66–5	19	Adams: 0–7–0	11,239
Apr. 5	Low 23/31 (40:00) Adams 12/14 (20:00)	@MTL	L	2–10	18	45	7–67–5	19	Low: 7–36–2	16,910
Apr. 6	Low	PIT	W	8–4	29	32	8–67–5	21	Low: 8–36–2	9,061

Appendix: Statistics

Kansas City Scouts Game-by-Game Summary

1975–1976 Season

Date	Goalies	Opp.	Res.	Score	SF	SA	W–L–T	PTS	Goalie Rec.	Att.
Oct. 8, '75	Herron	NYI	T	1–1	20	26	0–0–1	1	Herron: 0–0–1	6,850
Oct. 11-	Herron	VAN	W	4–2	37	30	1–0–1	3	Herron: 1–0–1	9,683
Oct. 14	Herron 10/14 (20:00) McKenzie 17/18 (40:00)	@STL	L	1–5	27	32	1–1–1	3	Herron: 1–1–1	16,294
Oct. 18	Herron (59:00) 1 ENG	ATL	L	3–5	20	31	1–2–1	3	Herron: 1–2–1	7,036
Oct. 22	McKenzie	@WSH	W	4–2	20	20	2–2–1	5	McKenzie: 1–0–0	6,418
Oct. 23	Herron	@BOS	W	3–2	17	37	3–2–1	7	Herron: 2–2–1	12,717
Oct. 25	Herron	CHI	L	0–4	25	34	3–3–1	7	Herron: 2–3–1	10,111
Oct. 29	McKenzie	@MIN	L	0–2	24	25	3–4–1	7	McKenzie: 1–1–0	8,335
Oct. 30	McKenzie 21/25 (40:00) Herron 3/5 (20:00)	WSH	L	2–6	32	30	3–5–1	7	McKenzie: 1–2–0	5,127
Nov. 1	Herron	@TOR	L	0–3	22	44	3–6–1	7	Herron: 2–4–1	16,364
Nov. 2	McKenzie	@PHI	L	0–10	19	51	3–7–1	7	McKenzie: 1–3–0	17,007
Nov. 5	Herron	CAL	W	3–2	25	28	4–7–1	9	Herron: 3–4–1	5,937
Nov. 7	Herron	TOR	T	3–3	34	36	4–7–2	10	Herron: 3–4–2	7,156
Nov. 12	Herron	@ATL	L	1–2	29	40	4–8–2	10	Herron: 3–5–2	9,989
Nov. 13	McKenzie (59:43) 1 ENG	@DET	L	3–6	35	29	4–9–2	10	McKenzie: 1–4–0	10,115
Nov. 16	Herron	@BOS	L	2–4	30	44	4–10–2	10	Herron: 3–6–2	14,525
Nov. 19	Herron	@NYR	W	6–4	35	46	5–10–2	12	Herron: 4–6–2	17,500
Nov. 22	Herron (59:38)	@NYI	L	2–5	37	36	5–11–2	12	Herron: 4–7–2	14,865
Nov. 23	McKenzie 17/19 (20:00) Herron 23/27 (40:00)	@BUF	L	2–6	29	46	5–12–2	12	Herron: 4–8–2	16,433
Nov. 26	Herron	@STL	T	3–3	28	23	5–12–3	13	Herron: 4–8–3	8,500 (est.)
Nov. 27	Herron	STL	W	3–2	22	23	6–12–3	15	Herron: 5–8–3	10,137
Nov. 29	Herron (59:00) 1 ENG	DET	L	3–5	25	32	6–13–3	15	Herron: 5–9–3	9,437
Nov. 30	Herron	@CHI	T	1–1	22	40	6–13–4	16	Herron: 5–9–4	n.a.
Dec. 3	Herron	MTL	W	6–5	25	42	7–13–4	18	Herron: 6–9–4	7,638

264 Appendix: Statistics

Date	Goalies	Opp.	Res.	Score	SF	SA	W–L–T	PTS	Goalie Rec.	Att.
Dec. 5	Herron	NYR	L	2–3	29	30	7–14–4	18	Herron: 6–10–4	8,372
Dec. 6	Herron	@MIN	L	0–4	31	33	7–15–4	18	Herron: 6–11–4	9,244
Dec. 9	Herron	PIT	W	3–2	32	33	8–15–4	20	Herron: 7–11–4	6,127
Dec. 11	Herron (59:00)	MIN	L	3–5	28	15	8–16–4	20	Herron: 7–12–4	5,783
Dec. 13	Herron 27/30 (59:11) 1 ENG	@MTL	L	1–4	37	31	8–17–4	20	Herron: 7–13–4	15,575
Dec. 16	Herron (59:10)	@ATL	L	1–3	23	39	8–18–4	20	Herron: 7–14–4	9,834
Dec. 17	Herron	VAN	W	6–5	37	33	9–18–4	22	Herron: 8–14–4	5,583
Dec. 19	Herron	DET	W	4–1	33	34	10–18–4	24	Herron: 9–14–4	6,733
Dec. 20	Herron	@TOR	L	1–5	37	36	10–19–4	24	Herron: 9–15–4	16,313
Dec. 23	Herron 22/26 (40:00) McKenzie 9/10 (20:00)	BUF	L	1–5	37	36	10–20–4	24	Herron: 9–16–4	6,018
Dec. 27	McKenzie	@LA	L	4–9	20	46	10–21–4	24	McKenzie: 1–5–0	13,470
Dec. 28	Herron (59:51)	@CAL	W	3–1	29	43	11–21–4	26	Herron: 10–16–4	4,749
Dec. 30	McKenzie 14/16 (32:23) Herron 13/16 (27:27)	@VAN	L	2–5	36	32	11–22–4	26	McKenzie: 1–6–0	15,612
Jan. 1, '76	Herron (59:00) 1 ENG	PHI	L	2–4	39	34	11–23–4	26	Herron: 10–17–4	10,137
Jan. 3	Herron (59:05) 1 ENG	ATL	L	4–6	30	36	11–24–4	26	Herron: 10–18–4	9,139
Jan. 6	McKenzie	@NYI	L	1–8	22	42	11–25–4	26	McKenzie: 1–7–0	14,865
Jan. 7	Herron	LA	L	2–5	26	25	11–26–4	26	Herron: 10–19–4	6,273
Jan. 10	Herron 16/20 (28:50) McKenzie 14/18 (31:10)	NYR	L	4–8	28	38	11–27–4	26	McKenzie: 1–8–0	10,143
Jan. 14	Herron	@DET	L	3–8	25	30	11–28–4	26	Herron: 10–20–4	8,472
Jan. 15	McKenzie	TOR	L	4–6	34	31	11–29–4	26	McKenzie: 1–9–0	6,656
Jan. 17	Herron	PHI	L	1–7	24	41	11–30–4	26	Herron: 10–21–4	12,037
Jan. 21	McKenzie	STL	L	2–4	26	32	11–31–4	26	McKenzie: 1–10–0	7,143
Jan. 23	Oleschuk (59:57)	@CAL	L	1–4	35	52	11–32–4	26	Oleschuk: 0–1–0	6,096
Jan. 25	McKenzie	@CHI	L	1–3	33	33	11–33–4	26	McKenzie: 1–11–0	12,000 (est.)
Jan. 28	McKenzie	@MIN	L	3–9	35	28	11–34–4–	26	McKenzie: 1–12–0	8,035

Date	Goalies	Opp.	Res.	Score	SF	SA	W–L–T	PTS	Goalie Rec.	Att.
Jan. 29	Herron	@PIT	L	2–6	22	36	11–35–4	26	Herron: 10–22–4	8,360
Jan. 31	Herron	PIT	T	4–4	25	35	11–35–5	27	Herron: 10–22–5	12,471
Feb. 4	Herron	STL	T	3–3	22	42	11–35–6	28	Herron: 10–22–6	5,938
Feb. 7	Herron	WSH	W	5–1	30	33	12–35–6	30	Herron: 11–22–6	9,947
Feb. 12	Herron	NYI	T	2–2	19	29	12–35–7	31	Herron: 11–22–7	5,837
Feb. 14	Herron (59:00)	CHI	L	4–5	25	38	12–36–7	31	Herron: 11–23–7	9,126
Feb. 15	Herron (59:57)	@NYR	L	1–5	26	49	12–37–7	31	Herron: 11–24–7	17,500
Feb. 17	Herron	@PIT	L	1–6	26	41	12–38–7	31	Herron: 11–25–7	8,679
Feb. 18	McKenzie	BOS	T	3–3	21	26	12–38–8	32	McKenzie: 1–12–1	6,561
Feb. 20	McKenzie	ATL	L	1–3	34	38	12–39–8	32	McKenzie: 1–13–1	6,842
Feb. 22	McKenzie	MIN	L	3–6	36	23	12–40–8	32	McKenzie: 1–14–1	7,145
Feb. 25	Herron	MON	L	1–3	17	36	12–41–8	32	Herron: 11–26–7	6,129
Feb. 26	Herron	@NYI	T	2–2	17	41	12–41–9	33	Herron: 11–26–8	14,865
Feb. 28	Herron	BUF	T	4–4	26	40	12–41–10	34	Herron: 11–26–9	8,435
Mar. 4	Herron	PHI	L	1–6	28	40	12–42–10	34	Herron: 11–27–9	7,123
Mar. 6	Herron	VAN	L	3–5	25	36	12–43–10	34	Herron: 11–28–9	7,370
Mar. 7	Herron (59:53)	@PHI	L	1–4	23	51	12–44–10	34	Herron: 11–29–9	17,077
Mar. 10	Herron	@VAN	L	1–3	26	45	12–45–10	34	Herron: 11–30–9	15,612
Mar. 13	Herron (58:58) 1 ENG	@STL	L	3–5	26	45	12–46–10	34	Herron: 11–31–9	18,524
Mar. 16	Herron	CHI	L	3–6	35	27	12–47–10	34	Herron: 11–32–9	6,676
Mar. 18	McKenzie	BOS	L	2–5	20	32	12–48–10	34	McKenzie: 1–15–1	7,683
Mar. 20	Herron	CAL	T	2–2	29	30	12–48–11	35	Herron: 11–32–10	16,219
Mar. 21	Herron	@BUF	L	1–3	8	37	12–49–11	35	Herron: 11–33–10	16,433
Mar. 23	Herron (59:44)	@WSH	T	5–5	26	35	12–49–12	36	Herron: 11–33–11	11,235
Mar. 24	Herron 10/12 (24:11) McKenzie 17/19 (35:49)	MIN	L	1–4	31	31	12–50–12	36	Herron: 11–34–11	5,811
Mar. 27	Herron	@MTL	L	2–8	30	59	12–51–12	36	Herron: 11–35–11	16,847
Mar. 28	Herron	@NYR	L	2–4	34	53	12–52–12	36	Herron: 11–36–11	17,500
Mar. 30	Herron	LA	L	6–8	29	52	12–53–12	36	Herron: 11–37–11	7,123
Mar. 31	McKenzie (59:48)	@CHI	L	3–6	33	44	12–54–12	36	McKenzie: 1–16–1	9,000 (est.)
Apr. 3	Herron	@LA	L	1–5	14	43	12–55–12	36	Herron: 11–38–11	13,618
Apr. 4	Herron	@VAN	L	2–5	28	35	12–56–12	36	Herron: 11–39–11	15,612

Appendix: Statistics

Washington Capitals Game-by-Game Summary

1975–1976 Season

Date	Goalies	Opp.	Res.	Score	SF	SA	W–L–T	PTS	Goalie Rec.	Att.
Oct. 7, '75	Low (59:42)	PIT	L	2–4	28	23	0–1–0	0	Low: 0–1–0	9,375
Oct. 9	Belhumeur (59:19)	@PHI	L	4–5	28	50	0–2–0	0	Belhumeur: 0–1–0	17,077
Oct. 11	Low (59:21) 1 ENG	@PIT	L	5–7	29	40	0–3–0	0	Low: 0–2–0	11,834
Oct. 14	Belhumeur	@VAN	L	2–7	22	46	0–4–0	0	Belhumeur: 0–2–0	15,570
Oct. 15	Low	@LA	L	3–4	15	24	0–5–0	0	Low: 0–3–0	10,092
Oct. 17	Belhumeur	@CAL	T	3–3	18	29	0–5–1	1	Belhumeur: 0–2–1	7,996
Oct. 19	Low	@BUF	L	4–5	11	45	0–6–1	1	Low: 0–4–0	16,433
Oct. 22	Belhumeur (59:18) 1 ENG	KC	L	2–4	20	20	0–7–1	1	Belhumeur: 0–3–1	6,418
Oct. 24	Low 10/14 (42:31) 1 ENG Belhumeur 12/13 (17:13)	TOR	L	3–6	25	28	0–8–1	1	Low: 0–5–0	12,536
Oct. 26	Low (59:50)	@CHI	W	7–5	24	53	1–8–1	3	Low: 1–5–0	13,000 (est.)
Oct. 28	Belhumeur	@LA	L	0–6	16	40	1–9–1	3	Belhumeur: 0–4–1	8,412
Oct. 30	Wolfe	@KC	W	6–2	30	32	2–9–1	5	Wolfe: 1–0–0	5,127
Nov. 1	Belhumeur	@NYI	L	3–7	30	32	2–10–1	5	Belhumeur: 0–5–1	14,865
Nov. 5	Wolfe	LA	L	1–3	21	27	2–11–1	5	Wolfe: 1–1–0	12,527
Nov. 9	Low	STL	L	3–5	26	31	2–12–1	5	Low: 1–6–0	10,144
Nov. 12	Wolfe	PIT	T	6–6	25	37	2–12–2	6	Wolfe: 1–1–1	11,210
Nov. 14	Low 21/24 (38:43) Wolfe 13/14 (21:17)	ATL	L	1–4	22	38	2–13–2	6	Low: 1–7–0	9,206
Nov. 15	Wolfe 25/31 (40:00) Low 13/16 (20:00)	@STL	L	2–9	22	47	2–14–2	6	Wolfe: 1–2–1	17,466
Nov. 18	Low	@TOR	L	2–4	28	37	2–15–2	6	Low: 1–8–0	16,485
Nov. 19	Low	VAN	L	2–5	21	23	2–16–2	6	Low: 1–9–0	6,298
Nov. 21	Wolfe	CAL	L	0–2	22	26	2–17–2	6	Wolfe: 1–3–1	6,572
Nov. 26	Low	LA	W	7–2	21	29	3–17–2	8	Low: 2–9–0	6,282
Nov. 29	Low	@MIN	L	3–5	25	38	3–18–2	8	Low: 2–10–0	8,242
Dec. 3	Wolfe	BUF	T	4–4	25	37	3–18–3	9	Wolfe: 1–3–2	6,821
Dec. 4	Low	@BOS	L	2–3	13	43	3–19–3	9	Low: 2–11–0	13,621

Appendix: Statistics

Date	Goalies	Opp.	Res.	Score	SF	SA	W–L–T	PTS	Goalie Rec.	Att.
Dec. 6	Wolfe	@MTL	L	3–9	13	54	3–20–3	9	Wolfe: 1–4–2	14,424
Dec. 7	Low	@NYR	L	2–5	27	39	3–21–3	9	Low: 2–12–0	17,500
Dec. 9	Wolfe	@ATL	L	1–7	19	45	3–22–3	9	Wolfe: 1–5–2	9,877
Dec. 10	Low	CHI	L	2–7	33	34	3–23–3	9	Low: 2–13–0	6,502
Dec. 12	Low	DET	L	3–5	23	30	3–24–3	9	Low: 2–14–0	6,534
Dec. 14	Wolfe	MIN	T	4–4	22	26	3–24–4	10	Wolfe: 1–5–3	6,441
Dec. 17	Low	BOS	L	2–3	39	38	3–25–4	10	Low: 2–15–0	8,439
Dec. 19	Wolfe	PHI	L	5–7	22	54	3–26–4	10	Wolfe: 1–6–3	18,130
Dec. 21	Low 26/36 (48:00) Wolfe 10/14 (12:00)	@BUF	L	2–14	16	50	3–27–4	10	Low: 2–16–0	16,433
Dec. 26	Wolfe (59:39)	MIN	T	1–1	28	12	3–27–5	11	Wolfe: 1–6–4	11,881
Dec. 29	Wolfe	MTL	L	0–6	27	42	3–28–5	11	Wolfe: 1–7–4	10,358
Dec. 31	Low	@DET	L	0–4	23	31	3–29–5	11	Low: 2–17–0	11,115
Jan. 2, '76	Low 31/38 (45:00) Wolfe 12/13 (15:00)	CAL	L	5–8	31	51	3–30–5	11	Low: 2–18–0	12,262
Jan. 3	Low 10/15 (25:40) Wolfe 19/21 (34:20)	@MTL	L	0–7	28	36	3–31–5	11	Low: 2–19–0	15,293
Jan. 6	Wolfe (59:43) 1 ENG	VAN	L	3–5	24	37	3–32–5	11	Wolfe: 1–8–4	8,261
Jan. 8	Low	@STL	L	2–4	21	35	3–33–5	11	Low: 2–20–0	16,407
Jan. 9	Low	CAL	L	0–5	24	31	3–34–5	11	Low: 2–21–0	7,426
Jan. 11	Low	BOS	L	4–7	23	49	3–35–5	11	Low: 2–22–0	8,078
Jan. 13	Wolfe	MTL	L	2–3	13	29	3–36–5	11	Wolfe: 1–9–4	7,092
Jan. 15	Wolfe	@BUF	L	3–5	16	46	3–37–5	11	Wolfe: 1–10–4	16,433
Jan. 17	Low	@MIN	L	3–7	19	32	3–38–5	11	Low: 2–23–0	9,305
Jan. 21	Wolfe	NYI	L	2–5	21	28	3–39–5	11	Wolfe: 1–11–4	6,565
Jan. 23	Low	NYR	W	7–5	32	23	4–39–5	13	Low: 3–23–0	9,915
Jan. 24	Low 24/29 (40:00) Wolfe 8/11 (20:00)	@PIT	L	2–8	26	40	4–40–5	13	Low: 3–24–0	11,175
Jan. 27	Wolfe	@LA	L	0–2	25	30	4–41–5	13	Wolfe: 1–12–4	11,390
Jan. 28	Wolfe	@CAL	W	4–2	17	34	5–41–5	15	Wolfe: 2–12–4	4,274
Jan. 30	Wolfe	@VAN	L	2–4	16	44	5–42–5	15	Wolfe: 2–13–4	15,612
Feb. 4	Low	@TOR	T	4–4	23	41	5–42–6	16	Low: 3–24–1	16,307
Feb. 7	Low	@KC	L	1–5	33	30	5–43–6	16	Low: 3–25–1	9,947

Date	Goalies	Opp.	Res.	Score	SF	SA	W–L–T	PTS	Goalie Rec.	Att.
Feb. 8	Wolfe	@CHI	L	2–4	31	32	5–44–6	16	Wolfe: 2–14–4	12,000 (est.)
Feb. 10	Wolfe	LA	T	2–2	27	35	5–44–7	17	Wolfe: 2–14–5	7,243
Feb. 13	Wolfe (59:43)	STL	L	0–2	18	37	5–45–7	17	Wolfe: 2–15–5	8,111
Feb. 15	Low (59:55)	DET	W	8–5	28	34	6–45–7	19	Low: 4–25–1	8,467
Feb. 16	Wolfe (59:54)	TOR	L	1–5	32	42	6–46–7	19	Wolfe: 2–16–5	7,450
Feb. 18	Low	@NYR	L	4–11	33	42	6–47–7	19	Low: 4–26–1	17,500
Feb. 21	Wolfe	@DET	W	5–1	26	36	7–47–7	21	Wolfe: 3–16–5	9,872
Feb. 22	Wolfe	NYI	L	0–4	29	32	7–48–7	21	Wolfe: 3–17–5	9,850
Feb. 24	Wolfe (59:50)	PHI	T	5–5	19	41	7–48–8	22	Wolfe: 3–17–6	18,130
Feb. 27	Low (59:40)	BOS	T	3–3	26	28	7–48–9	23	Low: 4–26–2	13,153
Feb. 29	Wolfe (59:35)	CHI	W	4–1	30	43	8–48–9	25	Wolfe: 4–17–6	12,386
Mar. 6	Low	@NYI	L	3–6	27	48	8–49–9	25	Low: 4–27–2	14,865
Mar. 7	Low (59:10)	@BOS	L	3–4	24	29	8–50–9	25	Low: 4–28–2	13,994
Mar. 12	Low (59:26)	@ATL	L	1–4	26	38	8–51–9	25	Low: 4–29–2	12,154
Mar. 14	Wolfe 34/39 (57:59) Low 3/3 (2:01)	@MTL	L	1–5	22	42	8–52–9	25	Wolfe: 4–18–6	16,462
Mar. 16	Low	NYR	W	5–2	32	38	9–52–9	27	Low: 5–29–2	10,137
Mar. 19	Wolfe	PIT	L	3–7	28	31	9–53–9	27	Wolfe: 4–19–6	13,287
Mar. 20	Low	@TOR	L	3–7	32	50	9–54–9	27	Low: 5–30–2	16,485
Mar. 23	Low 6/10 (25:55) Wolfe 15/16 (34:05)	KC	T	5–5	35	26	9–54–10	28	Wolfe: 4–19–7	11,235
Mar. 24	Wolfe 17/22 (40:00) Low 15/17 (20:00)	@DET	L	3–7	28	39	9–55–10	28	Wolfe: 4–20–7	8,314
Mar. 26	Wolfe (59:23)	BUF	L	1–4	20	43	9–56–10	28	Wolfe: 4–21–7	12,961
Mar. 28	Wolfe (59:26) 1 ENG	ATL	L	1–3	29	38	9–57–10	28	Wolfe: 4–22–7	9,563
Mar. 30	Wolfe	DET	W	5–3	26	32	10–57–10	30	Wolfe: 5–22–7	8,036

Date	Goalies	Opp.	Res.	Score	SF	SA	W–L–T	PTS	Goalie Rec.	Att.
Apr. 1	Low	@PHI	L	2–11	23	62	10–58–10	30	Low: 5–31–2	17,077
Apr. 3	Low	@PIT	W	5–4	27	52	11–58–10	32	Low: 6–31–2	14,631
Apr. 4	Wolfe (58:29)	MTL	L	3–4	24	39	11–59–10	32	Wolfe: 5–23–7	18,130

Chapter Notes

Interviews: All quotes where a source is not indicated means that it has come from a personal interview with one of the following people:

Henry Boucha (March 23, 2021)
Robin Burns (December 17, 2014 and July 17, 2019)
Denis Herron (May 30, 2019)
Ron Lalonde (July 2, 2014 and September 4, 2019)
Mike Lampman (August 27, 2014 and October 9, 2019)
Jack Lynch (June 24, 2020 and March 26, 2021)
Bill Mikkelson (October 4, 2020)
Kris Wagner (November 19, 2020)
Bernie Wolfe (May 29, 2014 and December 17, 2019)

Preface

1. Robin Norwood, "McVie Is Proof That NHL Expansion Builds Characters," *Los Angeles Times*, April 18, 1993.
2. Alex Prewitt, "How the Washington Capitals turned in—and recovered from—the worst NHL season ever," *Sports Illustrated* (online, January 11, 2017.
3. Jeff Z. Klein and Karl-Erik Reif, *The Death of Hockey* (Toronto: Macmillan Canada, 1998), 13.

Chapter 1

1. Ray Ferraro, "How to Survive an Expansion Season," TSN.ca, September 20, 2017.
2. Ibid.
3. Just for the record, Mohns had two goals.
4. The last part of the parable, which alludes to the recent addition of twelve World Hockey Association teams, was omitted to better fit the content of this section.
5. Rick Pearson, "World Hockey Association Previews," *WHA Gameday* (Tucson: Purple Cactus Media, 2018), 272.
6. Stan Fischler, *Slashing!* (Toronto: Fitzhenry & Whiteside, 1974), vii.
7. Ibid., 237.
8. Alan Bass, *The Great Expansion* (Bloomington: iUniverse, 2011), 19.
9. David Cruise and Allison Griffiths, *Net Worth: Exploding the Myths of Pro Hockey* (Toronto: Penguin, 1991), 133.
10. Ibid.
11. Ibid.
12. Ibid., 133–134.
13. Ibid., 135.
14. Ibid., 131.
15. Alan Bass, *The Great Expansion*, pp. 18–19.
16. Bass, *Great Expansion*, 27.
17. Ibid.
18. David Cruise and Allison Griffiths claim the land was worth around $2 million.
19. Cruise and Griffiths state that Vancouver "turned down the proposition, mainly because of opposition to giving a carpetbagger a hand-out of downtown land." (*Net Worth: Exploding the Myths of Pro Hockey*, p. 132).
20. Cruise and Griffiths, *Net Worth*, 132.
21. I know what you're thinking: surely not *everyone* thought expansion was a *great* success. And you would be correct. Games between expansion teams were sinfully boring, and the Stanley Cup finals of 1968, 1969, and 1970 were terribly one-sided, anti-climactic affairs.
22. Klein and Reif, *The Death of Hockey*, 20.
23. Sean McIndoe, *The Down Goes Brown History of the NHL* (Toronto: Penguin Random House, 2018), 62.

Chapter 2

1. The Greyhound Bus Company invested in the club when the Pla-Mors ran into financial difficulties.
2. Greg Williams, "Edwin G. Thompson/President," *Goal* (Official NHL Program Magazine),

Professional Sports Publications, December 22, 1974.

3. Some sources indicated the group actually won all 16 votes.

4. Dick Mackey, "Kansas City Sweeps Into N.H.L. on First Ballot," *Kansas City Times*, June 9, 1972.

5. Williams, "Edwin G. Thompson/President."

6. Since 1899, the American Royal has been a popular annual livestock show, horse show, and rodeo in the Kansas City area.

7. Troy Treasure, *Icing on the Plains* (Bloomington: Balboa Press, 2018), 24–26.

8. *Ibid.*, 147–148.

9. Jay Greenberg, "Thompson Just Never Said Die," *Kansas City Star*, October 27, 1974.

10. Williams, "Edwin G. Thompson/President."

11. Chris Creamer and Todd Radom, *Fabric of the Game* (New York: Skyhorse—Sports Publishing, 2020), 101.

12. Jay Greenberg, "Scouts Have Abel, Baz Together Again," *Kansas City Star*, October 27, 1974.

13. "Loyalty before money puts Guidolin on top," *Vancouver Province*, February 6, 1973.

14. Jay Greenberg, "Guidolin Can Be His Own Boss Now," *Kansas City Star*, October 27, 1974.

15. "Bep Chucks Scouts Over Dispute," *Leavenworth Times*, January 22, 1976.

16. Jay Greenberg, "Guidolin Tells Scouts They Can Make It With Hard Work," *Hockey News*, October 11, 1974, 22.

17. Greenberg, "Guidolin Can Be His Own Boss Now."

18. Pun actually intended in this case; Guidolin believed Esposito had been fielding offers from Vancouver and Cincinnati of the WHA, but in the end, Espo never signed with the rebel league.

19. *Ibid.*

20. "Capital Centre success quiets critics," *Baltimore Sun*, February 4, 1974.

21. "Contest set to name new team," *Annapolis Capital*, January 2, 1974.

22. "Pandas" was actually the second most popular choice, believe it or not. It was a reference to the two bears President Richard Nixon brought back with him from China.

23. Creamer and Radom, *Fabric of the Game*, 234.

24. "Washington fans after tickets for new NHL 'Waterskates,'" *Montreal Gazette*, January 17, 1974; D. Farquharson, "The fans know what's up," *Calgary Herald*, January 29, 1974.

25. Milt Schmidt profile, *Goal* game program from December 2, 1975 game versus Buffalo.

26. Leigh Montville, "Milt Schmidt: 'Flyers' success tremendous omen for us,'" *Boston Globe*, May 19, 1974.

27. Dan Proudfoot, "And the Last Shall Be First," *Weekend Magazine*, April 12, 1975.

28. Garry Brown, "Springfield pro hockey great Jimmy Anderson dies at 82," *Springfield Republican*, March 10, 2013.

29. One would think that placing Vancouver, Los Angeles, and Oakland (California) together in the same division would have made sense, but the NHL put each of them in *separate* divisions.

30. Daniel L. Taylor, "Scouts Can Figure on Rude Debut," *Springfield News-Leader*, October 8, 1974.

31. "Scouts' Abel predicts success for new team," *Manhattan Mercury* (KS), June 23, 1974.

Chapter 3

1. Ken Dryden, *Scotty: A Hockey Life Like No Other* (Toronto: McClelland & Stewart, 2019), 7.

2. Luckily, a saviour in the form of Denis Potvin was available with the first overall draft pick in 1973, so the Isles didn't remain doormats very long.

3. In 1973-74, the NHL had 16 teams, and the WHA had another 12. The following year, when the Capitals and Scouts joined the NHL, the WHA also expanded, to Phoenix and Indianapolis, bringing the total number of teams to 32.

4. Attendance was nothing to write home about. In 1973-74, the Vancouver Blazers led the WHA with an average of 9,356 per game. That same season, 15 of 16 NHL teams had a higher average attendance.

5. Treasure, *Icing on the Plains*, 37.

6. Future Capitals goalie John Adams once claimed he was actually still in the net when the puck went in, but he may have been pulling everyone's leg. (Bob Fachet, "Ron Low and Bernie Wolfe—Holding down the fort," *Washington Capitals 20th Anniversary souvenir magazine*, 1994.)

7. "Plasse fulfills dream of goalies," *Jefferson City Post-Tribune*, February 22, 1971.

8. Hal Bock, "NHL Preview," *Hockey Sports Stars of 1975*, 1974.

9. *Ibid.*

10. Joe Posnanski, "Scouts Were a Disaster," *Kansas City Star*, July 8, 2007.

11. Jay Greenberg, "Rejected by Cup Flyers, Nolet Named to Lead K.C.," *Hockey News*, October 25, 1974.

12. *Ibid.*

13. Jim Proudfoot, *Pro Hockey NHL 76-77* (Markham, ON: Simon & Schuster, 1976), 167.

14. Jim Proudfoot, *Pro Hockey '74-'75* (Markham, ON: Simon & Schuster, 1976), 99.

15. Andrew Podnieks, *Players: The Ultimate A-Z Guide of Everyone Who Has Ever Played in the NHL* (Doubleday Canada, 2003), 192.

16. Ken Rudnick, "Milkshake Diet Added Extra Pounds, Helped K.C. Goaler Herron Win Job," *Hockey News*, January 16, 1976.

17. Ken Rudnick, "Croteau's Hustle Makes Him Regular With Scouts," *Hockey News*, January 23, 1976.

18. Proudfoot, Jim, *Pro Hockey NHL 76-77*, 167.

19. Steve Marantz, "Scouts' Rota Proving Size Not a Handicap," *Hockey News*, March 26, 1976.

20. *Kansas City Scouts Premiere Season Yearbook, 1974-75*, 40.

21. Podnieks, *Players*, 489.
22. Jay Greenberg, "Burns Puts Out for New NHL Team Despite Wearing No. 13," *Hockey News*, December 27, 1974.
23. *Kansas City Scouts Premiere Season Yearbook, 1974–75*, 31.
24. Ibid., 41.
25. Jay Greenberg, "Scouts Finally Have Hitting Defenseman in Murray," *Hockey News*, January 31, 1975.
26. Stephen Laroche, *Changing the Game: A History of NHL Expansion* (Toronto: ECW Press, 2014), 241.
27. Jay Greenberg, "Gilbert Proof Expansion Draft Isn't All Bad," *Hockey News*, January 24, 1975.
28. *Kansas City Scouts Premiere Season Yearbook, 1974–75*, 35.
29. Leigh Montville, "Milt Schmidt: 'Flyers' success tremendous omen for us," *Boston Globe*, May 19, 1974.
30. Podnieks, *Players*, 454.
31. Ron Weber, "Labre Delivers for Fans Despite Blueline Miscues," *Hockey News*, November 28, 1975.
32. Podnieks, *Players*, 462.
33. Weber, "Labre Delivers for Fans Despite Blueline Miscues."
34. Phil Hersh, "Laframboise Hopes NHL Holiday Is Over," *Baltimore Evening Sun*, September 23, 1974.
35. Podnieks, *Players*, 169.
36. Ibid., 73.
37. Glenn Dreyfuss, *The Legends of Landover* (self-published, original publication date not indicated), 12.
38. He was referring to the ongoing Watergate scandal.
39. Joe McGuff, "Sporting Comment," *Kansas City Times*, February 6, 1975.
40. Dreyfuss, *Legends of Landover*, 12.
41. Ibid., 10.
42. McGuff, "Sporting Comment," *Kansas City Times*, Feb. 6ruary 1975.
43. Prewitt, "How the Washington Capitals turned in—and recovered from—the worst NHL season ever."
44. No one picked was older than 26.
45. These totals exclude goaltenders.
46. Dreyfuss, *Legends of Landover*, 10.
47. Ibid.
48. Bill Heufelder, "Bastien Contends NHL Erred Tossing Caps, Scouts Scraps," *Hockey News*, August 1976.
49. Dreyfuss, *Legends of Landover*, 10.
50. Ibid., 27.
51. Laroche, *Changing the Game*, 260.
52. *Lora Evans and Paul Patskou Hockey Zoomcast: Capitals Stories*, September 24, 2020.
53. Russ White, "Capitals' Marson First Black to Make NHL in 15 Seasons," *Hockey News*, October 25, 1974.
54. Ken Rudnick, "Guidolin Turns Paiement Loose After Medical OK," *Hockey News*, October 24, 1975.
55. Greg Oliver and Richard Kamchen, *Don't Call Me Goon: Hockey's Greatest Enforcers, Gunslingers, and Bad Boys* (Toronto: ECW, 2013), 140.
56. Ibid., 141.
57. Jay Greenberg, "Guidolin Admits Kids Like Paiement Making It All Worthwhile with K.C.," *Hockey News*, December 6, 1974.
58. "Scouts on way," *Iola Register* (KS), September 7, 1974.
59. Bill Grigsby, *Grigs! A Beauuutiful Life* (Sports Publishing, 2004), 122.

Chapter 4

1. Jeff Z. Klein and Karl-Eric Reif, *The Klein and Reif Hockey Compendium* (Toronto: McClelland and Stewart, 1986), 58.
2. Dreyfuss, *Legends of Landover*, 9.
3. Bock, "NHL Preview."
4. Ibid.
5. Glenn Cole, "Schmidt's Happy with Discards," *Winnipeg Free Press*, June 13, 1974.
6. Klein and Reif, *Death of Hockey*, 82.
7. Klein and Reif, *Klein and Reif Hockey Compendium*, 57.
8. Prewitt, "How the Washington Capitals turned in—and recovered from—the worst NHL season ever."
9. "Mohns' 22nd year stars with rooks," *Vancouver Sun*, September 10, 1974.
10. Prewitt, "How the Washington Capitals turned in—and recovered from—the worst NHL season ever."
11. Ibid.
12. Dreyfuss, *Legends of Landover*, 19.
13. Laroche, *Changing the Game*, 250.
14. Bob Fachet, "The Team That Couldn't Shoot Straight," *Inside Hockey*, May 1989.
15. Russ White, "Dupere Showing Knack for Putting Puck in Net," *Hockey News*, January 10, 1975.
16. Russ White, "Anderson Enthused by Capitals' Showing in First NHL Camp," *Hockey News*, October 11, 1974.
17. Fachet, "The Team That Couldn't Shoot Straight."
18. Russ White, "Caps' Atkinson Benefits from Demotion," *Hockey News*, December 3, 1974.
19. White, "Anderson Enthused by Capitals' Showing in First NHL Camp."
20. Russ White, "Washington Fans Thrilled by Opening Night Tie Game," *Hockey News*, October 18, 1974.
21. Prewitt, "How the Washington Capitals turned in—and recovered from—the worst NHL season ever."
22. Phil Hersh, "So Far Joly Isn't Earning Salary," *Baltimore Evening Sun*, September 23, 1974.
23. Ibid.
24. White, "Capitals' Marson First Black to Make NHL in 15 Seasons."
25. Fachet, "The Team That Couldn't Shoot Straight," *Inside Hockey*, May 1989.

26. "Capitals are beaten," *Annapolis Capital*, October 10, 1974.
27. *Ibid.*
28. Mike Vogel, "Caps History: Opening Night—Oct. 9, 1974," Washingtoncaps.com, January 30, 2017.
29. Russ White, "Scoring Capitals' First Goal Completes Hrycuik's Big Jump," *Hockey News*, November 1, 1974.
30. White, "Scoring Capitals' First Goal Completes Hrycuik's Big Jump."
31. "Capitals are beaten."
32. Russ White, "Caps Have Problems Both Winning Games and Attracting Fans," *Hockey News*, November 8, 1974.
33. *Ibid.*
34. White, "Dupere Showing Knack for Putting Puck in Net," *Hockey News*, January 10, 1975.
35. Dreyfuss, *Legends of Landover*, 17.
36. Laroche, *Changing the Game*, 261.
37. Associated Press, "Expansion Capitals taste fruits of victory," *White Plains Journal News*, October 18, 1974.
38. Russ White, "Saving's Big Thing with Capitals' Fans," *Hockey News*, November 15, 1974.
39. Joe Gross, "Around the sports world and back," *Annapolis Capital*, November 5, 1974.
40. White, "Dupere Showing Knack for Putting Puck in Net," *Hockey News*, January 10, 1975.
41. Fachet, "The Team That Couldn't Shoot Straight."
42. Bob Greene, "Washington No Match for Boston," *Hagerstown* (MD) *Daily Mail*, November 8, 1974.
43. It should be noted that Gerry Cheevers was still playing in the WHA in 1974-1975. The goalie on record in Boston's 10-4 win was actually Ross Brooks.
44. Dreyfuss, *Legends of Landover*, 18.
45. Prewitt, "How the Washington Capitals turned in—and recovered from—the worst NHL season ever."
46. Greene, "Washington No Match for Boston."
47. Jerry Langdon, "'Mad Dog' Kelly Excites Flyers' Fans," *Fort Myers News-Press*, January 2, 1975.
48. Don McDermott, "For Capitals, the future is player draft," *Wilmington* (DE) *Morning News*, November 12, 1974.
49. *Ibid.*
50. Russ White, "Caps Only Six Games Shy of Non-Winning Record," *Hockey News*, February 7, 1975.
51. Dreyfuss, *Legends of Landover*, 9.
52. *Ibid.*, 31.
53. Russ White, "Caps' Fans Puzzled by Fast Departure if Veteran Seiling," *Hockey News*, November 22, 1974.
54. *Ibid.*
55. *Ibid.*
56. Dreyfuss, *Legends of Landover*, 36.
57. "Marson depends on ability," *Baltimore Sun*, November 28, 1974.
58. *Ibid.*
59. *Ibid.*
60. Cecil Harris, *Breaking the Ice: The Black experience in professional hockey* (Toronto: Insomniac Press, 2003), 66.
61. *Ibid.*, 67.
62. Dreyfuss, *Legends of Landover*, 26.
63. Harris, *Breaking the Ice*, 66.
64. William Douglas, "Washington Capitals to salute Mike Marson, the NHL's 2nd black player." TheColorofHockey.com, posted March 24, 2016.
65. Neil Campbell, "Marson leads Caps to win over Seals," *Ottawa Journal*, November 20, 1974.
66. Russ White, "Stripper's Record Much Better Than Capitals,'" *Hockey News*, December 20, 1974.
67. "Martin's 4 goals beats Caps," *Annapolis Capital*, December 4, 1974.
68. Bob Greene, "Sabs' 'French Connection' Bombs Caps," *Salisbury* (MD) *Daily Times*, December 6, 1974.
69. White, "Stripper's Record Much Better Than Capitals.'"
70. Francis Rosa, "Bruins bomb two goalies in 12-1 romp," *Boston Globe*, December 15, 1974.
71. *Washington Capitals 1977–78 Yearbook and Media Guide*, 22.
72. "Caps 'advance' despite 4-0 defeat," *Annapolis Capital*, December 23, 1974.
73. "Capitals play to first sellout crowd," *Annapolis Capital*, December 27, 1974.
74. Russ White, "Caps' Coach Anderson Makes Plea for Time," *Hockey News*, January 24, 1975.
75. *Ibid.*
76. Russ White, "Mohns Suddenly Named Captain of Lowly Caps," *Hockey News*, January 17, 1975.
77. Dreyfuss, *Legends of Landover*, 22.
78. Proudfoot, "And the Last Shall Be First."
79. Associated Press, "Scouts Beat Bruins for Road Victory," *Corpus Christi Times*, January 24, 1975.
80. He was referring to his own players.
81. "Rough Flyers Rout Caps," *Annapolis Capital*, January 17, 1975.
82. Russ White, "Mohns' Pep Talk Spurs Caps to Fourth Victory," *Hockey News*, February 14, 1975.
83. *Ibid.*
84. White, "Caps Only Six Games Shy of Non-Winning Record."
85. Milton Richman, "Capitals' chant: 'We're number 179,'" *Ottawa Journal*, February 11, 1975.
86. Russ White, "Fans Hang 'Blood Line' Tag on Capitals' New Ice Unit," *Hockey News*, January 31, 1975.
87. Laroche, *Changing the Game*, 253.
88. Ron Weber, "Capitals' Lynch Looking Hopefully to Future," *Hockey News*, May 21, 1976.
89. Ron Weber, "Pyatt Working Way Up Capitals' Talent Ladder," *Hockey News*, December 12, 1975.
90. Russ White, "Pyatt Turns New Fans on With Penalty Shot Goal But Caps' Plight Worsens," *Hockey News*, April 4, 1975.

Notes—Chapter 4

91. Alan Maki, "-82," *Toronto Globe and Mail*, September 30, 2006.
92. Michael Farber, "Hockey's Minus Man," *Sports Illustrated*, July 9, 2012.
93. Dreyfuss, *Legends of Landover*, 25.
94. Farber, "Hockey's Minus Man."
95. Russ White, "Scarred Players Still Haven't Quit Working," *Hockey News*, March 7, 1975.
96. *Washington Capitals 1977-78 Yearbook and Media Guide*, 14.
97. White, "Scarred Players Still Haven't Quit Working."
98. Ron Weber, "Gilbertson's Scoring Spurt Encourages Washington," *Hockey News*, November 21, 1975.
99. Fred Rothenberg, "Caps Suffer Another Loss on the Road," *Hagerstown* (MD) *Daily Mail*, February 10, 1975.
100. Richman, "Capitals' chant: 'We're number 179.'"
101. Proudfoot, "And the Last Shall Be First."
102. *Ibid.*
103. *Ibid.*
104. *Ibid.*
105. Russ White, "Washington Trades Off Top Scorer, Replaces Anderson with Sullivan," *Hockey News*, February 28, 1975.
106. Proudfoot, "And the Last Shall Be First."
107. "Capitals Win One for New Skipper," *Hagerstown* (MD) *Daily Mail*, February 12, 1975.
108. *Ibid.*
109. From an e-mail correspondance with Bill Mikkelson, February 22, 2021.
110. White, "Washington Trades Off Top Scorer, Replaces Anderson With Sullivan."
111. Ken Rudnick, "Caps Need More Than Coach," *Kansas City Star*, February 14, 1975.
112. Greg Enright, *The Pittsburgh Penguins: The First 25 Years* (Jefferson, NC: McFarland, 2020), 11.
113. *Ibid.*
114. *Ibid.*, 27.
115. William Barry Furlong. "A Trip to End All Trips," *Washington Post* (date unknown).
116. Proudfoot, "And the Last Shall Be First."
117. *Ibid.*
118. *Ibid.*
119. Prewitt, "How the Washington Capitals turned in—and recovered from—the worst NHL season ever."
120. "Capitals Win One for New Skipper."
121. Proudfoot, "And the Last Shall Be First."
122. Rudnick, "Caps Need More Than Coach."
123. White, "Scarred Players Still Haven't Quit Working."
124. Dreyfuss, *Legends of Landover*, 31.
125. Russ White, "New Caps Delight Fans with Muscle," *Hockey News*, March 14, 1975.
126. White, "New Caps Delight Fans with Muscle."
127. Klein and Reif, *The Klein and Reif Hockey Compendium*, 58.
128. Fachet, "The Team That Couldn't Shoot Straight."
129. Russ White, "Capitals, Fans Involved in Peculiar Love Affair," *Hockey News*, March 21, 1975.
130. Dan Donovan, "Penguins Storm Capitals, 12–1," *Pittsburgh Press*, March 16, 1975.
131. Jay Greenberg, "Resiliency Aside, Scouts Lose, 6–3," *Kansas City Times*, March 17, 1975.
132. Fachet, "The Team That Couldn't Shoot Straight."
133. Gordon Beard, "Caps Shatter Record," *Hagerstown* (MD) *Daily Mail*, March 21, 1975.
134. "Capitals Win One For New Skipper."
135. "Sullivan resigns," *Austin American-Statesman*, March 23, 1975.
136. Bob Fachet, "The trials and tribulations of the early Capitals," *Washington Capitals 20th Anniversary souvenir magazine*, 1994.
137. "Despite new coach Capitals lose again," *Frederick* (MD) *News*, March 24, 1975.
138. Russ White, "History Catches Up with GM As Caps Set Futility Record," *Hockey News*, April 11, 1975.
139. White, "Stripper's Record Much Better Than Capitals,'" *Hockey News*, December 20, 1974.
140. Russ White, "Caps Substitute Trash Basket For Cup," *Hockey News*, April 18, 1975.
141. Hugh McDonald, "NHL's Worst Team?" *San Mateo Times*, March 29, 1975.
142. Brad Kurtzberg, *Shorthanded: The Untold Story of the Seals* (Bloomington: Author House, 2006), 256.
143. According to Ron Low in a 2017 interview with Alex Prewitt of *Sports Illustrated*, it was Ace Bailey who came up with the idea of signing the garbage can.
144. White, "Caps Substitute Trash Basket for Cup."
145. When I interviewed Lalonde's friend and teammate, Jack Lynch, he told me that if there was one Capital who would have never been late for anything, it was Lalonde.
146. Furlong, "A Trip to End All Trips."
147. Rich Bercuson, "Canadiens go for broke against Capitals," *Montreal Gazette*, April 5, 1975.
148. Furlong, "A Trip to End All Trips."
149. Vogel, "Time CAPSule: 1974–75 Season in Review."
150. Russ White, "Disgruntled Gilbertson to Listen to WHA," *Hockey News*, April 25, 1975.
151. Gilbertson had never scored a NHL hat-trick before his four-goal outburst, and neither had Williams, but Williams had scored a hat trick April 12, 1973 as a member of the New England Whalers in the WHA playoffs versus Ottawa.
152. Terry Colvin, "Capitals capture finale," *Hagerstown* (MD) *Daily Mail*, April 7, 1975.
153. White, "Disgruntled Gilbertson to Listen to WHA."
154. Fachet, "Ron Low and Bernie Wolfe—Holding down the fort."
155. Garth Williams, "How They'll Finish in the NHL," *Argosy Hockey Yearbook 1975–76*, 1975.
156. White, "Pyatt Turns New Fans on with Penalty Shot Goal But Caps' Plight Worsens."

157. Russ White, "Low's Place of Future Employment Uncertain," *Hockey News*, March 28, 1975.

158. Bob Fachet, "Ron Low and Bernie Wolfe—Holding down the fort," *Washington Capitals 20th Anniversary souvenir magazine*, 1994.

159. In the 1975-76 *Argosy Hockey Yearbook*, an unfortunate typo indicated the Capitals had lost 671 games. Anyone who actually played on that team would probably agree it felt like they lost at least that many.

160. They didn't win that road game until game number 81; the Capitals played just 80 games in 1974-75.

161. White, "Caps Only Six Games Shy of Non-Winning Record."

162. Milton Richman, "Hockey Capitals: worst of worst teams," *San Rafael Independent Journal*, January 27, 1976.

163. Russ White, "NHL Caps Confident They'll Be No. 1," *Hockey News*, February 21, 1975.

164. White, "Scarred Players Still Haven't Quit Working."

165. Robert Fachet, "Analyzing Milt Schmidt's hardly-capital hockey team," *Boston Globe*, January 2, 1976.

166. Fachet, "The Team That Couldn't Shoot Straight."

167. Fachet, "Analyzing Milt Schmidt's hardly-capital hockey team."

168. Dreyfuss, *Legends of Landover*, 10.

169. Prewitt, "How the Washington Capitals turned in—and recovered from—the worst NHL season ever."

Chapter 5

1. Jim Tibbetts, "Grigsby to Speak at Rotary," *Leavenworth Times*, May 7, 1974.

2. "Construction strike delays opening of KC hockey arena," *Salina Journal*, May 22, 1974.

3. "No More Delays for Scouts," *Atchinson Daily Globe*, May 31, 1974.

4. "Scouts' Abel predicts success for new team," *Manhattan Mercury*, June 23, 1974.

5. Williams, "Edwin G. Thompson/President."

6. "Scouts' Abel predicts success for new team."

7. Jay Greenberg, "Reluctant Scout to Defect—Either Sooner or Later," *Kansas City Times*, September 17, 1974.

8. Dennis Feser, "Thoughts of Kansas City brought Paul to Blazers," *Vancouver Sun*, September 19, 1974.

9. Greenberg, "Reluctant Scout to Defect—Either Sooner or Later."

10. Jay Greenberg, "Hughes Still Giving 100 Percent to NHL Scouts," *Hockey News*, February 28, 1975.

11. Fischler, *Slashing!*, 84.

12. Treasure, *Icing on the Plains*, 49–50.

13. Jay Greenberg, "Guidolin Admits Kids Like Paiement Making It All Worthwhile with K.C."

14. Jay Greenberg, "Guidolin Tells Scouts They Can Make It with Hard Work," *Hockey News*, October 11, 1974.

15. Greenberg, "Guidolin Tells Scouts They Can Make It with Hard Work."

16. Greenberg, "Hughes Still Giving 100 Percent to NHL Scouts."

17. Jay Greenberg, "Scouts Start on Low Key," *Kansas City Times*, September 16, 1974.

18. Treasure, *Icing on the Plains*, 62–63.

19. Proudfoot, *Pro Hockey NHL 76–77*, 166.

20. Treasure, *Icing on the Plains*, 50.

21. Jay Greenberg, "Scouts Take Ice for First Time," *Kansas City Times*, September 20, 1974.

22. Diane Herbst, "For the Devils, it's been a slow waltz to the top," *Asbury Park Press*, June 27, 1995.

23. Associated Press. "Hodge is hot in Bruins' win," *Vancouver Province*, September 27, 1974.

24. John Gilbert, "North Stars tie, rookie rolls on," *Minneapolis Tribune*, September 27, 1974.

25. Jay Greenberg, "Scouts' Sparkling Exhibition Play Surprises Everybody But Guidolin," *Hockey News*, October 18, 1974.

26. *Kansas City Scouts Premiere Season Yearbook, 1974–75*, 20.

27. Ibid., 14.

28. Jay Greenberg, "Scouts Take Another Look-See in Order to Use Ax," *Kansas City Times*, September 25, 1974.

29. Laroche, *Changing the Game*, 242.

30. Pearson, "WHA Feature," *WHA Gameday*, 284.

31. Jay Greenberg, "Toronto Ruins Scouts' Debut," *Kansas City Times*, October 10, 1974.

32. Jay Greenberg, "Scout Debut Disappoints Burns," *Kansas City Times*, October 11, 1974.

33. Joe McGuff, "Sporting Comment," *Kansas City Times*, October 9, 1974.

34. Greenberg, "Toronto Ruins Scouts' Debut."

35. Ibid.

36. McGuff, "Sporting Comment," *Kansas City Times*, October 9, 1974.

37. Greenberg, "Toronto Ruins Scouts' Debut."

38. Greenberg, "Scout Debut Disappoints Burns."

39. Greenberg, "Burns Puts Out for New NHL Team Despite Wearing No. 13."

40. *Kansas City Scouts Media Guide, 1975–76*, 1975, 14.

41. Podnieks, *Players*, 111.

42. Greenberg, "Burns Puts Out for New NHL Team Despite Wearing No. 13."

43. Jay Greenberg, "Nolet Makes Triumphant Return To Philly," *Hockey News*, November 1, 1974.

44. Jay Greenberg, "Rejected by Cup Flyers, Nolet Named to Lead K.C.," *Hockey News*, October 25, 1974.

45. Greenberg, "Nolet Makes Triumphant Return To Philly."

46. Jay Greenberg, "Scouts Finding Laughter Only Remedy on Devastating Eight-Game Road Start," *Hockey News*.

47. Hugh McDonald, "Seals Get a 'Boost,'" *San Mateo Times*, October 24, 1974.

48. *Ibid.*
49. *Ibid.*
50. McCreary was not officially the team's general manager because the Seals were owned by 15 other NHL teams. He did not receive the general manager's title until the following season, when the Seals were purchased by Melvin Swig.
51. Jay Greenberg, "Guidolin Irked by Johnston's Put-down As Scouts End Road Trip with One Point," *Hockey News*, November 15, 1974.
52. Jay Greenberg, "Another Oakland Rivalry Born," *Kansas City Times*, October 25, 1974.
53. "Flames turn back KC Scouts, 4–2," *Salina Journal*, October 20, 1974.
54. McDonald, "Seals Get a 'Boost.'"
55. Laroche, *Changing the Game*, 242.
56. Ken Rudnick, "Thanks to the Scouts, Giroux is Saved," *Kansas City Times*, October 31, 1974.
57. "Scouts, Arena Suffer from Growing Pains," *Springfield Leader and Press*, November 10, 1974.
58. Jay Greenberg, "Scouts Get Standing Ovation Despite Loss to Hawks," *Hockey News*, November 22, 1974.
59. Jay Greenberg, "Chicago Spoils Scouts' Home Opener, 4–3," *Kansas City Star*, November 3, 1974.
60. Rudnick, Ken. "Losses Follow Scouts Home," *Kansas City Star*, November 3, 1974.
61. Greenberg, "Scouts Get Standing Ovation Despite Loss to Hawks."
62. Dan Donovan, "Penguins Scout for Goaltender, Find Johnson," *Pittsburgh Press*. November 6, 1974.
63. Jay Greenberg, "Guidolin Contemplates Changes As Scouts Continue to Lose," *Hockey News*, November 29, 1974.
64. Steve Cameron, "Scouts Learning All the Time," *Maryville Daily Forum*, November 16, 1974.
65. Cameron, "Scouts Learning All the Time."
66. "Buffalo Ties Atlanta, 4–4, with Three Late Goals," *St. Louis Post-Dispatch*, November 23, 1974.
67. Chuck Newman, "K.C.'s Not-So-Good Scouts Lambasted by Flyers, 10–0," *Philadelphia Inquirer*, December 2, 1974.
68. Bill Fleischman, "Oh Boy, Scouts weren't prepared for the Flyers," *Philadelphia Daily News*, December 2, 1974.
69. Associated Press, "Philadelphia Flyers Trounce Scouts 10–0," *Emporia Gazette* (KS), December 2, 1974.
70. Newman, "K.C.'s Not-So-Good Scouts Lambasted by Flyers, 10–0."
71. Treasure, *Icing on the Plains*, 98.
72. *Ibid.*
73. Associated Press, "Chicago Black Hawks roll over Scouts, 7–3," *Sedalia* (MO) *Democrat*, December 5, 1974.
74. "Shabby Effort Yields 5–3 Loss for Seals," *Santa Cruz Sentinel*, December 13, 1974.
75. Jay Greenberg, "Scouts' 'Rocket' Not in Orbit Yet As Scorer," *Hockey News*, April 4, 1975.
76. "Deadmarsh's Play Turned Scouts Off," *Hockey News*, January 3, 1975.
77. McGuff, "Sporting Comment," *Kansas City Times*, February 6, 1975.
78. *Washington Capitals 1977-78 Media Guide*, 16.
79. Jay Greenberg, "Scouts See Trade As Upward Step," *Hockey News*, January 3, 1975.
80. Treasure, *Icing on the Plains*, 100.
81. Jay Greenberg, "Lagace Fills Scouts' Most Pressing Need," *Hockey News*, February 7, 1975.
82. "Herron Isn't Very Big, But He Fooled Rangers," *Poughkeepsie Journal*, November 20, 1975.
83. Rudnick, "Milkshake Diet Added Extra Pounds, Helped K.C. Goaler Herron Win Job."
84. *Kansas City Scouts Media Guide, 1975–76*, 1975, 24.
85. Rudnick, "Milkshake Diet Added Extra Pounds, Helped K.C. Goaler Herron Win Job."
86. Jay Greenberg, "Herron Getting Masochistic Wish with Scouts," *Hockey News*, February 14, 1975.
87. Greenberg, "Lagace Fills Scouts' Most Pressing Need."
88. Williams, "How They'll Finish in the NHL."
89. *Kansas City Scouts Media Guide, 1975–76*, 30.
90. Jay Greenberg, "Guidolin Returns to Haunt Former Employers," *Hockey News*, February 21, 1975.
91. Associated Press, "Bruins Ambushed by Fledgling KC Scouts," *Atchison Daily Globe*, January 24, 1975.
92. Jay Greenberg, "Scouts High After Upset," *Kansas City Times*, January 25, 1975.
93. Laroche, *Changing the Game*, 241–242.
94. Greenberg, "Guidolin Returns to Haunt Former Employers."
95. *Kansas City Scouts Media Guide, 1975–76*, 18.
96. Ken Rudnick, "Gary Croteau Lives Up to Name," *Kansas City Times*, January 31, 1975.
97. Rudnick, "Gary Croteau Lives Up to Name."
98. Treasure, *Icing on the Plains*, 123–124.
99. "Lucky shot lets Bruins tie Scouts," *Jefferson City Post-Tribune*, January 28, 1975.
100. Ken Rudnick, "Scouts Watch Bruins Forge 3–3 Tie at :46," *Kansas City Times*, January 28, 1975.
101. Jay Greenberg, "Scouts Gain Tie," *Kansas City Times*, January 30, 1975.
102. McGuff, "Sporting Comment," *Kansas City Times*, February 6, 1975.
103. Jay Greenberg, "Golden Age of Scouts' Hockey Shortlived," *Hockey News*, April 18, 1975.
104. McGuff, "Sporting Comment," *Kansas City Times*, February 6, 1975.
105. Jay Greenberg, "Scouts Acquire Buhr," *Kansas City Times*, February 6, 1975.
106. Greenberg, "Scouts Acquire Buhr."
107. Jay Greenberg, "Scouts Win 3–2; So Do Kings, 95–94," *Kansas City Times*, February 7, 1975.

108. Joe DeLoach, "Seals lose to KC, 2–1," *Hayward Daily Review*, February 10, 1975.
109. "Late Goal by Rangers Ties Scouts, 2–2," *Leavenworth Times*, February 19, 1975.
110. Chuck Newman, "Stephenson Gets Lonesome as Flyers Win, 3–0," *Philadelphia Inquirer*, March 2, 1975.
111. Jay Greenberg, "Johnston Ecstatic Over Return To NHL," *Hockey News*, March 21, 1975.
112. Greenberg, "Johnston Ecstatic Over Return to NHL."
113. Podnieks, *Players*, 410.
114. Hal Sigurdson, "Canucks scrape bottom for tie," *Vancouver Sun*, March 12, 1975.
115. Greenberg, "Golden Age of Scouts' Hockey Shortlived."
116. Jay Greenberg, "Scouts' Play Respectable for First-Year NHL Team," *Hockey News*, April 25.
117. Greenberg, "Golden Age of Scouts' Hockey Shortlived."
118. Jay Greenberg, "First-Year Scouts Resemble Rubber Band," *Hockey News*, April 11, 1975.
119. "59 shots too much for Scouts," *Sedalia Democrat*, March 31, 1975.
120. "Scouts Top Kings to End Dry Spell," *Emporia Gazette*, April 2, 1975.
121. Treasure, *Icing on the Plains*, 142–143.
122. Greenberg, "Scouts' Play Respectable for First-Year NHL Team."
123. Jay Greenberg, "Scouts' Owner Thompson Optimistic for Future," *Hockey News*, March 7, 1975.
124. Only California ever consistently drew crowds that small in their early days, and by 1974 they were in such dire straits the league eventually stepped in and bought them. The Seals were essentially an orphan team.
125. Jay Greenberg, "Opening Night Throng Leaves Scouts' Owner Asking Where Fans Are," *Hockey News*, December 13, 1974.
126. Jay Greenberg, "New Marketing Procedures Top Year Two Priority List of Kansas City Management," *Hockey New,*, May 9, 1975.
127. Greenberg, "Opening Night Throng Leaves Scouts' Owner Asking Where Fans Are."
128. Jay Greenberg, "Scouts Showing Encouraging Progress," *Hockey News*, March 14, 1975.
129. Greenberg, "Scouts' Play Respectable for First-Year NHL Team."
130. Klein and Reif, *The Klein and Reif Hockey Compendium*, 108.
131. Bob Verdi, "A puckish hockey list for Christmas," *Chicago Tribune*, December 25, 1974.
132. According to Jeff Z. Klein and Karl-Erik Reif, co-authors of *The Hockey Compendium*, "Between 1939 and 1942, 90 NHL players enlisted or were drafted into military service, which surely helped the Allied cause but devastated the level of play in pro hockey. Quality defence players—goalies, rearguards, and forwards who could backcheck—always at a premium, were replaced by bush-leaguers, and play became sloppier and more wide-open as the war raged on." (12) They further point out that "Bush-league players who had been allowed to invade the NHL and fill out expansion-era rosters watched as better players skated circles around them; their only resort was to hold, hook, clutch, and grab, and in the case of Philadelphia, to incite mayhem and thuggery as an intimidating tactic.... Other teams quickly followed suit; smart, clean, well-positioned defensive play began to devolve into clutch and grab, and bench-clearing brawls were almost a nightly feature through the mid-'70s." (15-6)
133. Mike Vogel, "Time CAPSule: 1974–75 Season in Review," NHL.com, Sepember 25, 2012.

Chapter 6

1. Fischler, *Slashing!*, 110.
2. *Ibid*.
3. Chuck Svoboda, "Quotable quotes in '75," *Montreal Gazette*, December 27, 1975.
4. Dreyfuss, *Legends of Landover*, 11.
5. Montville, "Milt Schmidt: 'Flyers' success tremendous omen for us.'"
6. Russ White, "Flyers' Loss—Capitals' Gain," *Goal* game program from December 3, 1975, game between Washington and Buffalo.
7. Unlike past and future drafts, not one player drafted in 1975 would end up in the Hockey Hall of Fame, and of all the draftees only Brian Engblom would be selected to an end-of-season NHL All-Star team (1981-82).
8. *Ibid*.
9. *Ibid*.
10. *Washington Capitals 1977–78 Yearbook and Media Guide*, 28.
11. Ron Weber, "Unique NHL Draft Put Caps' Monahan Back in Big Apple," *Hockey News*, April 9, 1976.
12. White, "History Catches Up with GM As Caps Set Futility Record."
13. Weber, "Pyatt Working Way Up Capitals' Talent Ladder."
14. Weber, "Gilbertson's Scoring Spurt Encourages Washington."
15. Proudfoot, *Pro Hockey NHL 76-77*, 50.
16. *Ibid*., 51.
17. Kathleen Maxa, "Everything's Not So Joly in Washington," *Hockey Digest*, May 1975.
18. Dreyfuss, *Legends of Landover*, 28.
19. Maxa, "Everything's Not So Joly in Washington."
20. Ken Rudnick, "Scouts' Newcomer McDonald Plays Hitting Game," *Hockey News*, October 31, 1975.
21. Phil Jackman, "Some People Got No Class," *Baltimore Evening Sun*, September 25, 1975.
22. Dick Draper, "Seals' Hopes Hinge on Discipline," *San Mateo Times*, October 18, 1975.
23. Frank Brown, "Surprise! Capitals Win on Road, Upset 'Hawks," *Salisbury* (MD) *Daily Times*, October 27, 1975.
24. Associated Press, "Capitals capture 6-2 hockey victory," *Hagerstown* (MD) *Daily Mail*, October 31, 1975.

25. Dick Irvin, *In the Crease: Goaltenders Look at Life in the NHL* (Toronto: McClelland & Stewart, 1995), 231.
26. Ron Weber, "Caps' Wolfe Enjoying Himself While Looking for Win No. 2," *Hockey News*, January 23, 1976.
27. Weber, "Caps' Wolfe Enjoying Himself While Looking for Win No. 2."
28. Canadian Press, "Low-ly Capitals nearly find miracle," *Edmonton Journal*, December 5, 1975.
29. Ron Weber, "McVie Frets As Inconsistency Follows Caps," *Hockey News*, March 12, 1976.
30. Ron Weber, "Caps Hope Bennett, Sirois Will Give Lift," *Hockey News*, January 16, 1976.
31. Weber, "Caps Hope Bennett, Sirois Will Give Lift."
32. Proudfoot, *Pro Hockey NHL 76-77*, 50.
33. *Washington Capitals 1977-78 Yearbook and Media Guide*, 34.
34. John D. Gates, "Flyers triumph 7-5," *Wilmington (DE) News Journal*, December 20, 1975.
35. Gates, "Flyers triumph 7-5."
36. "Caps Victims of Sabre Frustration," *Cumberland (MD) Evening Times*, December 22, 1975.
37. "Schmidt Resigns as Capitals' Boss," *Wilmington (DE) Evening Journal*, December 30, 1975.
38. Ira Lacher, "Yes Virginia (and Maryland and D.C.)—There Really is a Capital Improvement," *Action Sports—Hockey*, January 1978.
39. Ibid.
40. Ron Weber, "Caps' Futility on Ice Bewildering to McVie After Tough Takeover," *Hockey News*, February 6, 1976.
41. Bob Fachet, "Tom McVie—Taking the first steps forward," *Washington Capitals 20th Anniversary souvenir magazine*, 1994.
42. Dick Irvin, *Behind the Bench: Coaches Talk About Life in the NHL* (Toronto: McClelland & Stewart, 1993), 205.
43. Lacher, "Yes Virginia (and Maryland and D.C.)—There Really is a Capital Improvement."
44. Ben Olan and the editors of *Hockey Illustrated*, "Previewing the Topsy-Turvy World of The 1977-78 National Hockey League," *Hockey Illustrated, Special 77/78*, 1977.
45. Ibid.
46. In the article "Ron Low and Bernie Wolfe – Holding down the fort" from the *Washington Capitals 20th Anniversary* souvenir magazine, it is claimed Ron Low was the culprit who called the bus company the night before.
47. Weber, "Caps' Futility on Ice Bewildering to McVie After Tough Takeover."
48. "Wings spoil Tom's debut," *Dayton Daily News*, January 1, 1976.
49. "People Are Saying…," *Baltimore Evening Sun*, February 18, 1976.
50. Ron Weber, "Japanese Tour Honeymoon for Joly," *Hockey News*, April 16, 1976.
51. "Caps suffer 5-0 defeat to California," *Hagerstown (MD) Daily Mail*, January 10, 1976.
52. "Caps Seen Setting NHL Losing Record," *Cumberland (MD) News*, January 13, 1976.
53. "Gerry Meehan … 'Pack Your Bags,'" *Action Sports Hockey*, January 1978.
54. Ken Reid, *Hockey Card Stories* (Toronto: ECW Press, 2014), 118.
55. Ken Reid, *Hockey Card Stories 2* (Toronto: ECW Press, 2018), 130.
56. Milton Richman, "Hockey Capitals: worst of worst teams," *San Rafael Independent Journal*, January 27, 1976.
57. "Capitals erupt late, turn back Red Wings," *Hagerstown (MD) Daily Mail*, February 16, 1976.
58. Ibid.
59. "Rangers, Smash Capitals, 11-4; Stretch Skein," *Salisbury (MD) Daily Times*, February 19, 1976.
60. "Bernie's Back … and Fit to Be Tied," *Wilmington (DE) Evening Journal*, February 25, 1976.
61. Gordon Beard, "Capitals not satisfied with 3-3 tie of Bruins," *Hagerstown (MD) Daily Mail*, February 28, 1976.
62. "Caps Post Eighth Victory, But…" *Salisbury (MD) Daily Times*, March 1, 1976.
63. "Hustling Capitals Can 'Skate with Any Club,'" *Salisbury (MD) Daily Times*, March 17, 1976.
64. "Capitals tie Scouts," *Salina (KS) Journal*, March 24, 1976.
65. Gordon Beard, "Capitals' McVie talked too much?" *Hagerstown (MD) Daily Mail*, March 24, 1976.
66. From a short piece written by Morton S. Hodgson, Jr., for the *Coca-Cola Bottlers' Cup Pro Ice Hockey Series Official Program*, 1976.
67. Milt Dunnell, "Hockey for export brand X variety," *Toronto Star*, 1976 (exact date unknown).
68. Bill Davidson, "This spring storm figures, somehow," *Brandon Sun*, March 20, 1976.
69. Dunnell, "Hockey for export brand X variety."
70. Pete Mossey, "Only On Monday," *Medicine Hat News*, April 19, 1976.
71. Jim Taylor, *Vancouver Sun* column, April 5, 1976.
72. Gary Mullinax, "Flyers Feel Embarrassed Over 'Massacre' of Capitals," *Wilmington News Journal*, April 2, 1976.
73. Ron Weber, "Caps Ended Campaign with Close Games," *Hockey News*, Aprch 30, 1976.
74. Ron Weber, "McVie Not Satisfied Yet with Caps," *Hockey News*, May 7, 1976.
75. Ron Weber, "Caps Hoping New Men at Top Will Change Plight," *Hockey News*, January 30, 1976.
76. Weber, "McVie Not Satisfied Yet with Caps."

Chapter 7

1. Clancy Loranger, *Vancouver Province* sports column, November 22, 1975.
2. "Should NHL's rich brothers spread wealth," *Saskatoon Star Phoenix*, November 22, 1975.

3. Jay Greenberg, "Scouts' GM Sees Better Days With Right Off-Season Moves," *Hockey News*, May 16, 1975.
4. Jay Greenberg, "KC Lands Dupere, Patrick in Trade," *Hockey News*, July 1975.
5. Jay Greenberg, "Scouts Acquisition of Patrick Seen Move To Plug Left Wing As Abel Realigns Offense," *Hockey News*, August 1975.
6. Ken Rudnick, "Dupere's Freak Injury Fouls Up Guidolin's Plans," *Hockey News*, November 7, 1975.
7. Ken Rudnick, "Baumgartner Adjusting to Life Without Hockey," *Hockey News*, December 26, 1975.
8. Greenberg, "KC Lands Dupere, Patrick in Trade."
9. Ken Rudnick, "Scouts' Lament—Everybody Wants The Sky," *Hockey News*, September 1975.
10. *Kansas City Scouts Media Guide, 1975–76*, 12.
11. Nathaniel Oliver, "One for the Ages: Gary Bergman's 1975–76 Season," TheHockeyWriters.com, May 17, 2019.
12. Ken Rudnick, "Veteran Bergman Steadying Scouts' Young Legs," *Hockey News*, October 17, 1975.
13. Steve Cameron, "Scouts Draft Muscle, Bid for Star," *Maryville (MO) Daily Star*, June 12, 1975.
14. Howard Hoffman, "Scouts done hiding behind expansion tag," *Port Huron (MI) Times Herald*, September 17, 1975.
15. Rudnick, "Guidolin Turns Paiement Loose After Medical OK."
16. Ken Rudnick, "Bep Resorts to Line Switching with Scouts," *Hockey News*, November 14, 1975.
17. Ken Rudnick, "Charron Proving Wings Erred in Trading Him," *Hockey News*, December 12, 1975.
18. The shots on goal were 20-20 when the siren sounded to end the game. It was the *third* time in five games the Scouts recorded exactly 20 shots.
19. "Scouts Look Horrible," *Leavenworth Times*, November 3, 1975.
20. Ken Rudnick, "Rout by Cup Flyers Dimmed K.C. Hopes," *Hockey News*, November 21, 1975.
21. "Scouts Look Horrible."
22. Ken Rudnick, "Unproductive Start Proving Frustrating to Scouts' Paiement," *Hockey News*, November 28, 1975.
23. "Scouts' road trip starts with defeat," *Salina Journal*, November 13, 1975.
24. "Herron Isn't Very Big, But He Fooled Rangers," *Poughkeepsie Journal*, November 20, 1975.
25. Ken Rudnick, "Sophomore Scouts Come of Age on Road As Club Rides Emotional Roller Coaster," *Hockey News*, December 19, 1975.
26. "Scouts earn 1–1 tie with Chicago," *Sedalia Democrat*, December 1, 1975.
27. "Scouts blitz Montreal," *Neosho Daily News*, December 4, 1975.
28. "Guidolin presented 3–2 victory for birthday," *Sedalia Democrat*, December 10, 1975.
29. *Ibid.*
30. "Scouts Edging Up in Their Division," *Emporia Gazette*, December 18, 1975.
31. *Ibid.*
32. Ken Rudnick, "Scouts Sail by Detroit," *Kansas City Times*, December 20, 1975.
33. Rudnick, "Milkshake Diet Added Extra Pounds, Helped K.C. Goaler Herron Win Job."
34. Marantz, "Scouts' Rota Proving Size Not a Handicap."
35. "Six Canadiens Named All-Stars," *St. Louis Post-Dispatch*, January 7, 1976.
36. Ken Leiker, "Guidolin Gets Goon, Can Socialize Again," *Maryville Daily Forum*, January 13, 1976.
37. Posnanski, "Scouts Were a Disaster."
38. Steve Marantz, "Scouts Get Tough One," *Kansas City Times*, January 10, 1976.
39. Steve Marantz, "Explosive Shot Arnason's Key To Success," *Hockey News*, March 12, 1976.
40. *Ibid.*
41. "Guidolin raps Flyer tactics," *Manhattan Mercury*, January 2, 1976.
42. Steve Marantz, "Scouts Hope to Change Timid Character with Addition of Tough Defender Durbano," *Hockey News*, January 30, 1976.
43. Dave Wright, "You gotta have a goon," *Manhattan Mercury*, January 25, 1976.
44. *View From the Penalty Box* (podcast), episode 30, February 11, 2019.
45. Stan Fischler, *Hockey's Toughest Ten* (New York: Grosset & Dunlap, 1974), 80.
46. *Ibid.*, 81.
47. *Ibid.*, 83.
48. *Ibid.*, 84–85.
49. Leiker, "Guidolin Gets Goon, Can Socialize Again."
50. "Wings rout Scouts 8–3," *Manhattan Mercury*, January 15, 1976.
51. "Sees light at the end of tunnel," *Neosho Daily News*, January 16, 1976.
52. "Bep Chucks Scouts Over Dispute."
53. John Meagher, "Scouts played like cubs in K.C.," *Montreal Gazette*, February 2, 2007.
54. "Scouts' road trip starts with defeat."
55. Rudnick, "Milkshake Diet Added Extra Pounds, Helped K.C. Goaler Herron Win Job."
56. Steve Marantz, "Bep Raps 'Scapegoat' Role," *Kansas City Times*, January 22, 1976.
57. Steve Marantz, "Guidolin Resigns Amid Protests," *Kansas City Times*, January 22, 1976.
58. *Ibid.*
59. *Ibid.*
60. *Ibid.*
61. *Ibid.*
62. "Scouts' Guidolin Resigns," *Saint Joseph (MI) Herald-Palladium*, January 22, 1976.
63. Steve Marantz, "Bep Guidolin Quits as Scouts Coach," *Emporia Gazette*, January 22, 1976.
64. Steve Marantz, "Lack of Club Support Forced Guidolin To Quit," *Hockey News*, February 13, 1976.
65. Marantz, "Bep Raps 'Scapegoat' Role."
66. Cathie Burnes, "Scouts Stumble Again As

Abel Takes Helm," *Kansas City Times*, January 22, 1976.

67. Steve Marantz, "California Puts Heat on Scouts' Rookie, 4–1," *Kansas City Star*, January 24, 1976.

68. Marantz, "Lack of Club Support Forced Guidolin To Quit."

69. John Meagher, "'We Set Hockey Back 10 Years,'" *Vancouver Sun*, February 2, 2007.

70. Frank Brown, "Bush says he is not unhappy," *Neosho Daily News*, January 29, 1976.

71. Bob Whitley, "Pens Find Real Loser," *Pittsburgh Post-Gazette*, January 30, 1976.

72. Dan Donovan, "Fired-Up Scouts Tie Pens, 4–4," *Pittsburgh Press*, February 1, 1976.

73. Ken Leiker, "Things to Know from Leiker," *Maryville Daily Forum*, March 19, 1976.

74. "KC Scouts face 'crisis,'" *St. Joseph* (MO) *Gazette*, February 13, 1976.

75. Posnanski, "Scouts Were a Disaster."

76. "Scouts seek K.C. support," *Springfield* (MO) *News-Leader*, February 13, 1976.

77. Steve Marantz, "K.C. Cage Kings Shows Interest in Ice Scouts," *Hockey News*, March 19, 1976.

78. "Scouts Could Get League Help," *Leavenworth Times*, February 17, 1976.

79. "Montreal Breaks Down Scouts," *Leavenworth Times*, February 26, 1976.

80. "Scouts Tie Islanders," *Leavenworth Times*, February 27, 1976.

81. Podnieks, *Players*, 349.

82. "N.H.L. Ponders Aid to Scouts," *Kansas City Times*, March 9, 1976.

83. D'arcy Jenish, *The NHL: 100 years of on-ice action and boardroom battles* (Toronto: Doubleday Canada, 2013), 234.

84. "N.H.L. to Lend Scouts $300,000 So Club Can Finish the Season," *Kansas City Star*, March 10, 1976.

85. Steve Marantz, "Who's Minding the Store Scouts' Thompson Asks As Ticket Drive Stalls," *Hockey News*, April 2, 1976.

86. Marantz, "Who's Minding the Store Scouts' Thompson Asks As Ticket Drive Stalls."

87. Steve Marantz, "Scouts Laughing But Fans Not Amused," *Hockey News*, April 9, 1976.

88. Steve Marantz, "Scouts' Apathy Reflects At Home," *Hockey News*, April 16, 1976.

89. Archie McDonald, "Room at top for Canucks," *Vancouver Sun*, March 11, 1976.

90. "Hawks Dispatch Scouts," *Munster* (IN) *Times*, March 17, 1976.

91. James C. Fitzpatrick, "Fate of the Scouts Disappoints Star," *Kansas City Times*, June 8, 1976.

92. Marantz, "Scouts Laughing But Fans Not Amused."

93. "Coach of Scouts Blasts Officials After Loss Sunday," *Emporia Gazette*, Mar.ch22, 1976.

94. Henry Boucha, *Henry Boucha, Ojibwa: Native American Olympian* (self-published), 2013, 397–398.

95. "Coach of Scouts Blasts Officials After Loss Sunday."

96. Meagher, "Scouts played like cubs in K.C."

97. "KC Scouts fall to LA Kings," *Neosho* (MO) *Daily News*, March 31, 1976.

98. Treasure, *Icing on the Plains*, 235–236.

Chapter 8

1. "Sports Shorts," *Titusville* (PA) *Herald*, March 13, 1976.

2. Lee Kavetski, "NHL Caps, Scouts to Skate in Japan," *Pacific Stars & Stripes*, April 4, 1976.

3. Mel Tsuji, "Japanese Show Appreciation of NHL Exhibitions; Eyeing Kings, Seals," *Hockey News*, May 21, 1976.

4. Weber, "Caps Ended Campaign with Close Games."

5. In one photo provided by Robin Burns, the banner actually reads "Welcome to Japan the National Hockey League of Great Fighters and Sweet Ladies."

6. John Saar, "Respect Stuns Caps," *Washington Post*, April 14, 1976.

7. John Saar, "Caps, Scouts love Japan" (originally published in *Washington Post*), *Winnipeg Free Press*, April 15, 1976.

8. From an advertisement for the NHL Japan Series, courtesy of Ron Lalonde.

9. Saar, "Respect Stuns Caps."

10. "Caps Open Japan Tour with Win," *Pacific Stars and Stripes*, April 16, 1976.

11. John Saar, "Caps Palm Pearls," *Washington Post*, April 14, 1976.

12. John Saar, "Capitals Bow in Japanese Finale," *Washington Post*, April 18, 1976.

13. Ibid.

14. Lee Kavetski, "Capitals Pound Scouts 6–2," *Pacific Stars and Stripes*, April 19, 1976.

15. "President Admits Scouts Are Broke," *Emporia Gazette*, April 16, 1976.

16. John Saar, "Caps Win 6–2, as Fists Fly," *Washington Post*, April 15, 1976.

17. Mike Vogel, "Once Upon a Time in the West," DumpnChase.com (defunct website), posted January 14, 2013.

18. Saar, "Caps Win 6–2, as Fists Fly."

19. Vogel, "Once Upon a Time in the West."

20. Saar, "Respect Stuns Caps."

21. Saar, "Caps Win 6–2, as Fists Fly."

22. For those of you who are not scientifically literate, here is a quote from an article entitled "How Fast Does Light Travel?" by Nola Taylor Redd on Space.com to give you a better idea of how fast the speed of light actually is: "If you could travel at the speed of light, you could go around the Earth 7.5 times in one second." After reading the alternative facts in the program's translation, I suddenly felt very bad for every goalie who ever faced Bobby "Jull".

23. Kavetski, "Capitals Pound Scouts 6–2."

24. Ibid.

25. John Saar, "Capitals Go 3–0 in Japan," *Washington Post*, Apil. 17, 1976.

26. Ron Weber, "Caps Show Japanese Fans,

Scouts Their Best Shots," *Hockey News*, May 14, 1976.
27. Ibid.
28. Saar, "Capitals Go 3-0 in Japan."
29. Ken Rudnick, "Bergman Going All Out But Admits Legs Going in Windup With Scouts," *Hockey News*, January 2, 1976.
30. Saar, "Capitals Bow in Japanese Finale."
31. Ibid.
32. Lee Kavetski, "Scouts Top Caps 4-2 in Finale," *Pacific Stars and Stripes*, April 20, 1976.
33. Saar, "Capitals Bow in Japanese Finale."
34. Weber, "Caps Show Japanese Fans, Scouts Their Best Shots."
35. Weber, "Caps Ended Campaign with Close Games."
36. Tsuji, "Japanese Show Appreciation of NHL Exhibitions; Eyeing Kings, Seals."
37. Kavetski, "Capitals Pound Scouts 6-2."
38. Tsuji, "Japanese Show Appreciation of NHL Exhibitions; Eyeing Kings, Seals."

Chapter 9

1. Lacher, "Yes Virginia (and Maryland and D.C.)—There Really Is a Capital Improvement."
2. Proudfoot, *Pro Hockey NHL 76-77*, 50.
3. Bob Fachet, "Tom McVie—Taking the first steps forward."
4. Olan and the editors of Hockey Illustrated, "Previewing the Topsy-Turvy World of the 1977-78 National Hockey League."
5. Ibid.
6. Mike Shalin, "Guy Charron: A Capital Gain," *Hockey Illustrated*, April 1977.
7. On January 8, 1977, McVie started Wolfe against Montreal, then proceeded to switch goalies *eight* times before the final buzzer.
8. "Letter from NHL office encouraging," *Sedalia (MO) Democrat*, April 1, 1976.
9. "Scouts Create Sale Talk in Toronto," *Kansas City Times*, April 13, 1976.
10. "Scouts seek sale to K.C. Kings," *Jefferson City Capital News*, April 14, 1976.
11. Joe McGuff, "Kings' Offer to Buy Scouts Disclosed," *Kansas City Times*, April 28, 1976.
12. McGuff, "Kings' Offer to Buy Scouts Disclosed," *Kansas City Times*, April 28, 1976; Alice Hartmann, "New Hockey Lease Worked Out," *Kansas City Times*, May 20, 1976.
13. Hartmann, "New Hockey Lease Worked Out."
14. John T. Dauner, "Kings Fail on Lease Strategy," *Kansas City Times*, May 21, 1976.
15. John T. Dauner, "Kings Stop Plans to Buy Scouts," *Kansas City Times*, May 22, 1976.
16. "NHL Expected to Drop Kansas City Franchise," *St. Louis Post-Dispatch*, May 25, 1976.
17. "One Last Chance for Scouts," *Kansas City Times*, May 28, 1976.
18. "Scouts Franchise Prolonged—Briefly," *St. Louis Post-Dispatch*, May 26, 1976.
19. Joe McGuff, "Kings Reject Last Offer; Hockey Apparently Lost," *Kansas City Times*, June 2, 1976.
20. Ibid.
21. "Scouts Saved?" *Maryville (MO) Daily Forum*, June 12, 1976.
22. "Hoping to keep Scouts," *Neosho (MO) Daily News*, June 16, 1976.
23. Steve Marantz, "Late Bid to Move Scouts Finds Novorr Off Guard," *Kansas City Times*, July 1, 1976.
24. Ibid.
25. "Effort to Keep Scouts in KC Fails," *Mexico (MO) Ledger*, July 27, 1976.
26. Jeff Meyers, "Everything's Up to Date—Well Nearly," *St. Louis Post-Dispatch*, July 29, 1976.
27. Jay Greenberg, "Scouts Get Sobchuck—If…" *Kansas City Times*, December 14, 1973.
28. Meagher, "Scouts played like cubs in K.C."
29. Myron Welik, "65 Going on 35—Robin Burns," Medium.com, June 20, 2018.
30. Podnieks, *Players*, 111.
31. Meagher, "Scouts played like cubs in K.C."
32. Frank Brown, "The NHL… At the Crossroads," *Hockey News 1977 Yearbook*, 1977, 22.
33. "Colorado Rockies," *Hockey News 1977 Yearbook*, 1977, 93.
34. Currier, Steve. "Celebrating the 40th Anniversary of the Coca-Cola Bottlers' Cup," *The Hockey Research Journal XVIII (2014-15)*, Society for International Hockey Research.

Bibliography

Bass, Alan. *The Great Expansion*. Bloomington, IN: iUniverse, 2011.

Boucha, Henry. *Henry Boucha, Ojibwa: Native American Olympian*. Self-published, 2013.

Creamer, Chris, and Todd Radom. *Fabric of the Game*. New York: Sports Publishing, 2020.

Cruise, David, and Allison Griffiths. *Net Worth: Exploding the Myths of Pro Hockey*, Toronto: Penguin, 1991.

Dreyfuss, Glenn. *The Legends of Landover*. Self-published, 2020.

Enright, Greg. *The Pittsburgh Penguins: The First 25 Years*. Jefferson, NC: McFarland, 2020.

Fischler, Stan. *Hockey's Toughest Ten*. New York: Grosset & Dunlap, 1974.

_____. *Slashing!* Toronto: Fitzhenry & Whiteside, 1974.

Gassen, Timothy. *WHA Gameday*. Tucson: Purple Cactus, 2018.

Grigsby, Bill. *Grigs! A Beauuutiful Life*. Champaign, IL: Sports Publishing, 2004.

Harris, Cecil. *Breaking the Ice: The Black Experience in Professional Hockey*. Toronto: Insomniac Press, 2003.

Irvin, Dick. *Behind the Bench: Coaches Talk About Life in the NHL*. Toronto: McClelland & Stewart, 1993.

_____. *In the Crease: Goaltenders Look at Life in the NHL*. Toronto: McClelland & Stewart, 1995.

Jenish, D'arcy. *The NHL: 100 Years of On-Ice Action and Boardroom Battles*. Toronto: Doubleday Canada, 2013.

Kansas City Scouts Media Guide, 1975–76.

Kansas City Scouts Premiere Season Yearbook, 1974–75.

Klein, Jeff Z., and Karl-Erik Reif. *The Death of Hockey*. Toronto: Macmillan Canada, 1998.

_____. *The Klein and Reif Hockey Compendium*. Toronto: McClelland & Stewart, 1986.

Kurtzberg, Brad. *Shorthanded: The Untold Story of the Seals*. Bloomington, IN: Author House, 2016.

Laroche, Stephen. *Changing the Game: A History of NHL Expansion*. Toronto: ECW, 2014.

McIndoe, Sean. *The Down Goes Brown History of the NHL*. Toronto: Penguin Random House, 2018.

Oliver, Greg, and Richard Kamchen, *Don't Call Me Goon: Hockey's Greatest Enforcers, Gunslingers, and Bad Boys*. Toronto: ECW, 2013.

Podnieks, Andrew. *Players: The Ultimate A-Z Guide of Everyone Who Has Ever Played in the NHL*. Toronto: Doubleday Canada, 2003.

Proudfoot, Jim. *Pro Hockey '74–'75*. Markham, ON: Simon & Schuster, 1974.

_____. *Pro Hockey NHL '76–'77*. Markham, ON: Simon & Schuster, 1976.

Reid, Ken. *Hockey Card Stories*. Toronto: ECW, 2014.

_____. *Hockey Card Stories 2*. Toronto: ECW, 2018.

Sports Reference LLC. Hockey-Reference.com—Hockey Statistics and History. https://www.hockey-reference.com/. September 20, 2021.

Treasure, Troy. *Icing on the Plains*. Bloomington: Balboa Press, 2018.

Washington Capitals 1975-76 Yearbook and Media Guide. Ed. Chip Campbell, 1975.

Washington Capitals 1976-77 Yearbook and Media Guide. Ed. Pierce Gardner, 1976.

Washington Capitals 1977–78 Yearbook and Media Guide. Ed. Pierce Gardner, 1977.

Index

Numbers in ***bold italics*** indicate pages with illustrations

Abel, Sid 10, 17–18, 23, 28, 32–33, 41, 96, 97, 101, 102, 103, 109, 116, 117, 119, 120, 125, 133, 134, 135, 143, 174, 175, 176, 177–178, 179, 185, 186, 188, 189, 192, 194, 195, 216, 228, 234; coaching career 17, 196; playing career 17; resignation from Detroit Red Wings 17
Adams, John 66, 89, 272*n*6
Adams Cup *see* Central Hockey League
Ahearn, Kevin 53
Ahern, Fred 205
Ali, Muhammad 190
Amarillo Wranglers 32
Amateur Draft *see* National Hockey League
American Basketball Association (ABA) 21, 78, 210, 239
American Football League (AFL) 9
American Hockey Association (AHA) *see* United States Hockey League
American Hockey League (AHL) 8, 32, 33, 34, 37–38, 39, 53, 57, 61, 62, 74, 92, 100, 105, 112, 116, 120, 128, 130, 195, 238; Calder Cup 31; Hall of Fame 22
American Royal (event) 15, 272*ch*2*n*6; building 14, 96
Anderson, Jimmy 22, 51, 53, 54, 55, 57, 59, 61, 62, 67, 69, 70, 72, 73, 77, 78–79, 80, 81, 85, 141–142, 234; minor-league coaching career 22; playing career 22
Anderson, Murray 40
Anderson, Park 60
Anderson, Ron 39, 58, 82, 87, 142
Andrascik, Steve 105
Apps, Syl, Jr. 83, 110, 144, 198
Arbour, Al 78

Arnason, Chuck 90, 166, 188–189, 192, 193, 196, 198, 201, 204, ***223***, 226, 242, 245
Ashford, Malcolm 168
Atkinson, Steve 38, 54, 55, 64, 67, 81, 93
Atlanta Flames 3, 12, 13, 26, 29, 33, 39, 71, 74, 97, 98, 101, 108, 113, 120, 123, 124–125, 130, 138, 148, 149, 160–161, 175–176, 179, 181, 186, 190–191, 201, 228
Atlanta Thrashers 5, 6
Avco World Trophy (aka Avco Cup) 31, 98, 238; *see also* World Hockey Association
Axelson, Joe 240, 241

Bailey, Garnet "Ace" 67, 75–76, 88, 90–91, 93, 144, 148, 149, 150, 162, 166, 170; death 238–239; relationship with Wayne Gretzky 238; shenanigans 52, 76, ***77***, 84, 88, 94, 141–142, 157, 224, 239, 275*n*143
Ballard, Harold 10, 11
Baltimore Blades 94, 130; *see also* Michigan Stags
Baltimore Bullets 19–20; *see also* Capital Bullets; Washington Bullets
Baltimore Clippers 100
Bar, Jiri 53
Barber, Bill 143, 150, 180
Bastien, Joseph Aldege "Baz" 103, 120, 135, 168, 187, 216, 228, ***232***; career-ending injury 18; minor-league career 18
Batman 158
Bauer, Bobby 21
Baumgartner, Mike 34, 102, 103, 176
Bavis, Mark 239–240
Bealey, John 168
Belhumeur, Michel 36, 59, ***60***, 66, 67, 68, 81, 83, 88, 89, 90, 93, 143, 144, 145, 146

Bennett, Bill 149
Bennett, Curt 130, 181
Bennett, Harvey, Jr. 149, 150, 160, 163, 164, ***221***, ***225***, 226, 227, 231
Bennett, Harvey, Sr. 149
Bergeron, Michel 181, 187, 192
Bergman, Gary 1, 41, 103, 177, 178, 183, 187, 197, 198, 199, 205, 207, 215, ***223***, ***227***, 228–***229***, 230, 231, 242, 245
Berkley, Richard 240
Bernier, Serge 53
Berry, Bob 106, 117
Bishop, Jim 17
Bladon, Tom 164
Blehm, Irv 100
Blight, Rick 204
Blood Line 73; *see also* Bloom, Mike; Laframboise, Pete; Marson, Mike
Bloom, Mike 22, 38, 58, 61, 68, 73, 81, 82, 158
Boddy, Greg 113
Boileau, Marc 191
Boldirev, Ivan 109, 204
Bolonchuk, Larry 39
Bordeleau, Paulin 108
Borg, Bjorn 2
Boston Braves 18, 37, 53
Boston Bruins 6, 7, 18–19, 21–22, 35, 36, 37, 38, 39, 46, ***50***, 51, 52, 60–61, 63, 67–68, 71, 73, 75, 76, 77, 78, 82, 84, 94, 99, 100, 108–109, 115, 121–122, 123, 124, 125, 136, 148, 149, 150, 152, 159, 163–164, 168–169, 179–180, 182, 185, 194, 200–201, 205, 232
Boston University 39
Boucha, Henry 185–186, 195, 206, 245; assault by Dave Forbes 185, 201
Bouchard, Pierre 73
Bourne, Bob 47, 102, 176
Bower, Johnny, Jr. 53

285

Bowman, Scotty 17–18, 29, 155, 185, 235
Bozak, Ryan 168
Bradley, Brian 6
Bragnalo, Rick 170, 215, **227**, 231, 237
Brandon Wheat Kings 30, 39
Broad Street Bullies *see* Philadelphia Flyers
Bromley, Gary 66
Brooks, Gord 38, 81
Brooks, Ross 68, 274*n*43
Brossart, Willie 63, 93, 104, 145, 161, 162
Bryan, Gary 243
Bucyk, John 68, 121, 180
Buffalo Bisons 22
Buffalo Sabres 3, 12, 26, 30, 32, 38, 44, 54, 63, 64, 66–67, 69, 97, 98–99, 111, 120, 125, 133, 136, 143, 144, 148, 151–152, 160, 182, 187, 206
Buhr, Doug 125–126
Burdon, Glen 116, 177
Burnett, Red 104
Burns, Robin 17–18, 32–33, 101, 103, 104–105, 106, 109, 110, 111, 112, 113, 117, 118, 120, 123, 124, 127, 128, 129, 133, 146, 166, 175, 183, 184, 185, 193, 197, 198–199, 205–206, 207, 208, **214**, 219, 224, **225**, 226, 227, 228, **230**, **232**, 243–244; ITECH 244; Lange skates 197, 218–219, 244; Procure Walk of Courage 244
Burrows, Dave 144
Bush, Eddie 31, 196–197, 199, 201, 207, 212, 213, 231
Butler, Jerry 144

Cairns, Don 175
Calder Cup *see* American Hockey League
California Golden Seals 6, 28, 30, 37, 52, 66, 68, 72, 76, 85–86, 91, 107–108, 115, 117, 125, 127, 128, 131, 136, 138, 144–145, 158, 162, 171, 180–181, 187, 188, 196, 202, 205, 233, 234, 242, 245, 272*ch*2*n*29, 278*n*124; Oakland Seals 7, 79; white skates 50; *see also* California Seals; San Francisco Seals
California Seals 11; *see also* California Golden Seals; San Francisco Seals
Cameron, Al 74
Campbell, Clarence 10, 11, 26, 43, 60, 167–168, 191, 200, 202, 239; resistance to expansion 8–9
Campbell, Colin 144, 245

Canadian Amateur Hockey Association (CAHA) 44
Canadian Standards Association 244
Capital Bullets 20; *see also* Baltimore Bullets; Washington Bullets
Capital Centre 20, 58, 69, 70, 74, 78, 94, 135, 140, 159, 164, 237, 247; *see also* Washington Capitals
Carr, Gene 117
Cashman, Wayne 122, 124, 205
Central Hockey League (CHL) 14, 29, 32, 36, 39, 153, 243; Adams Cup 31
Central Red Army (team) 159
Charron, Guy 116–117, 121, 123, 124, **126**, 127, 128, 131, 133, 135, 175, 178, 179, 180, 181, 182, 186, 187, 195, 196, 198–199, 200–201, 204, 205, 215, **227**, 229, 231, 236–237, 238, 242, 243, 244
Cherry, Don 47, 148, 246
Chicago Black Hawks 6, 7–8, 11, 16–17, 18, 23, 27, 31, 33, 36, 44, 50, 51, 58, 59, 72, 82, 109–110, 112, 113, 114, 121, 125, 132–133, 145, 146, 162, 164, 168, 183–184, 185, 197, 200, 204, 228
Chicago Cougars 44
Chicago Stadium 132, 146
Chouinard, Guy 47
Choyce, John 175
Christison, Jimmy 168
Churchill, Winston 122
Clarke, Bobby 69, 100, 105–106, 139, 143, 150, 169, 180
Clarkson, William 242
Clement, Bill 62, 69, 71, 139–140, 141, 147, 150, 152, 160–161
Cleveland Barons (AHL) 8, 34
Cleveland Barons (NHL) 245
Cleveland Crusaders 191, 202
Clinton Comets 34
Coalter, Gary 30, 33, 126, 191
Coca-Cola 2, 3, 167, 221, 232; Coca-Cola Bottling Company 213
Coca-Cola Bottlers' Cup 1–2, 3, 4, 48, 166, 167, 172, 209, 212, 219, 221, 226, 230–231, 233, 234, 235, 237, 238, 247–249; *see also* NHL Japan series
Cole, Grant 143
Collins, Bill 116, 161
Collyard, Bob 39
Colorado Rockies 116, 243, 244–246; *see also* Kansas City Scouts
ColorMark 246; *see also* Hudson, Dave

Columbia Broadcasting System (CBS) 9, 11
Comeau, Rey 181
Concordia University 244
Connor, Cam 189–90
Conway, Tim (player) 53
Cournoyer, Yvan 112, 184, 201
Cowick, Bruce 38, 56, 67, 69, 72
Crashley, Bart 26, 102–103, 104, 106, 109, 110, 113, 116, 135
Crisp, Terry 129
Crosby Kemper Memorial Arena 1, 15, 111, 112, 118, 120, 124, 132, 134, 135, 186, 200, 201, 205, 207, 240, 241; construction workers strike 96, 109; cost 16, 109; opening night 109–110; *see also* Kansas City Scouts
Croteau, Gary 30, **31**, 41, 119, 121, 123, 130, 132, 145, 175, 178, 179, 186, 196, 198, 201, 205, 207, 219, 229, 231, 245, 246
Crozier, Joe 97, 98
Currier, Bob 38

Daigle, Alain 204
Dallas Black Hawks 36, 102
Dallin, Cyrus E. 17
David, Larry 54
Dayton Gems 22, 64, 69, 153
Dea, Billy 157–158
Deadmarsh, Butch 29–30, 97–98, 99, 103, 105, 108, 110, 115–116, 120
Dean, Barry 174–175, 245
Debenedet, Nelson 117–118
Delparte, Guy 53
Delvecchio, Alex 116, 157–158, 192
Denver Nuggets 239
Denver Spurs (CHL) 91
Denver Spurs (WHL) 29
Desjardins, Gerry 182
Detroit Red Wings 6, 7–8, 10, 17, 18, 23, 30, 32, 33, 55, 63, 65, 72, 73, 74, 86, 87, 89, 103, 109, 113, 116, 118, 121, 129, 130, 131, 133, 136, 139, 143, 153, 157–158, 162–163, 169, 177, 179, 181, 183, 185, 186–187, 188, 192, 193–194, 228, 239, 245, 246; Olympia Arena **165**
Dillon, Wayne 44, 161, 163
Dionne, Marcel 147, 177–178
Directors' Cup 14; *see also* United States Hockey League
Dowd, Edward 14
Drouin, Jude 188
Dryden, Dave 44
Dryden, Ken 26, 27, 28, 29, 54, 184, 238
Dube, Norm 33, 41, 101, 103, 109, 118, 124, 175

Dumart, Woody 21
Dunn, Dave 143–144
Dupere, Denis 38, 41, 53, 55, 58, 61, 64, 67, 68, 72, 75, *76*, 110, 175, 176, 178, 198, *225*, 227, *230*, 245
Dupont, Andre 129
Durbano, Nick 190
Durbano, Steve 189–192, 198, 199, 205, 206, 207, 217, 221, *223*, 224, 227, 231, 245

Eagleson, Alan 40, 98, 99, 134, 178
Ecclestone, Tim 63
Edmonton Oilers (WHA) 33, 175, 178, 238
Edur, Tom 44
Edwards, Gary 106
Egers, Jack 40, 41, 54, 58, 61, 93, 141–142, 144, 146
Ellis, Ron 68, 103, 127
Esposito, Phil 19, 22, 75, 77, 122, 124, 161, 163, 272*ch2n*18
Esposito, Tony 110, 145, 147
Evans, Chris 32, 109
expansion: definition 5; to Denver and Seattle 62; dilution of talent 3, 7, 12–13, 25, 43, 138, 278*n*132; draft rules 10–11, 24, 25, 26, 27–28, 49; franchise fee 10, 15, 27, 40, 43; impact on hockey 12, 13, 136–139, 278*n*132; in 1920s and 1930s 7–8; 1967 3, 10–11, 25–26; 1970 3, 11, 12, 26; 1972 3, 12–13, 26; 1974 2, 3, 13, 19, 27–44, 49; player opportunities 6, 12, 26, 27, 36, 62; quality of players 3, 5–7, 10, 24–25, 26, 40–44, 62; resistance 7–10; *see also* National Hockey League; World Hockey Association

Fachet, Robert 74
Fairbairn, Bill 161
Faubert, Mario 118
Favell, Doug 35, 36, 103, 104, 126, 133
Feldman, Skip 93–94, 130
Ferguson, George 68, 83
Ferguson, John 140
Ferguson, Norm 26
Ferraro, Ray 5, 6
Finley, Charles 37
Fischler, Stan 7
Fisher, Bob 244
Flaman, Fern 51
Fogolin, Lee 206
Forbes, Dave 185, 201
Foreman, Earl 19–20
Fort Worth Wings 32, 39
free shot experiment 101–102

French Connection Line 66–67, 69, 182; *see also* Martin, Richard; Perreault, Gilbert; Robert, Rene
Frig, Len 115
Fullan, Larry 40

Gagnon, Germain 58, 183, 185
Gardner, Dave 86, 192
Gardner, Paul 192, 245
Gare, Danny 47, 151, 182
Garpenlov, Johan 5
Gassoff, Bob 144, 182–183
Gazelle Line 64; *see also* Dupere, Denis; Kryskow, Dave; Williams, Tommy
Geoffrion, Bernie 140
Giacomin, Ed 56, 57, 81, 181
Gilbert, Ed 34–35, 41, 103, 107, 108, 110, 111–112, 113, 115, 116, 118, 121, 122, 123, 127, 133, *174*, 182, 183, 189, 198
Gilbert, Gilles 133
Gilbert, Rod 56, 128, 132, 163
Gilbertson, Stan 75, 76–77, 82–83, 86, 88, 90–91, 141–142, 144–145, 146, 147, 149, 275*n*151; career-ending car crash 149
Gillies, Clark 47
Girard, Bob 158, 205
Giroux, Larry 109, 116, 135
Glazer, Stan 14, 15
Gordon, Jackie 52
Gould, John 108
Graham, Dale 117, *230*
Graham, Rod 124
Grant, Danny 185
Gratton, Gilles 183
Gratton, Norm 63, 128–129
Graves, Hilliard 238
Green, Rick 238
Greenberg, Jay 99, 114
Greschner, Ron 47, 163
Gretzky, Wayne 238, 246
Grigsby, Bill 16
Gryp, Bob 37, 54, 88, 90, 143
Guevremont, Jocelyn 160
Guidolin, Armand "Bep" 18–19, 21, 71, 84, 99, 100, 106, 108, 109, 111, 112, 114, 121–122, 123, 128, 129, 146, 173, 177, 178, 179, 180, 181, 183, 186, 187, 188, 189, 191–192, 193–195, 196, 197, 234, 272*ch2n*18

Hadfield, Vic 83, 90, 110–111, 131, 144, 186, 197
Hajt, Bill 182
Hall, Glenn 8
Hamilton Red Wings 190
Hammarstrom, Inge 104, 126–127
Hanna, John 191
Harkness, Ned 17

Harlem Globetrotters 54
Harper, Terry 192
Harris, Billy 118
Harris, Cecil 65
Harris, Ron 161
Hart, Gerry 102
Hart Trophy 17
Harvey, Fred "Buster" 176, 178, 180, 181, 182, 192
Heft, Arnold 19–20
Henning, Lorne 201
Herron, Denis 119–121, *122*, 123, 124, 125, 126, 127, 130, 133, 135, 177, 182, 184, 186, 187–188, 192, 196, 197, 198, 199, 201, 204, 205, 206–207, 215, 226, 228, 229, 231, 242, 243, 244–245
Hershey Bears 32, 57, 105, 111, 120, 219
Hess, Paul 15
Hextall, Dennis 65
Hicke, Ernie 73
Hickey, Pat 163
Hinky Dinky 15
Hodge, Ken, Sr. 22, 39, 68, 121, 164, 200
Hodgson, Morton S., Jr. 167
Hogaboam, Bill 72, 158, 192
Holmes, Arthur 217
Holt, Gary 145
Holtby, Braden 248
Horbul, Doug 35, 109
Hornung, Larry 26, 176
Houde, Claude 34, 116, 128, 129, 176
Howatt, Garry 118
Howe, Gordie 10, 17
Howe, Mark 44
Howe, Marty 44
Hrechkosy, Dave 107, 115, 144
Hrycuik, Jim 56, 57, 68, 93, 110
Hudson, Dave 33, *34*, 103, 105, 107, 112, 116, 118–119, 123, 126, 133, 145, 179, 182, 196, 204, 205, *226*, *230*, 231, 245, 246; ColorMark 246
Hughes, Brent 30, 41, 103, 118, 123, 128; contract with San Diego Mariners 98, 100, 129, 176
Hughes, John 89
Hull, Bobby 8, 29, 36, 168
Hull, Dennis 58
Hurlbut, Bob 38
Huston, Ron 107
Hynes, Dave 68

Indianapolis Racers 3, 272*n*3
Ingarfield, Earl 79
Inness, Gary 83, 110, 111, 131, 144, 198
intra-league draft 57, 140; *see also* National Hockey League
Irvine, Ted 183

Index

ITECH 244; *see also* Burns, Robin

Japan National Hockey League 167; *see also* NHL Japan Series
Jarrett, Doug 58, 161
Jarvis, Doug 201
Jennings, Jeff 15
Jennings, William 9–10, 15
Johnson, Bob 110
Johnson, Jim 53
Johnson, Tom 18
Johnston, Ed 35, 112, 133, 183
Johnston, Larry 129–130, 176, 177, 183, 193–195, 204, 205, 218, *223*, *227*, *229*, 231, 237, 245
Johnston, Marshall 107–108, 115
Johnstown Jets 130
Joly, Greg 44–45, 47, 53, 55, 64, 87, 90, 93, 110, 142–143, 144, 147, 150, 154, 158, **159**, 161, 171, 226, 227, 238; salary 45, 55, 94
Jones, Ron 73, 93

Kansas City Blues 14, 16, 32, 39, 96
Kansas City Builders Association 96
Kansas City Chiefs 15
Kansas City Kings 15, 135, 239–242
Kansas City Pla-Mors/Greyhounds/Americans 14
Kansas City Scouts: arena issues 14, 96, 109; average attendance 127, 135, 138, 199, 239; criticism of expansion draft 43, 173; Crosby Kemper Memorial Arena 1, 15, 111, 112, 118, 120, 124, 132, 134, 135, 186, 200, 201, 205, 207, 240, 241; debts 200, 240; difficulty drawing fans 134–135; expansion draft picks 29–35; expansion draft strategy 41–42, 125, 135; financial issues 16 119, 134, 199–200, 202, 228, 239–240, 241, 243, 245; first line-up 103; loan from NHL 202–203, 216, 228, 240, 241; logo 1, 109; 1974 Amateur Draft 46–47; 1975 Amateur Draft 174–175; origin of team name 16–17; ownership 1, 15–16, 134, 200; player contract issues 97–99; players' curfew breach 193–195; potential sale to Carl Scheer, Jr. 239; potential sale to Gene Novorr 242–243; potential sale to Kansas City Kings 239–241, 242; potential sale to Ted Tobias 239; sale to Bud Palmer 242–243; season-ticket drive 200, 203, 239, 241–242; season-ticket sales 96–97, 199, 203; training camp and pre-season 99–100, 177–178; uniforms 1, 104, 109; *see also* expansion; National Hockey League
Karlsson, William 6
Kea, Ed 130
Kearns, Dennis 108, 176
Kehoe, Rick 83, 111, 131–132, 198
Kelly, Bob 83, 114
Kelly, Red 104
Keon, Dave 35, 83, 103, 104
Ketter, Kerry 33
Kilmer, Billy 76
Kindrachuk, Orest 164, 180
King, Wayne 145
Kinsella, Brian 53
Kipp, Robert 240, 241
Korab, Jerry 148
Koroll, Cliff 110, 145, 204
Kraus, James 117
Kraut Line 21
Kryskow, Dave 36, 41, 56, 64, 65, 66, 68, 70, 72, 73, 74, 110, 118

Labre, Yvon 36–37, 51, 55, 64, 80, 82, 83, 90, 120, 127, 142, 145, 152, 162, 163, 170, 171, 198, 219, 231, 238
Lafleur, Guy 18, 61, 70, 71, 132, 170, 207, 237, 238
Laframboise, Pete 37, 66, 71, 73
Lagace, Jean-Guy 119, 120–121, 124–125, 128, 131, 132–133, 135, 176, 177, 186, 204, 217, **225**–226, 227, 242
Lalonde, Bobby 113, 204
Lalonde, Ron 62, 68, 72, 73, 87, 88, 90, 91, 118, 141, 147, 149, 161, 163, 164, 171, 219, 224, *225*, 227, 231, 275n145
Lambert, Yvon 70, 170, 184, 201
Lampman, Mike 39, 41, 141, 148, 156, 157, 161, 170, 217, ***224***, ***226***, 227, 229, 231, 236, 238, 239
Lange skates 197, 218–219, 244; *see also* Burns, Robin
Laperriere, Jacques 29
Lapointe, Guy 29, 71
Lapointe, Rick 192
Larocque, Michel 27, 170, 184, 237
Larose, Claude 41
Larouche, Pierre 47, 68, 83, 118, 162, 186
Lavender, Brian 127
Laxton, Gord 144
LBJ Line 53; *see also* Bernier, Serge; Johnson, Jim; Lesuk, Bill
Leach, Reggie 69, 71, 114, 150, 164, 169
Leblanc, J.P. 163
Lefley, Bryan 32, 103, 104, 128, 244
Lefley, Chuck 67, 118
Lemaire, Jacques 35, 71, 113, 184
Lemelin, Roger 125–126, 245
Lemieux, Jean 160, 161, 163, 217, 227, 229, 231
Lemieux, Mario 18
Lemieux, Richard 33, 103, 108, 110, 111–112, 115, 116, 119, 123, 127, 175–176
Leonsis, Ted 247
Lesuk, Bill 53, 68, 69, 72, 89, 141
Lever, Don 130, 131
Lewis, Brian 69
Lewis, Dale 140
Lewis, Richard 87
Ley, Rick 35
Libett, Nick 158, 192
Lindsay, Ted 17
Litzenberger, Ed 168
Lockett, Ken 108, 113
Los Angeles Blades 9
Los Angeles Kings 5, 6, 11, 22, 23, 27, 30–31, 37, 39, 40, 53, 57–58, 59, 68, 71, 72, 78, 106, 117, 125, 131, 132, 139, 140, 144, 146, 147, 162, 167, 168, 178, 187, 207, 233, 234, 238, 272ch2n29; Great Western Forum 78, 212
Los Angeles Sharks 102
Low, Ron 35–36, 53, 56–57, 58, 59, 60, 63, 66, 67–68, 69, 72, 74, 80, 82, 83, 86, 88, 89, 90, 91–***92***, 93, 128, 143, 145, 146, 147–148, 151, 158, 165, 166, 170, 217, 229, 231, 235, 237
Luce, Don 133, 151, 182
Lundrigan, Joe 38, 56
Lynch, Jack 63, 73, 74, 142, 147, 152, 156, 162, 163, 166, 167, 198, 219, 227, 238
Lysiak, Tom 125, 148

MacAdam, Al 158
MacDonald, Lowell **60**, 131
MacLeish, Rick 71, 129, 139, 150, 151
Macmillan, Billy 118
Madison Square Garden 12, 81, 132, 163
Mahovlich, Frank 44, 97, 116
Mahovlich, Peter 35, 70, 71, 112
Maine Mariners 152
Major League Baseball 8–9, 78, 210
Malarchuk, Garth 143
Maloney, Dan 106, 181, 192
Manery, Randy 181

Maniago, Cesare 67
Marchant, Gordie 106, 117
Marcotte, Don 68, 71, 124, 205
Margolin, Robert 240–241
Marks, John 114
Marotte, Gilles 22, 63, 128
Marsh, Brad 6
Marson, Mike 45, 53, 55–56, 61, 66, 67, 69, 71, 73, 80, 81, 82, 90, 94, 118, 142, 143–144, 146, 215, 238; victim of racism 46, 64–**65**, 66; salary 55, 64, 94
Martin, Lawrence 104
Martin, Pit 22, 204
Martin, Richard 66, 151
Maruk, Dennis 196
Mattiussi, Dick 79
McCreary, Bill 86, 107, 277n50
McDonald, Jiggs 47
McDonald, Lanny 35, 103, 147
McDonald, Terry 143
McDonald's (restaurant) 220
McDuffe, Peter 29, 101, 103, 113, 114, 118, 123, 125, 127, 128, 129, 130, 131, 132, 133–134, 177
McElmury, Jim 102, 103, 108, 110, 111–112, 115, 128, 176, **221**, 229, 231, 245
McFadden, Edgar "Lefty" 58, 61, 62, 63, 150
MCI Center 247; see also Washington Capitals
McKechnie, Walt 181
McKenney, Don 51
McKenny, Jim 104
McKenzie, Bill 145, 175, 177, 180, 181, 182, 188, 201, 205, **230**, 246
McLean, Don 139
McManama, Bob 83
McMorran Arena (Port Huron, Michigan) 99
McNab, Max 153, 160, 161, 168
McNab, Peter 151, 182
McRae, Gord 74
McSheffrey, Bryan 160
McVie, Tom 1, 2, 153–157, 158, 159, 161, 162, 163, 164, 165, 166, 170, **171**, 172, 212, 213, 215, 218, 219, 224, 226, 230, 231, 234, 235, 236, 237, 238, 282n7
Medicine Hat Tigers 174
Meehan, Gerry 160, 161, 162, 163, 164, 170, 217, 231
Meloche, Gilles 107
Memorial Cup 45
Merrick, Wayne 158
Micron skates 197, 244; see also Burns, Robin
Middleton, Rick 56, 161, 162, 163, 182
Mikita, Stan 51, 59, 114
Mikkelson, Bill 39, 41, 51, 56, 58, 67, 74–75, 76; plus-minus record 75
Milford, Jake 167
Minnesota Fighting Saints 185–186
Minnesota North Stars 6, 11, 23, 34, 39, 40, 41, 51, 52, 57, 62–63, 64, 67, 72, 84, 101–102, 103, 112, 118, 123, 128–129, 131, 133, 136, 137, 152, 176, 185, 186, 188, 197, 201, 238
Miron, Ray 244, 245
Moffat, Lyle 104
Mohns, Doug 6, 51–52, 53, 60, 63, 67, 69, 72, 81, 271ch1n3
Monahan, Garry 108
Monahan, Hartland 140, 142, 143–144, 145, 146, 149, 161, 164, 170, 218, 235, 236
Montreal Canadiens 6, 8, 9, 23, 27–28, 29, 31, 34–35, 40, 44, 53, 54–55, 59, 60, 61, 70–71, 73, 82, 88–89, 94, 102, 112–113, 115, 116, 117, 118, 128, 131, 132, 133, 136, 138–139, 148, 152, 155, 160, 165–166, 170, 179, 182, 183, 184–185, 186, 189, 201–202, 207, 209, 235, 237–238, 282n7;
Montreal Forum 37, 87
Montreal Maroons 8
Moore, Jay 202
Morris, William S. 14
Morrison, Lew 39, 68, 83, 90, 198
Moxey, Jim 205
Municipal Auditorium (Kansas City) 14
Murphy, Mike 117
Murphy, Neil 53
Murray, Ken 33–34
Myers, Bob 104
Myre, Phil 124, 190–191

National Basketball Association (NBA) 15, 20, 21, 78, 94, 135, 210, 239; NBA-ABA merger 239
National Football League (NFL) 9, 15, 78
National Hockey League (NHL): Amateur Draft 27, 28, 29–30, 34, 44–48, 87, 98, 102, 139, 153, 174, 192, 238, 241; attendance 138; divisional realignment 22–23; franchise instability 202; free shot experiment 101–102; increase in violence 189–190; intra-league draft 57, 140; Next Six 6; NHL Players Association (NHLPA) 40, 134, 167, 234; Original Six 6, 7, 8, 10, 13, 26, 35, 52, 185; parity 6, 8; player salaries 8, 27, 94, 98, 193, 199–200; salary cap 3; television contract with CBS 10, 11; see also expansion; Western Hockey League; World Hockey Association
National Hockey League Players' Association (NHLPA) 40, 134, 167, 222, 234; see also National Hockey League
Neilson, Jim 145
Nesterenko, Eric 168
Nevin, Bob 40–41, 117
New England Whalers 52, 275n151
New Haven Nighthawks 34, 40
New Otani Hotel 214, 232
New Westminster Royals (WHL) 153
New York Americans 8, 50
New York Islanders 3, 12–13, 26, 27, 28, 32, 33, 38, 39, 70, 73, 78, 80, 102, 105, 112, 115, 118, 125, 131, 136–137, 160, 163, 164, 175, 176, 179, 188, 199, 200, 201
New York Raiders (WHA) 12
New York Rangers 6, 8, 9, 12, 15, 29, 30, 35, 40, 56–57, 63, 72, 77, 78, 80, 81, 85, 115, 118, 128, 132, 137, 140, 149, 161–162, 163, 165, 168–169, 178, 181, 182, 188, 190, 192, 200, 207; Madison Square Garden 12, 81, 132, 163
Newman, Chuck 114
Newman, Murray 15
NHL Japan series 3; attendance 216, 221; concerns 167–169; culture shock 215, 220; description of Sapporo 220–221; description of Tokyo 220–221; extracurricular activities 213–214, 232; fan reaction 212, 216, 218, 220; financing 167, 168, 213–214; future series 232, 233–234; game one 215–217, game two 216–218; game three 219–228; game four 228–230; media reaction 212, 216, 218–219, 220, 227; player fraternization 219; playing conditions 1, 209, 222–**224**, **230**; prizes 215, **223**, 228, 230; promotion 168, **210–211**, 213, 219–220; purpose 2, 167, 169, 209–210; reasons for inviting Scouts and Capitals 212, 234; sponsors 166–167; ticket prices 215; treatment of players 213–214, 233, 234; trip to Hawaii 232; Yoyogi National Stadium 221, 247;

see also Coca-Cola Bottlers' Cup
Nicholson, Jack 155
Nicholson, Paul 53, 68
Nikkan Sports 167
Nixon, Richard 153, 272*ch2n*22
Nolet, Simon 29, 41, 103, 105–106, 107, 108, 110, 111, 112, 113, 114, 115, 117, 118, 120, 123, 125, 126, 128, 131, 133, 175, 178, 179, 180, 182, 183, 186, 189, 243, 245
Norris, Bruce 17
Norris, Jack 22
Norris, James 11
Norris Division 23, 59, 117, 132, 138
Norris Trophy 6, 51
Nova Scotia Voyageurs 31, 38, 40, 53, 179, 189
Novorr, Gene 242–243
Nowak, Hank 72, 205
Nystrom, Bob 118

Oakland Seals *see* California Golden Seals
Oddleifson, Chris 108, 204
O'Flaherty, Gerry 113
Oglethorpe, Ogie 109
Oklahoma City Blazers 28
Oleschuk, Bill 196, 246
Olesevich, Dan 158
Omaha Knights 29, 31, 102, 160
O'Malley, Peter 140
O'Reilly, Terry 38, 39, 63, 205
Original Six 6, 7, 8, 10, 13, 26, 35, 52, 185; *see also* National Hockey League
Orr, Bobby 22, 45, 60, 67, 75, 84, 109, 121, 122, 125, 171, 180, 193, 194, 195, 239
Ottawa Senators 6, 93
Ovechkin, Alexander 87

Paddock, John 53, 54, 142, 149
Paiement, Rosaire 47, 98
Paiement, Wilf 46–47, 98–99, 101, 103, 106, 107, 108, 110, 111, 112, 113, 115, 121, 123, 127, 130, 132, 133, 134, 145, *174*, 175, 177, 178, 179, 180–181, 182–183, 184, 186, 187, 189, 192, 193, 198, 201, **230**, 243, 244, 245; assault of Dennis Polonich 246; salary 47, 98, 99
Palazzari, Doug 67
Palmer, Bud 242–243
Pappin, Jim 59, 109, 114, 158
Paradise, Bob 161, 190
Parent, Bernie 35, 71, 100, 139, 143, 164, 204
Park, Brad 56, 201
Parr, George 247
Pashby, Tom Dr. 244; *see also* Burns, Robin

Patey, Larry 107
Patrick, Craig 166, 175, 178, 182, 184, 186, 187, 199, **224**, 229, **230**, 231, **233**, 242, 245
Patrick, Lester 175
Patrick, Lynn 175
Patrick Division 114, 161, 181
Patterson, Dennis 34, 112, 124, 127, 128, 166, 176, 182, 227, 231, 245
Patterson, Jack 53
Peloffy, Andre 54
Peluso, Tom 33
Penn Valley Park 17
Perreault, Gilbert 66, 151
Philadelphia Flyers 6, 8, 28, 29, 35, 36, 38, 53, 58, 61, 62, 69, 71, 84, 99–100, 105–106, 114, 115, 123, 125, 128, 129, 133, 136, 139, 144, 149, 150–151, 152, 160, 163–164, 169–170, 174, 176, 180, 188, 189, 190, 204, 209, 246, 278*n*132; Philadelphia Spectrum 61, 65, 69, 105, 129, 216
Philadelphia Quakers 85
Philadelphia Spectrum 61, 65, 105, 129, 216
Phoenix Roadrunners 3
Picard, Robert 238
Piggott, James 9
Pilote, Pierre 168
Pinder, Gerry 191
Pittsburgh Hornets 18
Pittsburgh Penguins 6, 7, 23, 32, 36, **60**, 68, 73, 78, 79, 80, 83–84, 85, 89, 90–91, 100–101, 108, 110–111, 112, 117–118, 119, 120, 125, 131–132, 133, 134, 137, 139, 144, 149, 162, 165, 170, 184, 186, 188, 189, 191, 197–198, 200, 202, 228, 244–245
Pittsburgh Pirates (NHL) 11
Plager, Barclay 67
Plager brothers (Bill, Bob, and Barclay) 190; *see also* Plager, Barclay
Planes, Trains & Automobiles 89
Plante, Jacques 35
Plasse, Michel 27, 28–29, 101, 102, 103, 104, 107, 111, 114, 117, 119, 134, 135, 144, 186, 198, 245, 246
Polis, Greg 56, 128
Pollin, Abe 19–21, 46, 49, 73, 81, 93, 94, 140
Pollock, Sam 28, 189
Polonich, Dennis 181; assault by Wilf Paiement 246
Popein, Larry 108
Portland Buckaroos 102
Potvin, Denis 272*n*2
Potvin, Jean 102

Powis, Lynn 31, 101, 103, 104, 113, 114, 125, 128, 130, 132, 133, 175
Price, Noel 124
Price, Pat 44
Procure Walk of Courage 244; *see also* Burns, Robin
Production Line 17; *see also* Abel, Sid; Howe, Gordie; Lindsay; Ted
Pronovost, Jean 110, 186, 198
Pulford, Bob 59, 132
Pyatt, Nelson 51–52, 74, 86, 141, 144, 145, 147, 158, 161, 163, 235, 237, 245

Queen Elizabeth Hotel 28, 88
Quinn, Pat 181

Ramsay, Craig 151, 182
Randall, Ed ***171***
Redmond, Mickey 116
Rhoades, Dr. Arthur 14–15
Richard, Henri 35, 61, 197
Richard, Jacques 130, 190
Richardson, Ken 118
Riley, Bill 65, 69, 237
Riley, Jack 79
Risebrough, Doug 35, 71, 112, 113
Robbins, Tony 236
Robert, Rene 66
Roberto, Phil 192, 196, 201, 207, **226**, 227, 231, 245
Roberts, Jim 113
Robinson, Larry 29, 70
Robitaille, Mike 160
Rochefort, Leon 131
Rosenberg, Paul H. 240, 241
Rota, Darcy 82, 114, 145
Rota, Randy 30–31, 41, 101, 103, 104, 113, 114, 115, 121, 127, 128, 131, 132, 133, 175, 179, 180, 182, 186, 201, 205, 226, 227, 229, 231, 245
Russell, Phil 82

Sabourin, Gary 158
Sachs, Jerry 20, 58
St. Catharines Black Hawks 46
St. Laurent, Andre 118
St. Lawrence University 30
St. Louis Blues 6, 11, 14, 15, 17, 23, 29, 31–32, 38–39, 40, 67, 75–77, 84, 91, 108, 109, 111–112, 118, 132, 133, 134, 137, 143, 144, 156, 158, 162, 175, 178, 179, 182–183, 186, 187, 190–191, 192, 196, 198–199, 200, 204, 209, 240, 245; St. Louis Arena 11
Salming, Borje 35, 103
Salomon, Sid, Jr. 11
Salomon, Sid III 11

Index

San Diego Gulls 38, 153
San Diego Mariners 12, 98, 176
San Francisco Seals 11, 153; *see also* California Golden Seals; California Seals
San Jose Sharks 6, 93
Sanderson, Derek 22, 81, 183
Savard, Andre 68, 164
Savard, Serge 29
Scamurra, Pete 164, 215, 231
Scheer, Carl, Jr. 239
Schmautz, Bobby 39, 47, 205
Schmidt, Milt 35, 40, 43, 51, 52, 53, 55, 57, 62–63, 64, 65–66, 68, 70, 73, 74, 78–79, 80, 84, 85, 86, 89, 92, 94–95, 116, 139, 141–142, 146, 148, 149, 173, 231, 234 ; coaching career in Boston 21–22, 46; departure from Capitals 152–153, 187; general manager of Boston Bruins 22; Kraut Line 21; playing career 21
Schock, Ron 83, 111, 112, 131
Schultz, Dave 71, 164, 174
Schurr, George 244
Scooter Line 51; *see also* Mikita, Stan; Mohns, Doug; Wharram, Ken
"The Scout" (statue) 17
Seagram's 16
Seiling, Rod 56, 63, 94
September 11, 2001, terrorist attack 238–239
Serviss, Joe 240, 241
Sheppard, Gregg 164, 205
Shero, Fred 29, 36, 62, 71, 114, 133, 139, 169, 180
Shewchyk, Dave 124
Shutt, Steve 170, 184, 237
Simmer, Charlie 47, 86, 127
Simmons, Gary 127, 181
Sirois, Bob 149–150, 161, 164, 166, 215, 217, 226, 227, 231, 238
Sisyphus 5
Sittler, Darryl 35, 103, 104, 127, 143–144
Smith, Billy 38
Smith, Dallas 201
Smith, Gary 113, 130, 133
Smith, Gord 37–38, **60**
Smythe, Stafford 10, 11
Smythe Division 22, 99, 103, 119, 125, 130, 132, 137, 164, 178, 179, 183, 185, 186, 187, 204, 245, 246
Snell, Ted 32, 103, 110, 113, 116, 135
Snider, Ed 11
Sobchuk, Dennis 44
Society for International Hockey Research (SIHR) 3
Soviet Wings 159

Spencer, Brian 206
Springfield Kings/Indians 22, 33, 37–38, 39, 176, 194
Stackhouse, Ron 90, 198
Stanfield, Fred 22, 62–63, 151
Stanfield, Jim 38
Stanley Cup 2, 6, 4, 8, 10, 12, 17, 18, 19, 21, 22, 23, 25, 35, 36, 48, 54, 58, 62, 86, 94, 98, 99, 106, 109, 125, 129, 133, 136, 143, 144, 146, 148, 150, 153, 162, 169, 172, 173, 185, 197, 209, 212, 213, 229, 237, 247, 248, 271*n*21
Stemkowski, Pete 17, 182
Stephenson, Wayne 105–106, 129, 147, 150
Stewart, Blair 73, 93, 150, 154, 158, 160, 161, 166, 218, 224–**225**, 226, 227, 232
Stewart, Bob 107, 196
Stram, Hank 15
Sullivan, George "Red" 78, 79–82, 83, 84–85, 127
Sullivan, Peter 53, 94
Sutter, Brian 175
Swig, Melvin 202, 242, 277*n*50

Tallon, Dale 145
Tampa Bay Lightning 6
Taylor, Billy 146
Terbenche, Paul 30, 41, 97, 98, 99
Thompson, Edwin G. 15, 16, 17, 98, 99, 109, 134, 178, 199, 200, 202, 203, 216, 239
Thompson, Hunter F. 198
Thomson, Floyd 111
Tobias, Ted 239
Toronto Maple Leafs 6, 8, 9, 10, 18, 35, 36, 38, 53, 63, 68, 74, 82–83, 92, 103–104, 125, 126–127, 129, 131, 137, 142, 143–144, 147–148, 160, 162, 163, 165, 180, 187, 189, 193, 194, 245, 246; Maple Leaf Gardens 103, 104, 180
Toronto Marlboros 104, 192
Toronto Toros 44, 239
Torrey, Bill 102
Tremblay, Mario 47, 70–71, 112
Trevelyan, Tom 38
Trottier, Bryan 47
Tucker, Tanya 198
Tulsa Oilers 130
Turnbull, Ian 104

Ullman, Norm 35, 103, 178
Unger, Garry 17, 67, 118, 182
United States Hockey League (USHL) 14; Directors' Cup 14
United States Olympic Hockey Team (1960) 52
University of Missouri 30

Vachon, Rogie 147
Vadnais, Carol 68, 124, 182
van Boxmeer, John 28, 170
Vancouver Blazers 44, 47, 97–98, 115–116, 272*n*4, 272*ch*2*n*18
Vancouver Canucks (NHL) 3, 11, 12, 23, 26, 28, 32, 33, 35, 39, 47, 64, 68, 82, 107, 108, 111, 113, 125, 127, 130–131, 137, 156, 160, 162, 176, 179, 186, 204, 207, 238, 272*ch*2*n*29; Pacific Coliseum 157
Vancouver Canucks (WHL) 9, 153
Vegas Golden Knights 6, 173
Veisor, Mike 58
Ververgaert, Dennis 108
Vickers, Jack 244
Vickers, Steve 132, 161, 163
Victoria Cougars 175
Video Promotions 167, 233
Villemure, Gilles 81, 133
Vogel, Mike 247

Wagner, Kris 2, 247–248
Walsh, Father John 244
Ward, Richard 240
Washington Bullets 19–20, 58, 94, 140
Washington Capitals: average attendance 58, 94, 138; average player salary 94; Capital Centre 20, 58, 69, 70, 74, 78, 94, 135, 140, 159, 164, 237, 247; criticism of expansion draft 43, 61–62; expansion draft picks 35–41; expansion draft strategy 41–42, 94–95, 153; fan club 92, **171**; financial concerns 94; "Guaranteed Win" night 147, 152, 165–166, 170; logo 21, 50; MCI Center 247; 1974 Amateur Draft 28, 44–46; origin of team name 20–21; players' behavior and attitude 79, 80, 141–142, 152–154, 156–157, 235; players' conditioning 79–80, 153–156, 157, 163, 212–213, 226, 231, 235–236; record winless streak 164; road losing streak 67, 77, 83, 85–86; season ticket sales 58, 93, 94; Stanley Cup garbage can 85–86, 146, 162; training camp and pre-season 53–54, 55, 141–142, 143–144; uniforms 49–51; *see also* expansion; National Hockey League
Washington Capitols 21
Washington Caps 21
Washington Generals 54
Wasson, Terry 53
Watson, Bryan 192

Watson, Jim 69
Watson, Phil 21–22
Watters, Bill 99
Wayne & Shuster 136
Weber, Ron 83, 84–85, 87–88, 94
Weir, Stan 107
West, Steve 39
Western Canada Hockey League (WCHL) 30, 39, 174, 175
Western Hockey League (WHL) 11, 29, 38, 45, 102, 153; competition with NHL 9
Wharram, Ken 51
Wheeler, Charles, Jr. 96, 203, 239, 241–242
White, Bill 114
White, Tony 142, 143, 144, 145, 146, 147, 149, 151, 158, 161–162, 166, 170, 215, 226, 235
Wicks, Ron 170
Widing, Juha 106, 117
Wilbur Mills-Fanne Foxe sex scandal 85
Wilkins, Barry 83, 111
Williams, Dave "Tiger" 126, 162, 239
Williams, Tommy (L.A. player) 71
Williams, Tommy *50*, 52–53, 54, 62, 63, 64, 71, 72, 77, 81, 82, 90–91, 93, 130, 141, 143, 145, 146, 149, 159, 179, 275n151
Williams, Warren "Butch" 86, 115
Wilson, Doug 6
Wilson, Dunc 35, 161, 182
Wilson, Johnny 245
Wilson, Murray 70
Wirtz, Arthur 11
Wolfe, Bernie 46, 143, 146–147, 148, 149, 150–151, 158, 162, 170–171, 213, 215, 223, 226, 227, 228, 235, 237, 238
Wolfson, Robert L. 11
World Hockey Association (WHA) 3, 12, 30, 33, 39, 44, 49, 52, 78, 91, 92, 94, 97, 98, 100, 102, 103, 115–116, 129, 137, 141, 173, 176, 178, 185–186, 202, 210, 232–233, 238, 239, 244, 245, 271ch1n4, 272n3, 272n4, 272ch2n18, 274n43, 275n151; Avco World Trophy (aka Avco Cup) 31, 98, 238; expansion 3, 7, 272n3, 136; salaries 12, 18, 27, 199; signing junior players 44, 47, 234; talent raids on NHL 12–13, 25, 26, 27, 35, 43, 72
World War I 216
World War II 6, 18, 114, 136, 241
Wright, John 31–32, 103, 109
Wyrozub, Randy 38

Yake, Terry 5
You Only Live Twice (film) 214
Young, Garry 37
Youth for Christ 244
Yoyogi National Stadium 221, 247; *see also* NHL Japan series

Ziegler, John 243

www.ingramcontent.com/pod-product-compliance
Lightning Source LLC
Chambersburg PA
CBHW060336010526
44117CB00017B/2854